The Story of Pau

Voyages on All the Great Rivers of the World

Paul Boyton

Alpha Editions

This edition published in 2024

ISBN : 9789362923431

Design and Setting By
Alpha Editions
www.alphaedis.com
Email - info@alphaedis.com

As per information held with us this book is in Public Domain.
This book is a reproduction of an important historical work. Alpha Editions uses the best technology to reproduce historical work in the same manner it was first published to preserve its original nature. Any marks or number seen are left intentionally to preserve its true form.

Contents

CHAPTER I. .... - 1 -

CHAPTER II. .... - 13 -

CHAPTER III. .... - 25 -

CHAPTER IV. .... - 34 -

CHAPTER V. .... - 49 -

CHAPTER VI. .... - 69 -

CHAPTER VII. .... - 89 -

CHAPTER VIII. .... - 101 -

CHAPTER IX. .... - 113 -

CHAPTER X. .... - 121 -

CHAPTER XI. .... - 126 -

CHAPTER XII. .... - 143 -

CHAPTER XIII. .... - 151 -

CHAPTER XIV. .... - 156 -

CHAPTER XV. .... - 163 -

CHAPTER XVI. .... - 175 -

CHAPTER XVII...- 186 -

CHAPTER XVIII...- 203 -

CHAPTER XIX. ....- 212 -

CHAPTER XX...- 245 -

CHAPTER XXI. ....- 251 -

CHAPTER XXII..- 279 -

CHAPTER XXIII..- 296 -

CHAPTER I.

One bright day in July, 1858, two women carrying well filled market baskets, were crossing the old Hand Street bridge that spans the Alleghany River between Pittsburgh and Alleghany City, Penn.

"Oh, Mrs. Boyton, do look at that child in the middle of the river paddling around on a board."

"Well," said the one addressed as Mrs. Boyton, "I'm glad it is none of mine. My son Paul, loves the water dearly, but I took the precaution to lock him up before I started for market."

After observing the child, who was evidently enjoying his aquatic sport, for some time, the two women proceeded on their way. On reaching home, Mrs. Boyton, with a feeling of remorse for keeping her young son so long in captivity, went up stairs to release him, and to her consternation found that he had escaped. Three minutes later an excited woman stood on bank of the Alleghany, vigorously waving her hand and hailing the youthful navigator. The forward end of the one by twelve inch board was reluctantly headed for shore, and slowly idled in. As the child reached land, he was grasped by the angry and anxious mother, who beat a merry tattoo on a tender portion his body with a shingle.

This was not the first time that the young hero had received punishment for loving the water. His home was within one block of the clear and swift flowing Alleghany; and whenever he could escape the vigilant eye of his mother, he was found either on the bank or in the water. One day, Mrs. Boyton, who had a continual dread of his being drowned, was going on a visit, and she determined to secure Paul against accident. She took him upstairs, undressed him and removed his clothes from the room. She locked the door and went away content.

The day was lovely; the water lay clear and blue in sight and Paul could hear the delighted cries of the boys as they plunged into its refreshing depths. The temperature was too strong. Paul searched the room carefully and to his joy, discovered a pair of his father's drawers. He got into them and tied the waist-string around his neck. Then forcing a window, he slid down the convenient lightning rod like a young monkey, and was found in his usual haunt by his astonished mother some hours later. From this time on, she gave him more liberty to follow his natural bent. From early May until late in October, when not at school, Paul spent most of his time in the water.

In those days, driftwood, consisting of slabs, logs and boards, were continually floating down the river from the headwaters, where the great forests were being cut down. When he saw a nice piece of wood, Paul would cut through the water like a young shark, and swim with it ahead of him to the shore, where his lumber pile was a goodly sized one. He kept his mother's cellar well supplied with firewood and sold the surplus to the neighbors; the proceeds of wich were devoted to gingerbread and even at that early age to the abominable roll of tobacco known as the "Pittsburgh Stogie."

Great rafts of lumber were coming down the river daily and a favorite amusement when he saw one, was to run up the river bank about a quarter of a mile, swim off and board it. In this way he became acquainted with many of the hardy "buck-tail" boys who piloted the huge rafts down the river. His knowledge of the different bars that were formed by the bridge piers was utilized, and often proved of great assistance to his friends, the raftsmen. One day, he boarded a raft, the captain of which was evidently a stranger to the channel in the vicinity of Pittsburgh, and Paul saw that it was certain to run aground. He told the captain and was so earnest in his manner, the course was ordered changed. Less than 500 yards further down, the ugly bar showed up not five feet from the side of the raft, as it went gliding by. The raftsman insisted on keeping the little fellow by his side until he was safely moored to the Pittsburgh shore; then as a reward for his services, presented Paul with a little flat boat about twelve feet long by five feet wide and ordered two of the crew to tow it with a skiff to the Alleghany side.

The generous present was most joyfully and thankfully received, for Paul's sole and only ambition for a long time had been to own a boat. As the two sturdy oarsmen with the boat in tow, neared the Alleghany shore, Paul stood erect in the stern, his eyes shining with triumph and satisfaction, and loudly hailed his playmates to come and see his prize. It is safe to say, that no commander of a vessel, ever viewed his craft with more pride, than Paul did his little flat-bottom boat. He named her "Gray Eagle." He was ever tired of overhauling, scrubbing and cleaning her. All the money realized by the capture of drift-wood, was devoted to the purchase of paint. He selected and shipped a crew from among his playmates. They were soon able to drive her where they liked upon the river with long poles and paddles, and many a successful battle royal was fought with their old enemies across the river, the Pittsburgh boys. The "Gray Eagle" was generally half loaded with nice, round stones that served as ammunition.

The "Eagle" would be carefully poled up the Alleghany shore against the current, then headed out and vigorously paddled towards the Pittsburgh side. Nearing the enemies' headquarters a skirmish would be opened by a shower of stones sent into their ranks. If the Pittsburghers were not sufficiently numerous to repel the invasion, the "Gray Eagle" was landed.

The majority of the crew pursued the flying enemy up the back streets, while the balance remained and hastily loaded up the best of the driftwood from the piles gathered by their antagonists. When their cargo was secured, the skirmishers were called in. All leaped aboard, and the "Eagle" headed for Alleghany, where the wood was carefully stored, far beyond the reach of a probable invasion by the Pittsburghers.

About this time a new enterprise opened for the commander and crew of the "Gray Eagle." The city commenced to pave the streets with large round stones called "Pavers," many of which were found in pockets at the bottom of the river. One day a contractor met Paul on the bank and said:

"Say, son, could not you boys gather a lot of pavers? I will buy them from you and give you thirty cents per hundred."

The offer was eagerly accepted. Next day the "Eagle" was anchored with a piece of rail-road iron, over a pocket, and the crew engaged in diving through the transparent water to the bottom, where they would gather one or two pavers, return to the top, and drop them into the boat. Paul had much difficulty in teaching his companions to keep their eyes open while under water. This occupation was pursued with varying success during the summer months of '59. The contractor came down every week to cart the "pavers" away; and many a dispute the boys had with him over the count. The dispute was generally decided by the carts driving off, and the contractor paying whatever he pleased. The boys discovered a rich pocket right near the old Aqueduct bridge. They worked it enthusiastically and were loath to leave such a find, until they had overloaded the Eagle. When all the divers climbed aboard, the additional weight almost swamped her. The strongest swimmers were compelled to go overboard and resting their hands gently on the gunwale, they propelled her by swimming toward the shore. They had not proceeded far when the bottom of the well-worn "Eagle" fell out and the cargo disappeared. While the boys hung on to the framework of their wrecked craft, their enemies across the river observed their predicament and sallied forth in a skiff to chastise them. The Alleghany boys swam for their own shore as rapidly as possible. On gaining shallow water, they faced about on their assailants and a battle was fought that was long remembered by the inhabitants on both sides of the river. In the meantime, the wreck of the "Gray Eagle" floated gently down to the Ohio, where the powerful current caught it and hurried it off to the southward.

After the loss of the "Eagle" the boys resumed their old sport of swimming and gathering wood. About this time, owing no doubt to the complaints of the riverside inhabitants, the city authorities determined to stop all further rows and displays of nudity. The orders against naked bathing were strictly enforced by a constable named Sam Long. Before the boys got thoroughly acquainted with him, he often captured an offender's clothing, which he detained until the boy came ashore. Then Sam would escort him to the Mayor's office to receive a stern reprimand, or his parents would be compelled to pay a small fine. Paul was never caught, for he was always on the outlook for the watchful Sam. On the constable's approach he would swim rapidly to his wardrobe which always lay conveniently close to the water. As it was neither weighty nor large, he would pile it on his head, tie it with a string under his chin; then swim swiftly off to the first pier of the bridge. This was fully fifty yards out in the stream, and here Paul would sit on the abutment rocks until Sam's patience was worn out and he would depart. Then Paul would swim leisurely to the shore, dress himself and go home.

Paul's elder brother, Michael, was a studious sedate boy who took no pleasure in the sports and adventures of his aquatic brother. But Paul's glowing descriptions of the pleasures of plunging and paddling in the cool, clear river, at last induced Michael to join in the watery gambols. One warm afternoon he accompanied his brother to the riverside. Paul slipped out of his clothes and was soon disporting himself in the refreshing water, while he shouted encouraging remarks to his hesitating brother to follow his example. Michael slowly disrobed and cautiously stepped into the water. He was no swimmer; but being surrounded by Paul and his companions, he grew bolder, waded farther out from shore, where he was soon enjoying himself as heartily as any of them.

Suddenly the cry of "Sam Long" was raised. Many of the boys seized their clothing and disappeared in the direction of their homes. The hardier swimmers, with Paul, struck out for the abutment on the pier in their usual way and poor Michael was left alone. Sam gently gathered up Michael's clothes, and retired to a lumber pile where he leisurely seated himself and waited for the owner to land. Michael had often heard of the terrible Sam Long so he did not go ashore, though Sam called him frequently. At last growing weary, the constable walked away with the captured wardrobe. As he disappeared, Michael started on a dead run for home. His clothes were recovered; but it was some time before Michael was inclined to calculate how many cubic feet of bread Paul would consume in a week, or to reckon how much time he lost from his studies by going into the water, as had been his custom. It is needless to add that it was many moons ere Michael went swimming again.

It was the custom then, as it is at present, to run enormous tows of coal barges, propelled by a powerful tug, from Pittsburgh to New Orleans. These grim and heavily loaded fleets had an intense fascination for young Paul. Many and many a day he spent in assisting the inland sailors in lashing boat to boat and diving overboard after spars, etc., that had slipped into the river. He often dreamt of the time when he would be large enough to go down the mighty Ohio and the great Mississippi. He made many friends among the coal men and eagerly devoured their stories of danger, of voyages down the river and of the comical "darkies" in the far off south. Time after time he implored permission from his mother to go away on one of those barge trips, but she would never consent. One day while assisting as usual on a fleet that was about to depart, a great, dark whiskered man named Tom, who was his particular friend, said: "Why don't you come with us, Paul? We will take good care of you and bring you safe hme again."

The temptation was strong, but the thought of his anxious mother deterred him. Tom still urged and the wonderful stories he told about brilliant New Orleans and the mighty "Father of Waters" rapt Paul's attention so that he did not at first notice that the tug "Red Lion" was driving the huge fleet of barges ahead of her. Would he jump into the river and swin ashore or would he go ahead?

"He who hesitates, is lost."

"Paul remained on board. Tom took him to the lookout far ahead on the tow and Paul forgot all about home and gave himself up to the delight of watching the swiftly passing banks while he listened to the swish, swish of the water as it beat against the bows of the barges. He was seated with the men on the watch, who passed the time telling stories and laughing at rough jokes. When it was getting late his big friend Tom, said:

"Now Paul, it's time you turned in. There's your bunk," pointing to a shelf in the dark and damp look-out house. Paul prepared to retire while the men continued their stories. The river-men of that time were rather given to profanity, so their yarns were freely interspersed with oaths. Suddenly Tom said in a loud whisper:

"Dry up! Don't you see the youngster is saying his prayers?"

A hush fell on the group, all looked around. Paul, kneeling on the damp, dirty beam alongside his bunk, was repeating the prayers learned at his mother's knee.

With the return of daylight, the remorseful feeling of a runaway boy came strongly upon him and Paul thoroughly realized how cruel he had been to his dear mother. He begged his friend Tom to get him back or to send a letter home. Tom dissuaded him from returning, but helped him write a letter which was posted at Wheeling, Va. This informed his mother that he was safe and would be taken good care of. Much relieved in mind, Paul was soon enjoying again the beautiful scenery and bright sunshine along the

Ohio. His work was to carry the coffee to the forward men on the lookout, and to help in many other little ways.

When nearing Evansville, Indiana, about seven hundred miles below Pittsburgh, a great shock was felt on the fleet, and a shower of coal was sent flying into the air. The cry "Snag! Snag!" was heard on all sides, the big engines of the "Red Lion" were stopped and reversed and the headway of the fleet was checked, as it slowly swung to the shore. All hands rushed to the damaged barge and found that a snag, a sunken log, had penetrated the bottom. Fearing that she would go down and drag other barges with her, she was detached and a line passed to the shore, then luckily near. A crew shoveled the coal from the ugly rent. The snag was cut away and vain attempts were made to pass a tarpaulin under and so stop the hole. Paul stood near his friend Tom, and suggested that he dive under, take a rope with him, and so enable them to pass a canvass below.

"Do you think you can do it without drowning?" said Tom.

"I am certain," was the response.

Tom handed him the end of a rope. Without hesitation Paul sprang into the water and dove under the then sinking barge. The rope was hauled up and another passed to him with which he repeated the operation. Two ropes were fastened to the tarpaulin, two more fastened to the other corners. The canvas was lowered into the river and the men on the opposite side hauled it under the ragged hole. As the canvas covered it, the inflow of water was instantly checked. With a loud cheer, the crew sprang to the pumps. When the water got low enough, the carpenters nailed planks over the hole. The barge and the valuable cargo of coal were saved. In less than three hours from the time the snag had struck, the injured barge was again lashed to the fleet and on her way down the Ohio. Paul was the hero of the hour. The Captain of the "Red Lion" solemnly transferred him from his damp and grimy quarters on the head to the comfortable cabin and pilot house. He confessed to the kind Captain that he had run away from home and how anxious he was about his mother. That day the Captain wrote a glowing letter to Mrs. Boyton and posted it at Paducah, Kentucky. From that time, he took great pleasure in teaching Paul how to steer, and many other arts in river craft. Paul keenly enjoyed this first voyage down the Mississippi. The strange scenes on the river were of deep interest; but he never tired of watching the slaves, either at work in the fields, or at play on the banks of an evening.

At last the "Red Lion" and her tow were safely moored at New Orleans. The Captain found a letter waiting from Mrs. Boyton requesting that Paul be sent back by the first mail packet. While waiting her departure, the Captain took Paul out to see the great city. Among many places of interest they visited that day, the slave mart at the foot of the fine statue erected in honor of Henry Clay, lived long in Paul's memory. Numbers of slaves were to be sold. The Captain and Paul pushed their way well to the front, so that they stood near the auctioneer. With feelings hard to describe, Paul saw slaves disposed of, singly and in parties. Fathers, mothers, sons and daughters were bid for and sold, and the critical purchasers examined them as if they were prize cattle. While the sale proceeded, Paul spelled out the inscription on the monument which said "that if he (Henry Clay,) could be instrumental in eradicating this deepest stain, slavery, from our country, he would be prouder than if he enjoyed the triumphs of a great conqueror." Even to his childish mind this seemed sadly inconsistent with the surroundings. The auction concluded with the sale of three boys, who seemed to be brothers, or at least close friends for they wept bitterly when parted. As they moved away, Paul's eyes were full of tears at the agony of the unhappy creatures, and turning to the Captain he said:

"Do you think this is right?"

"No," responded the Captain, "I'm darned if I do. It is an outrage and a shame that human beings should be sold like cattle, but—Great Scott! Did you notice what big prices they brought?" then added reflectively; "I'm blessed if it wouldn't pay me better to run a cargo of them down from Pittsburgh, than a tow of coal barges!"

Late that evening the Captain and Paul returned. As they approached, they saw an excited crowd, pushing their way through near the boat. They met the mate on the gang-plank keeping the people back.

"What's the matter?" demanded the Captain.

The mate explained that there had been a fight on the levee, and that big Tom had been stabbed, he feared fatally. Paul rushed into the cabin where his friend lay helpless and gasping.

"Tom, Tom!" he wailed.

"Ah! Paul, my boy," faintly responded Tom, "I fear I'm about to slip my cable. I want you lo help me say a few prayers. Just ask the good Lord not to be hard on me. I've been rough and careless all my life, but I never meant to be really bad. You talk for me."

The doctor came in and pushed the weeping Paul aside. One half hour later Tom had quietly floated out to eternity.

No one knew his full name or where his people were, so next day they buried him, the entire crew attending the funeral, and fervent were the prayers poured out then and often afterwards by little Paul for the friend so much beloved and so deeply mourned.

The Captain secured passage for Paul on a Northern bound boat and bought him many little presents ere wishing him God speed. Among them and prized most highly, were two red birds and a young alligator. At five o'clock that evening came the order: "All aboard! Haul in your gang-planks!" Just then a weird musical chant was struck up by the slaves working on the levee, which was answered by the boat's crew, as she backed out into the river and headed away on her long northern trip. Paul had snug quarters and spent much of his time feeding the red birds and playing with his alligator. He saw great fun ahead in the tricks he hoped to spring on his sisters and friends with the cunning little reptile. Whenever the boat made a landing, he was always on deck watching the negroes, as they rolled bales of cotton down the steep bluffs or struggled with the refractory hogs who refused to come aboard. The loud commands and fierce oaths of the mate made him feel very grateful that he was not a roustabout. About five weeks from the time he had so thoughtlessly embarked on the coal fleet, he stood hesitatingly half a block from his mother's home, holding in his hand the cage containing his red birds, while snugly stowed away in the bosom of his shirt was his much cherished pet, the alligator. He was not sure of the reception he would receive; but at length he steeled his nerves for whatever was in store and made a rush for the house. The delighted mother folded him in her arms and covered his face with kisses. His brothers and sisters grouped around with words of welcome for the prodigal.

"Thank God that you are safe home again, dear Paul," exclaimed his mother, as she embraced him again and again.

"But what's this?"

She started back, for she had felt something squirming inside of his shirt.

"Oh, that's my dear little alligator," and Paul put in his hand and pulled out his pet. His sisters ran screaming away. His mother gazed sternly at him and said:

"Put out that ugly reptile!" Paul placed it tenderly on the floor beside the red birds' cage and received from his fond mother a well merited castigation. That evening, however, all was forgotten and Paul entertained his family with stories of his adventures and was doubtlessly looked upon by the little group, as a wonderful traveler or a hardened young liar.

Paul's father, a traveling man, came home a few days after this. He had a long consultation with his wife regarding the escapade of their venturesome son. They came to the decision that they had better move from the vicinity of the river and so wean him from his unnatural love of the water. A week later found the family at the head of Federal Street, about as far as they could get away from the river and still remain in the city. Paul spent his last night before moving on one of his friends' woodpiles; (his own had been pirated during his absence,) and bitterly bemoaned the fate that took him so far away from his beloved element.

A rigid discipline was now pursued in regard to Paul. He was given a certain space of time to go and return from school. After that he was expected home and made to stay there. He studied hard all winter and advanced rapidly. But he had to cross a bridge going to and coming from school. He would always stop to gaze into the water he loved so well, even if had to run to make up for lost time. Spring came on and the longing increased to enjoy again the piney smell of the newly arrived rafts, to dive into the clear depths, and revisit his old friends the "pavers." He took off his shoes and felt the water's temperature. "In two weeks," he thought with rapture, "In two weeks I can take a plunge."

In less than two weeks he enjoyed this plunge and finally remembering that he had to be at home by four o'clock, he scrambled onto a raft and discovered that his body was covered with some unknown, greasy, tar-like substance. He could not get it off, and at last asked a raftsman, who stood by, what it was:

"Why, son," answered the lumberman; "That is petroleum. Don't you know that they struck oil at the head of the river and great quantities are pouring into the Alleghany above. It will be a long time before the river will be as clear as she used to be, and you, my little man, will have a nice job getting that off your skin."

When Paul reached home, his mother's scrutiny revealed the fact that something was wrong.

"Have you been swimming again, despite your promise?"

Paul murmured something that might be either "yes" or "no." His hat removed, showed his hair quite damp further investigation revealed the fact that his shirt was on wrong side out, while round his neck was a well defined dark line from the oil cakes he struck while swimming against the stream. His sister Teresa revenged herself that evening for many a raid on her dolls by scrubbing him into the appearance of a boiled lobster, so that he would be neat and presentable for school next day. Even this lesson did not teach him. One warm day while on his way to school, he lingered so long on the bridge that the tower clock struck ten, and then he argued that it would be useless to go until the afternoon session, when he could easily hoodwink his teacher with an excuse. But the afternoon came, and the wild boy was still in the water, too deeply interested in the navigation of a plank to realize that he was playing "hookey" and risking its shady consequences.

About two o'clock he heard loud cries from the St. Clair Street bridge. Looking up, he saw an excited crowd gathering. The object of their excitement was a little boy who had waded out on a shallow bar above the bridge until he had stumbled into deep water and was being carried away by the strong current. Paul caught one glimpse of him as he disappeared and springing from his plank he swam out with a strong, steady stroke to his assistance. The crowd on the bridge shouted loud cries of encouragement. As Paul reached the spot where the body went down, he could find no traces of him. A man on the bridge shouted:

"A little farther down! A little farther down! I can see him at the bottom."

Paul swam in the direction indicated and at the cry, "there, there," dove to the bottom like a seal. He came directly on the body which was doubled up against a large boulder. He grasped it by the arm and rose with it to the surface. Loud ringing cheers from the crowd above, encouraged him. He swam with one arm, supporting the body with the other. They were being rapidly carried away down the stream, when a boat which had been sent out, reached the almost exhausted boy. Paul and the unconscious boy were taken ashore and conveyed to the back room of a saloon where a doctor soon revived both. He then proposed that, some token of recognition should be presented by the assembled crowd to the brave little fellow who had made the rescue. Paul's hat was taken and soon filled to the brim with silver. Then the two boys were loaded into an express wagon and escorted by a policeman, they started for home. When the wagon reached the house of the boy who had been rescued, the policeman lifted him out carefully and carried him in, while the mother's affrighted cries alarmed the neighborhood. The officer assured her that there was no danger, so she grew calmer and helped to roll her son into a warm blanket and tuck him snugly in bed. The old grandmother, who was blind, heard the story and asked that Paul be brought to her. Her trembling hands were passed over his face and head. She blessed him fervently and then to the delight of the grinning urchins, looking in at the door and to Paul's intense embarrassment, she kissed him several times. At last the policeman told him to come on and Paul and his silver continued their homeward journey. When Mrs. Boyton saw her truant son under police escort, she turned pale, but the officer called out, "Don't be frightened, ma'am, he's all right. You ought to be proud of this boy," and he told her the story of the rescue and handed over the silver. The mother's eye's beamed with pleasure as she listened. She praised her gallant little son and thanked the officer for his kindness. After he was gone she put the silver carefully away and interviewed the hero, as often before, with a shingle.

"Not only for playing hookey," she said; "but for going into the water at all."

The little fellow rescued that day is Thomas McCaffery, now a member of the Alleghany City Fire Department. Many years afterwards he gave Paul a gold medal in remembrance of their first meeting.

In vacation Paul started out to look for work, for with all his wildness he was industrious. He secured a place in a paper box factory at the princely salary of fifty cents a week. His business was to lower great packages of boxes from the upper story to the ground floor. He thought how delightful it would be to go down himself on the rope. One day he induced a small boy who worked near, pasting, to mind the windlass while he descended by hanging on above the usual pits of boxes. The sensation was novel and pleasing and it became exciting when the boy above leaned over and shouted: "The boss is coming, look out for yourself. I'll have to go." An instant later Paul and the boxes crashed together on the bottom floor. The proprietor dragged him out of the ruin he had made and assisted him energetically to the street, without even the hint of a recommendation.

As Paul slowly and painfully wended his way home, a lady called him: "Little boy, do you want a job?" Paul said he did and was put to work. He had to sprinkle the street and keep the brick sidewalk clean in front of her house. He was happily aided by a long hose, so that he thoroughly enjoyed his new work and gave entire satisfaction. About ten days after, Mrs. C., his employer sent him to escort her son to the house of a relative living in Lawrenceburg, a village a few miles up the river from Pittsburgh. She warned Paul to be careful of her little boy, who was a delicate child about his own age and gave him street car fare to pay his way up and down. Her last instructions were to leave Harvey at his aunt's and return as soon as possible. When Paul was about to take the car back, he thought of a pleasanter way, one in which he could save his car fare, too. So he went to the river where he selected a large sized plank and a piece of driftwood for a paddle. Then he piloted himself down in safety and was back in time. A few days later, the trusty little messenger was sent to Lawrenceburg to bring Harvey home. Instead of taking the cars as instructed, Paul induced his charge to go with him to the river. The little boy was very timid and refused to embark on a steering oar that Paul found near the shore. A steering oar consists of a plank securely pinned into a spar about thirty feet long and used on stern and bow of a raft to guide it. Paul at last half forcibly seated him on a block of wood on the steering oar and procuring a pole they started on their voyage. All went well until they had passed under the old Aqueduct Bridge. Then a crowd of Pittsburgh boys who were in a skiff recognized Paid as the leader of their enemies from Alleghany and opened up hostilities. Paul bravely kept them off with his pole and whenever the chance offered propelled it nearer and nearer to his own side of the river. When almost ashore they rammed the steering oar with the bow of their skiff, struck Paul with the oar and tumbled poor Harvey into the river. Paul never thought of himself; but seizing the son of his aristocratic mistress, he swam in for the shore, then only a few feet away. The Pittsburgh boys were satisfied with the prize they had captured in the steering oar and towed it away to their own side of the river. They were followed, however, by a shower of rocks hurled by the infuriated Paul. A sad looking pair greeted the maid who answered their ring. Paul turned young Harvey over to her, then sneaked around to the alley to await developments. Hearing loud lamentations coming from the direction of Mrs. C.'s room, he started for home where he told his mother that the work was too severe for him and fearing the lady would refuse to let him go, he left without bothering her for a reference.

About this time the war of the rebellion broke out and the fever burned fiercely in Pittsburgh and vicinity. Paul longed to join the great bodies of troops that were being hurried to the front, especially so, when he saw boat loads of his old friends, the gallant "buck-tail" boys coming down the river to enlist. He spent all his spare time hanging around the headquarters of the forming regiments. One day he asked a recruiting officer if he needed a drummer boy. "You are pretty small, sonny," said the soldier, "can you drum?" "No," said Paul, "but I can learn mighty quick." Pleased with the answer, the soldier took him to his headquarters and said: "Here is a little volunteer." Paul was closely questioned and untruthfully assured the officers in charge that his mother would be glad to get rid of him. That night he was enrolled in Colonel Cass' Regiment. Next day he began his drum practice, an exercise that was rudely interrupted by the appearance of his mother, who lead the "warrior bold" home by the ear.

CHAPTER II.

His parents now decided to send Paul away to school. The college they selected was situated in the heart of the Alleghany Mountains about four miles from the Pennsylvania Railroad. It was far from any water course or river, and surrounded by a dense forest of pines. Paul's mother accompanied him to the college. She told the faculty of his peculiar passion for the water and the dread she had of losing him. Mrs. Boyton was assured that her boy would be taken good care of. Paul was permitted to escort her as far as the village where she took the stage for the rail road again. Their farewell was most affectionate. Paul cried bitterly, not only for the parting from his mother whom he loved so well, but for the feeling that he was being exiled for all his crimes and misdemeanors. The fall session had not yet begun so he had ample time to become acquainted with the few boys who were already at the college and to explore the dark pine woods that seemed a new world to him. Paul inquired eagerly if there was any water in the vicinity. The boys told him there was a place called the "swimming hole" about two miles from the college. Next day he coaxed some of his companions to show him the way. He found a pond, little larger than a hole, surrounded by heavy vegetation and inhabited by a colony of frogs. He was soon swimming in its depths and had induced two or three of the boys to follow his example. Day after day he visited the hole and made out to enjoy a swim; but he always thought longingly of the far off, bright Alleghany.

One day a teamster who sometimes came to the college, told Paul of a sheet of water that was much larger than the swimming hole. He called it "Bruce's Dam." Next morning Paul and a Philadelphia boy named Stockdale, who was his particular chum, obtained permission to go out of bounds. They had managed during breakfast to appropriate a sufficient supply of bread and butter for all day. They started out to find Bruce's dam. A long and weary tramp they had over the mountains. They turned aside often to chase the gray squirrels that abounded in that country, and they wasted much time in a fruitless attempt to dig out a red fox, that had crossed their path and shot down a hole in the ground. They were so long reaching the dam that they thought they must have been misdirected. They were about to return, when Paul suddenly said, "Hark! I think I hear water!" They listened intently for a few seconds. A sound again came through the woods. They struck out a little to the right and were soon at the long-sought, dam. It was a body of water about one hundred yards wide and five hundred yards long. Enormous pine stumps protruded through the surface.

There was a miserable looking saw-mill situated at the lower end. Two men were employed in drawing out logs and ripping them up into boards. Paul tittered a joyful cry as he perceived that the water was both clear and deep. Hastily he divested himself of his clothing and "Stockie" slowly followed his example. As they stood naked on the bank, before their plunge, a snake shot out almost from under then feet, and swam gracefully over the surface to a stump a little distance off. That was enough for "Stockie," who resumed his clothes. Paul did not like the idea of snakes in the water, still he had traveled far for a swim and he was resolved to have it and so he plunged headlong in. Round and round among the stumps he swam. He saw several snakes and also a number of water lizards. After his bath, Paul and "Stockie" went down to the mill and had some talk with the men engaged there. The latter assured them that the snakes and water lizards were perfectly harmless. This restored "Stockie's" courage. He agreed to try the water before leaving, provided Paul would go in with him. The two chums had a long, delightful swim and finally, as sunset approached, they suddenly thought that they might be needed at the college. It was dark when they got back. They both received a severe lecture for their long absence. Bruce's dam was several times revisited and always with great enjoyment. At last vacation was over and these pleasant pilgrimages came to an end. Paul kept the promise made to his mother. During study time he applied himself with all his energies to the task before him and so rapidly increased his store of knowledge; but, he was also learning many things outside the school room. The loneliness and surroundings of the college increased the natural wildness of his nature. When recreation time approached, Paul would pass the sign to the ever ready "Stockie." Then he would obtain permission to leave the room on some pretext, and the other, by some clever maneuver, would soon be after him. Then down to the dark, cool pine woods to visit their "figure four" traps which they had set in different places to catch squirrels. This trap consisted of a square box placed on a piece of board and set with a little wooden trigger. When a squirrel would enter to get the walnut fastened inside, he would spring the trap and would not succeed in cutting his way out before his young captor's arrival. They would slip a pillow-case, furnished unconsciously by the college, under one corner of the box, turning it off the bottom board until a little opening was made into the bag. The squirrel of course would jump in, and was grabbed and twisted until it was squeezed down to one corner. Then his captors would get a firm grip on the back of his neck. If the squirrel proved to be a young one, they would put on a collar and little chain, that they had always ready, and keep him to train for a pet. Once Paul caught a gray squirrel kitten so small and young that he had to feed it on milk and crushed walnuts. He called it May. The tiny creature lived in his pocket and desk and shared his bed at night. It would sit on the off page of his book whilst he studied and comb its little whiskers and brush its tail in perfect contentment. Every one marveled at the affection of his pet and at the control he had over it. Paul would let it loose in the woods, it would run up a tree and at his call, "Come May," it would return at once and with a chuckle drop into his pocket. Paul kept this squirrel until after he had left college. The crowded streets of the city seemed to bewilder it, and it jumped from his pocket to the sidewalk. A man passing struck it with a cane and killed it. Paul grieved long over his pet; but from this experience he acquired a great control over animals and always had a supply in hand to train. He carried snakes and bugs and mice and lizards in his pockets and at one time had a white rat that came very near to filling the place of the lost May. If the boys captured an old squirrel, they generally let it go; but sometimes it was retained for another purpose.

It would be taken back to the college and that evening put down through a knot hole in the study-hall floor. The hole was carefully covered by a small piece of board with the leg of Paul's desk to keep it down. Next morning when all would be deep in their studies and a profound silence filled the hall, Paul would quietly slip the board away from the hole. Attracted by the light, the squirrel would soon come out. The studious (?) boys who were posted, kept one eve on their books and one on the hole. When the squirrel appeared, as it usually did in a short time these would start up with well feigned cries of alarm. In a moment the entire study-hall was in an uproar, all pursuing the bewildered squirrel. The first or second time this occurred, the staid professor took active part in the exciting chase. The frequent recurrence of squirrel hunts in the study-hall awakened suspicion in the minds of the faculty. An investigation was made, Paul and Stockie were called to the president's room and interviewed regarding squirrels and their habits. After this, the study-hall was no longer disturbed by these little denizens of the forest.

About the last time that Paul went swimming to Bruce's dam, a decayed thorn was driven into his foot, a portion of which he was unable to remove. This troubled him occasionally. During the month of November the foot commenced to swell in an alarming manner. He had to remain in the dormitory for over a week. While he was still an invalid, a box arrived from home full of cakes, candies, preserves and many other goodies dear to a school-boy's heart. In the box was also a present from his younger brother. It had been packed in without the knowledge of his mother. It was a large Chinese firecracker. Paul carefully concealed this precious gift until a grand occasion would come to fire it. At recess many of the boys came up to see him, and incidentally to share in the delicasies he had received. Stockie came also and told Paul that their crowd had discovered a tale-bearer in the person of a youth from Johnstown, Penn. He wound up by adding:

"And how are we to fix him?"

Paul answered mysteriously: "Leave it to me. I have it; bring me all the string you can find."

From day to day Stockie produced liberal supplies of the desired article. No doubt most of it belonged to the boy whose innocent pastime was that of flying kites during recess. Paul wound this string firmly and tightly around the Chinese cracker until it had assumed considerable proportions. He argued on the principle that, if paper resisted the force of the explosion, the additional binding of string would cause a much louder one. The bomb was at last completed and Stockie received a hint to keep his ears open for music that night. The little iron bed of the doomed talebearer was not far distant from Paul's, and between them was a stove in which burned a brisk fire every night to drive out the chill mountain air. When all were asleep, Paul slipped from his bed, and touched the fuse to the red hot side of the stove. Then he placed the ignited bomb under the tell-tales bed and hastily scrambled back to his own. He had just time to roll himself up in the blankets, when there was a flash and terrible explosion. The bed of the tell-tale turned a complete somersault, while the entire building trembled with the concussion and a shower of broken glass was scattered around. No serious damage was done; but Paul was horrified and frightened half to death at the result of his first essay with explosives. The boys in the dormitory were only too glad of an excuse for excitement. They immediately began the usual battle with pillows accompanied with the wildest yells and whoops, until they were suddenly quieted by the entrance of the officials. No one could find out the culprit, so the investigation was postponed until morning. Classes were suspended next day. Every student, including the invalid, was present in the study-hall. The entire faculty sat in judgment. The president opened the meeting with a severe lecture, during which he quoted that it "was better that ten guilty ones should escape rather than that one innocent person should suffer." He called urgently upon the guilty ones to stand up and declare themselves. His invitation was not accepted.

"Now boys, you know that it is a strict dormitory rule that no one there shall speak above a whisper. The noise you made last night was heard distinctly in the village a mile away. All of you who did not break the rule last night put up your hands."

Every boy's hand in the study hall was at once raised. The president looked perplexed, and said: "Perhaps you misunderstood me. To make it plain to you, I want every boy who did not raise his voice above a whisper after retiring last night to stand up."

The first on their feet were Paul and Stockie, whose good example was followed without any exception by every boy in the school. The president was dumbfounded. He shook his head sadly. After a brief consultation with the professors he remarked. "The young men now before me are grievously lacking either in understanding or veracity." Numerous were the mishaps that befell Paul and his companion Stockie, owing to their love of wandering through the woods. When they were missed, a professor was generally sent after the fugitives. In visiting their squirrel traps they often separated, Stockie examining one trap, Paul another. They would appoint a place of rendezvous, close to some well known giant pine. The one to arrive first would call the other by a loud whistle in close imitation of a quail. The other would answer by a similar whistle. One day when about to mount the tree and give his usual signal of recall, Paul discovered the professor, who had been sent after them, approaching. Quickly he climbed into the tree and concealed himself in the dense foliage. At this moment he heard Stockie's familiar signal quite near the rendezvous, and to his dismay, the professor, hidden behind a tree close by, repeated the quail call, thus leading the unsuspecting Stockie to his doom. As Stockie neared the tree in which Paul was hidden, he shouted: "I've got two!" The professor stepped forward and said: "I have one!"

Paul could distinctly over-hear the professor question Stockie in regard to his chum's whereabouts, all knowledge of which the latter loyally but untruthfully denied. He had grasped the situation at a glance. The professor with his captive remained a long while and the latter was compelled to repeat the quail call time after time in hopes that the other victim would respond. But the moaning of the pines was the only answer. Finally the professor and his prisoner started for the college. Paul slid down the tree and taking a shorter cut, was deep in his books when they entered. Though strongly suspected, he escaped that time, the poor captive receiving a double dose. Stockie was generally unfortunate enough to get more than his share of punishment, but he was thoroughly loyal to his friends and never murmured. It was customary, when a boy had misbehaved himself or broken any rule, to send him to the president's room where either reprimand or a thrashing awaited him. One day a professor called Stockie during recess and said:

"As you are a good, swift runner, I want you to go over to the President's room and ask for his letters. I want to put them in the mail bag. The coach will be starting in a few minutes."

The president was not in his room and Stockie availed himself of the chance to view the pictures hanging around the walls. The president had just made the discovery that several of the boys had utterly ruined some growing tobacco that he had been experimenting on, so he was in bad humor when he entered his sanctum.

"What! You here again?"

And without permitting the astonished Stockie to speak he began to administer a severe thrashing. The door was opened by the professor who wanted the mail.

"Has he been in mischief already? Why I told him a few moments ago to come here and get your letters." "Oh," exclaimed the president, "I thought he had been sent here as usual, for punishment. Well, if he does not deserve it now, he certainly will before the week is out."

Paul had organized a company of choice spirits who were known by the title of the 'Wild Geese'. Each member named himself after his own particular hero, such as Dick Turpin, Jack Shepard, Capt. Kidd and other distinguished gentleman freebooters. The headquarters of the association was in an abandoned log house about three miles from the college. On half holidays the company would escape out of bounds by different ways and assemble at headquarters. The cabin consisted of one large earthen floor room with a loft above. The stairs leading up to this loft had been cut away and a light ladder that could be easily hauled up, substituted. The aperture closed down by a rough trap door made for the purpose. This was done to afford concealment, in case any of the professors should come looking for them, or protection against a rival organization of larger boys, known as the "Wild Hens." When the company assembled, it was customary for Paul, who was their chosen chief, to detail parties to different duties. While some would be cutting and collecting wood to burn in the huge fire-place in the lower story, others would be off through the surrounding farms on a forage for chickens, potatoes, apples, etc., etc. All the money in the society would be entrusted to a committee of the most reliable members. These would be dispatched to the village store to purchase cheese, crackers, ginger-bread and other delicacies for the banquet. The village store was owned by an old fellow by the name of Philip Hardtsoe. He had expelled both Paul and Stockie from his territory on account of an incident which had happened some time previous. The two chums went in one day to buy a few cents worth of candy. They were difficult to please and insisted that Philip should hand them some from a jar on an upper shelf. While his back was turned Paul reached far into a barrel where a few nice, red apples lay on the bottom. As he balanced on his stomach over the chime of the barrel, Stockie saw his opportunity for mischief and gave him a push that toppled him down on his head. The noise caused old Philip to turn around. He thought the lads only intended to fool him when they asked for the candy. He rushed from behind the counter, easily capturing Paul, who was helpless in the barrel, while Stockie dashed through the door roaring with laughter. This was the reason that Philip would never allow either boy in his store, so Paul and Stockie had to buy their candy by proxy.

But to return to the "Wild Geese." As the various committees reported, they would find a roaring fire and everything ready for cooking. The banquet table was generally prepared in the upper story or loft and consisted of two long boards on trestles. The seats were round blocks of wood. The chief luxuries of the banquet itself, besides the store supplies, were chicken and potatoes. The chickens had been prepared by rolling them in mud; then baking them. When fully cooked the feathers came off. A sharp knife ripped them open and the baked entrails were easily removed. The potatoes were simply roasted in the hot ashes. The commoner articles of the banquet menu, such as bread, butter, salt and pepper were always appropriated from the college table. The first banquet that ever took place in the old log cabin followed the election of officers. Paul was unanimously elected chief and escorted to the head of the table. Stockie and Billy O'Meara, of Washington, as first and second lieutenants, sat on either side. It is doubtful if ever a pirate captain looked with more pride on his gallant crew, or if a real banquet was ever more thoroughly enjoyed by the participants.

Several times during the winter the "Wild Geese" were attacked by the "Wild Hens." They were always repulsed excepting one day when the latter were re-enforced by an alien crowd. The "Wild Geese" defended their cabin bravely, but, were driven foot by foot, until they wore compelled to retreat to the loft and draw up the ladder. The lower portion of the cabin was in full possession of the besiegers, who demolished everything they could lay their hands on, with much gusto. They did their utmost to pry up the trap door, but were beaten back. Suddenly to the "Wild Geese's" surprise, the lower part of the cabin was abandoned by the Hens. They thought it a ruse to draw them out, so I they lay quiet for some time. There were no windows in the loft. Bye and bye Paul knocked a hole through the shingles of the roof. Protruding his head he saw the Hens in a wild flight towards the forest. He could see no cause for this until he knocked a hole through the other side of the cabin roof. What he beheld was not calculated to cheer his heart. Eight or ten of the professors were almost on the cabin. There was no time or chance to escape. Paul commanded all hands to lie down and keep still while himself and lieutenants sat on the trap door. The house was quickly entered by the professors. Remarks such as "They must be here," "The fire is still burning," "See the chicken feathers," etc., etc. ascended to the trembling urchins above.

"Is there no loft or upper story?" said one finally.

"I don't think so," responded another; "There is no means of getting up there. They have all left. Here is their trail in the snow leading to the woods."

All would have been well with the "Wild Geese" had not the unlucky Stockie at this moment, given a loud sneeze. At which some of the minor members of the company giggled. The chief looked sternly at the culprit. He saw Stockie about to repeat the involuntary sneeze and grabbed him by the nose and throat. Too late! The noise had been heard below and the imperative command was given to "come down." Slowly the trap-door was opened and the ladder descended. Then a scuffle ensued to see who would go down last. The consequence was that two or three of the Geese went down at the same time. Slowly and sorrowfully the prisoners marched to the college where to add to their misery they beheld the faces of the smiling and triumphant "Wild Hens." These had regained "bounds" without being discovered and their loud cackling grated discordantly on the nerves of the late banqueters. That evening, singly and in pairs were the "Wild Geese" called over and interviewed by the president. On their return to the study hall their flushed faces and reddened eyes accompanied by rapid, mysterious signals, gave warning to the waiting ones of the wrath to come. Paul and Stockie were the last to be summoned. They found the president and the prefect of studies in the star chamber.

"Be seated" was the brief command. "Do either of you know anything about a secret organization called the 'Wild Geese'?"

The culprits saw that the customary denial of everything would not answer in this case. They acknowledged that they had heard of such a society. The President was satisfied that he had learned from the other members about all the information that he needed, and that the present interview would not add much to his knowledge, so he turned to the two boys with a kindly smile and gave them a fatherly lecture on the error of their ways. He urged them to promise that in the future they would be more faithful to study and more obedient to the rules of the institution. His kind tones made Paul and Stockie feel ashamed and inspired them with the hope that this gentle lecture would be their only punishment. They glanced congratulations at each other out of the corners of their eyes.

"Now boys," said the president in conclusion, "you have promised me faithfully to mend your conduct. To keep this promise fresh in your memory, I have something to give you. My motto is to leave the best for the last, so Master Paul will retain his seat. Take off your jacket, Stockdale."

Disappointment and dismay were depicted on the two faces. Stockie made many fruitless attempts to unbutton his jacket, unbuttoning two buttons and buttoning one. At last the president's patience gave out and he rushed on his victim with the strap. Now, in the room was an old-fashioned bed, in which ropes were fastened from side to side, in lieu of slats. To escape the strap, Stockie dove under this bed. The president, who was somewhat rheumatic, could not reach him very well, so he called upon the prefect and Paul to assist him in removing the bed. They moved it from side to side around the room in vain, for Stockie was holding on to the bed cords. Paul felt like an executioner to his friend; but life is sweet. He glanced furtively at the prefect and saw him convulsed with smothered laughter. The president made frantic attempts to dislodge Stockie and Paul dashed through the door to liberty. Later, Stockie appeared and cheered Paul with the information that his punishment would come when he had gone to bed. Paul looked the situation over and at last thought of a plan of escape. He sent Stockie into the hall to call out an unsuspicious youth whom he named. This boy soon appeared and Paul told him all about the tribulations of the "Wild Geese." He said he was certain he knew the informer, the villain who had brought all this dire disaster. He had a plan to punish the tale-bearer. He would like to exchange beds that night with his listener, so that he would be near the villain's bed. Then he would put a handful of red pepper over the mouth and nose while he snored. Was his friend willing? His friend thought the cause a just one and readily agreed to the proposed arrangement. That night the innocent youth slipped into Paul's bed and the avenger joyfully nestled in his, at the other side of the dormitory. About an hour after the boys had retired, a tall figure, with stealthy step passed in the direction of Paul's bed. There was a suppressed scuffle and the clear sound of a strap coming in contact with its victim, while a low, stern voice was heard saying: "Not a word sir; not a word. Don't dare to raise your voice above a whisper. You deserve it all and more." After a few moments Professor Justice retired with the same stealthy step. There was convulsive sobbing in Chief Paul's bed, and the other boys covered their heads with their blankets in dread of a similar visitation.

The boy who suffered that night is now a brilliant judge and well known politician. But he always believed that he had been punished for changing beds and wondered not a little that his companion had escaped similar castigation.

The boys were obliged to rise very early in the morning. The first duty of the day was to proceed to the chapel for prayers, and religious instruction. But many of the lads preferred to gather around the red hot stove of the study hall where they could tend to their devotions with more liberty and comfort than in the chilly chapel. If they were missed, a professor was sent to ascertain their whereabouts. He was generally discovered in time by the boy detailed by his companions as look out. The study hall and dormitories formed a building separate from the rest of the college. As the professor approached from the main building, the boys would leap from the low windows of the study hall into the snow. Sometimes the professor was suspicious and would reconnoiter outside the study hall; but the boys were alert and as he passed around a corner, they would get around another and so they often escaped to the chapel. One morning the president missed several of his jewels and started himself for the study hall determined to capture them. As usual, the boys clambered through the windows and escaped in different directions always keeping the hall between them and their pursuer. Stockie, Billy O'Meara and Paul adopted the old rule of sneaking away from one corner of the hall, while the president advanced around another. The pursuit was very close, for the president was sure from the tracks in the snow, that some of the boys were dodging him.

Stockie and O'Meara broke for the shelter of another building; but Paul continued to dodge around the study hall. Once the president failed to appear at the expected corner. Paul feared that he might be doubling on him and so crept cautiously on all fours back to the corner he had left to take a look around that side of the building. As he warily put his head out to take the observation it came in hard contact with that of the president, who had adopted Paul's own tactics to catch him. The situation was so ludicrous that even that austere gentlemen burst out laughing and Paul scampered away to the chapel.

A favorite resort for the boys during winter weather was a barn where they had rare sport tumbling over the great quantities of hay in the loft. A party of them were one day enjoying this pastime, when a stern voice below commanded them to "descend immediately," supplemented by the ominous and oft repeated expression, "I know you all, I, have your names." Some of the boys descended, but Paul and four companions clambered out on the roof of a wagon shed. This roof was very steep and was covered with about three feet of snow. Here they squatted down and awaited results. The professor took the names of the boys who had descended and ordered them to the study hall. This gentleman, by the way, was very successful in discovering culprits, and was known facetiously by the boys as the "bloodhound." He was sure he had not found all the truants, but he saw they were not in the loft, so he began a tour outside of the barn to ascertain how they had escaped. Slowly he walked around the wagon shed carefully scrutinizing every place in which he thought they might be concealed. The snow, loosened by the heat and extra weight of the unlucky boys, gave way and precipitated them over the head and shoulders of the astounded professor.

One form of punishment inflicted by the faculty was termed "corrence." The culprit was deprived of his meals mid compelled to remain at study in the hall while the others enjoyed their repast. This was a severe punishment to healthy, growing boys, whose appetites were whetted by the keen mountain air. On the "corrence" list one day appeared the names of William O'Meara and Paul Boyton. This was no infrequent occurrence. These boys did not seem much distressed. There was a secret understanding among the then suppressed "Wild Geese" that none of their number should suffer the pangs of hunger while provisions could be obtained from the table. The faculty must have found out this fraternal understanding, for on the day in question every boy was examined as he left the refectory and everything eatable in his possession confiscated. The day was hard for Billy and Paul. By night they were wild with hunger and vowed to make a raid on the kitchen or die. The kitchen in question was in the deep basement of the main building, lit up by small windows fully six feet above the floor. When the cooks had retired, Billy and Paul made their way to one of these windows. They pried it open. Paul persuaded his companion to crawl into the window head first, while he lowered him by holding on to his legs and feet. He instructed Billy that when the floor was reached he could with the aid of a chair easily pass out the much needed supplies. Billy began his descent. When lowered as far as Paul could reach he said:

"I can't feel the floor, pull me up."

Just then there was a deep growl heard in the kitchen and footsteps approaching from the outside. Paul did not have time or strength to haul Billy up again, so letting him go by the run, he started to his feet and disappeared in the darkness. Billy was seized by a large Newfoundland dog that held him fast until discovered by the cooks who came down to find out the cause of the noise.

The refectory of the college was a long, narrow room with a table extending its entire length. Each boy was supposed to stand in his place with folded hands and bowed head, while grace was being said by the professor at the end of the table. But such keen appetites could hardly wait for the blessing to be called. While one hand was devoutly raised, in case the professor would look down along the table, the other grasped a fork and all eyes were fixed of the dishes of meat. Smothered exclamations of "That's my piece with the fat;" "The middle piece is mine," "I like the lean," etc., passed along the line. As the amen rang out, every fork was darted into the longed for meat, as a harpoon is sent into a whale.

Not far from the college lived an irascible old gentleman who owned a rich farm and some very fine horses of which he took great pride. Paul and his chums looked on these lovely animals with envious eyes, and often wished that they could capture one and enjoy a ride. One day Stockie and Paul went to the woods at the bottom of a field that led by a gentle ascent to the farm house. They had with them a pillow-slip half full of oats. They were trying to induce a magnificent looking colt to approach them. The colt was shy, but the oats were tempting. He came near enough to taste them and submitted gently to the boy's caresses and even permitted them to lead him around by the forelock. "Now Stockie," said Paul, "I will hold him by the nose and mane. You jump from that stump and take the first ride."

With a spring, Stockie mounted the animal's back. The colt broke from Paul and dashed madly away, Stockie clinging to him like a cat. The creature never stopped in its mad career until it had reached the farm yard. With a terrific leap it unseated Stockie, who tumbled uninjured but paralyzed with fear, into a pile of manure from which he was dragged by the enraged farmer. As his friend disappeared, Paul made a beeline for the college. Soon after poor Stockie was brought in by the farmer and delivered into the hands of the president. It was some time before the victim was able to sit at his desk with any degree of comfort.

With such adventures as these, two years of college life glided by and then the parting came. Paul had progressed rapidly in his classes for his was a character that applied itself to books, as devotedly as it did to play. His best loved study was navigation, and he often surprised the gray-haired old professor by his knowledge in this quarter. His open, fearless nature had endeared him to his teachers and despite the punishments; he had learned to love the college life so his going was viewed with regret by both sides. The college was in its infancy when Paul's name was on the pupil's roll. He returned to visit it some years ago, to find it grown into one of the great educational institutions of the land. Many of our brightest and best men lovingly roll it their Alma Mater. The venerable president received him with open arms. He put Paul's picture in his gallery of the boys who were a credit to the institution, and both talked over old times and life's many changes with emotion, and laughed heartily over certain well remembered experiences. Paul felt a deep pang of remorse at the praise and the welcome, for his memory bore another record.

During Paul's sojourn at college, his family had moved from Alleghany to New York. His father was an importer of sea-shells, corals, marine curiosities anal oriental goods, of which he made annual sales in the chief cities of the country. He took Paul with him and gave him the first lesson in business. Travel suited Paul immensely; but business was irksome and the civil war was still raging. Stirring accounts of the conflicts in the south, and the martial air that pervaded the entire country, filled Paul's soul with longing to go to the front.

CHAPTER III.

On the morning of April 15th, 1864, young Boyton presented himself at the Brooklyn Navy Yard, and was enrolled in the United States Navy as a sailor before the mast. After a few weeks drilling he was transferred to the United States Steamer, Hydrangea, Captain W. Rogers in command. Paul was now in his fifteenth year. He had no difficulty in passing the scrutiny of the enlisting officers. He was of a powerful build and very muscular. His outdoor life in the woods and on the river made him look older than he really was. The Hydrangea was ordered to Fortress Monroe, and Paul received his baptism of fire while the steamer was running up the James river past Malvern Hill, where a confederate battery was stationed. Much has been written about the war, and as this is simply a story of adventure, it will be left to better writers to record war history many of whom have already described scenes enacted in that vicinity during the year 1864. The last engagement Paul was in, was the memorable assault on Fort Fisher. When the war closed, he was mustered out. At that time he held the position of yeoman.

Mr. Boyton discovered that Paul did not have much aptitude for commercial pursuits, so he sent him to the West Indies for the purpose of collecting and shipping all kinds of marine curiosities. Paul's companion was a submarine diver whom his father had engaged. They took passage on the bark, "Reindeer," bound for the Barbadoes. They had all kinds of the latest dredging apparatus, including submarine armor and pumps in their outfit. After a tedious voyage of twenty-seven days, the "Reindeer" cast anchor in Bridgetown. Paul and the diver, whose name was Tom Scott, were kindly welcomed by the merchant, an old friend of Mr. Boyton's, to whom they carried letters of introduction.

His father's instructions were to charter a fishing boat, or some suitable vessel at Bridgetown for a six month's cruise among the keys and islands surrounding, for the purpose of fishing up coral, shells and other curios that he could gather. A few days after his arrival, Paul engaged a staunch little sloop commanded by a negro, who was assisted by four strong sailors also colored, as crew. The first cruise was around the island of Barbadoes. Several curios were collected and purchased and a goodly shipment sent back by the "Reindeer." When he received them and read Paul's accompanying letter, Mr. Boyton was satisfied that his son was now engaged in a business that thoroughly suited him. The Cayosa, for such was the name of the little sloop, was then provisioned for a voyage to the group of islands that lay to the westward, and where it was said rare shells would be found. For a small consideration the captain had agreed to bunk forward with crew, leaving Tom Scott and Paul his little cabin all to themselves. This cabin was thoroughly scrubbed and cleaned by the pair, after which they fitted it up and placed therein their baggage, rifles, fishing gear, plenty of reading matter and their private stores.

While in port, Paul remained the guest of Mr. C., the merchant, whose home was a beautiful villa situated a little way out of town. The merry, bright-eyed daughters of his host made sad havoc in the susceptible heart of young Boyton. At last all the stores were aboard and everything was ready. One bright morning the anchor was weighed, and the sloop stood away on her cruise to the island of Vincent, which lay about one hundred miles to the westward. During this voyage a heavy tornado tested the little sloop to her utmost. She was driven far out of her course. It was four days ere they reached Kingston on the southward of the island, instead of Richmond whither they were bound. They spent a few days in the quaint, old town and picked up several curiosities. The sloop was then headed for the Cariacou islands, a large group which dot the ocean between St. Vincent and Granada. Many of these islands are uninhabited by human beings. They are low and loaded down to the water's edge with rich, tropical vegetation. The sloop spent six weeks in this group. Every available part of the boat was packed with coral and all kinds of curiosities. A run was then made to Charlottetown, Granada, where the collection was discharged, cleaned and packed in hogsheads all ready for the first boat that would call, bound for New York. Here the sloop was again provisioned, then she set out for Tobago about one hundred miles southeast. A cruise was made around the entire island, but the collection was not remunerative. The sloop was then headed to Trinidad, and along the north coast, valuable specimens were picked up. In this same locality they struck on a reef of exquisite brain coral, with which they loaded the sloop. Sail was then made for Port of Spain, the principal town of the island. In going through the Dragon's Mouth, a narrow, dangerous passage between the mainland of South America and Trinidad, the Cayosa was nearly wrecked. A sudden change in the wind when they were rounding the point drove her into the breakers. Her mast was badly sprung and only with the utmost difficulty was she saved. Under shortened sail she entered Port of Spain, a curiously picturesque old town. Here the collection was discharged as before and the Cayosa beached for an overhauling. Among those employed to assist in the repairs were three English sailors who were held prisoners on the charge of mutiny. The prison regulations in Trinidad were very lax, so much so that the three mutineers were permitted to come down daily and take a hand in the sloop's overhauling. They were from Liverpool and hard characters. The captain of their vessel delivered them over at Trinidad preferring to go shorthanded rather than have them aboard. On the shady side of the sloop, that was then high up on the beach, they entertained Scott and Paul with their varied adventures. One day Paul expressed astonishment that being prisoners, they were allowed such unusual liberties. One of them, Dick Harris by name, answered:

"We are a burden to the authorities here. They would be glad to be rid of us without the trouble and expense of sending us to England, where, no doubt, we would get the rope's end of the law. Last night when you paid us off, we stayed out late. When we got back at the jail we had to knock again and again. At last the jailer called out: 'Who's there?' We gave our names, when he exclaimed: 'Now if you blasted shell-backs can't get home at a reasonable hour, you can stay out. This is the last time I will be disturbed from my slumbers to let you in.'"

The three worthies implored Paul to take them away on the Cayosa. I referred them to the negro captain. The latter earnestly assured them that, he would sooner run a cargo of scorpions than risk himself and crew to the tender care of the mild mannered Liverpool tars.

When the sloop was fully repaired, she started on a trip around the island, but the breakers were too heavy for successful work. She directed her course northward and soon reentered the Cariacon group. A couple of months were spent in those lovely islands. The great breakers that swept in along the coast of Trinidad, Tobago and Granada were missing. In the tranquil bays and inlets, they pursued their occupation of bringing up the natural treasures of the deep with more profit and less risk. They would anchor the Cayosa as near shore as possible, in some well sheltered bay. Here soundings wouid be taken, and the vicinity thoroughly inspected. When the bay gave promise of shells and coral, a camp was made on the silver-like beach under the shade of the towering cocoanut trees. The mainsail was detached and carried ashore to serve as an awning. The large sheet-iron boilers were also landed. While two of the crew gathered wood and decayed vegetation for fuel, the others were busy erecting a crude fire-place with rocks, over which the boilers were set. The shore camp being ready, the submarine pump would be lowered into the yawl and with Tom Scott, encased in his diving armor, would be conveyed to the most likely place on the bay. When this was reached, a kedge anchor was dropped, the face piece of the armor screwed on, the pipes attached and Tom quietly slipped over the side and descended to the reef. Two of the crew turned cranks to force air down to him, while Paul seated in the stern held the life line. When the diver reached bottom, he gave the signal to shift the boat wherever his explorations led him. When a lot of shells or curious objects were found, several pulls on the line were given indicating, "to anchor and send down the bucket." This bucket was a huge iron affair, holding about five bushels. It was sent to the bottom. Tom soon filled it with living and dead specimens of brilliant and beautiful shells. Then it was hoisted and the contents transferred aboard. In the clear waters on the coral reef, Paul, by hanging over the stern, could distinctly see Tom on the bottom moving around in his ponderous dress. He longed for the day when he could go down and behold the strange sights below in the green, transparent water. At last, the yawl was loaded. Tom came up and the helmet of his suit was removed and he enjoyed the pure, salt air once more. The boat was headed for shore and the treasures landed. All living shells were quickly transferred to the boilers full of hot water. They were left to simmer over the fire for a couple of hours, after which they were dumped on the sands. The thoroughly cooked inhabitants were easily removed and the shells sweet and clean and glowing with all the beautiful tints of the rose and lily, were placed in piles under the shade of the awning.

While the crew was engaged in this latter occupation, Scott, and Paul, armed with rifle and shotgun, would saunter through the heavily perfumed tropical forests in search of any game they could find. In expeditions of this kind, they captured three young monkeys and a couple of parrots, who were soon trained pets on the Cayosa, furnishing all hands with amusement. Scott and Paul shot many iguanos. These are huge lizards that abound in the tropics. The captain and crew considered this game a great delicacy and broiled and ate them with relish. It was a long time ere Scott or Paul would touch the reptiles. One day the black captain offered all a young lizard, daintily broiled. He assured them that it was as sweet and tender as an angel's dream. They tasted it and found it really excellent, and from that time on partook heartily of the dish, whenever it was on the table. At night they frequently stretched their hammocks from tree to tree for their cabin was uncomfortably hot. After a refreshing bath in the cool phosphorescent water and a scamper up and down the level sands in lieu of a towel, they would turn in and enjoy a sound sleep. They were generally awakened before daylight by the shrieking and chattering of the parrots and monkeys. Then with a spring from their hammock, they would dash merrily in to the reviving water. After this they donned their white canvas suits and were ready for another day. Breakfast was taken on shore. This consisted of fresh fish, coffee, cocoanuts, pineapples and bread fruits. Abundance of this fruit was found on all the islands they visited. On some of the islands they could not enjoy their nights in the cool hammocks, owing to the attacks of the malicious jigger spider and ferocious mosquitoes.

One day while at anchor over a coral reef at the southern part of Vequin, Torn Scott agreed to give Paul his first lesson in diving. Tom had been feeling sick and feverish for some days so it made him willing to let Paul take his place for once. He gave Paul full instructions how to act, especially warning him not to gasp in the compressed air, but to breathe naturally and easily. When the helmet was screwed on, Paul felt a smothering sensation but it soon passed. Encouraged, he stepped down n the rope ladder over the side of the sloop and slowly slipped to bottom about five fathoms below. The descent was easy, but bewildering. When his heavily leaded feet struck on the coral, it seemed to him as if the top of his head was being lifted off. For the moment he wished to regain the surface, but Scott's advice to keep cool and steady came back to him and he quickly regained control of his nerves. He peered through the heavy plate glass visor curiously around at the strange sights under the green water. The bottom was as white as snow drift and the powerful sun lit lip the water so That he could distinctly see all objects within twelve or fifteen feet of him. He signaled "all right" to Scott with the line and started to walk around. The signal line and hose were played out to him, so that he could take a wide scope around and under the sloop. Notwithstanding the enormous weight of lead attached to the diving dress, Paul found that he had to walk as easily and lightly as if there were egg shells under his feet; the least little pressure on the bottom had the tendency to send him up. After a half-hour below, during which he thoroughly enjoyed his novel surroundings, he felt an oppression on his chest and signaled "to haul up." The strong arms of the crew helped him regain deck, the helmet was removed and his flushed and eager face exposed. He remarked to Tom that "diving was glorious." After a rest of two hours, the sloop having been shifted to another anchorage, he again descended. This time the bottom had a different aspect. It was full of dark rocks over which grow great masses ofsea weeds. A few feet from where he descended, sprang up a reef of branch coral which extended as far as he could see on either side. This coral grew like shrubbery. It was hard to believe that, all this was the product of an invisible insect, instead of being a miniature forest turned into pure white stone. The scene was surpassingly beautiful; coral branches ran up to a height of eight or ten feet from the bottom, where they locked and wove together like vines. Paul walked to the edge of this reef and gazed with delighted eyes into its liquid depths. Schools of bright colored fish were swimming gracefully in and out through the delicate coral branches. Some, more fearless than their companions, swam round and round Paul's copper helmet, and looked into the thick glass at the front. When Paul made a sudden move of his hand, they darted away; but returned soon again to satisfy their curiosity and ascertain what strange monster had invaded their fairy land.

Three sudden jerks of the life line held in the hands of the anxious Tom, recalled Paul to his work. The three pulls meant, "Where are you? Is everything right?" He then signaled for the bucket to be lowered. Taking his pry he broke off some exquisite specimens of the undergrowth coral, which he loaded in and sent up. He then explored on the side of the coral forest until he came to a small portion of the bottom, covered with sand and surrounded with rocks. Under the growth of marine vegetation, he passed his hand, and pulled from the rock a living shell. Paul had been fully instructed by his father in the science of conchology, so he recognized this specimen as very rare and much sought after. It was the shell called "voluta musica." This was the first one of those shells found during the expedition. After a careful search he found twenty-three more of the same kind, and several large shells known as "Triton's trumpet." The bucket was filled. Paul followed it to the surface well satisfied with his first day's work as a submarine diver.

Scott was not enthusiastic over the "volute musica", but the captain of the Cayosa was delighted. He knew the value of the shell. He told Paid he had sold many of them to the tourists and collectors in Barbadoes receiving from fifty cents to a dollar and a half apiece. He also said that where one of those shells was found there was generally many in the vicinity, and advised Paul not to move the sloop that night, but to descend again the next day.

When the sun was sufficiently high the next morning, Paul again donned the armor and resumed his search for the voluta. Not thirty yards from where he had discovered the first one, he found a basin in the rocks filled with sand. From around this basin he took out two hundred and forty specimens of the desired shell. Afterwards it was ascertained that no greater find of this species had ever been made. Scott was not pleased with Paul's success. He grew more sullen every day. Several times he tried to resume his position as chief diver, but his strength was not equal to the strain, and Paul gladly took his place, which only made Scott furious. The abuse and curses he heaped upon captain and crew would have resulted in something serious only for Paul. The captain wanted to maroon the growler, that is, to place him on an island with some provisions and sail away. To this Paul answered that he would blow off the head of the man that attempted such a thing. He then tried to restrain Scott but with poor success. There was no other way out of it, so Paul decided to end the cruise. The sloop had a pretty fair cargo so he ordered the captain to make sail for Bridgetown, Barbadoes. They arrived there a month before the charter expired. Mr. C. settled to the satisfaction of the Cayusa's Captain and Scott was placed in the Marine Hospital. Three weeks later, after intense suffering from fever, the poor fellow died. Then Paul understood all his growls and abuse and was sincerely sorry. The collection was boxed ready for shipment and Paul had a pleasant time on the island, while waiting for a northern bound vessel.

One day while sitting at the mole, fishing, he saw a staunch little schooner with dilapidated sails bear into the harbor. When her anchor was let go, a boat was lowered into which two sailors and a man evidently the captain, entered. Paul, folding his fishing line, sauntered down to find out who the new arrivals were. A custom house officer standing by, hailed the stranger as he came ashore with, "Why, Captain Balbo. I am delighted to see you."

"Shure it does me eyes good to see yureself," said the new arrival, in a rich Irish brogue. "Me papers air all right, so we'll have no trouble. O'ive just called in to get a bit av fresh wather, an' if the Lord's willin' somethin' a little stronger."

"You're always welcome," responded the officer, "even if you do neglect to get your clearances. You know there is no love lost between you and the custom house."

The schooner captain way a stout, thickset man with a face bronzed to the color of mahogany and a head of hair as red as a Pittsburgh furnace at midnight. His blue eyes sparkled with good nature and merriment, and a continual smile hovered over his massive mouth. After several hearty greetings to acquaintances on the landing, the captain proceeded to the warehouse of the merchant, where Mr. C. soon afterward introduced Paul to the jolly old sea dog. When Captain Balbo learned that Paul had come down after seashells and curiosities, he was delighted and invited the boy to come aboard.

"O'im in the same line meself. But instead of lookin' afther dirthy, bad-smellin' sea shells, it's afther the shells of ould Vessels Oi am."

Paul gladly promised to go aboard that afternoon. The captain purchased a supply of provisions and made arrangements for his casks of fresh water and "stronger stuff," but in vain Mr. C. entreated him to remain over and take dinner with himself and Paul. The captain declared he could "fill himself up at the hotel with more liberty and less embarrassment." Mr. C. told Paid that Captain Balbo was a good natured old wrecker and treasure hunter, well-known in all the West India Islands. Late that afternoon Paul rowed out to the schooner, and received an enthusiastic welcome from the captain, who had evidently been enjoying himself "without restraint or embarrassment." He took Paul into a roomy cabin, and introduced him to his wife, a Very obese yellow woman, who was reclining on a sofa. The woman was undoubtedly of negro blood; but to Paul's profound astonishment, she had as fine a brogue as her husband. After some conversation Paul ventured to ask the captain how this happened. The latter laughed heartily and answered:

"Me wife wuz born far enough away from dear ould Ireland. Oi'll tell ye how it wuz. Many years ago a parthy of immygrants left county Kerry for Nassau, New Providence oisland. Their ship wuz driven far out av her way in a sthorm an' wrecked on a small oisland in Flamingo Bay. A few av thoze thet survived, settled on the oisland, an' soon had foine homes on its fertile soil. They found only a few nager inhabitants, an' shure they tuk thim fur servants. Me parents were among the survivors from the ship an' Oi wuz born about a year afther the wreck. As toime went on, the nagers gradually acquired the accent of their masthers. Whin Oi grow up Oi shipped on a tradin' schooner in which we wus cast away near Nassau. There Oi joined an English ship; n' fur foive years put in the loife av a sailor forninst the mast. Me heart always longed fur the sunlit, happy oisland an' me people an' at lasht Oi got back there, an' there Oi married Betsy thet ye will see on her beam ends on the sofia. Soon afther, in company with others, Oi bought fur a trifle, a schooner that wuz wrecked on the Keys. Afther hard wuerk we got her afloat, an' re-masted. We did good wuerk in her as a wrecker. Wan be wan Oi bought me comrades out, until to-day Oi am masther av the good little craft that's under yez. Me wife is always the companion av me voyages. Ehen she has the will to shake hersel', she can put more weight on a rope then the balance av the crew. An' there's not a cook in the gay city of Paris that equal her. Me business is tradin' and wreckin.' Mr. C. tould me that ye had submarine armour an' some improved dredgin' appyratus. Now Oi know where both will be useful to ye an' to me. There's many a wreck that Oi know, that's out av me reach wid the appliances Oi have. Wid your appyratus we can get treasure in abundance."

His stories of wrecks and treasures were of deep interest to Paul. Gladly would he have joined the captain, but his father owned the submarine armour and apparatus and he felt that he ought to consult him first. But he promised to answer Captain Balbo later on. A was about to leave the schooner, he remarked, "Your good lady sleeps very soundly, but she is very fat."

"That fat, me b'y," responded Balbo, "is av great valey to me. The English law makes us to give wan fourth av all treasure trove; but it's devilish little they find on board the 'Foam' afther me wife lands. They ofthen remark to me, that it's queer how fat Betsy is whin she goes ashore an' how much flesh she loses afther a short sojourn. Now, me b'y, Oi'll meet ye to-morrow. Oi loike ye an' Oi hope ye'll jine me. Ye'll niver regret the day ye do. An' now ye black devils," he said, turning to the boat's crew, "set this young gintleman safe ashore, er be the port bow av Noah's ark. Oi'll break ivery bone in yer black shkins. Good night, God bless ye, me son," was shouted over the dark waters as the boat shot away to the landing.

That night Paul entertained Mr. C. with an account of his visit to the "Foam" and his interview with the captain. Mr. C. assured Paul that Balbo was reliable and thoroughly honest in his dealings. At the same time he strongly advised him to take passage in the brig that had just arrived in the offing bound for New York and consult his father before embarking in the enterprise proposed by the wrecker. The next day Mr. C., the captain and

Paul dined together. Paul promised the captain, that if he would consent to his gathering curiosities during the voyages they would make together and give him a share of all treasure recovered, he would lay the matter before his father on his arrival in New York. If Mr. Boyton consented he would join him in Nassau, with all the improved apparatus he could secure for the business. The form of agreement was drawn up and a bargain concluded subject to the approval of Paul's father. Three days later Paul sailed for New York on the brig Saco, and after a quiet voyage arrived safely at home once more. The collection of curios he had with him and the previous shipments he had made convinced his father that in no other position would Paul be so valuable to him. He was delighted with his success and allowed him a liberal sum for his labors. Paul was glad to be with his family once more and proved to his much loved mother that he had not forgotten her in all his wanderings as he had a splendid collection of the richest, rarest and most beautiful specimens he had gathered during his voyage as a present for her. The liberal supply of money obtained from his father's generosity was recklessly divided between his sisters. A few days after reaching home, he broached the subject of Captain Balbo's proposition to his father. Mr. Boyton did not like the idea of wrecking or treasure hunting, but he was perfectly content that Paul should join the captain for the purpose of collecting curiosities, and was willing to supply him with money and all the improved apparatus required for that purpose. Paul promised his father that the outlay would be applied according to his directions; but made the firm resolve to himself that he would tackle the treasure ships mentioned to him by Balbo.

CHAPTER IV.

A month after he reached home, young Boyton started again for Nassau where had sent several letters to the captain of the "Foam" informing him as to when he might be expected to arrive. He sailed on a trading schooner, and when they entered the harbor at Nassau, he was glad to find the "Foam" at anchor there. As the schooner glided past the "Foam," Paul loudly hailed her. Captain Balbo protruded his red head through the gangway. When he recognized Paul, he greeted, him with a burst of semi-nautical and semi-scriptural eloquence and shouted: "Oi'll sind a boat afther ye. Come aboard quick as ye can."

As Paul could not leave the schooner without first having his effects passed through the Custom House, the captain himself came ashore. He nearly dislocated Paul's arm with his vigorous hand shaking and said that he had been waiting at Nassau a week for him. The apparatus being duly passed, all embarked in the captain's yawl and were speedily conveyed aboard the "Foam." There he received the same warm welcome from the captain's good natured wife, who had a neat little cabin prepared for him. After supper the captain and Paul had a long talk on deck where they sat smoking cigars under the brilliant starlight. Paul described fully his father objection to his embarking in the wrecking business, though he was willing to enter into the arrangements, providing his share would be the shells and curiosities, which the captain regarded as so much trash.

"Now, Paul, me b'y," said Balbo, after listening intently to his proposition; "Oi'm an old man an' Oi consider meself an honest wan. Ye can have all the shells an' other things ye consider curiosities that we pick up; but ye must also have share in anything valuable we recover, an' ye can depind on me to give you a shquare dale. As fur that paper Mr. C. drew up, there is no occasion fur it. Oi'm not fond o' papers av ony koind fur Oi've always had more or less throuble wid im. Oi give ye me wurrd an' Oi've yure wurrd an' that is sufficient. The paper can go to the shaarks where it belongs."

He then descended into the cabin and returned with the paper they had signed, which he tore in two and cast into the sea. The next morning the Captain and Paul went ashore for the clearance papers and that afternoon anchor was weighed and the "Foam" stood away for the south. Island after island was visited in the Great Bahama group. Many wrecks well known to the captain were visited and worked successfully. Anchors, chains, windlasses, etc., were found in abundance until the "Foam" was well loaded and sail was made for Kingston, Jamaica. Off Morant Point they picked up a negro pilot in his little canoe far out at sea. The pilot wore a pair of blue pants, white shirt and stove-pipe hat, given him no doubt by some passenger or captain of a merchantman. He gravely saluted all on deck as he passed his bare feet over the bulwarks and turning to the captain said in the peculiar dialect of the Jamaica negro:

"Does yo want er pilot, sah?"

"No," responded the captain, "Oi know this coast well enough, but Oi think ye had bother hoist that craft av yure's on boord an' come wid us into Port Royal. There is signs av a cyclone if Oi'm not mishtaken;" an invitation which the pilot gladly accepted. His outlandish attire and quaint English greatly amused Paul, who after supper, sat beside him on the deck and plied him with questions about Jamaica. The pilot told him many interesting tales, among them one of a famous shark known as "Port Royal Tom" who was supposed to inhabit the waters of Kingston's beautiful bay. "Tom, sah, was a pow'ful shahk, 'bout thirty feet long; but nobody know how ole he was. In de ol'en times big fleets ob English men-ob-war use to anchoh off Port Royal, an' dat shahk got fat on de refuse dat was frown ovahboahd. Sometimes de sailors would heah de yallow gals laughin' an' dancin' on de shoah at night an' dey longed fur to jine dem. Dey wasn't 'lowed to go of'en in dose days 'cause de yallow fevah was dere; but when de sailor boys got a chance dey would slip sof'ly down de side an' strike out fur de shoah. Tom, he know dis custom, an' he kep sharp eye on de boys, an' I 'shure yo' sah, dat dat shahk gobbled up moah seamen dan 'uld fill de bigges' ob de Queen's men-ob-wah. As lots ob de sailors went ashoah fur 'sertion as well as fur 'musement, de navay people winked dere lef' eye at de tricks ob ole Tom. After a while de sailors got to belibe dat he wah under de pay ob de gove'ment, an' many a red-hot cannon ball ware sec'etly dropped ober de side to Tom, yafter firs' temptin' him wid nice pieces ob salt junk. I nab neber seen ole Tom myself, sah, but dey say dat he is 'round heah yet. Lucinda Nelson, de great fortune tellah an hoodoo 'oman done tole me dat Tom's now livin' in a big ware-house down in ole Jamaica an' dat he sel'om comes out 'cause he's getting' quite ole. Ole Jamaica, yo' mus' remembah, sah, is fifteen fathom below de ocean now. Great earthquake come up one night an' swallowed de whole town an only a few yeahs ago, when de watah was right cleah, yo' could see de tops ob some ob de houses still standin' at de bottom. I belibe Lucinda Nelson, sah, fur she's a great 'oman an' known a heap ob tings. Niggah folks all go to her fur hoodoos an' chahms an' I reckon she mus' be close on two hun' yeahs ole."

Captain Balbo who was laying close by did not seem to pay much attention to the story of Port Royal Tom. He had heard it often before; but he pricked up his ears when Lucinda was mentioned and eagerly questioned the pilot as to her present whereabouts. Turning to Paul, he said: "Oi've heard a good dale about, this fortune-teller, an' Oi intind to visit her; she may be able to put us onto somethin' good" Paul laughed at the idea of her knowing anything about wrecks or sunken treasure; but the captain persisted in his determination to find her when they landed.

The wind having dropped, the schooner was becalmed and lazily pitched around on the gentle swell. The captain called loudly to his help-mate Betsy to bring up some fresh cigars and a bottle of grog and settled himself more comfortably on deck to enjoy the pilot's stories.

"Have you ever seen Port Royal Tom?" Paul asked the captain.

"No," responded the Captain; "but a frind av moine did an' ye may rest ashured that he is around here somewhere. Oi wouldn't be surprised if he were in the ould ware-house that our frind, the pilot mintioned."

"I guess yo' see a great many shahks in yoah time, massa Cap'in:" said the pilot.

"Yis," responded the captain, "Oi saw lots av thim." He nudged Paul with his foot and a merry twinkle lit his eyes. "They're curious brutes an' not built like human bein's."

The pilot and Paul were now all attention as the captain seemed inclined to spin a yarn.

"Whin Oi wuz a shtrapping young fellow about eighteen, Oi wuz sailin' aboord a trader. Wan day we were layin' becalmed, as we air now, off Turk's Island. While we were quietly sittin' on the bulwarks, we saw a monstrous shaark off our starboard beam. The ould mon at the toime was snorin' away in his cabin, an' it was a foine chance to have a little fun. We out wid the shaark hook and havin' baited it wid a temptin' piece av junk, attached it to a shtrong line which we rove troo the davitts. After smellin' round it, the shaark turned on its side an' swallowed it. All hands clapped on to the rope an' we hoisted him clear out av the wather. A bowline wuz passed over his tail an' we got him on boord an' a few blows wid the axe along the spine quited him down. His floppin' on the deck niver woke the skipper, so we cut him open. We shlit him from close under the mouth to near the tail and overhauled everything that wuz in him. In the stomach we found a collection of soup an' bouillon cans an' bottles enough to shtart a liquor house. As we wuz examinin' the stuff, the ould man came on deck an' thundered out:"

"'What the blazes are ye doin' there messin' me decks up! Get that brute overboord quick an' wash down.' We histed the carcass av the gutted shaark an' passed it over the side. We watched the body as it struck the wather. It remained still fur a few minutes, thin, to our amazement, turned over an' began swimmin'. He casht his eye inquiringly up at the crew, who were all standin' along the rail lookin' at him, as though he wanted somethin'. The skipper himself was so overcome at the shtrange soight that he furgot, fur the toime bein', all about the disgustin' state av the deck. Quickly recoverin' himself, he hoarsely ordered the crew to git the stomach and internals av that shaark overboard and git cleaned down. Three av us grasped the shaark's insides an' liftin' thim to the rail, cast thim into the say. Whin they shtruck the wather they were grabbed be the shark an' swallowed. As his belly was cut wide open, they went through him an' came to the surface. Three times he done this, but did'nt succeed in holdin' thim in their proper place. At this toime all hands were on the rail watchin' the sport an' ivery wan laughed loud at his maneuverin'. The shaark seemed to grow more vexed at each failure an' to resist the merriment of the crew for he cast many furious and malicious glances at the vessel. Once more he backed off fur a charge to swallow thim an' this toime succeeded in holdin' thim in be a nate trick. Instid av turnin' partly on his side an' showin' his dorsal fin afther he had swallowed he kept bottom up and swam slowly away waggin' av his tail with a gratified air while a huge grin spread over his repulsive countenance."

"Great lo'd, sah," said the pilot, "dat was wonderful indeed!"

The captain gazed sternly into the pilot's eye to see if there was the glimmer of a doubt therein, while Paul tumbled into the cabin to suppress his fit of convulsive laughter.

During the night the threatened cyclone made its appearance and the "Foam" let go her anchor in Kingston harbor just time to escape the full fury of the storm. After some considerable trouble at the Custom House, the cargo of the "Foam" was landed and disposed of; except the shells and curiosities gathered in the months' run through tint islands. Those as usual were cased and left in the hands of a merchant for shipment to New York. The sale of the wreckage amounted to three hundred and twelve dollars. After deducting the stores consumed on the vessel, the captain offered half the balance to Paul, who refused, as the shells obtained were equal in value to the wreckage. The captain insisted that he should at least accept one hundred dollars. All business was concluded and the "Foam" provisioned; but the weather was still stormy and unsettled so they decided to remain over until it cleared up. The captain and Paul made many excursions around Kingston. One of them was to the camp of the English soldiers. It was situated on a plateau above the town about four thousand feet from the sea level. To reach this camp they had to charter jackasses. Captain Balbo was not at home on this stubborn craft. All went well on the plains below; but when they reached the steep path up the mountain side the captain could not hold his seat. His fat body would continually slip down on the flanks of the donkey, who would begin to practice as though he wanted to kick a hole in the sky. Three times the captain was unseated but finally he struck a plan of holding on to the donkey's tail and in this manner was towed up the mountain. The magnificent sight from the camp amply repaid them for their arduous ascent. They could distinctly see every part of Kingston as it lay stretched along the shore of its superb bay, while on the other side, a long tongue of land covered with cocoanut trees reached out and almost made the harbor a lake. At the extreme point was the entrance out into the ocean, where immense naval store-houses covered the beach and off them were moored great hulks belonging to the British government. They thoroughly enjoyed the beautiful view and did not regain the town until almost nightfall. Instead of going aboard, the captain proposed to have dinner at a hotel; after which he persisted in making a visit to the fortune teller. The pilot was easily found and consented to act as a guide to the cabin of the dark seeress. Along tramp through the narrow streets and a little out in the country brought them to the habitation of this famed dealer in "Black Art." The house was almost buried by banana trees and heavy vines. In response to the captain's impatient knocks, the door was opened by a little girl, who said:

"Gran won't see any one to-night, no use in trying."

"We must see her fur we're goin' away to-morrow an' won't have another chance," urged the captain.

A querulous voice from the inside was heard saying: "Come Captain, come in if you insist," an invitation which was quickly accepted by the captain who was followed by Paul and the pilot. On entering the back room, a curious sight presented itself. The seeress looked far different from the picture Paul had formed of her in his mind. She was not over five feet high and so thin and wrinkled that she resembled a mummy rather than a human being. On her head she wore a turban formed of some bright colored cloth, while the balance of her apparel consisted of a dark robe embroidered with snakes and other reptiles. The room was adorned with skins of serpents, bunches of herbs, and many weird looking objects.

"So, Captain Balbo, you came to see me at last," exclaimed the old crone; "and who is that young stranger from the far off north that I see at your side?"

The captain was dumbfounded at hearing his name announced by a person whom he had never seen before, but shrewdly remarked:

"If ye know me, why is it ye don't know this young stranger?"

"Ah," responded the fortune-teller, "if he sought me I would know him. He has simply accompanied you as a sightseer. Now, Captain, what can I do for you?"

"How ye know me, Lucinda, is morn than Oi can comprehend, Oi've often heard av ye. As ye know me ye must be aware av me business an' can also tell phat Oi'm here fur."

"Yes, Captain, I know both and the yellow curse you are after lays in a little bay in sufficient quantities to satisfy you on the most southern island in a group of three that bear the same name."

The captain pondered for a while, then said, "It must be the Caicos, for they're the only three islands in a group that bear the same name that Oi know of."

She then went on in a mysterious way to describe to the captain a rock-locked bay, giving him points and descriptions by which he easily recognized the island of East Caicos. She ended the conversation abruptly and ordered them out. Before leaving the captain placed a sovereign in her hand and came away deeply impressed with what the fortune-teller had revealed to him. For quite a distance he remained profoundly silent, then turning to Paul he said: "Oi know the exact place the old devil manes. Though she didn't name the island she described it so closely that it is impossible to mishtake it. It is East Caicos, Oi know the bay well an' it has a great reputation of bein' a resort fur pirates in olden days; an' mark me wurrd, b'y, the visit to that old black will be the means av makin' our fortune. Instead av headin' fur Little Cayman to-morrow mornin', we'll pint her fur East Caicos. It is over fure hundred miles north by east from here; but it will pay us to make the run."

Next morning being fair, the "Foam" left Jamaica and stood off in the direction of the island. They had good weather and fair winds. In four days they passed Cape Maysi, the most easterly point or Cuba. Here they met head winds that caused them to tack four more days, then they got under the lee of the Great Inagua island. The weather was very threatening and every indication pointed to another cyclone, so they decided to run the sloop into one of the sheltered bays that abound on those coasts. Here they lay for two days while the wind whistled and shrieked through the naked rigging. As they were about to get under way the third morning after the dropped anchor, a native came off in a canoe containing pineapples and cocoanuts which he exchanged for a few biscuits. The captain questioned him closely in regard to wrecks around the island and was told about a large Spanish ship that went down years ago on the southeast coast and it was a legend among the inhabitants that she contained a vast amount of treasure. None of her crew ever reached shore so the information was rather vague. Nevertheless, the captain determined to make a try for it. The Indian swore that he knew about the exact location and for the promise of a dollar a day he agreed to pilot them to the place. After a cruise of about thirty miles eastward, they came to the place where the Indian said the wreck had occurred and taking sounding they found bottom a little over nineteen fathoms. The weather being fine they hove to and the yawl containing the diving pump was lowered.

"This is a pretty deep dive," remarked the captain to Paul as he was equipping himself in his armour.

"It is," responded Paul, "the deepest I ever made; but nothing risk, nothing win. Fasten on the face piece and you yourself attend to the signal line."

He dropped overboard and commenced descending slowly, while the captain anxiously and watchfully plied out the signal line and hose. He reached bottom which was full of rocks covered with a slimy growth of marine vegetation; the pressure on him was something enormous. It was very dark and he groped for some time without discovering anything. He signaled the boat to move with him as he pursued his explorations. At last his heart was gladdened by the sight of a wreck overgrown with a heavy mass of weeds and sea plumes. After a closer investigation he was disappointed to find that she was not nearly as large as the vessel described by the Indian; but by her appearance he judged she must have been under water many, many years. All the iron work was eaten away and the timbers badly decayed. He gave the signal, "kedge and buoy." The answer from above was "all-right," and soon after he grabbed a kedge that slowly and silently descended near him. Having fastened it to the wreck, he signaled "haul away," and was soon to the surface and helped aboard the yawl. When the helmet was removed he was very much exhausted. The captain was enthusiastic over his discovery, but was rather disappointed when told of the dimensions of the wreck. The schooner was then hailed to come alongside and all sails were lowered. One of the largest dredges was sent down and Paul descended after it. He used the dredge to clear away the masses of vegetation which covered the wreck. He fastened the claws in the decayed wood and signaling them to haul away, an entrance was at last effected into the hull. He found nothing there to reward him for his trouble and work except long white rows, which on examination proved to be grinning skulls and bones and the traces of rusty iron chains that bound them together in life. Paul was horrified at his ghastly discovery and signaled "haul away." On reaching the dock be informed the captain of his find.

"A slaver, be the mizzen top av the ark," he exclaimed. "There's no use av huntin' through that fellow. They would have no cash aboard if the skeletons are there. They'd have to sell the nagers before they'd have anything av value."

Three days were now spent in looking for the phantom treasure ship, but the captain lost patience finally and unceremoniously kicked the Indian overboard into his canoe and the "Foam" bore away with a fair wind to the island of East Caicos.

The second morning after, East Caicos lay under their port bow. It towered high and forbidding far up in the mist. They beat around to the bay which the Captain supposed was the one described by the fortune- teller. The schooner was anchored to the lee of a reef, while the captain, Paul and two of the crew embarked in the yawl on a tour of investigation. They pulled close under the cliff and into an inlet between two great jaws of barnacle-covered rock that towered high above them. Paul was astonished to see the exact reproduction of the word picture painted by the black fortune-feller of Jamaica before his eyes. They rowed through the inlet on the swell and entered a bay that was perfectly landlocked. All around it to the height of a couple of hundred feet arose a mass of irregular rock, out of which great flocks of gulls and other sea birds flew and angrily circled around the intruders. "This is the place shore enough, Paul. There's no other place loike it on the oislands, Oi could'nt be mishtaken."

At this moment one of the oarsmen exclaimed: "Almighty Lord, Captain! Look over there! See the sharks!"

A short glance was sufficient to reveal the fact that the water was full of these wolves of the deep and they commenced to gather around the yawl in alarming numbers.

"Be careful there, Paul," cautioned the Captain, "keep yure hands in boord," as he hurriedly ordered the crew to swing around and pull out. By this time fully a hundred pair of hungry eyes were following in the wake of the boat. As she retreated, the sharks grow bolder and approached closer; many of them diving from side to side under the boat, while one of them made a snap at the oars. It did not require much encouragement for the black sailors to pull, as their eyes were standing out of their heads at the time and the muscles showed up on their arms like whip cords as they sent the boat flying to the schooner. They reached the side in safety and then every fire-arm and harpoon on the "Foam" was called into play on the ferocious brutes. Many and fervent were the prayers that the captain sent up for the welfare of the black witch at Jamaica, whom he swore he would kill on sight.

After this adventure the schooner was headed to the northwest and for four months the islands and keys wre thoroughly worked. During that time, three trips had been made to Nassau and valuable cargoes of recovered articles discharged. No treasure of any account was found, with the exception of one enormous piece of coral, in which were embedded a number of old Spanish dollars. This object was sold to a tourist at Nassau for the suns of $250. Experience convinced Paul that the tales of vast treasure in the Indies were more fabled than real; still, strange to say, old Balbo firmly believed in them. Every time the water closed over Paul's copper helmet, his sanguine nature firmly expected that untold wealth was about to be opened up to them. During this cruise Paul had neglected no opportunity to secure rare specimens of shells and other marine novelties. In a letter he received from his father during his last visit to Nassau, he was informed that his share of the goods shipped had covered the cost of the submarine armour, dredging apparatus, etc., and that he had placed eight hundred and sixty dollars to his credit in a New York bank. This letter he showed to Balbo who to use his own expression, was "thrown on his beam ends" with astonishment. Paul now persuaded him to give up the dredging of wreckage and treasure hunting and devote the whole time to seeking curiosities. The old man was loth to give up his pet ideas of treasure-hunting and of making long, useless voyages in quest of phantoms. Paul assured him that there was more chance of finding treasure ships by systematically working one locality, so he agreed to turn the schooner into a "shellhunter" as he sarcastically termed it. Everything was ready for another cruise through the Keys and small islands, when the captain, who had secretly been interviewing another fortune-teller, announced his intention of sailing to the coast of Mexico. The first point sighted was Cape Catoche, the northeast point of Yucatan. Along this coast they were most successful and soon filled the schooner with a large and valuable collection of curios with which they sailed to Campachie where they were transferred to a vessel bound for New Orleans. While at Campache, news came in of the wreck of a Mexican brig that occurred on the Alakranes Bank.

The daughter of a rich planter living near Merida, Yucatan, was one of the lost passengers and her father offered one thousand dollars reward for the recovery of her body. An agent was sent down from Sisal to negotiate with Captain Balbo, with the result that the "Foam" bore away to the north taking along one of the surviving sailors of the brig. They sailed to the Alakranes Bank that lay about eighty miles off the mainland. They arrived there on a Saturday night and soon found anchorage. Sunday morning the sea was as smooth as a pond of quick- silver. When they embarked in the yawl and commenced their search, the Mexican sailor was confused owing to different conditions of the water. When he been there last, a wild sea broke over the reefs. In the afternoon they discovered a dark object below, which proved to be the ill-fated brig. Her bottom was almost completely torn out by her contact with the reef so that she sank instantly to the leeward. Through the clear water they could distinctly see her two masts standing while her shattered sails lay thick and tangled through the rigging. Next morning the schooner was taken out and anchored close by and Paul descended to the wreck. As he struck the bottom a few feet from her, he found her heavily canted to star-board. He walked around taking care that his hose pipe would not become entangled in the rigging and clambered over her side. Two good sized sharks shot away from the deck when they heard the hissing of the air escaping from his helmet. He could see very clearly all around, owing to the direct rays of the sun reflecting on the coral reef. On gaining the deck which lay at an angle of about 35 degrees he discovered the iron pumps detached from their place and pinning to the bulwark the body of a dead sailor, or rather part of a body as his legs and stomach had been eaten away. This sight rather unnerved Paul, but he worked his way aft to the cabin hatch which he found securely fastened. A few blows with his pry forced it open and descending the gangway he found himself in a cabin with four state rooms on each side. The rooms on the tower side were rather dark but he opened each door and carefully felt the bunks and bottoms for the body he was in quest of. Finding nothing in the first four state- rooms, he tried the upper ones. There was much more light in these as the sun shone down through the green, clear, water and in through the glass port holes. Everything buoyant in the staterooms had floated up against the deck so that he had to haul and pull them down for examination. The third door he reached he could not open. It was fastened by a bolt on the inside, but with the aid of his pry he soon shot it back. Then swinging the door impatiently toward him, the eddy brought out the upright body of a young woman in her nightdress. Her hair floated around her head like golden sea-weed as it came forward and fell against the glass face-piece of his armour. For a moment he was paralyzed with the shock, but, he quickly regained his nerves, and gently placing his arm around the dead body, he reverently bore it to the deck. Her hands were clasped as though in last supplication to the great power above, while her eyes protruded with terror at the fate she had met. Hastily signaling those above to lower a line, he laid the body carefully against the shattered rigging while he went to grasp the rope. Passing it under her arms and putting two secure half hitches on it, he signaled again to haul away. It gently ascended through the clear water, while a school of fish played around her as though sorry to see her go. Paul followed after and found all on deck solemn and silent, while the captain's good-natured wife was in the cabin wrapping the corpse in a sheet. That night a rude coffin was made in which the remains were placed and the schooner headed for Sisal, where she sailed in with her flag at half-mast. The father faithfully paid the promised reward and the schooner under charter, returned to resume her work at the wreck. Out of this job the captain and Paul made about nine hundred dollars each.

A cruise was then made around the Gulf of Campechie which was most successful. The catch was landed at Vera Cruz whence it was shipped to New York. Sometime before this, Paul had informed his father of the changed condition of his contract with Captain Balbo and requested him to forward the captain's one-half of the proceeds of the goods shipped. At Vera Cruz they found letters, one containing a robust check for Captain Balho, which so pleased that worthy individual, that he determined to spend at least one week ashore and enjoy hotel quarters for which he had a weakness. The gamblers, who abound in Vera Cruz, found a rich victim in the captain, who parted with all the money he could conceal from the watchful eyes of his wife, Betsy, with the guilelessness of a boy ten years old.

A cruise was now made along the coast of Mexico; but the collection of curiosities did not pay for the time engaged, so they concluded to abandon it and stand away again to the islands. At Tuxpan, where they landed for fresh water, they received information of a steamer that had been burned and sunk near Tampico, so they headed the schooner for that port. The steamer had been burned about three weeks before and the hull lay on a bank in eight fathoms of water. The agent offered to engage them to recover the safe for which he would pay them five hundred dollars, or they could have the usual salvage, ten per cent. As it was reported around the port that the safe contained over thirty thousand dollars, besides a number of valuable packages belonging to the passengers, they concluded to take ten per cent. For four days they worked hard on the wreck, removing the confused mass of iron, which was twisted into fantastic shapes by the action of the fire. On the forenoon of the fifth day, Paul sounded something solid and heavy with his pry, far down through the debris near the keel, and after about an hour's hard work sent up the joyful signal: "I've got it," which was received on deck with loud cheers. The chain hooks were now sent down and after a lashing was placed around the safe, the order to "haul away" was given. All hands manned the windlass and the safe was soon suspended between the bottom and the surface. Paul now went up to assist in getting it aboard. Sail was then Made and with light hearts they stood in for the port. The safe was locked and to all appearances uninjured.

"There is three thousand dollars there fur us, Paul me b'y," said the captain as he patted the safe affectionately.

On arriving at the dock, the safe was transferred to the ware-house, where it was forced open and to their dismay and disgust found that it contained nothing of any value. It was subsequently found out that the purser, seeing the ship in danger, had quietly transferred the safe's money to himself and when he landed had vanished and so all the hard work of raising the safe was in vain. Paul laughed at their bad luck, while the captain swore picturesquely in several languages. Preparations were again made for the voyage to the islands which had been postponed on account of this misadventure. One evening the "Foam" stood away to the east. Three o'clock the next morning a furious gale set in and increased hourly until the vessel was under bare poles and scudding for the coast. It was impossible to attempt to beat against the storm, so they stood away helplessly before it, running on to a very dangerous coast. At six o'clock that evening, she stuck in the breakers on the beach opposite Pueblo Viego. Enormous seas poured over her and swept everything from the decks. A boat was lowered but immediately smashed to atoms. In this critical position, the coolest person aboard was Betsy. She a life preserver strapped firmly around her and was covered with one of the captain's oil-skins.

"I guess it is a matter of swim for it," roared Paul to the captain, "as she won't stand this very long."

At this instant the mainmast went and as it swung clear, the stays were hastily cut by the captain and Paul. The captain frantically motioned Betsy to grab one of the lines attached to the mast. The next moment a sea broke over her that carried the three of them, with two of the crew hanging on to the mast, which, clear of the wreck, was rapidly driven towards the shore. Once a great sea broke Paul's hold and he found himself unaided swimming in the mad surf. He was fortunate enough to catch a hatch that was floating near which supported him to the shore where he was thrown with considerable violence and half stunned. He managed to stagger up the beach and in a few minutes discovered Betsy dragging the insensible form of the captain out of the reach of the sea. The captain was not dead, but very near it. One of the crew had an arm broken while the other landed without injury. The three men left on the wreck were lost. When the skipper recovered consciousness he was inconsolable at the loss of his craft. That night the party found shelter in a house about half a mile from the beach where they were hospitably entertained. At the break of day the captain and Paul were on the beach. The sea was still breaking heavily and all that was left of the staunch little "Foam" were her timbers scattered far up and down on the sands. Among them were found the bodies of two of the men, the other was never heard of. So sudden and unexpected was the loss of the vessel that Paul never thought of his money he had safely stowed away in the cabin and he stood on the beach that morning without a cent in his pocket. The loss of his armour and apparatus grieved him deeply but he felt a keen sorrow for the distress of his old friend Balbo. Yet in a way, the captain was more fortunate than himself as Betsy had carried all their earnings safely ashore, stowed away in the voluminous folds of her dress. All day long the Captain, Betsy and Paul and the uninjured seaman, patrolled the beach in the hope that something valuable might wash up. But outside of a few articles of clothing and some casks, nothing came ashore. In the evening they gave it up in despair and returned to the house that had sheltered them the previous night. The next morning after another visit to the beach a conveyance was obtained for Tampico, where they arrived the same evening.

For some days they were at a loss what to do until a vessel appeared in harbor bound for New Orleans. On this the Captain, Betsy and the two seaman procured passage and they vainly urged Paul to do the same; but he had a lingering hope that he might yet recover his apparatus with the aid of the primitive dredgers of the Mexican fishermen, so he refused to leave. He saw them on board the ship and took an affectionate farewell of his old friends. Before parting, the Captain insisted on his accepting a small loan which he said he could return to Nassau whenever he felt like it. There was a suspicious dimness in his eyes as he crushed Paul's hand in his own, while Betsy cried outright as she heartily kissed him good-bye. When the weather became mild again, Paul engaged a small fishing craft and went down the coast to the vicinity of the wreck but his efforts were in vain. His armour by that time was buried far below in the quicksand so he abandoned the search and went back to Tampico.

While sitting disconsolately on the piazza of the little hotel in Tampico, he was approached by an American: "Well young fellow I've heard that you have had pretty hard luck. What do you intend to do?"

"That's just about what I would like to know myself."

"Well, I think I can post you," said his new acquaintance as he leisurely seated himself and hoisted his heels on the rail. "There is a good chance for active young fellows just now. I presume you never did much soldiering, but I guess you can fire a gun."

"Why yes," responded Paul, "I think I could manage that."

The stranger then told Paul that he was connected with the Revolutionists, whose headquarters were then at Palmas and assured him that he would be well taken care of. Paul, who was at the time, open for anything that would turn up, quickly accepted the proposition. The next morning he and fourteen others mounted on mules, and conveying a pack train were pursuing their way up the mountain road in the direction of the headquarters. His filibustering friend furnished Paul with a pretty good rifle and revolver, and informed him that they were on their way to join a party under the command of General Pedro Martineze. He also told him that his own name was Colonel Sawyer; that he had been born in Texas, but had spent most of his life on the frontier and was concerned in many of the Revolutions that disturbed the Republic of Mexico. His principal occupation was running arm and ammunition from the coast to the Revolutionists in the interior. For three days they pursued their journey, camping every night. About ten o'clock on the morning of the fourth, they were stopped by the cry of "Halts, halta." Looking up from where the hail came, they saw the muzzles of thirty or forty rifles pointed at them. Colonel Sawyer loudly cried in answer to their command, "Amigos." In a few moments they were surrounded by a skirmishing party of Revolutionists and conveyed to the camp. Here Paul found several Americans, all soldiers of fortune, none of whom gave him very encouraging accounts of the prospects. Two weeks were spent in the camp from which small expeditions were sent out every day. Paul accompanied one of these to the National road running from Tampico to Monterey, and between the villages of Liera and Maleta. They had a skirmish and succeeded in capturing a carriage, hauled by four horses which contained some person of importance as he was treated with the utmost respect by the Commander and conveyed a prisoner to the camp. The horses were unhitched from the carriage which was left on the road. Soon after Paul and a party under the command of Sawyer, were sent to the town of Bagarono where a cargo of arms had been landed. These by the aid of pack mules were safely transferred to the camp. Soon after there was a heavy engagement in which the entire body of Revolutionists participated near Ciudad Victoria. The revolutionists were badly repulsed and retreated to the mountains. After this it was nothing but a series of raids which were both laborious and unsatisfactory. Paul was fast tiring of this semi-barbarous mode of warfare so that he and four of his companions decided to discharge themselves on the first favorable opportunity. It came sooner than they expected. They were sent under command of Sawyer and others to Metamoras for ammunition. On reaching there, they found the schooner with the promised supply had not arrived. After waiting for some days news came that the Revolutionists had again been repulsed and were all in retreat. This decided Sawyer, who said:

"Boys, the jig is up and the best thing we can do is to get across the river and into the United States."

That night they crossed the Rio Grande in an old tub of a boat that they expected would go to the bottom every moment and landed in safety at Brownsville, on the American shore. Here Paul wrote letters home and requested his father to send him a remittance to Galveston. With the little money they bad, mustangs and provisions were purchased and they started on a long ride to Corpus Christi. It was a wild journey through the chaparral, over the burnt and dried grass of the prairie, across swamps and rivers; but they made the two hundred miles in eight days. Here they separated. While his companions sought employment with the ranchers, Paul for consideration of his mustang, rifle and revolver, induced the captain of a coaster to give him passage to Galveston. He arrived in Galveston and found himself without a cent. He opportunely remembered that his father had a friend there in the person of ex-Governor Lubbock, whom he hunted up. He was cordially received by the Governor, who not only supplied him with all he wanted, but insisted upon his remaining in his house until his correspondence should arrive. In ten days the long looked for letter and remittance came to hand, and Paul lost no time in securing a passage on the steamer Haridan for New Orleans, and from there to New York, where he arrived June 2d, 1867.

CHAPTER V.

He was warmly received by his family and found that his father had a smug sum to his credit in the bank. Paul was now in his nineteenth year; he was strong and so bronzed with the sun that he looked fully twenty-five. For some time after his home coming he was unsettled what to do, and once or twice was on the point of investing in a new outfit and re-embarking for the West Indies. But the pleadings of his mother to abandon the wandering life he liked so well, and to settle down to a steady business prevailed, and his father assisted him to open a store in Philadelphia for the sale of curiosities and Oriental goods. A branch at Cape May was also opened. It was very successful and disposed of large quantities of goods to the visitors there. For two years he successfully pursued this mercantile life and was establishing a good business; but while at Cape May during the summer time his old love for the water drew him continually to the beach, where his magnificent and fearless swimming attracted the attention of all. At times he would swim so far out in the cool, dancing waves that the people could not see his head. His extraordinary power in this line, proved of great value to many unfortunate bathers who were carried out by the under tow and were in danger of drowning. Paul always swam to their assistance, and the first season he spent on the beach, he succeeded in saving fourteen who would certainly have lost their lives had it not been for his help. Many testimonials were presented to him for his bravery. He became very popular with the visitors, but not so with the native boat men who looked upon life saving and the perquisites attached, as their own, and wondered how a volunteer dared to do better than they. His second season on the beach was still more successful in both life-saving and business, and he met with many curious individuals in the persons whom he had saved. One day an excursionist swam far out over the breakers. When he turned to come ashore, he was alarmed either at the distance he found himself out, or feeling the under tow against him, he lost his courage and cried loudly for help. Paul was on the beach at the time, and, quickly divesting himself of his clothing, he sprang away through the breakers to his assistance. The man was very difficult to handle, for he was thoroughly frightened. He would obey none of Paul's injunctions, but persisted in clambering on his back. After extraordinary difficulty Paul succeeded in landing him. The man was unconscious and Paul himself thoroughly exhausted. The same afternoon, while Paul was standing talking to a group of gentlemen, the rescued excursionist appeared, and, calling him to one side, said:

"Say, mister, I hear that you are the man who saved me this morning, and I tell you I am very much obliged to you. I am going home now, and if you ever catch me in that darn water, I'll give you leave to drown me. Before going, I wish to present you some token of my esteem and regard."

Paul assured him that he required nothing, stating that the knowledge he had saved his life was sufficient reward in itself. The persistent individual was not satisfied. He slipped his hand in his pocket and drew forth a pocket-book, from which he extracted a dilapidated looking fifty-cent note. Fervently pressing it into Paul's hand, he said:

"You take that and remember me."

Paul was surprised at the liberal present, but quickly recovering, he said to the departing excursionist: "Hold on, my friend, you are forgetting something." Carefully counting forty-nine cents from a handful of change he drew out of his pocket, he handed it to the rescued man and remarked: "I could not think of taking a cent more than your life is worth."

On another occasion, Paul succeeded in rescuing a young lady who was being rapidly carried out to sea and who would certainly have been drowned but for his aid. In his struggles to get her ashore, he was compelled two or three times to grasp her roughly by the hair. When landed, she was unconscious and in that state was conveyed to her hotel. Paul met a friend of the lady on the beach and inquired, how Miss —— —— was getting along. "Oh very well," was the response; "but she is a very curious young lady."

"How is that?" asked Paul.

"Well, when I visited her this morning I remarked that she ought to be very grateful to you for saving her life. 'I am,' she hesitatingly answered. 'But I think he might have acted a little more gentlemanly and not caught me by the hair. I have a frightful headache.'"

There is an old saying, "That if you wish to make enemy of a man, just save his life or lend him money." Paul's experience convinced him that the saying was true. Many and many a person has he saved from a watery grave, who never even took the trouble to seek him out and thank him.

In the Fall of 1869 Paul lost everything he had in the world by a great fire at Cape May and he left there heavy hearted and disgusted with business. Soon after, his father died and the home was very, very lonely. When the estate was settled up, Paul's old love for travel and adventure came strongly back to him. The Franco-Prussian war broke out. He believed that it was the opportunity that he was looking for. He embarked from New York to Liverpool, thence to Havre, where he presented himself at the Hotel de

Ville and offered his services as an American volunteer. At this time the French military authorities were not accepting volunteers as readily as they did later on, so Paul had much difficulty in getting rolled in the service as a Franc-tireur. A few days after he had landed in Havre, he was marching away with a chassepot rifle on his shoulder and a knap-sack and blanket on his back. His uniform consisted of a black tunic with yellow trimmings, blue pants with wide red stripe along the side, a red sash bound around the waist, over which circled the belt which supported his sabre, bayonet and revolver. It also held an arm, the only one of the kind in his company, viz: a bowie knife which he had carried from America. Shoes, leather gaiters and kepi or cap completed the uniform. The company was about sixty strong, all picked men and Paul was the only foreigner in the lot. It was known as la Deuxieme Compagnie Franc-tireurs du Havre. The only visible difference between the regular and the irregular army was the lack of regulation buttons on the latter, and that they had no commissary department and had to provision themselves as they went. Their pay was thirty sous (cents) per day and they received their salary every morning. Out of this they were supposed to support themselves. Notwithstanding this small pay it was the highest given to any body of troops in the French army, as the regulars received but six cents per day, but the Government furnished them with provisions. The company was divided into six messes of ten men each. One of the ten had to act as cook when it came his turn, while others were told off to visit the farm houses in the vicinity of the camp to purchase the necessary provisions. At this time Paul's knowledge of French was very limited; but the Marschal de Logis, a petty officer and a Havre pilot named Vodry could speak English after a fashion. They acted as interpreters for him and gave him instructions in French. In the few weeks the company was camped near Havre, Paul acquired a little knowledge of the most necessary words and learned thoroughly to understand the commands given in French. He was instructed in the manual of arms by the Marschal de Logis. The command from his instructor such as "portez armes," "armes a gauche," "a droit" sounded strangely in Paul's ears. During his previous military career with the freebooting revolutionists of Mexico, there had been no drill whatever. Before the orders arrived to proceed to the front, he was sufficiently acquainted with the commands and terms to pass muster with any in the company. While still in camp, the news of the fall of Sedan was received and the tireurs were hurried forward to the vicinity of Paris on which the Prussians were rapidly advancing. Their first engagement was at Creteil. They did skirmishing for the army of General Vinoy, who had about fifteen thousand men. This was on the 11th of Dec., 1870. The engagement opened early in the morning by the Franc-tireurs and skirmishers on the hills of Mely. They were soon dislodged by the powerful artillery fire of the enemy and retreated to Charenton. Five of Paul's company were killed in the engagement and several wounded. After this they were engaged almost daily in skirmishing and light engagements around Paris. During those stirring times all was pleasant confusion. Paul knew nothing of what was going on, except through the reports of his comrades and they were but half understood; but that they were being slowly and surely driven back was apparent to him. In many of the engagements with the enemy, while several of their skirmishes were successful, he noticed that the tireurs never pursued them in the direction in which they retired. One day near Evereux the company to which Paul belonged saw a balloon coming towards them and a cloud of dust on the road far below showed them that a party of Uhlans were pursuing. At the time the balloon was rapidly descending. The company was ordered into ambush on each side of the road, while the Uhlans with upturned eyes and the occasional popping of a carbine at the balloon, dashed along the road unconscious of the hidden enemy. As they rode past the ambush, the order was given to fire. Twenty riderless horses dashed madly up and down the road, while the balance of the Uhlans sought safety in flight. The balloon descended but a short distance from thee scene of the engagement and was found to contain a man named Du Norof. He had with him dispatches from Paris which was then besieged. Their next engagement was at Martes. They were then under command of General Mocquard, a brave soldier who was always seen well to the front mounted on a little wiry Arab steed. Soon after this engagement the company, to which many new faces had been added to fill up the gaps caused by the shot and shells of the enemy, was joined to the Arme de la Loire.

On the 7th of October, the Franc-tireurs skirmished and opened the engagement at Tourey. This struggle lasted from seven in the morning until noon and many of their number bit the dust. Here for the first time Paul saw the Turcos, a French-African regiment, who distinguished themselves during the fight. Forty-seven prisoners were conveyed from the field by the survivors of Paul's company. On the 9th of October the great battle of Orleans commenced, which lasted for two days. The battle was a desperate one, and losses on both sides were great. The enormous armies engaged in this battle, the marching and counter-marching so rapid, and the deafening roar of the artillery, all added to confuse Paul, and he did not know that the army was in retreat until told by one of his companions. From that time until January, '71, the Franc-tireurs were engaged in many skirmishes and harassed the enemy whenever an opportunity presented itself. But they were slowly and surely driven back by the great and well disciplined army of Germany until they crossed the Seine and found themselves in the Department of Seine Inferieure, that was then invaded by the advance corps of the enemy. Notwithstanding all the scenes of carnage that Paul witnessed, and the dangers surrounding them, he has remarked that those were the happiest days of his life; free from all business troubles and with no property on earth except that contained in his knapsack. The old spirit of mischief that deeply imbued his nature was continually asserting itself, and he was always happy, no matter how somber were his surroundings. Notwithstanding all the dangers he had passed through, he only received two slight wounds, which quickly healed on his healthy body. In the part of France they were now encamped the peasants were rich though very economical. They had a holy horror of the Franc-tireurs, and when they heard of a company approaching, orders were given to the sturdy servant girls to convey all poultry to a place of safety. The place selected was generally the bedroom of the farm house, where the fowls roosted in tranquility on the head and foot of the bed while the disappointed Franc-tireurs searched in vain for material for their soup. As before stated, when the Franc-tireurs camped, parties were detailed to purchase provisions for the different messes. Two would go after bread and beef, two after coffee, sugar, etc., and yet another two after potatoes and vegetables. The last detail was always the favorite of Paul and his friend Vodry, the pilot. The majority of French peasants generally believed Americans were wild Indians. Paul and his friend utilized this belief to their own advantage in this fashion: Taking a sack with them they would depart for one of the surrounding farm houses; concocting a scheme on their way that invariably met with success. Before reaching the house they separated, Vodry going in advance with the sack. When he entered the kitchen of the spotlessly clean Normandy farm house, he would politely remove his cap and in a most courteous and insinuating manner inform the inmates that he was from the Franc-tireur's camp, and came for the purpose of purchasing some pommes de terre (potatoes). At the announcement that he was a Franc-tireur, his reception was never cordial; but knowing that they were compelled by the government to sell provisions to this branch of the army, as a general thing they sullenly complied with the request. Vodry's good manners and pleasing address usually caused them to relent. While the potatoes were being gingerly measured out, he would have them interested in some story of the war, which would invariably end up with the query: "By the way, did you know that we had an American in our company?"

This information immediately aroused their curiosity and they showered questions on him in regard the customs of the wild creature. Vodry then entertained them with the tale of how Paul had left his distant home, thousands of miles away and crossed the ocean to fight for La Belle France. He generally finished by saying: "Perhaps you would like to see him; he accompanied me on my way over, but as a general thing he does not like to come into a house so he remained outside while I came in."

Then without waiting for an answer he would step to the door and loudly hail the American. Paul would quickly appear from around some out-house or hay stack. Hi appearance would be far different from that which he presented at roll call. A slouch hat filled with feathers waved around his head in graceful confusion, a silver gray poncho blanket covered his uniform, outside of which was wrapped his revolver and bowie knife. Several daubs of wet brick dust and blue pencil marks adorned his face. In response to Vodry's call he would bound in with a yell that made the windows in the farm house rattle. He saluted the farmer with a vigorous shake of the hand and gracefully kissed the hand of the good dame of the house and her daughters, if she happened to have any, then stolidly walking around the kitchen he would examine all different utensils and instruments with an absorbing interest as if he never saw such things before. While observing him both with awe and admiration for his devotion to France, they would exclaim, "What a good child, what a brave fellow," etc., etc.

Finding that the time for action had arrived, Paul would approach the farmer and while ringing his hand, would say in broken French: "Cognac bon, cognac bon." The enthusiastic and sympathetic mistress of the house would immediately say:

"Ah, the poor boy wants a drop of cognac! Get him some father!" The reluctant farmer procured a big bottle and a very diminutive glass known as the "petit verre," which held about a thimbleful. Paul would congratulate the good dame on her keen perception. At this period Vodry would generally object saying:

"It is not good to give him cognac as the Americans can not control themselves when they take liquor."

His objections were over ruled and the farmer presented Paul with a miserable little glass full to the brim. This Paul insisted that the matron should drink first and on its being replenished he more emphatically insisted that the farmer should drink before him. While the farmer was drinking, Paul generally secured the bottle as if to relieve him from its charge while drinking. The moment he secured it he gave a wild whoop and placing it to his lips took a seemingly long swig, after which he executed a fantastic war dance around the kitchen to the alarm of the farmer and his worthy family who were only to glad to see him disappear through the door, Vodry remaining to remonstrate with them in regard to their folly in having given fire- water to this untutored child of the forest. He assured them that if he could procure the liquor he would return it, and then shouldering his bag of potatoes expressed the most profound sorrow at the occurrence. He would not proceed far until he was waylaid by Paul who was concealed in some hedge or dyke and the two conspirators resumed their way to the camp. That evening Paul's mess enjoyed the much cherished coffee and cognac so dear to every French heart.

The Gardes Mobiles, a large number of which were in this part of France, were regiments formed of clerks, lawyers, merchants and other citizens, many of whom volunteered and were formed into an army to assist the regulars and Franc-tireurs in repelling the invasion. They were brave fellows but unsophisticated in the ways of war. They were well supplied with nice blankets and abundance of provisions as they were never camped far from their native places. This branch of the service was looked upon by the fight-worn and weather beaten Franc- tireurs as their lawful prey. To be camped near one of them was looked upon as a direct gift from above. At such times the Franc-tireurs never thought of cutting wood for themselves. They frequently changed their dirty and dilapidated blankets for the fresh warm ones of the inexperienced Mobiles.

Hares abound in this part of France and many of them helped to make soup for the freebooters. So frequently had the shots been heard and needless alarms raised that a strict order was given out that there was to be no firing unless at an enemy. One day Paul was doing duty as a sentinel on an outpost, when a large, fat hare appeared on a little hillock not thirty yards from where he stood. Before he remembered about the order he had raised his rifle and sent a bullet crashing through its body. Paul had no time to pick up the hare before he saw the relief advancing on "double quick." So he stood on his post, saluted the officer in command, and in reply to his inquiry said that his gun had gone off accidentally. The officer scrutinized him closely, then looking around soon discovered the cause of the accident. He sent a soldier for the hare, examined it, and placed Paul under arrest, at the same time remarking "that for an accidental discharge of a gun it had a most remarkable effect and that only an American could cause such an accident." After a few hours detention in the guard house, Paul was allowed his liberty. Being the only foreigner, he was a favorite in the company and many of his escapades were overlooked, if a Frenchman had been guilty of the same he would have been severely punished. The captain of Paul's company at this time was an officer whose voice was very weak, and he could never finish a command in the same pitch he had started. He invariably broke down, and the command which was commenced in a stentorian voice was ended in a hoarse whisper. This peculiarity often caused the Franc-tireurs to smile. One morning the company was ready to march; the captain, mounted on a powerful horse, was at their head. Wheeling about and drawing his sword he gave the orders: "Attencion compagnie! En evant." He then suddenly broke down and paused to recover his breath and Paul in a low undertone and in exact imitation of the captain, added the word that ought to follow, "Mar-r-che!"

This drew forth a smothered laugh from the whole company. The captain turned fiercely around and demanded to know who it was that mimicked him. Dead silence prevailed. He gave them a lecture on the respect due to an officer and stated that the next offender of this kind would be severely punished; then added: "I can't find out who it was, but on my soul I believe it was that sacre American."

After this the company took part in many engagements through Normandy, principally at St. Roumain, Beuzeville, Yvetot, Rouen and Bulbec. The company suffered severely and in the last battle were a mere handful. There they lost their brave lieutenant Boulonger, who was shot through the breast. Paul and a party of his companions were detailed to convey the body to Havre, his home, where he was well known and respected. Here Paul saw for the first time in his life the French military burial Mass. This was the most solemn ceremony he had ever witnessed. The great cathedral was draped in crape, which added to the already somber appearance of the surroundings. The coffin of the lieutenant was carried on the shoulders of four Franc-tireurs and deposited on a bier near the altar. The soldiers then retired and joined their comrades. Every gun was polished and every bayonet shone as the Franc-tireurs and about four hundred of the mobiles and regulars marched with military precision into the cathedral. No soldier's cap was removed, while the citizens stood around with bare heads. An officer occupied a position on the steps of the altar and with unsheathed sword faced the soldiers, then standing in the body of the church. He gave orders in a loud voice at intervals during the service and his commands sounded strangely through the echoing arches of the cathedral. At the order "restez armes," the iron shod butts of the muskets dropped together on the stone floor, reminding those present of the stern realities of war and the sweet consolations of religion.

At the elevation of the sacred host, came the orders "Portez armes," "Presenter armes," "a genoux." Every soldier's right knee touched the floor and remained there while the muskets were held "a presenter." The solemn tones of the gong floated through the cathedral. When they ceased, the sharp order of "debout" rang out and all were on their feet in an instant. At the conclusion of the ceremony, the body was again carried out; a line was formed while the band struck up a mournful dirge, and they marched to the cemetery as escort of their lost and well loved officer.

The survivors of the company to which Paul belonged were now drafted into the regular army in the section known as "Bataillon Des Tirailleurs." Paul did not relish the change from the free and easy life of the Franc-tireurs to the strict discipline of the regular army. The company to which he was joined had two "Gatling guns" or "Mitrailleuses" as the French called them. It was drill, drill all day long and as the pay was now only six cents a day and payments only once a week, they had but little chance to play their favorite game of "Petit paquet," a game that had been more regular than prayers in the camp of the "Franc-tireurs." Having become thoroughly drilled in the use of the "Gatling gun" the company was ordered to the front. One evening a comrade said to Paul: "We will have bloody work tomorrow. General Menteuffel's army is advancing and all the out posts have been driven in." But the expected battle was never fought. That night news came that caused a heavy gloom to settle on the camp. No longer the laughing joke passed from comrade to comrade. No longer the patriotic songs were heard through the camp. Bronzed heads were bowed in sorrow and tears trickled down many a cheek. Paul anxious to know the cause of the general depression, asked an officer what was the matter and received the answer: "Paris has fallen." Soon after came the news of the armistice and that no more fighting should take place for thirty days. Notwithstanding the armistice and the conditions that neither army should move, the "Mitrailleuses" were advanced to a favorable point nearer the enemy and the heavy and constant drill resumed.

All expected that hostilities would continue at the close of the armistice. The two armies lay within plain sight of each other. Discipline was strictly enforced; several French soldiers were executed for neglect and disobedience of orders. One cold night Paul stood two hours guard over a Gatling gun that was placed in a shed with no sides and the fierce, cold wind whistled and penetrated his very bones. He was worn out with a heavy day's drill and concluded that he could watch the gun as well above in the shelter as by standing alongside. He mounted the beam and stretched himself out on a board. He knew, that it was instant death to be caught sleeping on guard, but he could not refrain from closing his eyes and was soon in a fretful slumber from which he was awakened by the crunching of the frozen snow under the feet of the advancing relief. Quick as lightning he dropped to his post and sang out the hail: "Halt, who comes?" the answer sounded, "France." On being questioned by the officer why he did not hail them sooner, according to orders, he assured him that, "the words had been frozen down his throat and he could not get them out sooner." The gay Frenchman laughed at his unique excuse and relieved him; but it was a close call for Paul. Before the armistice was ended, the news of the peace declared arrived in camp and soon after orders were given to march for Havre.

The discipline of the regulars was never enjoyed by Paul, neither was their commissary department. Horse flesh was served out three times a week. On other days they received pork and beef. Coffee, sugar, rice, bread and wine were served every second day. The two day's rations of wine never lasted over fifteen seconds. The trade in tobacco is monopolized by the French

Government. Who ever bore an order from his commanding officer could receive a certain amount by simply paying for the tax stamp. On railroad trains the regulars could ride for one third and gain admission to theatres and amusement halls at about the same rate, so that the munificent salary they received of six cents per day enabled them to enjoy themselves in a very limited manner. Every barracks and military building in Havre was overflowing with soldiers; and when Paul's company arrived they could find no place to sleep. So they received a document entitled a "billet de logement" that entitled them to a bed in the house on which it was drawn. Sometimes they received an order on the houses in the poorer part of the town and again in the most aristocratic mansions. As a general rule, when a billet carried by two war-worn Franc-tireurs was presented at the door of a chateau, the proprietor would gracefully excuse himself with many suave and flattering expressions. He would present the soldiers with two francs each and request them to get a room at the hotel, at the same time expressing regret at his inability to oblige the gallant defenders of Le Belle France. His house was just then filled by the unexpected arrival of some relatives. Feigning sorrow at being deprived of the supreme honor of sleeping under his roof, the Franc-tireurs would make their adieux. As the door closed they kicked each other for joy because they had obtained what they appreciated more than a nice soft bed. They could sleep as soundly in any of the parks or on the lee side of hogsheads, or on bales of cotton on the quay, after they had enjoyed spending the proceeds of the "billet de logement." The army was now quickly disbanded and Paul found himself once more a citizen. He still retained his uniform, for without it he would have been devoid of clothing.

At this time the Communes were causing the government great trouble in Paris and regiment after regiment was being hurried thither. With one of these regiments Paul managed to reach the capital. Being left to his own resources he was greatly bewildered. The nature of the stirring and exciting scenes he little comprehended. One evening while passing along the boulevard near the Madeleine, a soldier wearing the uniform of the Foreign Legion peered into his face and eagerly inquired if he could speak United States. Paul answered, "yes." The soldier seemed delighted and said, "Have you got any money? I am from Baltimore," all in the same breath. Paul told him that he had a few francs and that he was perfectly willing to divide and invited him to take dinner.

"I will take dinner gladly with you," responded his new acquaintance, "but we had better strike some cheaper quarters than our present surroundings."

So the two turning off the boulevard, pursued their way along the narrow streets until they struck something more in keeping with their financial standing. Here they entered a modest looking cafe and ordered a ragout.

While seated at the table they continued their conversation in English. The sour looking landlord after taking their order eyed them suspiciously for a few moments, while trying to understand their conversation. Rushing to the door of an adjoining room he loudly called:

"Corporal, come here. Prussians!"

The room was quickly invaded by a Corporal and one of his friends with drawn sabres in their hands. Paul and his companion, who saw that they were about to be attacked, grabbed chairs and backed into a corner, where they defended themselves against the onslaught. Paul asked them in his best French what they meant and assured them that they were not Prussians but American volunteers. On receiving this information the sabres were lowered and their assailants put them through an examination. Receiving satisfactory answers to all their questions and convinced that Paul and his friend were what they represented themselves to be, the Frenchmen gravely begged to be pardoned and warmly invited them into the adjoining room to take supper in their company. During supper Paul ascertained that their entertainers were officers in the Communes that were organizing in all parts of Paris. They were invited to join the ranks of the "liberators" as the called themselves; after the reception they had received from the gentlemen they wisely thought they had better acquiesce, so they were duly enrolled. That night they had a good lodging provided for them and were told to report at ten o'clock next morning. During the night Paul and his Baltimore friend had a long talk over the situation but they were far from satisfied. Leonard, the Baltimorean, suggested that before they took arms up against the government; they had better investigate a little further. With this intention they rose very early and started for a more respectable quarter of the city. On turning the corner they were amazed to meet the gentlemanly Corporal, who was trying the night before to slit their throats. He wanted to know where they were going. They plausibly assured him that "as they could not sleep in their lodgings on account of fleas they had decided to take a mouthful of fresh air." "Well" responded the Corporal, "you better take a mouthful of something else. Come with me and have a 'petit verre'." They accompanied him to the café and pretended to enjoy themselves, which however, they were far from doing. After some conversation the Corporal said:

"Mes enfants you must be around here at ten o'clock". They assured him that they would be on hand and to have no fear. When he had departed they quietly stepped out of the café and resumed their walk towards the Tuilleries. They wandered round and round through the narrow streets until they utterly lost their bearings. They came at last to a wide avenue in which there seemed to be great excitement. The cafés were all full of men and women, the sidewalks were thronged with a mad crowd, while cries of

"Vive la Commune" were heard on all sides. Through the crowds on the sidewalks and cafés they observed many soldiers of the "Gardes Nationales" who were well under the influence of liquor. The names of "Lecompte," "Thomas" and "Darboy," Paul heard frequently, mentioned by the half drunken and excited crowd. Then a fierce cheer echoed along the street. The women of Monmartre with long ropes attached to cannons came streaming up the boulevard. It was a wild and never to be forgotten sight. Many of the women wore army coats over which their hair floated loose. While one upraised hand grasped a naked sword or sabre the other held a rope that dragged the cannon. Through such exciting scenes as these, Paul and his Baltimore friend lost all count of the hours. It was noon before they thought about their ten o'clock engagement. Even had they desired they could not have found the place owing to their bewilderment. Wandering round, they came to the boulevard near the Rue de la Paix. In this vicinity they saw the first engagement which took place between the Communists and a body of citizens called "Les Hommes d'Ordre." While the firing was going on they stepped in a door way that sheltered them from the flying bullets. Shortly afterwards they found themselves on the Rue Rivolo. Here they saw great bodies National troops. As they were marching past a large building, Paul noticed an officer whom he recognized as his former Marechal de Logis in the Franc-Tireurs. Calling to his companion he quickly entered the same building, where they were confronted by a sentinel. They were permitted to pass in, when they informed him that they wished to see the officer who had just entered, but they failed to find him. As they we about to retire they were stopped by the sentinel, who refused to permit them to leave.

He called for the Corporal du garde who placed both of them under arrest and marched them into a room where many officers were seated. Among them, Paul discovered the one he sought, who also immediately recognized him and advancing asked him how he came to be in Paris. Paul told him he had come to Paris simply through curiosity and if necessary to take a hand in anything that was going on. Paul and his friend were then introduced to the officers present. One of them, a gray headed old fellow said:

"Well boys, I think we will find something for you to do; but as this is a quarrel among Frenchmen, I don't like the idea of any foreigners being mixed up in it. However as you are here we might as well use you."

Paul and his companion looked at each other with perplexity for they did not really know what they were about to join. Turning to his friend the Marechal de Logis, he told him in English of their adventures of the night before and asked him if this was the same army as the other. The officer laughed heartily and translated the story for the benefit of the others, who all joined him in his mirth. The gray haired man who had first spoken to Paul and who was evidently an officer in high rank said in pure English:

"Sons, I think you have done enough for France and it is best for you to leave Paris and go home."

Then calling an orderly he gave instructions that they should be taken to the rail road station and sent to Havre. Before leaving, he presented each with twenty-five francs and instructed the orderly to secure them transportation to the seacoast. The orderly who accompanied them to the station was an enthusiastic admirer of everything American. He had a brother in Quebec, which city he thought was about fourteen miles outside of New York. So vehement was the hospitality he had pressed on Paul and his companion that when he entered the station his military dignity was lost and nothing remained but his idea of treating his American friends to the best in the land. He placed them in a first class compartment against the remonstrance of the guard, whom with drawn sabre, he defied to eject them. As the train rolled out of the station cries of "Vive la France," "Vive l'Amerique," were exchanged.

At Rouen, then held by the Germans who had military guards all around the station, the train was detained for over half an hour owing to an accident. While waiting, Paul and his companion left the station to procure some tobacco. They passed a German soldier on guard at the gate who did not intercept them. On returning, the sentinel stubbornly refused them permission to enter notwithstanding the fact that they showed him their pass-ports and transportation; but they could not persuade him either in French or English to let them pass. At this moment a German officer arrived, when Paul advancing told their situation in French. Taking the transportation card from Paul's hand he showed it to the sentinel, and after many harsh sounding remarks in German he struck him with his open hand across the face. The soldier, still presenting arms to his superior officer showed no sign of resentment; not even a flush mounted to his cheek. The officer passed them in and Paul remarked to him:

"No French soldier would have stood that treatment."

"Possibly not," answered the officer, "but German soldiers know what discipline is."

On arriving in Havre, Paul found many volunteers placed in the same position as himself. All were waiting a chance to return to America; most of them looking to the French government to assist them home. While waiting for these orders that were very tardy in coming, Paul made the acquaintance of a Danish Count who had served all through the war. His quiet, gentle manners and evident embarrassment at being surrounded by the rough crowd of adventurers and soldiers of fortune with whom Fate had thrown him, appealed to Paul's sympathy, He said to the Count: "Come with me and I will take care of you." They secured lodging together on the upper story in a house in the Rue de l'Hospital for the princely consideration of one franc a week, which the landlady informed them must be paid in advance. With the air of a millionaire, Paul paid the rent for the first week and cheerfully intimated to the landlady that they would require the best room in her house as soon as their remittances arrived. Their room was a miserable affair in the attic, lit up with one small window. The scant bed clothes often compelled them to sleep in their uniforms of a cold night. When they reached their apartment they compared notes and found that all the money they had between them amounted to eight francs and seventy five centimes, (about $1.75).

"We must sail close to the wind now, Count," said the ever cheerful Paul to the despondent Dane. "With good management we can live high on a franc a day."

They did not live high, but they subsisted. Paul had entire charge of the household affairs and he drove hard bargains with those whom he favored with his patronage. The little square, two cent cakes of sausage were eagerly scrutinized while he weighed the one cent loaves of bread in his hand. Every two cent herring was examined as closely as a gourmand would a porter-house steak or some rich game. When the provisions were secured, Paul returned to their apartment where he generally found the Count with his head between his hands, seated near the window. "Now for the banquet," he would exclaim as he lit up a sou's worth of wood with which to fry the herring. The little squares of sausage would be placed on the soap dish. At times he prevailed on the Count to go down and get the cracked pitcher full of water, which made up their morning drinking cordial, while Paul was frying the herring. After it was cooked, it was scrupulously divided into two equal parts and they seated themselves. After meals they generally went out to ascertain news from the government in regard to sending them home. Some days they treated themselves to a regular table d'hote dinner at a little eating house kept by a widow on the quay. The cost of this dinner was thirteen sous and they could not often indulge in such a luxury. As time advanced things were getting more and more desperate. The Count was so gloomy and despondent that Paul feared he would end his life as he had threatened to do several times unless something turned up. They were now indebted to the landlady for two weeks' room rent. She had a very sharp tongue and used to fire a broadside at them every time she would meet them. In passing her door while ascending or descending, they generally removed their shoes as they did not wish to disturb her ladyship for whom they entertained great respect. Things continued to grow worse and worse until at last Paul spent the few last sous they had on two small loaves and a herring. They did not have even wood to fry the herring and were compelled to use the stump of a candle, which remained, to cook it with. Before retiring that night, Paul suggested to the Count the necessity of their trying to get some work, to which the Count replied that he would prefer death any time to the idea of going to work. Long before daylight Paul slipped quietly out of bed, dressed himself in his old uniform and proceeded in the direction of the docks. Near one of the bridges he saw a large group of men standing. He joined them and learned that they were all waiting for work, and that they expected the contractor along in a few minutes. The boss soon made his appearance and commenced reading from a slip of paper: "I want ten men at such a dock, five men at another place, eight men at another place and twenty-five men at the dry docks." The crowd separated itself into gangs, Paul joining the one that was called last. As the men passed the contractor, each one was handed a slip. When Paul's turn came to get his slip, the contractor looked at him curiously and said:

"Why, you are an American volunteer, what do you want here?"

"I want work," answered Paul, "and pretty badly too."

"Well," said the contractor: "I am sorry that I have no better job to give you today, but by to-morrow I will have something better."

Paul followed the gang to the dry docks where a large steamer had been hauled up. On exhibiting his piece of paper to the foreman, he received a three cornered scraper, a piece of sharp steel with a handle about eighteen inches long. He was told off to a certain plank suspended by ropes down the side of the vessel in company with two old dock rats who eyed him rather sullenly as though he was an intruder. Paul quickly slipped down the rope and seated himself on the plank, while the two professors climbed leisurely down and took a seat on either end, he occupying the middle. The side of the ship was thickly studded with barnacles and other shell fish. She had just returned from a long voyage to the tropics and was very foul. The air was chilly and raw down on the dark, damp stone dock. Paul was anxious to warm himself, so made a furious onslaught on the barnacles and soon had them flying in every direction. He stopped for breath and found his companions, instead of following his example, were gazing at him with looks of disgust and astonishment. One of them exclaimed:

"Regard him, look at him!"

While the other, with feigned pity, tapped his forehead with the tips of his fingers, as much as to say, "He is crazy, my brother." One of them then placed his hand on Paul's arm and asked him how long he had been engaged in scraping ship's bottoms.

"This is my first day," answered Paul, thinking he might have done something wrong.

"I thought so," responded his questioner. "A few more mad men like you would ruin our work in the dock. Why, at the way you are going the ship's bottom would be clean before night fall. This is the way to do it," and he put his scraper against the side of the vessel and slowly and laboriously removed a single barnacle. Then he laid the scraper on the plank beside him and drew out his pipe which he leisurely filled with tobacco and lighted. After taking a few whiffs he asked Paul where he was from and what caused him to seek work there. Paul fully explained his position and the cause that compelled him to work. After this, his two companions seemed to thaw out and entertained him with words of advice, instructing him in many methods of killing time when the foreman was not around. At noon all hands were called up out of the docks and each received a card to the value of two francs, which the foreman told Paul he could have cashed at the canteen by purchasing a dish of soup or a small piece of bread. Paul indulged in a five cent dinner and deeply regretted that the Count was not there to share it with him. He received one franc and seventy five centimes which he carefully stowed away. After dinner the plank was shifted and they resumed work at the barnacles. Before the six o'clock bell rang to cease work, Paul and his two preceptors were quite friendly. They told him that if he intended to pursue the business he should remember one thing:

"Never do what you did this morning, that is slip down the ropes first, particularly when there are three men to work on a plank, for," they gravely explained, "the two coming down last would occupy seats close to the ropes that net only act as a back brace when resting yourself, but would also be a means of saving your life in case the plank broke; when you could grab hold on the rope and the man in the middle would drop to the stones below and be killed. Of course the two clinging to the rope could be hoisted to the deck or be carefully lowered to the bottom."

At six o'clock Paul received a ticket for two more francs. To get it cashed, he purchased a glass of wine for two sous and then started on a run for his lodgings where he fully expected to find the Count dead. He ran the blockade of the landlady's door without the formality of taking off his shoes. Dashing into the room he exclaimed:

"Count! Count, where are you?"

"Here I am," exclaimed a faint voice from the bed.

"Well, I'm glad you are not dead, we dine at the widow's to-day. Look at this."

The Count started up and gazed on the seventy-three cents Paul exhibited with eager eyes, then looking reproachfully at him he said:

"Paul, I hope you have not taken to the highway." "No," said Paul, "I worked for that and hard too, so come on and we will have such a dinner as we have not had in two weeks."

Under the genial influence of the banquet, the Count confessed to Paul that he had retired to bed in the hope of dying quietly of starvation, providing the landlady had not disturbed him as he felt convinced that Paul had abandoned him. That night the landlady received one week's room rent and graciously gave them three days more to settle up in full. Paul was out again before daylight and sought out the contractor. This day he got a job on the ship Fanita of San Francisco, discharging grain. It was much cleaner and easier than scraping the steamer's bottom. His job was to guide the sacks of grain out of the hold while a horse on the dock attached to a long line passed over a block hoisted them up. While at this work the two mates of the ship stood near the hatchway and commenced making remarks about Paul whom they thought was a Frenchman.

"There is one of those French soldiers," said one.

"Yes," added the other; "he looks pretty hungry and thin; it is no wonder the Dutch licked them."

Paul smiled, but said nothing until a better opportunity presented itself, when he entered into conversation with the mate, who was much surprised to find that he was an American. At dinner time he was invited into the galley and regaled with a sea-pie until he was scarcely able to hail "Allons" to the driver of the horse on the dock, when he resumed work in the afternoon. That evening he was engaged by the captain of the vessel to keep tally on the sacks at five francs per diem. A few days later an order was issued from the Hotel de Ville that all foreign volunteers should assemble there. A hundred and twelve responded to the call and a motley group mustered from all quarters of the globe, representing every branch of the French service and wearing every conceivable kind of a uniform. Notwithstanding the fact that some of them were from Norway, Sweden, Denmark, Ireland, Belgium, etc., they all wanted to be sent to America. The mayor informed them that arrangements had been made to transport them there at the expense of the French Government. He also said that he was authorized to give each volunteer the sum of twenty-five francs, a mattress, blanket and a supply of tin-ware. This joyful news was received with loud cries of "Vive la France! Vive la Republique!" and three hearty cheers were given for the mayor. As the volunteers joyously dispersed, an officer informed Paul that the mayor wished to see him in his private office. When he entered, His Honor informed him that he desired him to take charge of the men on their passage over.

"I know they are a pretty wild lot, and no doubt will not obey orders, still I will depend upon you to do your utmost to keep them quiet, and not have them disgrace the uniform they wear."

He then gave Paul a strong letter of recommendation commending him for his courage and service to France, also presenting him with the arms he bore in the service. To this day Paul retains his chassepot as a memento of the happy, careless days he passed, while serving under the Tricolor of France.

Two days after, all the foreign volunteers were mustered to embark on the steamer Stromboli, the authorities taking the precaution not to give them the promised twenty-five francs until they had passed up the gang-plank. As the steamer moved out of Havre the citizens turned out in large numbers to bid them God speed. And when the bows of the steamer were kissed by the waves of the channel, the boys were all pretty hoarse shouting "Vive la France" in exchange for the cries of "Vive l'Amerique," that was sent over the water to them from the mighty crowd on shore.

The voyage to Liverpool was an uneventful one and the volunteers behaved well with the exception of emptying a cask of wine which they conscientiously filled again with water. This was the property of two French passengers who spent most of their time playing cards on deck and whose amazement when they discovered that their wine bad turned into water, knew no bounds. When the volunteers arrived in Liverpool they found that the steamer England of the National, which was to convey them to the United States was broken down, so they were compelled to remain in Liverpool several days at the expense of the steamship company, until the Virginia of the same line was ready to sail.

While in Liverpool they were treated very well and aroused a great deal of interest owing to their varied uniforms and war-stained appearance. While Paul and three of his companions were slowly sauntering one morning watching the sights, they beheld smoke proceeding from the basement of a rubber store from which the affrighted employees were madly rushing. Paul grabbed one of them and asked him if there was water anywhere around, and was informed that there was both water and hose attached in the basement, but that he would be smothered if he attempted to reach it. Without hesitation, Paul plunged into the basement, and fortunately came on the hose. Turning on the water he pushed his way back through the thick smoke and soon had the fire under control. It was a heap of rubbish and scrap rubber that emitted far more smoke than flame. When the fire engines arrived, it was found that they had nothing to do and the proprietor was so well pleased that he gave Paul five pounds.

When the Virginia was ready to sail, all the soldiers were transferred off to her in lighters. On reaching the deck they were all examined for revolvers and other weapons that when found were immediately placed in the charge of the quarter-master to be returned on reaching New York. There were a number of German emigrants and the steamship officers thought there might be some trouble. Besides the soldiers, there were eight hundred emigrants from different parts of Europe, mostly from Ireland and about fifty cabin passengers. The voyage was very rough and occupied twenty-one days. Many a wild trick was played in that steerage. Many a skirmish was nipped in the bud through the watchful care of the officers of the Virginia, which otherwise might have led to bloodshed. The favorite amusement was cutting down hammocks. Dark forms might be seen on all fours making their way on the greasy and slippery deck in the direction of selected victims. The sharp blade of a knife would be drawn across the taut cord that supported the hammock. Then an uproar that awakened the entire steerage would take place. If the one who was cut down happened to be an Irishman, he would loudly challenge all the passengers to come up and fight him, not caring whether they came in ones or hundreds. His invitation not being accepted he would generally pounce upon some unfortunate swinging near, and a scuffle would ensue in which the contestants were encouraged by hundreds of yells and cat-calls that would bring every steward on the ship into the steerage.

During the long voyage the soldiers suffered greatly from want of tobacco. The ship's doctor, a little Irishman from Dublin, often supplied them with the much needed article, and he had more influence over them than all the other officers on board. His quick wit one day prevented a fight that threatened to end most seriously. It was one of the few fine days that they experienced in the passage and all the hatches were being removed for fresh air. A German emigrant drew a knife on one of the soldiers and made a vicious slash at him. Sides were immediately formed between the soldiers and emigrants and the fight commenced right under the main hatch. It was interrupted by loud cries from above:

"Here you are! Here is what you want. Stop that fighting!"

Looking up they perceived the little doctor seated above with a large supply of tobacco, which he was throwing among the contestants. The fight stopped immediately, all scrambling for the much coveted weed. Before the supply was exhausted their good humor was restored and the fight forgotten.

On arriving in New York the volunteers scattered in every direction. Paul and his friend the Count started for his home. Their odd uniforms and equipments attracted much curiosity and comment. At this time, Paul's mother and elder brother owned a store on Broadway near Thirteenth street, and when he entered in his French uniform, his mother did not know him. On recognizing him she almost fainted. She had been told nothing about his being in the French army and believed he was off on one of his usual voyages. Paul discarded his uniform and was once more attired as a citizen.

While in New York, the Count received a heavy remittance from Denmark. He insisted that Paul must share in remembrance of the dark days when he had stood his friend, in Havre. He also consulted Paul as to what enterprise or adventure they should next embark. At this time expeditions were being secretly sent out from New York to aid the Cubans in their struggle for liberty. Paul thought this the most promising enterprise in which to engage and the Count readily acquiesced. They secured the address of an agent in the lower part of the city with whom they had a consultation and it was agreed that they should leave on the next expedition under General Jordan; but the expedition never sailed. The schooner was captured off Sandy Hook. They returned in company with a lot of others as violators of the neutrality law and spent two days in the Tombs. While there they were recipients of generous supplies of pies and other delicacies and beautiful flowers from fair Cuban sympathizers, and looked upon their discharge as a misfortune. After this the Count requested Paul to go to California with him, but the latter refused as he had decided to take another trip to the West Indies and pursue his former occupation of diving. He had sent letters to his old friend Captain Balbo with whom he often corresponded, and impressed the Count so with the description of the life they should lead among the sunny islands that he consented to join in the enterprise. They commenced negotiations for the purchase of the submarine armour and necessary appliances and only waited to hear from Captain Balbo before purchasing them. A letter from Nassau at last arrived informing Paul of the death of his old friend which caused him sincere regret and of course changed their plans. While still hesitating about what to do, a letter was received by the Count requesting him to return immediately to Denmark. It was so urgent and of such importance that he sailed by the next steamer.

CHAPTER VI.

After the Count's departure Paul joined a submarine company in New York and pursued the occupation of diver for over six months. He was wonderfully successful and when he resigned he had the largest salary of any diver in their employ. The cause of his resignation was the reports he had had heard about the diamond fields in South Africa. He determined to cast his fortune with the diamond hunters that were going from different parts of the world to the promised "Eldorado,"

Having secured a supply of implements and stores that he considered necessary, he took passage on the tall rigged ship Albatross, commanded by a friend of his. The Albatross was bound for China by way of Cape Town, and the captain promised to land him there. They had a long, pleasant voyage, during which Paul spent his time shooting at sharks over the side and trolling for fish. One day in the vicinity of the equator his hook was snapped by a dolphin, which he succeeded in bringing to the deck. It was laid on the shady-side of the galley and the sailors watched with great, curiosity the innumerable tints which radiated from its body. This transition in color was considered by the on-lookers as a visible evidence of the pain which it suffered. Picking up an ax Paul quickly dispatched it. In passing the equator the usual tom-foolery of receiving Neptune and baptizing those who had never crossed the line before, was enjoyed with one slight exception. The imitation of the god Neptune when coming out of the fore chains over the bow, missed his footing and fell into the sea. Fortunately for him the ship was becalmed at the time. With the aid of a line and a boat hook which one of his mates fastened firmly to his collar, he was drawn aboard. His appearance was certainly far from god-like. Paul often enjoyed the conversation of sun old sailor named Joe Clark. He was a misanthropist at the unjust inequality that existed in the conditions of life, and often sung a verse of his own composition which gave him intense satisfaction, as he chanted it while sewing sails or making sennet. It consisted of a few lines, the import of which was, that no matter how rich or gorgeous the outer apparel might be, all alike have to eat, drink and die. He was a typical tar and proved a source of continual amusement to Paul. He had sailed a long time with the captain of the Albatross on different ships, and the captain told Paul that he never made a voyage but that he did not express his determination that it would be the last one; and no matter what occupation he could get ashore, either street cleaning or farming he would take it in preference to going to sea again. After three days of shore life old Joe was tired of it and always headed for some outward bound ship. Once when

Paul and Joe were leaning over the bulwarks and gazing out on the glass-like surface of the equatorial waters in which they were then sailing, old Joe reflectively exclaimed:

"Mister Boyton, I wish I had a hundred thousand dollars. You may be sure that I would never make another voyage and it would save me from the fate of many an old shell-back that is dying around now."

Joe's firm belief was that every old sailor who died, turned into a sea-gull. Prompted by curiosity, Paul said: "Now, Joe, what is the first thing you would purchase supposing you had one hundred thousand dollars?"

"A quart of good Scotch whisky," promptly exclaimed Joe with a string of oaths to confirm his assertion, and he smacked his lips in satisfaction as though already enjoying it.

About two months after leaving New York, Table Rock was sighted and the same day anchor was let go off Cape Town. During this long voyage Paul improved the opportunity in studying and getting more practical ideas of navigation. By the time they cast anchor at Cape Town the captain assured him that he was as competent as himself and begged him to keep on with him to China as the man holding the position of first mate was very unskillful and he wished to get rid of him. Paul, however, had the diamond fever and no amount of persuasion could change his mind. He landed and secured quarters in Cape Town. With his usual happy-go-lucky disposition he had never inquired before leaving New York in regard to the location of the diamond fields, and he presumed that they were situated thirty or forty miles from the Cape. In Cape Town he became acquainted with an officer of the steamer Cambrian, named John Lord, who also had the diamond fever and intended going to the fields. Their pursuits being similar they naturally drifted into acquaintanceship. After a little conversation, Paul asked him how he was going up.

"Well," responded Lord, "I would go upon the regular wagon but my finances will not permit me. It costs twelve pounds and one is only allowed twenty pounds baggage."

"Twelve pounds? Sixty dollars? Why, good Heavens, how far is it? I was thinking about walking up."

"A little over seven hundred miles," was Lord's reply. Paul nearly fell over in his astonishment but said: "We are here and will get up no matter how far it is!"

On comparing notes they found that they could not afford to take the regular wagon that generally consumed twelve days in reaching the fields. They were told about another town named Port Elizabeth by going to which they could save three hundred miles of overland travel. Owing to the enormous fares charged in those times, they found it would be cheaper to go from Cape Town direct by ox trains. It took one of these trains from fifty to sixty days to get up and was anything but a comfortable trip. While waiting in Cape Town very much perplexed as to how they would get up, Paul made the acquaintance of an agent of Cobb & Co., who were engaged in the transportation business from the coast to the diggings. After some conversation, Paul was engaged to go as assistant superintendent of a heavy train which was about to start. On their long and tedious trip, the average time was about fifteen miles a day, when the order for outspanning would be given. This order meant to unhitch, dismount and camp for the night. As there were very few restaurants or hotels on the way, a large quantity of provisions was carried and like an army the train was made up in messes and did their own cooking. The Hottentot drivers and assistants made one mess, the passengers another, while those in command formed a third. Lord was also fortunate in getting transportation with the same train. This opening was looked upon as a Godsend as they not only got up themselves with their tools but had their provisions free. The train consisted of fifteen immensely long covered wagons of the stoutest build. Each wagon had between seven and nine thousand pounds made up mostly of provisions and for which the moderate price of nine dollars per hundred pounds was made for transportation. To each wagon was hitched a long line of oxen, harnessed to a strong chain. The Hottentot drivers were artists in handling their terribly long whips. Besides the oxen and fifteen wagons, was a mule team with the officers in charge. Three days after leaving Cape Town, the train drove into Wellington, fifty miles north. Soon after they entered the mountain, Bain's Kloof. They had great difficulty passing over this road through the mountains. Frequently they were obliged to double the ox teams on a single wagon in order to climb some steep ascent. The scenery through the mountains was exceedingly wild and picturesque, and the Hottentot driver with whom Paul was conversing, assured him that far away in the mountain tops were leopards and fierce baboons. The mountains being passed after a hard day's travel they entered the little village of Ceres where they outspanned for the night. From Ceres they passed on over a level plain occasionally passing a kail or cottage. At some places on the road the natives sold them hot coffee and cakes. The country over which they traveled was thinly populated. Occasionally a tramping adventurer or two would come with the wagons, all heading in the same direction. About ten days later the train entered Caroo Port, a vast desert, horribly desolate and forbidding. It was dead level and lay like a sea asleep. The heat was overpowering. Before entering the desert, a large supply of water was laid in and the order of travel was changed so that they ran at night instead of in the day time. This wilderness is about sixty miles wide and it took them five days to cross it Whenever a wind rose on this desert the mouth, eyes, ears and nose were filled with dust, making life miserable. At Durands, a solitary farmhouse stood like an oasis. They got a fresh supply of water there. After leaving the Caroo they entered a desert called Kope. In crossing this waste, they stumbled on many and many a skeleton of poor fellows, who had no doubt succumbed on account of the heat and lack of water. The crossing of these two deserts cost them many oxen. These were replaced at Beaufort by a relay that was in reserve for such an emergency. After leaving Beaufort they struck into a thickly wooded country that was a relief. Sometimes during the day, while the train was slowly wending its way onward, the superintendent and Paul would ride ahead for a hunt. They got some antelope and a large number of partridges. Paul was much surprised to find that game was much scarcer than he had been lead to believe by reading about South Africa.

They now entered a country where there were many ostrich farms, a business which was very remunerative. Ostrich chickens cost from twenty-five to fifty dollars apiece. In three years they will furnish plumage worth from twenty-five to thirty dollars each year. A Hottentot told Paul that many of the ostriches that then stood around in sight had been hatched by fat old Hottentot women who took two or three eggs away from the hens and lay with them in feather bed until they were hatched. The truthfulness of this story, Paul never verified.

After passing Victoria they wended their way slowly through great plains covered with a stumpy herbage. Here they saw large numbers of secretary birds and bustards and maramots and springbok antelope. Several of the latter were shot and added greatly to the comfort of the mess. Every few days they met the up or down carts, going or coming from the diamond regions. These would sometimes stop and give the news of above or below. It did not take much penetration to know the successful from the disappointed, coming from the mines as they got out of the train to stretch themselves. Forty days after leaving the Cape, they outspanned on the banks of the Orange river, into which Paul, without any ceremony, plunged with eagerness and enjoyed his first swim in Africa. Here they had to ferry and a slow and tedious occupation it was. About a week later they entered Pneil to which place the freight was consigned. The village was a small one, more like a camp. Down a steep ravine tents were pitched on every available spot, where a level surface afforded a floor. They were raised without regard to symmetry or order. Paul and his friend Lord looked around the camp and secured lodging with an old Californian who agreed to board them during their stay for ten shillings a day. At the same time he assured them that he did not intend to remain long there as the diggings were nearly played out and he was going to shift the following week to

Dutoitspan. After prospecting for several days and finding that they could not get a claim unless it was for an exorbitant price, they decided to adopt the Californian's idea and start over for the "dry diggings" at Dutoitspan. On arriving there they met a sorter who assured them that he was fully posted in regard to claims, the value of the stones found and everything else and agreed to enter partnership providing they purchased the outfit. After some hesitation and examination, they agreed to this. They bought a sieve, sorting table, and tent with cooking apparatus, etc., and started for a claim. They were fortunate in getting one about thirty feet square. There they erected their tent, under the supervision of the sorter who unceremoniously made himself head of the camp and who did more talking than work. Then they began the digging of the trench around their claim. Their sorting table was set up and they went to work with a will that was backed with enthusiasm and hope. The result of their digging was turned into the sieve, which was suspended by a rope from a cross bar, with handles on one side. The digger would swing it backwards and forwards until all the loose fragments of earth were broken off and nothing remained but the small stones like line gravel. These were then carried over and dumped on the sorter's table, who examined them carefully and placed anything promising to one side. But for three weeks nothing of any value was found. The small specimens that were obtained were disposed of to the dealers who daily visited every camp and digging. The amount derived from their sales barely kept the diggers in provisions. About this time Lord fell ill of dysentery, which was prevalent in all the camps in this vicinity, and Paul had to do double work to give the gentlemanly sorter, who refused to do any digging, occupation. Being tired and worn with the two-fold labor, Paul was tempted many times to abandon the claim and take a rest, and was prevented only by the fear that jumpers would take advantage of the work already done. The unwritten law at that time was that if a miner ceased working his claim for a certain length of time it could be "jumped" by others. About this time Paul also began to suspect the honesty of the sorter and kept a close eye on him. These suspicions he communicated to Lord, then recovering and found that Lord entertained the same ideas. So one evening after a hard day's work they grabbed the sorter and held an inquest on his pockets after calmly seating themselves on his head and knees. Their suspicions were verified by discovering stones on him that were valued the next day at one hundred and ten pounds. The frightened sorter willingly surrendered all they found, and confessed under the pressure of a revolver that he had been systematically robbing them for some time. Though pleased that they had discovered so much, Paul and his friend were both discouraged and disgusted with the diggings and they agreed that the first good strike they made they would leave it. After that they acted as their own sorters but with indifferent success. A couple of weeks later, Lord who had been out to purchase provisions returned with a speculator who was willing to purchase the claim. A long talk followed. At last they disposed of it to him with all their outfit for the sum of fifty pounds which left them not much richer than when they had started for the diamond fields. A short time after that they were in Cape Town once more, smelling the fresh, salt air. Here Lord obtained a position on one of the Union Co.'s line of steamers, while Paul remained in the hope of finding some ship going to China or Japan. Paul remained in Cape Town three weeks; but no chance opened to go to the eastward. He embarked on a French vessel that came in shorthanded, bound for Marseilles. He went before the mast as there as no other position on her and he had had enough of South Africa.

After a quick passage along the west coast of Africa they reached the straits of Gibraltar and stood across the blue Mediterranean to Marseilles. While there, assisting to discharge a cargo, Paul fell through a hatch and was badly wounded on the leg by coming in contact with the ragged edge of a roll of copper. At first he did not think he was much injured but as his leg kept on swelling, the captain strongly advised him to go to the marine hospital and conveyed him there in a cab. The ward in which Paul was placed contained about one hundred and fifty little iron beds filled with unfortunates like himself. The hospital authorities ran the institution on the principle that the less they gave the patient to eat, the sooner he would recover and get out. Breakfast consisted of a slice of bread and a little cup of very weak wine; dinner of some very feeble soup, bread and the same kind of wine. The supper was a repetition of the breakfast. After a couple of day's sojourn in the hospital, Paul was ravenous with hunger and would have willingly left if he had been able to do so. In vain he assured the good sister in his best French that it was his leg and not his stomach that was ill. In response she would smile sadly as she placed the meager allowance on the little stand at the head of the bed.

Paul was in bed number eleven. Number twelve was occupied by a Frenchman, who was fast dying, and number thirteen by an English sailor with a leg and arm broken. The Frenchman was so far gone that his appetite had failed so that he could neither eat nor drink. Notwithstanding this, his rations were always left on his stand at the head of his bed. The invalid and his provisions were watched by the English sailor and Paul with deep interest. Two or three times by the aid of his good leg Paul succeeded in confiscating the major portion, before the sailor could reach his unbroken arm out. One day after a consultation, the doctor shook his head slowly and told the sister that number twelve would not much longer remain a charge in her hands. This news was gladly listened to by Paul and the sailor. His dinner was placed as usual at the head of the bed but the Frenchman paid no attention to it. His labored breathings showed plainly to the watchers that the end was near. A few convulsive heavings followed, then the English sailor remarked: "I think he has slipped his cable." Paul got quietly out of bed to ascertain the truthfulness of the sailor's remark and made a grab for the soup and bread at the same time the sun-bronzed arm of the sailor reached out for the wine. Soon afterwards the nurse discovered that the patient had passed away and his body was carried to the dead house.

A couple of weeks later Paul was discharged from the hospital thoroughly cured, and eager to embark in anything that promised adventure. He was anxious if possible to secure some ship bound for America, and for this purpose haunted the docks and watched every new arrival closely. While sauntering around one morning he was accosted by a rough looking man who inquired if he was a sailor and wished to ship, Paul answered yes but that he wanted to ship on a vessel bound for the United States. "Well," said the stranger, "I am the captain of the bark Pilgrim and am bound for Valparaiso, why not that trip?"

Paul absolutely refused to go around the Horn. The captain then told him that they intended to start that night; but on the way out would stop at Malaga where he could land, and by going to Gibraltar get a ship much easier. He promised to pay him well for the run, so Paul consented to go. The Pilgrim was then laying in the offing and when Paul went to the landing to take the small boat to go to her, he found two other sailors belonging to her, who were going to Malaga on the run, the same as himself. One of them confidentially informed Paul that she was a floating hell and that he might expect lively times on the run down. Paul responded that he could stand it if the rest could. The row boat containing the sailors ran along side and the line was passed down. One of the sailors jumped lightly into the chains and took hold of his mate's bag. He tossed it on the deck without looking where it was going. His own was then passed up to him which he mounted the rail and jumped on deck. He had no sooner reached it than he was struck a powerful blow on the face and knocked on his back. His companion jumped on deck and found his comrade lying bleeding and half stunned. Over him, as if about to kick him, was the form of a powerful looking man who proved to be the first mate.

"What's the matter," exclaimed the sailor last landed. "What's this?"

"Perhaps you would like the same kind of a dose my hearty," exclaimed the mate as he came towards him with clenched fists.

"Well, no," was the response, "I don't intend to take any, but I will give you one that will teach you not to bill sailors in open port," and he drew his sheath knife and made a lunge that would certainly have disemboweled the first mate had he not quickly dodged the thrust and retreated to the cabin.

While the sailor who had drawn the knife was bending over his wounded comrade, the captain appeared, and exclaimed:

"This kind of work won't do! What's the meaning of this row?"

The sailor who had been struck explained to the captain how he had accidentally hit the mate while throwing his bag aboard, and that his partner had only come to his assistance when he thought he had been killed.

"Go forward, boys, go forward," the captain said. "I'll see that no more of this occurs."

This scene had been witnessed by Paul as he sat quietly on the rail. When the men went forward he stepped down and approached the captain, saying:

"Captain, I have been informed that your ship is a pretty wild one and by what I have seen I think she bears out her reputation all right. Now I consider myself fully competent to do my duty and will do it; but I want to give you fair warning that if I am molested by either of your bully mates, as I presume you have two of them, I will take good care of myself. The days when an officer can treat sailors with impunity are a thing of the past."

To which the captain responded: "You'll be all right, go away forward and stow your things."

When Paul entered the forecastle he found that the crew consisted of nine men seated on their sea chests and bunks, holding a council of war. They all agreed that it was a pretty bad ship and they determined to stand by one another. The council was broken up by a gruff voice:

"Come my hearties. Turn to with a will. Get your hand spikes and man the windlass."

All hands sprang out and quickly the clanking of the windlass chain was heard coming in. "Look over the head, young fellow," said the mate to Paul, "and see how she is." Paul complied and reported, "straight up and down." Soon after a tug came alongside, the line was passed over to her, the anchor catted and the Pilgrim stood away on her voyage. All hands were sent aloft to shake out sail and everything was ready to sheet home when the tug slacked up and cast off the cable. As the tug came around and returned to port she passed close alongside and the captain saluted the commander of the Pilgrim who was then showering oaths on the quarter deck and said sarcastically:

"My brave and gentle captain, the Lord have mercy on the unfortunate sea-infants who have trusted themselves in your hands."

Paul, who stood near by, overheard the tug captain's farewell and it convinced him that the Pilgrim's commander bore an unsavory reputation with sea-faring men. Every sail being set and lines coiled the decks were washed down. The crew, except Paul, who was at the wheel, were called up and ranged in a line along the deck. The two mates then advanced and tossed up a coin for first choice. The first mate won and said, "I'll take the man at the wheel." The second mate's choice then fell to a sailor at the right end of the line. Then they selected men alternately until they were divided into two equal parts. The first mate's watch being known as the starboard and the second mate's as the port watch. One watch was then ordered below while the other remained on deck. Soon after Paul was relieved from the wheel by another seaman and walking forward met the sailor who had been knocked down by the first mate as he came aboard. This man called him aside: "Did you notice that the first mate selected myself and mate in his watch? He evidently intends to do my friend some mischief for the slash he made at him."

He also informed Paul that he had a strong suspicion, which was shared by his mate that it was the captain's intention to take them all out to Valparaiso and not allow any to land at Malaga. This suspicion was confirmed next day in Paul's mind by the captain who sent for him to come aft. When he entered the cabin the captain said: "Young fellow, I like your appearance and wish you would change your mind and come on out with me to Valparaiso, I carry no boatswain, but I will give you that position and a pound a month extra, providing you can induce those two shell-backs who came aboard with you to do the same."

To gain time, Paul answered that he would speak to them and report in the evening. It was at that moment the farthest thought from his mind. After a consultation with his shipmates, both of whom assured him they would never consent, it was agreed that they should feign willingness to go. They knew that the captain had the power to hold them in the offing and prevent their landing so they determined to escape at the first opportunity at Malaga. The captain was so delighted with Paul's report that he insisted on his having a glass of grog, and was in such good humor that he went on deck and amused himself by smashing the nose of an unfortunate Norwegian, who was then at the wheel. This was a favorite pastime of both captain and mate's, but it was generally practiced on those whom they knew would never resist their cruelty. The Pilgrim was a brute to steer and a very slow ship, notwithstanding they had a fair wind it took them ten days to reach Malaga, where they anchored well off the shore. She then commenced to receive the balance of her cargo of wine by means of lighters. The crew were closely watched during the day. At night the oars were removed from the gig, swinging at the stern and as an extra precaution a heavy chain and padlock were passed around it. For three days the lighter came alongside but no chance presented itself to Paul and his companions to get ashore. Seeing that the cargo was about completed and that it would only take a few more lighters to fill her, Paul determined to leave that night. A large plank that acted as fender was stretched along the side. This he concluded to use for the purpose of getting his companions and bags ashore. He advised them to have everything stowed away in as small a space as possible and to have as large a supply of sea-biscuit and salt meat as they could secure. It was Paul's anchor watch that night, from one to two. When he came on deck he found it a clear, brilliant star-light night and the sea as smooth as a cup of milk. After walking around for about a quarter of an hour he stepped softly in the direction of the after cabin and listened intently. He was satisfied that all aft were sound asleep. Coming forward to the forecastle he found the two sailors all ready to join him. Their clothing and provisions were firmly lashed up in pieces of tarpaulin. The three silently and cautiously crept to the side; a sharp knife severed the rope that held up one end of the fender and the other was lowered quietly until the plank was afloat on the surface. A couple of turns were taken in the rope that held it over a belaying pin, and Paul said:

"Now is the time, one of you slip down the rope and deposit the bags on the planks. Then get in the water and rest your hands on the side." The water was very phosphorescent and the fish left trails of light after them as they dashed hither and thither below. Just as one of the sailors was about to step over and descend, either a porpoise or some large fish shot from under the vessel and left quite a trail of light in its wake. The sailor hesitated: "That must be a shark," he said, "if we get in that water we are bound to be eaten up."

Time pressed and Paul remonstrated with him in vain to get down. Any moment either the captain or the mate might wake up and discover them. To show an example that there was no danger Paul grasped the rope and slipped silently into the sea. He was followed by one of the sailors, but the other could not overcome his fear and decided to remain. His decision was irrevocable for he cast off the line and said:

"Good-bye boys, I am sorry that I can't go, I dare not risk it."

Paul and his companion pushed out and quietly passed under the stern and until sufficiently far away from the vessel, they were very gentle in their movement. Feeling more secure they struck out with powerful strokes driving the plank that supported their bags, ahead. The mountains that surround Malaga on all sides and tower far up in the starlit sky seemed only a few hundred yards away; but it was a full mile before the end of the plank grated on the shore and the sailors scrambled out on the slippery and weed covered rocks. They landed a little to the north of the city and grasping their bags commenced the ascent of the mountain. This was very steep and rough and exceedingly dangerous work as it was not yet daylight. Having gained a good height up the side they rested. A faint glimmer was just then tingeing the sky and everything around them was still as death. The gentle lapping of the waves against the rocky shore, the barking of the dogs in Malaga, and the occasional crow of a rooster rang out with wonderful distinctness. The anchor light of the ship about one mile away twinkled as though only a little distance off. Not yet feeling secure they began climbing upwards. The progress was arrested by a hoarse sound coming from the direction of the ship. As they sat on the rocks to listen, they heard the voice of the mate baying out oath after oath, calling the watch and asking:

"Who was the last on watch? Where is the watch? Turn out all hands!"

Then oaths from another voice came floating up and they had no difficulty in recognizing the choice maledictions of the captain as he rushed on deck to ascertain the cause of the disturbance. After this a confused murmur arose from the deck through which they fancied they could hear the blows of massive fists rained down on the heads and faces of the unfortunate seaman. They distinctly heard the sharp order: "Lower away the gig!" The click, click of the cleat as the rope ran through the blocks sounded alarmingly near to them. Soon after, advanced daylight revealed to them the boat as it was swiftly rowed to the shore. They recognized the captain seated in the stern and laughed heartily over the thought of the great rage of the commander whom they knew was eating his heart out. They surmised that his mission was to go to the Consul and report them as deserters and also start the Carbineros in search of them, by means of a reward for their capture. But they felt secure in the place they had selected, far up on the mountain. They quietly enjoyed the scenes below and watched the lighters as they carried out the last of the cargo. They laughed as they saw the captain's gig shoot fretfully from ship to shore many times during the day, while they enjoyed their pipes and ate with relish their salt beef and seabiscuits. Late in the afternoon they observed with glee the last lighter leave the side of the Pilgrim, the captain's gig hoisted on board, and the heavy sails loosened and dropped down. The clanking of the anchor chain was joyful music as it was taken on board and the Pilgrim under full sail soon glided away on a tack to the eastward. That night they decided to camp in the mountains, but it proved so chilly and uncomfortable that when the hour of three boomed out from the clock below, they decided to move. They carefully descended the mountain side until they found a road. This they followed until they entered the town which they passed through without molestation. They took the road to the south which they thought led to Gibraltar. By daylight they were well out of Malaga and walking rapidly along. During the day they met many peasants and exchanged the "buenos dias" and proceeded on their way undisturbed. That night they came to a monastery, where a peasant assured them they could find rest and supper. They were hospitably received in the traveler's quarters. The assistant did not seem to comprehend the Mexican-Spanish which Paul brokenly spoke. He finally succeeded in making the monk understand that he could speak French and that if there was any one around who could understand that tongue he would be more at home. In response to his request the assistant disappeared and soon returned with a venerable looking priest who spoke French fluently. Paul explained to him that they were seamen en route from Malaga to Gibraltar and that they wished to get some information as to the road, also hospitality for the night. Their request was complied with and they were assured that they were perfectly welcome. Paul then questioned the priest in regard to the Carlos revolution and said that he would just as soon join that as join a ship. The priest, who proved to be an ardent admirer to Don Carlos, assured them that it was impossible, as the seat of the revolution was away in the north and too far for them to hope of reaching it by foot. He advised them to continue on their way. Next morning after breakfast they resumed their march and two days after entered the gates of Gibraltar. Here they proceeded to a sailor's boarding house, where they were assured they would have no difficulty in getting a ship. Next day while hesitating over an offer they had from the captain of a fruiter to run down to the Grecian Islands where he intended to load with dry fruit and return to New York, a little English bark entered the bay. Her first mate was so ill that they decided to land him and leave him in the hospital. Paul sought out the captain and after a close examination was engaged in the position vacated by the sick man. The bark was the George, of North Shields, England. Paul induced Captain Moore also to ship his companion before the mast. The same day she weighed anchor and stood away on her course to Alameira. The crew of this little bark was a happy family. The captain was an easy, quiet humane man and a thorough sailor; the second mate was the owner's son who came out more to gain experience than to do duty as an officer. This was a far different craft from the blood-stained and wild Pilgrim that was then ploughing her way to the westward. An oath or an angry word was newer heard on the decks of the George, and the sailors seemed to do more work than the sullen and harassed seamen on the Pilgrim. They sailed up the beautiful coast of Andalusia and close in to the foot of the mountains that towered from the clear blue, waters of the Mediterranean far above the clouds, where their snow-white caps were cool and refreshing to look at from the burning deck below. The bark was laden with coal consigned to a firm in Alameira and the captain's instructions were to bring back a cargo of Spanish grass and copper ore. At Alameira they had to anchor in an open roadsted and the George's cargo was discharged into lighters. The method of discharging coal where there are no steam engines or docks to run alongside, is rather primitive and is known as "jumping." An upright stairs or ladder is made on the deck by lashing spars together. A block is fastened far above in the rigging over the hatch through which a rope is rove leading down into the hold. The end of this rope is fastened to a long spar just the height of the ladder and terminating in a number of lines called whips. These are grasped by six or eight sailors who climb the ladder, made of spars, that has been set over the hatch. When the large bucket is filled with coal below, the order is given to jump. The seamen simultaneously spring from the spar while banging on to the whips, and their combined weight brings up the huge tub of coal, which is grasped by the lighter men and dumped over the side into their boat. When the cargo of coal was discharged they commenced taking in copper ore until she was sufficiently ballasted to proceed up the coast to Motril to finish her cargo with Spanish Grass. This article is a coarse grained material something like a rush and of the nature of willow and bamboo combined, and is used extensively in England in the manufacture of mats, chair bottoms, etc. It was put up in bales and proved a most disagreeable article to stow away in the hold.

The cargo being completed, anchor was weighed to the cheerful sound of "homeward bound" and the George started on her voyage to Newcastle, England. Owing to head winds the bark had to tack all the way to Gibraltar. Sometimes close under a mountain and again far out in the Mediterranean, she beat her way down the coast. The weather was clear and beautiful and the crew did not have much to do outside of cleaning her down, mending and making sails. All who could handle the needle well were engaged in that occupation. They sat on the quarter deck and sewed industriously while the boatswain chalked and cut the lines for them. Good natured Captain Moore spent his watch on deck, chatting away with them and listening to their yarns. He thoroughly enjoyed their jokes and superstitions with winch many of their quaint stories were intermingled. While doing so he usually smoked a long clay pipe and being a very forgetful man the moment he laid it out of his hands he never remembered where he had left it. He was also a very short sighted man and the boys often had a quiet joke on him by shifting the pipe from place to place while he was looking for it. Once the boatswain, named Smith, who was as mischievous as a monkey, thought he would play a good joke on the captain. Seeing him lay his pipe on the lattice work aft of the wheel and run down into the cabin to get his glasses, Smith jumped up and threw his pipe overboard and sketched one in chalk in the same place. On mounting the deck the captain took a long look at the stranger that had just hove in sight over the starboard bow; then laid his glasses on the skylight and looked around for his pipe. When he saw the sketch he reached forth his hand to pick it up. Being convinced by the suppressed murmur of merriment he heard among the sail-sewers that they knew of the joke, he quickly disappeared down the hatchway. The sailors drove sail needles into each other in their hilarity. As he captain made no remark, the incident was forgotten.

The following Sunday morning the captain called Paul down and told him to order all hands on deck and get the chain hooks. This order surprised Paul as it was very unusual for any work to be done on Sunday except to stand watch, steer and trim sail. He made no remark, however, but proceeded to the deck and ordered all hands out. The men let their washing, sewing, and other domestic duties to which they generally devoted their attention on Sunday, and came on deck more astonished than Paul was. He then told the boatswain to get out the chain hooks. The captain now appeared and gave the order to "hoist away that starboard chain and trice it along the deck." This was a terrible job as fully sixty fathoms of the heavy anchor chain lay stowed away in the chain locker below. The men sprang to work and fathom after fathom of the chain was pulled up with the aid of the hooks and tried in lengths along the deck. When the boatswain reported "all up, sir," the order was given, "Get up the port chain." The men groaned, but complied without a murmur and link after link of the heavy chain from far below was drawn up through the iron bound hole in the deck. It was almost noon when the perspiring and worn out sailors had it all up. Again the report, "It is all up, sir," was given to the captain:

"That's impossible Mr. Smith, look down and see if you can't find more."

In compliance with the order, Smith applied his eye to the hole and again assured the captain that it was taut.

"Look again and see if you can't find it."

"Find what?" irritably enquired Smith.

"Why, my pipe to be sure. You can now let the crew go below."

Notwithstanding their fatigue, the boys had to laugh and all agreed that that was one on the boatswain.

The crew was great on debating and many and many a foolish question came up in the forecastle. After long argument, Paul was generally made referee. One evening during the dog watch he could hear a violent debate in the forecastle and wondered to himself what ridiculous question would now be presented to him for decision. He was quickly enlightened by seeing two of the sea-lawyers approaching the quarter deck. One of them was named Hiram Young, a very ignorant but positive American sailor, the other named Daniel Sneers, an Englishman equally ignorant and if possible more positive. When they neared the quarter deck Paul asked: "Well what is it?"

"We want you to decide a question sir," said Young, "this 'ere Sneers says and maintains as what England put in a challenge in the paper and kept it in for six months, offering to fight any country on the face of the earth, and I argues as she never put it in a American paper or she would a' been snapped up like that," demonstrating his remark by snapping his forefinger and thumb.

Paul tried to show them the difference between nations and prize fighters, but neither of them seemed thoroughly satisfied with the explanation given. As they walked back to the forecastle, Paul overheard Young remark, that "She might a put it in French or a Italian paper, but he was d—d if they ever put in a American paper!"

When they reached Gibraltar a heavy west wind was blowing in through the strait. Under lowered top-sails they were compelled to beat up and down under the shelter of the rocks. A large fleet of weather bound vessels kept the George company. It is too deep to anchor here, so the vessels are compelled to keep moving up and down until they get a fair wind to go through the straits into the Adriatic. While cruising about, the vessels passed so closely that the crews could hold conversation with each other, and many a friend was recognized and hailed. Their second morning under the lee of the rock during Paul's watch the large bark Culpepper, commanded by a very irritable old mariner was slowly passing. The angry voice of the captain, as he heartily cursed his crew was plainly heard on the George. In a lull in the torrent of abuse an Irish sailor who was leaning over the George's rail, said derisively:

"Hould on, hould on Captain, till the waters bile and Oi'll go over and shave ye."

The remark was overheard by the captain of the Culpepper who cried loudly and angrily:

"Bark ahoy, there! Bark ahoy, there."

"What do you want?" responded Paul coming to the side.

"Are you the captain?" demanded the infuriated ruler of the Culpepper.

"No," said Paul, "he is below."

"Then call him up," he thundered.

At this moment, Captain Moore, who had heard the conversation, protruded his head through the hatch and Paul informed him that the captain of the Culpepper desired to speak to him. He hailed the Culpepper and desired to know what was wanted.

"Why one of your ——— shell-backs insulted me," was the answer that floated across the water.

"What did he say?" inquired Captain Moore.

"Why he told me to wait till the water boiled and he would come aboard and shave me," thundered the angry captain of the Culpepper.

"And why the blazes don't you wait, it would add to your personal appearance considerably," said Captain Moore as he disappeared down the gangway.

About noon the wind changed and the long looked for easterly breeze came rippling over the waters of the Mediterranean. All sail was made and the fleet stood away through the straits. The Culpepper stood side by side for about five miles during which time the crews keenly enjoyed the broadside of compliments that was hurled from vessel to vessel by the two commanders. The George made a fair run and in due time entered the mouth of the Tyne and was soon after moored at the docks at Newcastle where Paul left her. He was loth to do so as it was the pleasantest vessel, captain and crew he had ever shipped with.

He then engaged himself as first mate on the ship Campbell, a Nova Scotia boat bound from North Shields to Philadelphia with a cargo of chemicals. When a couple of days out he discovered that the second mate was more brutal than either of the worthies on the Pilgrim. He was always below during the second mate's watch on deck so he had no chance of witnessing any acts of brutality, but he was posted on the subject by the men in his own watch, whom he always treated with kindness and consideration. He informed the captain about the reports he had heard. The latter agreed that it was wrong to maltreat sailors; but Paul felt sure that he closed his eye to many strange doings on his ship and that when a man representing himself to be a sailor came aboard and proved incompetent, there was no punishment considered severe enough for him. Three such unfortunates were aboard this ship, one in Paul's watch and two in the second mate's watch. Paul soon discovered that the man was unskillful. He could neither steer, reef nor splice so he set him to scrubbing, and by a few encouraging remarks got him to work harder than any one on the watch. The unfortunate would-be sailors in the second mate's watch did not fare so well. He instructed them in the mysteries of navigation through the agency of his fists. While the watches were being relieved, Paul noticed their blackened eyes and swollen cheek that evidenced all too plainly the effect of the second mate's bad temper. One night during the second mate's watch, the vessel was struck by a number of baffling squalls that seemed to come from every direction. This necessitated constant trimming of the sails and the men were kept hard at work. Every few minutes one could hear the hoarse orders given as the men scampered hither and thither to man the ropes. The oaths, blows, and fighting on this watch, kept both the captain and Paul awake. Seeing the captain turn out of his bunk and light his pipe, Paul remarked: "They are having a pretty warm time on deck."

"Yes," responded the skipper, "I presume Stanley is drilling some of those landmen."

At eight bells, when Paul's watch on deck commenced, he relieved the second mate, who was in a towering rage at the stupidity of his watch. The vessel was then under reefed topsails only and prepared for the uncertain squalls that were driving all around. At daylight Paul ordered hands aloft to shake out the reefs and set top gallants. As the top sail was raised he noticed dark blotches all across it and hailing the man aloft he asked him what caused them.

"Blood, sir," answered the sailor.

Paul well understood the meaning of it and knew it to be the work of the second mate, who had beaten the men over the head with a belaying pin while they were reefing. Shortly after the captain came on deck, Paul called his attention to the blood-stained sail and said: "This work has got to be stopped."

The captain shrugged his shoulders. "What can we do?"

"That's for you to say," answered Paul. "You're in command here."

"Well, I'll have to talk with Stanley when he turns out."

At seven bells the order: "Pump ship, call the watch," was given. The watch was called but failed to respond. The sailor sent to call it again reported that port watch did not intend to turn out. It was now eight bells and time for Paul's watch to go below. The captain came on deck followed by the second mate, with whom he had been remonstrating. Paul reported that the watch had been called out but refused to come. The second mate with a terrible oath started forward saying:

"I'll have the dogs on deck mighty soon."

He reached the forecastle door and flung it back. The same moment both Paul and the captain saw him stagger and fall to deck. He bellowed lustily for help. The captain and Paul rushed to his assistance and found him bleeding profusely from knife wounds in the breast and abdomen, while the port watch with drawn knives stood sullen and determined looking in the forecastle. This sight staggered the captain who exclaimed:

"Mutiny by the eternal!" and called loudly for the steward to bring him his revolver.

Paul ordered some of his watch to carry the mate, who was groaning, aft, then advancing to the forecastle door said:

"Boys, this is not right. This must not be. Put up those knives. If you have any grievances come out like men and give them to the captain."

"Oh, we have nothing to say against you or the captain," responded the leader, "but we have determined to die before we turn to under that man again."

Paul requested the men to keep calm and cool and he would speak to the captain who, during this interval, had slipped back to the cabin to arm himself. Paul advised the captain, as he met him coming out of the cabin with a revolver in each hand, not to go to the men in that shape.

"I am sure those men are determined. Their bloodshot eyes and frenzied manner convince me that they have not slept a wink during the watch below and have deliberately planned this outbreak and mean mischief. I cannot guarantee that my watch will not join them as they are all heartily sick of the second mate's inhumanity."

The captain thought it over for a few minutes and said, "You go forward and find out what they want."

When Paul returned to the forecastle he informed the men that the captain was anxious to hear their complaint and see that they were righted, and advised them to walk aft in a body and speak for themselves, assuring them at the same time that they would receive justice. After some hesitation they agreed to go aft. Paul preceded and told the captain that they were coming and he could hear their complaints for himself. At first the captain seemed inclined to bully the men and assert his authority; but the determined look caused him to change his mind, and he was very diplomatic in his treatment of them.

"Boys," he said, "I have sailed the seas for many a year and always like to treat my men well. One thing I object to and that is murdering mates. Now you are all in open mutiny and I am authorized by law to shoot you."

Here the men laughed derisively.

"Now," he continued, "I am against bloodshed and I want to know just what you men want and what I can do for you."

They looked at each other and to the one whom they regarded as leader. He was a sturdy, powerful Scotchman who stepped forward and said:

"If you were against bloodshed, why didn't you come out last night when the second mate tried to kill some of us. We are willing to turn to again; but not under that hound. We meant to kill him, he deserved it and if he is not dead it is not our fault. We are well aware that there is no law for a sailor before the mast, so at times the sailor has to take the law in his own hands. Now me and my mates are willing to work ship under you and the first mate but you must keep that brute out of sight providing he recovers."

The captain made another speech to the sailors in which he promised them that they would not again be molested by the second mate. He also stated that Paul could take the port watch and he would take the starboard watch. The men appeared well satisfied with this arrangement and turned to with a will. The captain and Paul walked up and down the quarter deck talking over the situation. The determined attitude of the men seemed to have caused a change in the captain's opinion, so much so that he gave Paul a long lecture on the duty of superior officers to treat their men kindly.

An examination of the second mate proved that he had been cut in five different places. All the simple remedies in the sea-chest were applied to relieve him from his sufferings. Neither the captain nor Paul had sufficient medical knowledge to know whether he was seriously wounded or not. They ad the steward wash the cuts which they covered liberally with plasters to stop the bleeding. The captain then insisted on giving the wounded man a tumblerful of strong whisky, saying "that it was the best thing in the world to kill a fever." They came to the conclusion that there was no danger of the mate passing away quickly owing to the savage kick he made while laying in his bunk, at the head of the inoffensive steward who was doing all he could to help him. But his wounds proved so severe that he was not able to leave his bunk until the vessel reached Philadelphia. Owing to the new arrangement, everything went well. There was no more fighting, cursing, or driving and the work on board was done promptly and cheerfully.

In a conversation with one of the two young fellows who were the special victims of the wounded mate's ferocity, Paul ascertained that he was a delicate and well educated youth from Hartford, Connecticut, whose romantic dream for years had been to go to sea. He ran away from home and fell into the hands of the master of a sailor's boarding house who robbed him of all he could and put him aboard a ship bound for Hull. The captain and officers of this ship proved humane, and though not absolutely ill-treated or beaten, his life was a misery. From Hull he went up to the Tyne on a coaster, where he joined the Campbell. He assured Paul with tears in his eyes, that several times before the outbreak in the forecastle he had concluded to dive overboard and swim far down in the sea to end his misery. He is a type of the many boys who think there is nothing but pleasure and romance in connection with life on the sea.

About this time heavy westerly winds set in against the Campbell and drove her far out of her course and for weeks she beat about in the most horrible weather. To add to their discomfort some of the water casks were stove, so that the crew were placed on short allowance until they were relieved by a barkentine named, The Girl of the Period. She was from Palermo with fruit, sixty-three days out and bound for New York.

In exactly seventy-one days after the Campbell had made sail out of the mouth of the Tyne she tied up at the docks at Philadelphia. Paul left this ship thoroughly satisfied with his experience and with the firm resolution never again to tread the plank of a ship either as sailor or officer.

CHAPTER VII.

While in Philadelphia he met the President of the Camden & Atlantic Railroad Company, who was desirous of negotiating with him in regard to taking charge of the life saving service at Atlantic City, a great watering place at the ocean terminus of the road. After a few interviews, the arrangements were made and the contract signed. Paul was installed as captain of a station built out on the beach and equipped with all kinds of life saving apparatus. During the seasons of 1873 and 1874 he held this position and so careful his watch and so efficient his system that not a single life was lost, and when he left the service he had the glorious record of having saved seventy-one lives. He also spent much of his time perfecting his appliances. It was while in this service that his attention was first attracted to the life saving dress in which he afterwards became so famous. As this dress will often be alluded to in the pages to follow, it may be well at this time to give its description:

It was invented by C. S. Merriman of Iowa, and consists of a pants and tunic made of highly vulcanized rubber. When the pants are put on the tunic is pulled over the head and down over a steel band at the upper part of the pants where it is firmly secured by a rubber strap. All portions of the body are covered except the face. There are five air chambers in the costume; one at the back of the head which acts as a pillow and when fully inflated it draws the thin rubber around the face so that no water can wash down. The other chambers are situated in the back, breast, and around each leg from the hip to the knee. The entire dress weighs about thirty-five pounds. When in water, the wearer of this suit can be horizontal or perpendicular on the surface. When standing upright, the water reaches to about the breast. When voyaging, he propels himself by a light double bladed paddle six feet long. He assumes the horizontal position feet foremost and some times uses a sail to help him along. During the winter of 1873 and spring 1874, Paul devoted much of his time to experimenting in this dress and became very expert in its use. His fearlessness in the water was no doubt of great aid to him. Many a fine, warm summer night he spent far out at sea in his dress and dreamed of the many voyages he would make in the future; but he never for a moment imagined the fame he would acquire in after years or the extraordinary voyages he would make through its means; but he thought of the thousands of lives that would be saved by this dress if properly introduced to the world. With the confidence of youth and the strength of manhood he was willing to take any chances to attain this object. At this time his passion for life saving amounted to a craze. He studied long and deeply on the best method to attract the world's attention. At last he struck upon a plan which he considered a good one and which he determined to put into execution at the close of the life saving season.

In the fall of 1874 he proceeded to New York. He spent a week with his mother, to whom, however, he did not confide his intention, fearing that it might worry her. His plan was to take passage on an outward bound vessel and when two hundred miles off the American coast to drop overboard and make the best of his way back to land. For this voyage he secured a rubber, water-tight bag with air chambers sufficient to support about fifty pounds of provisions. It also contained a compartment for fresh water. Into this bag he packed sufficient provisions in a condensed form to last him ten days; also two dozen signal lights with striker for same, some rockets, compass and a knife. Besides this his baggage consisted of his suit, a strong double bladed axe to be used for protection against sharks or sword fish. He innocently boarded several vessels and confided his intentions to the captains. They unanimously agreed that no attempt at suicide should be made off their vessel, for such they termed his enterprise. The newspapers at this time got hold of the plan and made it a subject of fun. Tired at failure to get a captain to take him off shore, Paul decided to adopt another plan. So on Saturday, October 11th, 1874, he quietly walked up the gangplank of the National Line Steamship Company's steamer The Queen. He carried his little store of baggage as if it was the property of one of the passengers. He walked forward and deposited his stuff; then mingled among the crowd. It was not his intention to cross the ocean so he neglected the necessary form of purchasing a ticket. When The Queen steamed away from her dock, Paul descended into the steerage and stowed away his outfit in an unoccupied bunk. From that time until Sunday evening, he kept very quiet and no one on board knew of his intentions. About eight o'clock he slipped on deck and under the shelter of a life boat commenced to dress himself in the suit. The weather had been fair and the steamer was making good headway so he calculated she was at that time two hundred and fifty miles out. He was quickly dressed in his armor, and with the rubber bag in one hand and the paddle in the other he was about to make a leap into the sea, when a hand was laid roughly on his shoulder and a gruff voice said:

"Here, where are you going?"

Paul mildly explained that he was going ashore. The deck was all excitement in a moment as the deck hand loudly reported to the officer on the bridge.

"Bring him aft," was the command.

Equipped in his strange looking dress, bag in one hand, paddle in the other and an ax strapped to his side and firmly gripped by two sailors, Paul was ushered back. They were followed by a crowd of curious passengers. On the captain perceiving him he exclaimed:

"Ah! Boyton you are aboard of me. Take off that suit and pass it over to the steward."

Paul remonstrated and told the captain that he had no ticket to Liverpool. He thought this confession would excuse him and cause the captain to assist in his return to America; but the captain would not even let him put himself off. Paul was compelled to undress and his entire outfit was turned over to the steward with orders to place it in the captain's cabin. The latter then took Paul into the chart room, where he had a long conversation with him. All Paul's pleadings and excuses that he was not prepared and that he would get safely back on shore were made in vain. The captain told him not to worry about his ticket, and requested the steward to give him an unoccupied bunk in the officer's quarters.

Paul's disappointment could not be described in words. He was in no way prepared for the enforced voyage to Europe having but one suit of clothing and only fifty dollars in cash. He had presented his entire salary with the exception of the money he had, to his mother before leaving New York, with the excuse that he was simply going down the coast and did not need it. The quarters given to him by Captain Bragg were very comfortable and his treatment was of the kindest. The next day the captain sent for Paul and they had a long talk. The captain drew from him many of his former experiences and adventures and was favorably impressed by the frank, open nature of the young fellow. He sympathized with him in his too apparent disappointment and shared his earnest desire to introduce an apparatus that would be the means of saving the lives of many sea-faring men. The captain promised that should they reach the Irish coast in good weather, he would allow Paul to go off and thus carry out his original idea on the European coast, which he assured him would be just as effective as on the American side. During the trip across, Paul spent much time with the captain in the chart room. While they studied over the charts, the captain pointed out to Paul one place off the Irish coast and several in the Irish sea where he could make a landing in either Ireland or England. The place selected by Paul was off the coast of Ireland in the vicinity of Cape Clear, as he was assured he could get under the lee of the island in case of a high wind from any direction. The news of the captain's permission to Boyton to leave the vessel when off the Irish coast, was spread among the passengers and every one, both fore and aft, manifested the most lively interest in the experiment. Some of the officers protested vigorously against it. Captain Bragg was a determined man and when he gave the word the only course was to obey him. On the evening of Tuesday, the 21st, the captain called Paul into the chart room and said:

"We are now nearing the Irish coast and the barometer is as low down as I have seen it for many a year and there is every indication of a gale. The coast you intend to land on acts as a breakwater for all northern Europe and the waves that pile up on it during a storm are something astounding. The cliffs that resist them are from one hundred and eighty to three hundred feet high and they are as straight up and down as a mainmast in a calm. Cape Clear that I expect to sight soon lays several miles off the mainland. On it is a powerful light that will guide you. The gale may not break for some time yet if you can make the Cape, you can drop around to leeward and land on it. And when the weather clears you can cross to the main."

Having thus explained the nature of the coast they were then rapidly approaching and the possibility of a gale which might dash him to pieces against the cliffs, the captain requested Paul to defer his experiment until they reached some part of the Irish sea where a landing could be made with more safety to himself. Paul was anxious and eager to get overboard and firmly held the captain to his word.

"As I have promised I will stand by it," said the captain.

At nine o'clock that night Paul fully prepared, with ax, paddle and bag securely lashed to him, was ready to leave. It was a wild, dark night. Great swells caused The Queen to roll heavily. In a few moments the cry of "A light on the port bow, sir" rang over the decks.

"That's Cape Clear," said the captain, "Now, Boyton, if you are ready, I'll stop her."

"Ready and willing," was Paul's response.

At this moment the first officer approached and earnestly remonstrated with the captain saying:

"This will cause us all trouble. This man will surely lose his life."

The answer to his protestation was:

"On the bridge there, stop her."

The great screw ceased to beat the foaming water behind and The Queen glided along with her own impetus.

"Good night captain! Good night ladies and gentlemen," said Paul as he stepped over the rail and grasping a rope commenced to descend the side. The vessel rolled heavily to port; he felt the sea around his feet, then up to his armpits. He let go the rope and kicked himself vigorously off the side. A loud cheer of farewell echoed over the waters. The vessel driving rapidly forward soon left Paul behind. He stood upright in the water and shouted cheerfully.

"All right captain, I'm all right."

His cheery call was echoed by the command "All right, go ahead."

A few moments after the lights of the Queen disappeared, and Paul was alone on the dark, rolling sea. From his position on the deck before going overboard, he could distinctly see the gleam of the Cape Clear light; but on the sea far below he could not find it. He knew the direction of the wind, that was then south west and guided his course accordingly. On every mighty swell that lifted him high up, he looked eagerly in the direction of the light and soon discovered it ahead. Perfectly content and without a fear of danger he kept paddling along occasionally cheering himself with a few snatches of a sea song as he drove his paddle strongly in the water and propelled himself toward the light which he observed more frequently when raised high up on the swells. The wind was steadily increasing and soon burst into terrible gusts. The long lazy roll of the sea changed and sharp, snapping waves continually broke over him. These grew larger and more powerful every moment. About two hours after he left the Queen the gale was on him in all its fierceness and the light was lost to his view. The heavy rain that accompanied the gale almost blinded him, and the seas grew so high that he abandoned paddling and sought only to keep his head against the overpowering waves that then drove down on him. An indescribable feeling of loneliness came over him. Once his paddle was wrenched from his hand by a heavy sea, but he fortunately recovered it. At times a great wave would completely submerge him. Then he would shoot to the crest where he would have time to breathe before he was again hurled down a sloping mass of water that seemed to him fully a hundred feet to the bottom. During this terrible ordeal, he has since confessed that he firmly believed that his last hour had come. He thought of all his transgressions. To use his own words:

"I recalled every mean trick I had ever committed against God and man in my reckless life and I did my utmost to remember the best and most effective prayer that I was taught when a boy."

For hours, that seemed weeks to him, he was driven along before the mighty seas. About three o'clock in the morning the water became more agitated and a booming sound struck Paul's ear. Coming to an upright position, he peered eagerly to leeward thinking he might be close to Cape Clear. He saw what seemed to him to be a dark mass of clouds banked up against the morning sky along which ran flashes of white. He quickly realized that he was nearing the cliffs and the flashes were the mighty waves that broke in fury against them. Knowing that to approach them would be certain death, he unlashed his paddle and made a frantic endeavor to back off through the enormous waves that were driving him slowly but surely to destruction. Notwithstanding his almost superhuman efforts he was carried in by an irresistible force closer and closer to the death dealing cliffs. At the same time he noticed by the changing head lands that the currents were driving him to the southward and hoping for an opening in the threatening wall of rock, he redoubled his efforts to gain more sea room. At times the enormous waves seemed to lift him almost to the surface of the cliffs, then again he sank far below while they seemed to raise like a cloud against the sky. Closer and closer he was driven in until their frightful roar almost deafened him. A streak of early daylight now showed through the black cloud of rock that was gradually approaching. He thought that this might be some cut in the cliffs and reversing his paddle propelled himself cautiously toward it. While hesitatingly examining the entrance a sea struck him. Another and another followed in quick succession and nearly in a senseless state, he was hurled into a little ravine. To save himself from the retreating wave he grasped a piece of rock. The next moment he was struck by another sea that sent him high up, and gaining his feet he rapidly reached a position in which he was safe from the surging breakers. He discovered that the cleft into which he was washed was the course of a fresh water creek which flowed into the sea. After resting himself for a short time on the rock, he examined his bag and found that it was all right. He then commenced to ascend the cliffs and on reaching their top the force of the gale almost blew him off his feet. He struck a signal light. This is a light made of chemicals which burns with intense brilliancy. Bracing himself against a rock he held it above his head. The flare lit up the surrounding cliffs. While it was still burning he turned to windward and looked down on the huge breakers that made the cliff on which he stood tremble as they dashed in against it. While gazing down on the mad water, he realized for the first time the terrible danger he had passed through in safety and recognized in his escape, the hand of the Great Pilot above. And as the flare died out and the beating gale struck him fun in the face, he sank to his knees and fervently thanked the good God who had so miraculously steered him to safety.

He had struck the light in the hope of attracting some coast guard's attention. He was not sure whether he was on the island of Cape Clear or on the mainland. Receiving no response, he started inland over the cliffs and found a well worn road. This he followed for some distance until he came to a place where it branched off, one road leading to the coast and one leading into the country. He chose the one running to the coast and soon afterwards entered the street of a village. No light was visible. The furious gale tore along the street carrying slates from off the roofs of the low houses. These crashed around him in an uncomfortable and dangerous manner. Rounding a bend to the village street he observed a light burning brightly in a window. To this he made his way hoping to find some one up. In answer to his repeated knockings a man appeared at the cautiously opened door. At this moment the force of the wind pushed Paul suddenly forward and carried the door and man bolding it heavily in. The affrighted expression of the man as he gazed on the strangely clad figure was ludicrous. While braced against the door he hesitated whether to close it or to let go and expel the intruder. Paul turned and helped him close the door against the fierce gusts of wind pouring in. The man recovered himself and inquired:

"Phere air ye frum?"

"New York," responded Paul.

"Phat air ye doin' here? How did ye come?"

Paul explained to him that he had left a ship that night when off Cape Clear.

"Phat did ye lave her fur?" questioned the perplexed life-guard for Paul had noted at once that he was in a life-saving station.

"Well, just to come ashore," said Paul.

"An' d'ye mane to say that ye came ashure in this gale?"

"I do."

"How many came ashure wid ye?"

"No one."

"Phere's ye're ship now?"

"God knows, I don't."

Question after question followed; but Paul was unable to convince the coast-guard that he had left the ship voluntarily and had landed in safety. The guard could not understand why any man should leave a vessel and come in on the coast of Ireland in such a gale unless he was shipwrecked. He thought Paul's brain had been injured by concussion with the rocks and a pitying expression came over his face as he said:

"Well, me poor fellow, 'ts no matther where ye're frum. It's me duty to help ye and yure mates an' if ye'll only tell me phere they air Oi'll collect the b'ys an' have thim out. Now tell me as calmly as ye can, how many is drohwned besides yureself?"

Paul saw his mistake and positively assured the guard that he was the only person to land, and that there had been no wreck and that the steamer had proceeded on her way to Queenstown. Notwithstanding all his protestations the coast guard could not realize the situation. The man before him was, however shipwrecked and in distress, so with the proverbial hospitality for which the Irish are famous, the guard said:

"Niver moind me lad how ye came ashure. Ye look tired enough. Come in here an' lay near the fire."

When Paul entered the warm room he removed his uncouth costume. He was thoroughly worn out buffeting the waves and with his long tramp down the road, so he gladly accepted the proferred bunk close to the fire and was soon in a sound sleep from which he was awakened by a kindly voice saying:

"Here me poor fellow, take this, 't will do ye good."

Before Paul could realize it he had poured a glass of whiskey down his throat, the strength of which raised every individual hair on his head. It was then about eight o'clock in the morning and the coast guard house was full of the villagers, men and women who curiously crowded around his bunk. They were a wild looking lot. Paul noticed the women particularly. They looked strong and rosy. They all wore long cloaks with a hood covering the head, and their feet were naked and as red as a pigeon's. From the expressions he overheard, he concluded that the coast-guard man had drawn on his imagination in explaining the stranger's appearance in the station.

"Did he railly swim from New York?" he heard time and again.

"Oh, thin he's not human if he could do that," and many other exclamations of like nature greeted the astonished Paul as he drowsily turned out of the bunk.

The coast-guard man now approached and driving the curious villagers out of the station, he invited him to breakfast in a little tavern across the way. The entire village was out. Crowds blocked their way as they crossed the street. While eating breakfast Paul learned that the most of the excitement was created by a report that he had swam all the way from New York. In conversation with the guard, he found out that the village was called Baltimore, a little coast town about thirty miles from where he had left the steamer; and also that there was no telegraph office nearer than Skibbereen, a distance of nine miles. There was but one conveyance in the village and as the driver was a very eccentric character, it was doubtful if he could be induced to go out on such a stormy morning. Paul requested that this man be sent for. Soon afterward he appeared pushing his way through the villagers. He was a strange looking man. The coast guard introduced him:

"Here is Andy," said he.

The latter acknowledged the introduction, by pulling his head forward with a lock of hair and exclaiming, as he eyed Paul curiously:

"Did ye railly swim from New Yark'"

Paul laughed, saying: "I hear you have a horse and I am anxious to get over to Skibbereen and send off a telegram. I would like to have you take me over there."

"It's no harse Oi have," he solemnly responded, "but Oi've wan av the finest mares in the south av Ireland an Oi'll drive ye over for six shillin'. But did ye railly swim from New Yark? Shure it's not natural."

Paul urged him to get his animal as quickly as possible and the driver rushed through the door only to be surrounded by a group of wild looking villagers, who questioned him both in Irish and English. Soon after Andy re-appeared coming down the village street driving a sorry looking nag. As he approached the tavern and saw Paul and the guard at the door, he shouted loudly to the crowd to separate, as though wishing to show Paul the blood in his favorite mare. He punched her with a little stick from which the sharp point of a nail protruded and by a dexterous movement dodged the flying hind feet that were aimed at his head.

"Phat de ye think o' that, sur? There's blood fur ye." A murmur of admiration stirred the crowd.

"But where is your cart? Hurry up and get her hitched," urged Paul.

Soon after Andy drove up to the door of the coast guard station with his jaunting car. The mare was hitched to the car with a curious combination of harness composed of twisted hay, rope, cords and leather. As nearly every one knows, a jaunting car is a two-wheeled affair. Over each wheel runs a seat, fore and aft, and in the centre is a little receptacle for small baggage, called the well. A car generally carries four passengers, two on each side. On such occasions, the driver sits on a little seat over the well, looking to the front, while the passengers' backs are turned toward each other. Having only one passenger, Andy decided to sit on the opposite side of the car to ballast her evenly. After Paul bid good-bye to the coast guard and thanked him for his hospitality, he placed his rubber suit on the forward part of the seat and sprung up behind. Andy seemed in no hurry to get under way. A multitude of knots in the harness required attention and he carefully scrutinized every part of the car while the villagers kept up a volley of comments such as: "Shure it's a quare customer ye have this mornin', Andy my b'y. The Lord betune ye an' harrum, Andy avick. Shure it's no human bein' ye're drivin' away wid." And many other remarks made in Irish, no doubt, of the same encouraging character.

"Come, come," exclaimed Paul impatiently, "let us get off?"

Andy reluctantly clambered on the opposite seat and commenced driving slowly up the village street, followed by a loud huzza. He seemed ill at ease and was loth to leave, driving so slowly that Paul had to urge him on. Reaching the last house on the straggling village street, he stopped the car and turning to Paul said: "Oi want to get a light fur my pipe, sur."

After a little time, during which Paul heard a vehement conversation going on inside, Andy re-appeared holding a coal of fire on the bowl of his clay pipe. He remounted again and slowly drove away followed by the shrill blessings and good wishes of the barefooted woman that stood at the door. Their way now lay along the cliff-road and squall after squall came bearing in from a roaring sea outside. At times Andy would reach across when the booming of the breakers could be heard coming up through ravine on the cliffs and say:

"Shure no human bein' could live in that sea, sur. Did ye come on top of the wather er under?"

"Oh, drive on, drive on," was the impatient response, "never mind."

Seeing one more than usually severe squall coming down on them from the sea, Paul, who was facing windward, thought he would be more comfortable if he would slip the rubber tunic over his head and shoulders. This he did without attracting the attention of Andy and he leaned forward pointing the comical shaped head-piece to the rapidly advancing squall. The head-piece not being inflated, the aperture for the face hung down like a great mouth. The car suddenly gypped and Paul felt his side sink a little. Turning around find the cause and pulling the head-piece from over his eyes, he saw the affrighted Andy about twelve yards away in a ditch. His eyes filled with terror, seemed to protrude from his head while he rapidly made the sign of the cross over his face and breast.

"What's the matter? What are you doing there?" thundered Paul. "Come on, get up, get up. What's the matter with you?"

"Och, shure, it's well Oi knew that it was no christian Oi had wid me this mornin'."

"Come on now, or I'll drive on without you," angrily exclaimed Paul, "don't you see that this is only a rubber dress that I put on to protect me from the rain."

After considerable persuasion, Andy was induced to remount and they continued through the heavy rain in silence. Soon after Paul asked:

"Andy, how far is it yet to Skibbereen?"

"About fure miles, ye're honor, and Oi wish it was only fure feet," In, added in an audible undertone.

Shortly after the houses on the outskirts of Skibbereen began to appear and Andy brightened up wonderfully and became quite communicative. He informed Paul that a friend of his had a hotel there and that it was a good one and that he would drive straight to it.

"Con Sullivan kapes the foinest hotel that mon er beast iver shtoped at," he concluded.

There were few on the streets as they drove up to the hotel. Paul dismounted and taking his suit into the hotel, asked for a private room. He then inquired of the landlord where the telegraph office was and started for it. He wrote a telegram, one to the captain of the Queen and one to the English office of the "New York Herald," Fleet Street, London. The lady operator scanned over the dispatch to London, then closely scrutinized Paul. Seeing her hesitation about accepting the telegram, Paul demanded to know what was the cause of it. "Excuse me, sir," said she, "but we have to be very careful about the nature of the telegrams we send out from here. I must first call the superintendent, before I can accept this."

When that individual appeared he looked it over and asked Paul if the contents were all true and correct.

"They assuredly are," impatiently exclaimed Paul, "I want you to get it off as quickly as you can," and he followed this up by several remarks not over complimentary to their methods of doing business.

Paul then returned to the hotel where he found Andy surrounded by a crowd to whom he was relating his adventures and giving a history of his eccentric passenger in his own way. When they saw Paul he was an object of the wildest curiosity. The crowd poured into the hotel after him and invaded the dining room, so he had to remonstrate with the landlord who unceremoniously shouldered-them out. The news of Paul's arrival on the coast seemed to have spread with the rapidity of a prairie fire all over Skibbereen, and people commenced gathering from all parts of the town around the hotel. One of the gentlemen who insisted on coming in was the superintendent of the telegraph, Mr. Jolly. He apologized for his seeming discourtesy at the office and assured Paul that the dispatch he had written seemed so improbable that he could not in justice blame them for not receiving it. He proved to be a very friendly, sociable gentleman and gave

Paul all the assistance and information he desired. He informed him that he would have to leave Skibbereen by stage which would depart in a couple of hours. This stage would convey him to the first railway station, some ten or twelve miles away where he could get a train in the afternoon for Cork. He urgently requested him to remain over for a few days and enjoy the hospitality of Skibbereen. Paul, being anxious to reach Cork, declined. He requested the landlord to send Andy in to settle up. As the hero was ushered in, it was easy to observe that the people had been filling him as well as pumping him.

"Here are your six shillings, I believe that is what you asked me."

"That's roight, sur," said Andy as he reached his hand, "that's fur meself, but how about me mare?"

"What have I got to do with your mare?"

"Shure, sur, ye don't want the poor baste to starve to death."

"Certainly not, she is yours and you ought to feed her."

"But, sur, Oi niver had a traveller yet as didn't pay fur the mare's eatin' an' drinkin' as well as moine."

Paul was amused at this new rule, but was informed by Mr. Jolly that such was the custom in that part of Ireland.

"Well, Andy," said he, "how much do you think it will take to keep your mare from starving until you get back to Baltimore? Here's your two shillings more."

Andy accepted the two shillings with evident satisfaction on behalf of the mare.

"That's the eight shillin' ye gave me fur the mare an' meself, an' Oi think yure honor ought to give me two more in consequince av the fright ye gave me. Shure it'll be a long day befure Oi git over it! Whin Oi turned an' saw that ingia rubber thing over ye Oi thought it was the very divil himself."

Paul laughed and handed him over the other two shillings, with: "Now, that's all you get."

"Well, good luck an' may the—" here his flow of blessings were cut off by Mr. Jolly who threw him out of the room.

When the stage coach drove up to the door almost the entire population of Skibbereen was out. Lusty cheers were given for Paul as he mounted the outside of the coach, in answer to which he fastened the American flag to his paddle and waved it to the cheering populace as he drove out of town. On reaching Dunmanway, Paul entered the train and started for Cork.

CHAPTER VIII.

Soon after Paul left the Queen, the gale that almost cost him his life, broke down on that gallant vessel. The captain put her nose in it and headed her off for sea. All night she ploughed against it while the huge seas burst over her and whitened her smoke stacks with salt to the very top. Not a soul on board believed that Paul would last in the gale half an hour after she broke out, and the captain blamed himself keenly for letting him go. The steamer did not succeed is reaching Queenstown harbor until noon next day. When the lighter came along side for the mails a man passed a telegram up to the captain. He feverishly tore it open and found with great relief that it was from Paul.

"Thank God that he is safe," he exclaimed, and he then read it aloud to the passengers.

Cheer after cheer went up as the news was spread along the decks. Having discharged her mail and passengers for Ireland, the Queen resumed her way to Liverpool, while the lighter steamed into Queenstown. Evidences of the ravages of the storm were visible on all sides. Dismantled ships, unroofed houses and vessels ashore told the story of its force in that vicinity. It was afterwards ascertained that fifty-six vessels were lost in the same storm on the southern coast of Great Britain that night. When the lighter reached Queenstown, the passengers were full of excitement in regard to Paul's wonderful feat and they spread the story broadcast both in Queenstown and Cork. To their disgust, they found that the people disbelieved them and laughed at them saying:

"This is a fine Yankee yarn you are springing on us now."

To convince the skeptical people of Cork, a party of them telegraphed all over the coast to see if they could not find Paul, to verify their story and from Skibbereen they learned that a man answering that description had passed through there and was now on his way to Cork.

When Paul arrived at the station he found himself surrounded by many of his late fellow passengers, who enthusiastically received him and escorted him to the hotel. The news of his remarkable adventure spread over Cork as rapidly as it had over Skibbereen, so that the hotel was thronged with eager people, the newspaper fraternity being well represented. It was late that night before he got through with his persistent interviewers and before he woke next morning, the story of his extraordinary adventure and daring was all over America. The Cork papers contained columns, describing his struggle with the ocean. Before he could dress himself, cards came showering into his room and when he went down he found the hotel packed with people eager to see him. For a few days Paul enjoyed the extravagantly warm hospitality of Cork. He was taken everywhere worth visiting, entertained with dinners, parties and receptions until his head swam with the whirl of attentions that he was so unaccustomed to. During his stay in the hotel a large party of huntsmen who came to Cork to participate in a grand hunt nearby, had a banquet to which he was invited. Paul was made the hero of the evening and so many were the toasts drank in his honor that he looked anxiously for a chance to escape the profuse but reckless hospitality. When an opportunity presented itself he slipped out and took a long walk in the night air. As he returned to the hotel and was about to ascend to his room, he could hear his late companions in one of their hunting songs enjoying themselves. Observing a stalwart porter connected with the hotel, laboriously bearing one of his late red-coated entertainers on his back as he mounted the stairs, Paul, thinking some accident had occurred ran to the porter and asked: "Why, what is the matter with the gentleman? Is he killed? Has there been a fight?"

"Oh, no sur, it's wan of the gintlemen, he's only a little overcome. Oi put them all to bed this way, yure honor, and moight ave had the pleasure av puttin' yureself to bed if ye had remained."

With sailor-like recklessness, Boyton never thought of how all this would end and he spent what money he had freely. One morning before rising from his bed, he began thinking the situation over. As he examined it closely and counted what money he had left, the outlook took on a most gloomy hue. He was confident that he did not have coin enough to pay half his hotel bill alone, not to think of getting home. After studying the matter over for some time he came to the conclusion that the only course he could pursue was frankly to confess to the landlord how he was situated and offer to leave his rubber suit until he could return home and send for it. Then he would go to Queenstown and see if he could not procure a position on some vessel bound for America. Just as he came to this conclusion he was interrupted by a knock at the door.

"Ten to one it's the landlord with my bill," thought Paul.

When he opened the door he was confronted by an energetic, little man who talked with great rapidity.

"Captain Paul Boyton, I believe, sir. Here is my card, I thought I would bring it up myself to save time. I have a great scheme for you. Go on, proceed with your dressing and I will talk about it. I am the manager of the Opera Company now playing at Munster Hall and I have a scheme by which you and I will make a considerable amount of money. I presume you are not averse to making money?" looking inquiringly at Paul.

"Well, no," responded Paul. "It's very useful at times."

"Well, sir, I have a great scheme. A great scheme, indeed."

"What is it?"

"You know all Cork is wild to see you, and my idea is that you shall give a little lecture. We can fill Munster Hall from pit to dome."

Paul looked at the man curiously for a few moments and made up his mind that he was crazy.

"Why, my dear sir, I am not a lecturer. I could not lecture. I never even made a speech in my life."

"That's nothing, that's nothing," responded the nervous and energetic little manager, "So much the better. I will do the lecturing for you. All you will have to do will be to stand there and exhibit your dress."

"Well, under those circumstances," responded Paul, who still considered the manager a little off, and seeing a probable means of paying his hotel bill, "What terms will you give me if I consent?"

"One half the house and I will do the advertising."

"And the lecturing too, remember," said Paul.

"Yes, yes, that's all right, we'll sign the contract immediately."

"But hold on," said Paul, "there is another question I want to ask you. How much do you suppose my share will be?"

"Between thirty and forty pounds. I am almost certain."

"Are you positive it will be twenty-five pounds?"

"Absolutely positive, confident my dear fellow."

"Then," said Paul "I will sign this contract on condition that you will pay me five pounds in advance."

Paul thought this stroke of policy would end the interview and rid him of his visitor. To his intense surprise, the five pound note was laid on the table without any hesitation. It was quickly transferred to Paul's pocket.

"Now make out your contract and we will sign it."

"Have done so, have done so; did it last night when I thought of the scheme. Have it all made out. Sign here."

Paul carelessly glanced over the contract an affixed his signature; after which the manager shook him warmly by the hand and congratulated him on having entered on such a brilliant enterprise, and said "I will now go and attend to the printing We will dine together," he added as he disappeared through the door.

"And remember you do the lecturing," Paul called after him as he rushed down stairs.

When he left, Paul locked the door, drew out the five pound note which he carefully examined to convince himself that it was genuine. He then in his great joy took two or three handsprings and made such a noise that the chambermaid rapped on his door and desired to know if the gentleman was knocking for anything. During the day, the manager visited Paul frequently and gave him encouragement. By evening the report of the intended lecture had circulated pretty well and Paul was frequently stopped on the street by acquaintances who assured him of their pleasure at having a chance to hear him speak. Paul took pains to tell all who questioned him in regard to it that it was not he but Mr. Murphy who was going to give the lecture. Next day Cork was covered with great bills announcing the lecture for the following evening and a feeling of nervousness overcame Paul as he beheld his name in such enormous letters. This nervous feeling was in no way allayed when he perused one of the bills and found that the enterprising manager, had not only promised that he would give a description of his landing on the Irish coast but that he would relate many thrilling adventures he had passed through in the American, French and Mexican wars; would describe time methods of life-saving in America, and compare it with the British method of life-saving service, and many other things that Paul did not dare to read, as he had sufficient. He sought out the plausible Mr. Murphy and vehemently went for him for deceiving the public.

"Never mind, my boy, never mind, the people all understand how it is. You will have nothing to do except to make a few remarks."

But Paul was not satisfied. He tried to commit to memory the few remarks he supposed he would have to make when he was introduced; but he would no sooner get them in ship shape than they would disappear again. The night of the, to him, terrible ordeal arrived. Manager Murphy took him to the Hall in a carriage. Great crowds surrounded the building and the manager assured him that it was already full inside. The arrangements were that Paul was to appear between the acts of the opera, which that night was "Madame Angot." Murphy took Paul to his own private office in the second story and encouraged him in every way he could. Paul listened to the music of the first act, as it rolled by with fearful swiftness. Never before in his life did he experience the feeling of nervousness which now seemed to possess him. Once during Murphy's absence from the office he raised the window and looked down into the river Lee that ran alongside the building and wondered if he could drop into the water without breaking his leg. All that deterred him was the thought of the five pounds that had been advanced. The fated moment arrived; the manager said:

"Your suit and paddle and appliances are out on a table on the stage. The curtain is down and the moment it rises you walk boldly out to the side of the table and I will follow you. Don't be afraid, the audience is most kindly disposed toward you and will give you a warm welcome."

Up went the curtain, Murphy's hand was laid on Paul's shoulder as he said:

"Now, my boy, step right out."

Paul braced himself and with his heart as near his mouth as he ever had it before during his existence, walked over to the table on which lay his suit, paddle, etc., etc.

The deafening roar of applause that greeted him set him more at his ease. He looked around for Mr. Murphy, but failed to see that worthy gentleman. So making a few steps towards the foot-lights he thanked the audience, in a trembling voice, for their kindness. He told them that he was no speaker and that Mr. Murphy had promised to do the lecturing part of the business. At this moment cries broke out all over the house:

"Brace up, Captain, never mind Murphy, its yourself we want to hear," and many other similar good-natured remarks.

This encouragement had the effect of steadying Paul's nerves and he calmly proceeded to give a vivid account of the terrible adventure he had passed through a few days before. He grew more confident as he proceeded and the frequent outbursts of applause gave him ample time to collect his thoughts and express himself with ease. His mind flew to what he had read on the bill and he traveled over the ground in a very thorough manner. When he concluded and bowed his thanks, the applause was as warm and loud as any ever heard in the Hall.

When he reached the wings he was embraced by the enthusiastic Murphy, who was vehement in his congratulations and easily smoothed Paul's feelings against him. To his intense surprise, Paul found that he had been speaking over one hour and he could not persuade his acquaintances but that he was an old hand at the business. Next morning Paul read his speech in the papers and it caused him as much surprise as it did Manager Murphy when he read it. His portion of the proceeds amounted to thirty-two pounds. When manager Murphy paid him over the balance after deducting the advanced five pounds, he felt more like a gentleman traveling in Europe for his health. On the same day he received three telegrams from Dublin all offering engagements to lecture; also an offer from the Cork Steamship Company to appear in Queenstown harbor in his suit where they would run excursions. The Dublin offers he left in the hands of Manager Murphy while he accepted the offer of the Steamboat Company. A couple of days after he appeared in Queenstown harbor and every steamer in Cork was loaded on that occasion. From this appearance he realized a little over ten pounds. In the meantime the story of his remarkable adventure on the Irish coast had been commented on by the English press and so many doubts cast on it, that prominent English papers sent their correspondents to Cork to investigate the matter thoroughly. These gentlemen questioned Paul closely and got his whole story. Then they went to Baltimore and got the testimony of the coast-guard. They thoroughly examined the coast and under the guidance of the coast-guard discovered the exact place be made his miraculous landing.

They learned that the place he came ashore was the only available landing for miles, the coast being formed by precipitous rocks and that if he had drifted one mile to the southward lie would have been cut to atoms on the sharp and dangerous reef known as the "Whale Rocks." Thoroughly satisfied with their investigation they returned to London and confirmed the story in every particular.

Paul next went to Dublin where he had a week's engagement to lecture in the Queen's Theatre. His reception was if possible more enthusiastic than in Cork. He cut his lecture out of one of the newspapers and studied it, so on that point he felt more easy. He appeared every night at the theatre, which was filled to its utmost capacity. At the conclusion of his lecture, he would bow his acknowledgements to the audience and retire behind the curtain, where a tableau was arranged.

It represented the scene of his landing, and he standing with uplifted paddle on which was tacked the American flag. A supe threw a bucket of water over him, previous to his mounting the imitation cliffs, the curtain would roll up and behold the hero as he just emerged from the sea in his glistening rubber suit. The applause was tremendous. The last night, every one being paid off and feeling good, Paul stepped behind the curtains in his suit to receive his customary ducking. The bucket of water was missing. The stage hand who was very mellow exclaimed:

"I had it here a moment ago but I can't find it now. Ah, here it is," and he drew a pail from under a table and deluged Paul. Up went the curtain, the audience screamed, Paul looked down on his armor in dismay, instead of water he was covered with white calsomine, when a voice from the gallery roared:

"That's the first rale white-washed Yankee I've ever seen."

A white washed Yankee is an Irishman who has spent about two years in America and returning to his own country apes the accent and eccentricity of the down east Yankee.

Before leaving Dublin, Paul gave an exhibition in the lake in the Zoological Garden, Phenix Park and so intense was the desire to see him in the water that the sum of seventy pounds was received from admissions. He also made a run down the Liffy through the heart of the city, during which time it is estimated that over a hundred thousand people turned out to see him.

On November 9th Paul made a swim from Howth Head to the historic Island of Dalkey, a distance of about ten miles. The following day he was presented with an illumined address signed by many of the most prominent people in Dublin, also with an elaborately worked American flag and gold medal. The address concluded with the following words: "The subscribers desire that Captain Boyton will regard this presentation as a reminiscence of his visit to Ireland and as a token of the high estimation in which they hold him as a fearless experimentalist in bringing under public notice the most valuable life saving apparatus that has yet appeared."

Paul made many good friends during his stay in Dublin and visited almost every point of interest in that historic city. He discovered a very original character in the car-driver who conveyed him to the theatre every evening. Whenever he had a leisure hour always spent it driving around he quaint old city with the driver, Pat Mullen, who entertains him with his stories and witicisms. While driving along the, Liffy one day Pat said:

"Would ye loike a little devarsion, Captain? If ye do, Oi'll take ye through Pill Lane; but ye must look out fur yure head, sur."

Pill Lane he described as a street mostly inhabited by fish-women who displayed their stock in trade on a tray on the head of a barrel, These ladies, like their sisters in Billingsgate, London, bad a great reputation for their vigorous use of the English language and the choice epithets that they often hurled at the heads of passers by who did not purchase from them. Pat explained that his method was to drive down the Lane at a good gait and by picking out two or three of the star performers he would arouse them by a method peculiarly his own. That consisted in driving quite close to these barrels and so near some of them that the step projecting from the side of the jaunting car would send the barrel and fish flying all over the sidewalk. Of coarse this was presumably quite accidental.

Paul consented to try the experiment, being assured that there was no danger in it. As they drove into the head of the Lane, he soon discovered that Pat was well known in that locally. The cries of:

"There's the the dirtily blaguard agin. Look out there, Mrs. Murphy, etc."

All these salutations were received by the imperturbable Pat with smiles and bows and a cheery remark, as he dodged a dead fish or some other missile aimed at his head. When little farther down the Lane, Pat said: "Look out now, Captain, do ye see the fat woman down there? She's a beauty an' Oi'n goin' to shtir her up. Ye'll hear a flow av iloquence such as ye niver heard in yure loife, sur. Oi'm sorry she's on yure side as the car, sur. Droivin' up, sur, ye wud not be so liable to get hit."

At this moment, by a dexterous twist of the horse's head, the iron step struck the barrel and scattered the contents, while Pat leaned across and said:

"Ye'll excuse me, Mrs. Olahan, that was an accident."

"Oh it's ye," exclaimed the lady addressed, as she hurled the cup that she was drinking tea out of at Pat. Then a torrent of language burst forth which could be heard far down the Lane as they drove quickly through; but not fast enough to escape the fusillade of decayed fish and every other missile, even to the head of a barrel, which could be hurled by Mrs. Olahan and her sympathizing friends. When they emerged from the Lane, Pat turned around and said:

"Air ye bruised, Captain?"

"No," said Paul, "but I don't want any more of that kind of diversion."

A long time afterwards, while in London, Paul read of a Dublin driver who was taking a party of women home one night and either through accident or design drove them all into the middle of the canal. Their loud outcries attracted people to the rescue and when they arrived on the scene, they found the driver seated high up on the seat trying to control the mad struggles of his steed, while he calmly requested the rescuers to "niver moind the women but to save the harse."

At the time Paul thought this must certainly be his old friend, Pat Mullen, and afterwards ascertained that he was correct in his surmise.

When his engagements in Dublin terminated, Paul went to London, where he found that interest in his exploit on the Irish coast was still manifested. He then began a series of experiments down the Thames and in the waters in the vicinity of London. The London papers were teeming with accounts of him and his adventures. About this time he formed the resolution to cross the channel from England to France and was busying himself in preparations. One morning he was surprised to receive an order from Osborne to appear before the Queen. Paul's friends assured him that this was a great honor and one which would be of much advantage to him in England.

The order was for him to appear before Her Majesty on the river Modena, East Cowes, Isle of Wight. He left London, having made his preparations Saturday morning and went to Portsmouth, where he was entertained by the Mayor, American Consul and members of the Yacht Club. The same night he crossed over to Modena on the Isle of Wight, where he took rooms in the hotel. Sunday morning he went aboard the royal yacht Alberta, and introduced himself to the captain, whom he found to be a jolly old sea dog. From a letter written home by Paul about this date, the following extract is taken: The yacht I boarded seemed as big as a man-of-war. A Marine stopped me on the gang plank with the question: 'Whom do you wish to see?'

'Why the captain of course.'

The sentry called to a petty officer, who escorted me to the captain. He conducted me to a gorgeously furnished cabin. When I introduced myself, the weather beaten tar grasped me warmly by the hand. He invited me to be seated and accept some refreshments. While discussing them, we also talked over my exhibition before the Queen the next day. I was anxious to acquit myself in the presence of royalty in a creditable manner, so I plied the captain with questions to obtain all the information possible. He told me that to please the Queen anything I did had to be done quickly. In answer to my question, how will I hail her, he said: 'In addressing Her Majesty, you must say first, Your Majesty. After that you can continue the conversation with the word madame.'

Well that won't be very difficult thought I, and I can get through with it all right. Before leaving the Captain, I requested him to send down a few men in the morning to help me get traps aboard. Returning to my hotel I spent most of the afternoon writing. I was interrupted by a waiter, who informed me that General Ponsonby, Private Secretary to the Queen, and two ladies desired to see me. I ordered them shown right in. The General, a fine, dignified old gentleman came in followed by two very handsome ladies. He introduced himself and the ladies saying: 'Captain, this is the Hon. Lady Churchill and this is the Hon. Lady Plunkett. The ladies curiosity was so great to see you that we came down from the Castle to have a little talk.'

I invited them to sit down and consider themselves at home. The General then put a number of questions in regard to my former life and Irish coast adventure. In a brief manner I gave them a story in the best way I could. It seemed to entertain them considerably as the ladies often laughed heartily. As they were about to leave the thought occurred to me, 'these are my guests, I ought to offer some hospitality. So backing up to the fire-place I took hold of the bellrope saying; 'General and ladies I hope you will mention what you will take.'

At this both the ladies laughed merrily and the General said: 'No, Captain, thank you. The ladies and myself have already been entertained handsomely.'

By the twinkle in the ladies' eyes I think they would have accepted my invitation and taken a drink if it had not been for the austere presence of the General. During the conversation I confided to them my trepidation about meeting the Queen, but they assured me that Her Majesty was a very kind lady and that I need have no fear, whatever, of any breach of court etiquette. After a warm handshaking, they bade me good-bye and said they would see me on the morrow.

After their departure I resumed my writing when I was again interrupted by the re-appearance of the General, who explained to me in behalf of the ladies that much as they would have liked to accept my hospitality, I must not feel hurt by their refusal. They were ladies of Honor to Her Majesty and it would be a terrible scandal if they accepted any hospitality in the hotel. 'But that won't prevent you and I, Captain, from drinking the ladies' good health.'

The General and I passed some time together and he gave me many useful hints. The next morning about twenty able-bodied British tars presented themselves at the hotel to transfer my effects on board the royal yacht. By their united efforts they succeeded in getting it aboard; but I could much more easily have carried the whole outfit myself. When on board I descended to the Captain's cabin where I donned my suit and got the appliances in the rubber bag. All this time carriages were rapidly driving up to the side of the yacht, which was moored at the dock; depositing their loads of courtiers, who came aboard and promenaded up and down the decks. I was standing forward with the Captain at the time and he told me the names of several noted personages and high officers who were pouring up the gang plank. One venerable looking man attracted my attention. I said:

'Holy blue, Captain, look at that man coming aboard now without any pants on.'

'That gentleman,' said the Captain, 'is John Brown, Her Majesty's most faithful servant and that is the National Scottish costume he wears.'

As I was gazing on John Brown with considerable curiosity, the Captain said:

'Stand by now. Her majesty is coming. When I tell you, you walk aft, bow to her and get over the side and do your work.'

The crowd on board obstructed my view so that I could not see the Queen come aboard. In a moment the Captain returned from the gang-way where he had been to receive her, and said:

'Walk right aft. Her Majesty is waiting for you.'

I might as well confess to you that my idea of a Queen had been formed by seeing the play of Hamlet, where the Queen of Denmark comes on the stage with long white fur robe, covered with pieces of cat's tails and a crown on her head. I certainly did not think that the Queen of England would dress in this exact way, but I thought she would have something to distinguish her from the coterie of ladies that surrounded her on deck. So I walked aft, paddle in one hand, rubber bag in the other and dressed in my suit. I came to a group of ladies, a little separate, around whom bare headed courtiers stood and was about to pay homage to a fine, grandly dressed maid of honor, when turning around I observed the face of the Queen which was made familiar by the thousands of photographs, which grace the windows in nearly every store in London. She is a stout, motherly woman, more plainly dressed than any one around her. I looked at her for a second and said:

'Your Majesty, I believe.'

With a kindly smile she answered, 'Yes.'

'Will I take the water, Your Majesty?'

I was confused by the mistake I came near making, in taking the maid of honor for the Queen.

'If you please,' she responded with the same kindly and encouraging smile.

It didn't take me long to get over the side of that vessel, you can rest assured. Remembering the Captain's injunction not to keep her waiting long, I drove through all the exhibition I could give and as I clambered aboard again the perspiration stood all over my forehead. On gaining the deck, I bowed to the Queen again and was about to go forward. The Queen stopped me and said:

'Captain Boyton, I am both delighted and astonished at your wonderful work in the water; I believe that dress will be the means of saving numbers of valuable lives.'

She asked me how old I was and many other questions. A handsome young lady who stood at her side said:

'Don't you feel very much fatigued after such an exertion and are not your clothes wet under your dress?'

'Oh, no, Miss, not the least.'

At this answer of mine a laugh went up from the royal group and I suspected that I had made some mistake. I added. 'To prove to your Majesty that I am perfectly dry underneath the suit, I am, with your permission going to take it off. You need not be afraid, I am perfectly dressed underneath.'

Seeing that she did not object, I quickly unbuckled the tunic and hauled it over my head cast it on the deck and kicking off my rubber pants, I stood in my stocking feet before them. The Queen examined the mechanism of the dress with much interest and said:

'I would like to have a suit made for the use of this yacht, and I wish you a safe journey across the channel.'

Seeing that the interview was about closed I said:

'Now, Your Majesty, I hope you will excuse any error I have made, for you see that you could not naturally expect me to be posted in court etiquette.'

The Queen laughed heartily in which she was joined by the surrounding crowd and said:

'You did very well, Captain.'

When she left I again joined Captain Welch, of the Yacht, who told me that Her Majesty was well pleased. 'You may be sure of a handsome present.'

I then asked him what was the cause of all the laughter. He said:

'Why that was the only mistake you made. You should have addressed Princess Beatrice as Your Royal Highness; but that is all right.'

Soon after, Paul received an elegant chronometer gold watch with motto and heavy chain by General Ponsonby from the Queen and with the request that he would send her his photograph.

CHAPTER IX.

Paul now commenced plans for his channel trip. He visited Boulogne, Calais, Folkestone and Dover and decided on taking a course from Folkestone to Boulogne. M. L'Onguety, the President of the Boulogne Humane Society, offered to give him the best French pilot on the channel and his lugger to steer him across. The steamer Rambler was also engaged to accommodate the press representatives and invited guests. The most intense interest prevailed not only in Europe, but in America. Letters and telegrams came pouring in on Paul to reserve space for the special correspondents of the most noted newspapers in the world. Mr. McGarahan, the brilliant and lamented correspondent of the New York Herald, who was one of the party on the Rambler, wrote the following account of this memorable trip.

"The start was to be made at 3 o'clock on the morning of April 10th, 1875, from Dover, that hour being set on account of the tide favoring. In order to be up in time, the newspaper correspondents and friends who were to accompany the intrepid voyager on the tug, did not go to bed at all, the hours intervening being spent in the parlors of the Lord Werden hotel. The morning was cold and raw and when the sound of a bugle apprised the crowd that the time for starting had arrived, there was a hustling for warm wraps. At the quay from which the start was to be made, a great number of people had gathered regardless of the unseasonable hour and the chill air. There was a most horrible din and confusion, caused by the shouting and rush of the people, the whiz of rockets, the puffing of steamboats and the hoarse sound of speaking trumpets, all amid the glare of Bengal lights and burning pitch. The firing of the tug's gun announced the start. A black figure, like a huge porpoise, could be seen in the cold, grey water and then disappear in the darkness. Those on the tug thought they would lose him; but at length his horn was heard far out on the water and the tug immediately headed in that direction in order to take the lead and show him the way. Pursuing slowly forward he was kept within hail, as the lights of Dover gradually grew dim in the distance and the lighthouse on the Goodwin Sands shone clear and bright like the star of morning."

"The pilot was one sent over from Boulogne by the French Societe Humaine, said to be the best on the French coast. The course agreed upon was as follows: Take the tide running northeast from Dover at three in the morning, which would carry them seven or eight miles in that direction somewhere off Goodwin Sands. Here the tide turns about six 'clock and runs southeast down the channel. They would follow this tide to a point considerably below Boulogne, where the current sweeps again to the east and flows into Boulogne harbor, which they hoped to reach about three in the afternoon, making a distance of sixty miles."

"At five o'clock in the morning, when daylight came, everything was going well and the exact course indicated by the pilot had been followed, except that the start been about twenty minutes late. Boyton now paddled alongside and called for his sail, which he adjusted to his foot by means of an iron socket without getting out of the water, lit a cigar and struck out again. The little sail instantly filled and commenced pulling him along in fine style, making a very appreciable difference in his rate of speed. At six o'clock they were off Goodwin Sands, a little short of the point that it had been planned to reach. The tide now commenced turning and they were soon running down the channel under a very favorable breeze; but a nasty sea and thickening weather. Nearly in the middle of the channel, there is a sand bank called the Ridge or, by the French, the Colbart, which splits the current in two, throwing one along the French coast and the other along the English. It was, of course, the intention of Boyton and the pilot to get into the French current; but either because the swimmer did not get far enough to the east, with the tide running out or what seems more probable, because the pilot, owing to the thick weather, which hid both the French and English coast, missed his reckoning, they were swept down the English side of the Ridge and all chance of reaching the French coast before night was lost. Paul resolutely attacked this ridge, hoping to get over it and reach the French current in time. It proved to be a terrible struggle. The sea here was foaming and tumbling about in a fearful way for the voyager. It was not a regular roll or swell, but short, quick, chopping waves, tumbling about in all directions, that whirled him round and round, rolled him over and over, rendered his puny sail utterly useless and blinded him with foam and spray. It was a strangely fascinating spectacle to watch him in his hand to hand struggle with the ocean. The waves seemed to become living things animated by a terrible hatred for the strange being battling with them. Sometimes they seemed to withdraw for a moment, as if by concert and then rush down on him from all sides, roaring like wild beasts. For two hours the struggle continued, during which time he did not make more than a mile; but at last he came off victorious and reached the current running along the French coast, where the sea, although nasty, was not so unfavorable. But it was now one o'clock and instead of being several miles south of Boulogne, as he had hoped, he was almost opposite and the current had already turned again to the north, thus carrying him far past the place. He determined, however, to push on and endeavor to land at Cape Grisnez, about ten miles north of Boulogne. He did not seem tired although he had eaten scarcely anything since taking to the water. The weather grew rainy, foggy, cold and miserable. Boyton worked steadily forward; but the pilot began to grow anxious. It was evident that he would not make the French coast before dark, and he expressed his determination to push on all night if necessary. The wind and sea were both rising, promising a bad night. It would be impossible to follow him in the darkness and fog. He would inevitably be lost and if he should miss Cape Grisnez, he would be carried up into the North Sea. At length, towards six o'clock, the pilot declared that he would not be responsible for the safety of the ship, so near the coast in the darkness and fog. The Captain was, of course, unwilling to risk his ship, and it was decided that the attempt would have to be given up. Paul and his brother, who was on the tug, both protested against this resolution in the most energetic manner. The former maintained his ability to finish his undertaking, declaring that he was not in the least fatigued, and to prove it swam rapidly around the ship. It was agreed that he had thoroughly demonstrated his ability to cross the channel and that it would be folly to risk the ship, the life of everybody on board, as well as himself by cruising along the coast all night in the fog and darkness. He at last agreed to go aboard and give it up maintaining, however, his ability to stay in the water all night. It was just half past six o'clock when he set foot on the deck of the tug, after having been a little more than fifteen hours in the water."

Paul felt keenly the disappointment at the failure of his first attempt to cross the channel, notwithstanding the telegrams of congratulation from the Queen, Prince of Wales and many high personages on both sides of the Atlantic. He firmly resolved to attempt it again. He was young then, only twenty-seven years of age and did not know what fatigue or fear was. When he returned to London, he received many offers to exhibit himself in his dress. He at last closed with a well known Manager for the sum of fifty guineas per day, about $250. At this time he did little more than paddle around in the water, fire off a few rockets and his exhibition would not last more than, perhaps half an hour. He has often laughed heartily since, to think of the miserable apologies for a exhibition that he then gave, when compared with the magnificent show that himself and company of water experts give at the present day. Notwithstanding his lack of knowledge of the show business, he always succeeded in pleasing the public, who gathered in enormous crowds wherever he was announced. His managers reaped a rich harvest through his work. Their share for three days' exhibition in Birmingham alone, amounted to over six hundred pounds, $3000.

Invitations showered in on him from every quarter for dinners, banquets, receptions and society gatherings of every description. Hundreds of these he was compelled to decline, on account of press of business. Notwithstanding all this flattering attention and flood of prosperity, he never lost his head or changed in either action or speech. He looked upon it as a matter of course and felt just the same as he did when diving with Captain Balbo, or bush-whacking under Colonel Sawyer. Towards the end of May he had his arrangements completed for his second attempt to cross the channel. This time he determined to reverse the course. Instead of starting from England, he decided to leave from Cape Grisnez, France, and land on any part of the English coast he could. A couple of days before the attempt, he went to Boulogne. It was arranged that he should leave at three o'clock in the morning, when the steamer containing the English correspondents would arrive.

John Laty, a well known London newspaper man wrote the following account of his second attempt:

"As we draw near Cape Grisnez light, aboard the Earnest, Capt. Edward Dane, preparations are made by Mr. M. Boyton for proceeding ashore to assist in his brother's departure. A boat is lowered from the davits. It is soon manned, your artist slipping down the rope with the agility of a sailor. He is the last straw. The boat is pulled off. The Earnest steams slowly on, for three o'clock is close at hand and that is the hour fixed for Captain Boyton's start from the Cran aux Anguilles, El Chine, about two hundred yards to the east of the Grisnez light.

"Three A.M.—A rocket rushes up from the boat sent ashore. It is the signal of Captain Boyton's departure. It is answered by a display of fire-works from the Earnest. A gun is fired and Grisnez light flickers and goes out. Day is breaking; but Captain Boyton is not discernable yet. Over the gray waters one sees through a good glass, the white fringe of surf breaking on the sandy beach, which is lined by a black mass of people behind whom is burning a large bonfire. A speck is at length made out to the right of the boat, 'three points off,' as the white haired old salt on board remarks. The sky gets lighter, the sea deep blue. We can now plainly see the dauntless Captain paddling actively away toward us, riding buoyantly over the swelling waves, and making good progress in his gray suit of india-rubber. His brother comes on board soon, with the news that the boat can not venture through the surf that foams up the beach. The stout little craft now receives a compass which is placed in the stern, where the mate takes his place to act as pilot. Off the boat puts once more, to act thence forth as Captain Boyton's guide.

"Four A.M.—We give the Captain a ringing cheer as he paddles alongside the Earnest. He answers that there are some people on shore who want to come aboard and that his sail too has been left behind. His message delivered, he paddles away again. In a few minutes he shouts out that if a boat is not sent off for those on shore he will turn back himself.

"If you don't do it," he says, "they will have to walk back to Boulogne, thirteen miles."

A crew having volunteered, Mr. Michael Boyton determines to brave the surf. The Earnest steams back as near as she can safely go to Cape Grisnez. A second boat is lowered. Before it can reach the shore a fisherman's skiff makes from the beach, and transfers to the boat of the Earnest the three or four drenched passengers invited by Captain Boyton to accompany him on his voyage. They are Baron de la Tonche (Sub-Prefect of Boulogne) Mr. Merridew, Pilot Mequin and others. It is a quarter to six by the time the Earnest overtakes Captain Boyton. He gives a cheery trump of satisfaction from his foghorn, when he learns that his sail and his guests have been fetched from land. He does not have recourse to his sail yet as the wind (w. n.-w.) continues unfavorable. He has nevertheless paddled to such good purpose by six o'clock that he has covered seven miles from Cape Grisnez, albeit he is but five miles from the French coast, having been carried up channel by the current. His plan is totally opposite from the one followed by him in his last voyage. Whereas he then went with the tide, he is now endeavoring to cut across the tides, in accordance with the advice of Captain Dane and the counsel of an eminent hydrographer, who had most courteously made out an elaborate chart and entered into the minutest details as to the channel currents, for Captain Boyton's guidance.

"Quarter to eight:—Boyton calls for his sail. The staunch little lath of a mast is fixed into the socket attached to one of his feet. The tiny sail fills; but sends him on a wrong tack, wind still blowing w. n.-w. Nothing daunted, Boyton paddles onward for another hour. He then sends the laconic message, 'All right!' by the first pigeon post of the Folkestone Pigeon Club. Wind w.s.-w. Captain Boyton hoists sail again at twenty-five minutes to ten and now scuds along beautifully, like some large sea-bird skimming over the blue waves. A critical time for him approaches. Captain Dane relieves the mate as pilot. When he is pulled out to Boyton, the daring voyager is paddling mechanically. He is very drowsy. Captain Dane's quiet, calm encouragement revives the failing Boyton. He feels greatly invigorated by the plain breakfast. No Liebig mess, this time, taken to him by Dr. Benjamin Howard, Honorary Secretary of the New York Humane Society. This morning meal and the two other meals taken by Boyton during his arduous undertaking cannot be considered very epicurean. Each frugal repast consists of nothing more than half a pint of good strong tea, green with a dash of black, and a couple of beef sandwiches. The tea wakes him up directly. Inspirited by the cup that cheers, he is roused to fresh vigor, and zestfully plies his paddle with wonted dexterity.

"Quarter to twelve.—Captain Dane says that Boyton is now in mid-channel. The tide has swept him north-easterly. The French cliffs are dim.

The white cliffs of Dover are not yet visible to the naked eye. In half an hour the coast line of England looms in sight. Clearer and clearer the cliffs grow out of the haze as the afternoon wears away. At twenty minutes from two a steamboat full of excursionists from Folkestone, decked with flags from stem to stern, sends a volley of rattling cheers across the water, and fair hands flutter handkerchiefs in honor of Captain Boyton, who runs up the stars and stripes in acknowledgement of their hearty encouragement. Another steamer proceeding across the channel is cheering Captain Boyton and dipping her ensign in his honor. More and more distinct grow the Dover cliffs. The outline of the Castle is clearly defined. 'Thou art so near and yet so far' might be appropriately struck up by the Captain, whose voice is strong and cheery whenever he exchanges a shout with us.

"6:30 P.M.—A calm and beautiful evening. Boyton sailing with a faint wind and in slack water. He has by this time crossed two tides. The flood up channel still. 8 P.M.—The ebb down channel to the Varne, being carried many miles north and south respectively by each, and is now in a fair way to reach England, being only four miles from Dover Castle, according to the encouraging news of Captain Dane. So clear is the air that Cape Grisnez and the Varne buoy are still in sight. The last pigeons are now dispatched. Twenty-nine in all have gone during the day. The longest three miles ever known are now entered upon. Hour after hour passes and three miles is ever the distance from shore, so says Captain Dane. The south Foreland lights flash out in our face. Dover lights shine brightly a little distance to our left. The interminable three miles are not lessened a jot. The crew of the Royal Wiltshire Life Boat, specially sent by the National Life Boat Association, warmly cheer the plucky Boyton. He again asks the distance.

"Three miles", shouts back Captain Dane.

"Ah," grimly answers Boyton, with a spice of the Mark Twainish humor peculiar to him, "that's about it. They've just told me from the life-boat its five miles, and, as your steamer is two miles long, we're right in our reckoning all around; but I don't care if it's twenty-five, I'm going to make it."

"Quarter to nine.—Boyton takes supper, lights a cigar and paddles perseveringly along, although he has now been close on eighteen hours in the water. Bravo heart! He is now paddling more strongly than he was in the morning. The three miles shrink, at last into two and three quarters and about this time the one sensational incident of this voyage happens.

"Captain Boyton's own words best describe the episode: 'About an hour before I got on land, I heard a tremendous blowing behind me. It startled me for the moment, for I guessed it was a shark. I instantly drew out my knife, but while I was in the act of doing this, a second snort came closer to my head. I out with my knife and instantly threw myself into a standing position, ready to strike if I had been attacked; but simultaneously with this movement of mine a tremendous black thing leaped completely over me and darted away like lightning. It was a porpoise.'

"The Earnest slowly steaming, Captain Dane casting the lead every few minutes, creeps so near to the towering South Foreland by 2 A.M. that one might almost throw a biscuit ashore. The feat is on the eve of being accomplished. The ebb is not yet so strong that he cannot make palpable progress through the tide. The curlews up in the cliffs are shrilly heralding the dawn, or welcoming Boyton, which you please. A fisherman's skiff has put off to show the safest landing place. The intensest interest is felt by the group on the bridge of the Earnest. Though day is breaking, the sea is still so dark that only the two boats can be discerned close to the shore. A cheer comes over the waters at half past two. Our hearts give a bound. We know the young hero has accomplished his daring task, and we send back our heartiest cheers to him. A rocket rushes up and curls in triumph over the cliffs. No one on board can be more exultant than Mr. Michael Boyton. Yet he coolly calls through the speaking trumpet, 'Come back now. That will do for to-night!'

"The rocky strip of beach on which the Captain has landed is in Fan Bay, a hundred yards or so west of South Foreland Lights. There from he is speedily rowed to the steamer. Receiving a fresh round of British hurrahs on nimbly embarking, he is warmly shaken by the hand, his comely, bronzed face lighting up with a modest smile, albeit his eyes and skin must be smarting terribly from the continual wash of the salt sea waves for twenty-three hours and a half.

"Captain Boyton is sufficiently recuperated before Folkestone is reached, to receive anew the homage which Englishmen are ever ready to pay to heroic pluck and endurance. Dover honors him with a salute of eleven guns as the Earnest glides by. Folkestone harbor is gained at last. Our adieux paid to Captain Boyton, no one seems loth to land." Paul received congratulatory telegrams from the Queen, the Prince of Wales and President Grant. Dover gave the Captain a dejeuner. Folkestone, or rather the South Eastern directors, entertained him at a banquet on Saturday evening, when he felicitously thanked Captain Dane and others for their generous services during his channel voyage.

After his successful attempt, which caused the wildest excitement over all the world, he rested a few days before resuming work, under his managers. Medals, flags, jewelry, addresses and presents of all kinds poured in on him. The Humane Society at Boulogne voted him their massive gold medal representing the First Order of French Life Saving.

All during the summer, Paul appeared in the different towns and watering places in England, getting his regular pay of fifty guineas a day, equal to $1,750 per week. In September his agent accepted of two week's engagements for exhibitions in Berlin at Lake Weissensee. The business that was done there was simply stupendous, and Paul's treatment by the inhabitants of Berlin will never be forgotten by him. For the first time in his life he fell in love. His inamorata was a blue-eyed young German lady, the sweetest and loveliest girl in Berlin; he carried her colors in many a lonely voyage in after years. But it never amounted to anything more than warm friendship, as his love for his free and adventurous life was much stronger than any chains Cupid could weave.

CHAPTER X.

At the close of his Berlin engagement, Paul determined to make a voyage down the Rhine. With that intention he started for Basle, Switzerland. Several correspondents of French, German and English papers desired to accompany him on his trip. As the river is very rough and swift between Basle and Strassburg, they decided to join him at Strassburg when he arrived there. In October, 1875, he started on his first long river voyage, four hundred miles, to Cologne.

At five o'clock in the morning he stepped into the rapid Rhine, with nothing but his bugle and paddle. His first run was to Strassburg, seventy miles below. News did not travel along the upper Rhine fast in those days and the peasantry did not know of his trip. His unexpected and strange appearance caused no little fright among the people along the banks. At one point he came on three workmen, engaged in mending an embankment. While approaching them on the swift current, he raised himself up in the water and blew a blast on his horn. The workmen looked around and seeing a strange figure standing in the water blowing a trumpet, perhaps thought it was old Father Rhine. They did not wait to investigate; but disappeared up the bank in a hurry. About noon Paul arrived at Breisgann, where he got some refreshments. The course of the river now ran along the Black Forest, and is much narrower there. The scenery is weird and somber and although the region is interesting, it is somewhat monotonous. People of the Black Forest are a dreamy and superstitious race; they would stand and look at the uncouth figure in the water for a moment and then run. One old man who was gathering driftwood was so surprised and frightened that he sprang from his boat and ran up the bank without waiting to secure it. At nightfall Paul was still driving along. He heard a peasant whistling and singing on the bank, he hailed him and inquired in German, how far Strassburg was below. "Eine stunde," (one hour,) was the reply.

He afterwards found out that it was the custom in that part of the country to give distance by time. In half an hour afterwards the lights of the bridge at Kohl showed up. There were two bridges there, one for the railroad and one a low pontoon bridge. While watching the high railroad bridge, as he was rapidly approaching on the current, he struck on one of the pontoons and was whirled under. On coming to the surface, he hauled for the shore and landed. It was then eight o'clock and no one was visible. Knocking on a door a woman opened it. She saw the dark figure all glistening with water and sent forth a series of yells that caused the entire neighborhood to turn out. A German policeman approached, took Paul in charge and conducted him to a hotel near by. He said:

"I recognized you, Captain, and your friends are all in Strassburg and do not expect you till to-morrow. The city is about three miles from the river. I will send immediately for a carriage."

When it arrived, he found that it contained three of his friends, who had been apprized of his landing. They drove to a hotel in Strassburg. The next day was spent in hunting for and purchasing a flat bottom boat for the reporters. The Berlin press was represented by Count Von Sierasowsie, an invalid officer with both legs cut off. He had to be carried around in a perambulator. He had a private soldier, which the German government allowed him, as a servant. The balance of the reporters were from France and England. A boat about forty feet long and eight feet wide was purchased and two men, who professed to know something about the channel of the Rhine, engaged to navigate it. It was nothing more than an open craft; no roof, so the correspondents put in straw and chairs to make themselves comfortable. A place was reserved in the bow for the Count's perambulator. The following day all the baggage was placed aboard. Paul had three trunks which had been forwarded from Berlin. Dr. Willis, the English correspondent, observed that Paul passed a strong line through the handles of his trunks and secured each firmly one to the other. Then he tied a buoy to the end of the line. The doctor inquired why he did so.

"Oh," answered Paul, "I always like to be prepared. In case this boat sinks I can easily find my baggage by means of this buoy which will float on the surface."

This remark had not a very encouraging effect on the doctor. That afternoon the voyage was resumed and they ran all night on a swift current. Great danger and difficulty were experienced from the floating mills. They kept the crew busy guiding the unwieldy boat out of danger. The reporters did not rest much. The only one on board who slumbered with pleasure was Simnick, the Count's servant, who seemed to take to sleep as naturally as a duck to water. Paul kept well ahead of the boat and warned them of dangers.

Next day came out clear and warm. As the approached Worms, they were met by gaily decorated steamers and large parties of ladies and gentlemen in small crafts. The burgomaster in an official boat was rowed off to Paul's side. His boat contained a liberal supply of the famous Lieb frauenmilch. He presented Paul with a magnificently chased goblet saying:

"Captain, you must accept the hospitality of Worms even if you do not stop," and filling the glass to the brim, also his own and the officials' who accompanied him and gave a "Lebenhoch."

The fairest and most interesting part of the Rhine was now reached, that which teems with historic and legendary associations; the part too, that possesses a population second to none in the Fatherland for generosity and hospitality. The whole voyage was now a continuous fete. At almost every place they passed the Burgomaster with his friends came out and invited them to drink a cup of wine for which every part of the Rhine is famous. All day they continued down the blue and rapid water and at three o'clock the next morning landed at Mayence, where they woke the sleepy inhabitants with rockets and bugles. The run from Strassburg lasted thirty-six hours; they were glad to get warm comfortable beds in the hotel where they rested till Monday. Before leaving Mayence, telegrams poured in from every point on the river below. One was signed Elizabeth, Princess of Schaumburg-Lippe, congratulating Paul and inviting him to stop at Wiesbaden.

The party left Mayence on Monday and continued dropping down the river. From this place on, the banks presented a very thronged and lively appearance. Perhaps no other river in the world could be found to equal that from Mayence to Cologne in the variety of its life and the multiplicity of its associations. Reception after reception was tendered the voyager and his party and every place seemed to vie with the others in the warmth and good will of its welcome. At Geisenheim, the committee who met Paul on the river, insisted that he must come ashore as a reception was prepared for him. They landed and found a number of Americans, including Consul General Webster. About twenty lovely girls dressed in white and carrying baskets of flowers met the party at the bank. They all implored Paul to come up with them and see their picturesque town and insisted that he must join in the parade. Paul was anxious to continue his way down the river; but the bright eyes and the sweet, soft tones of the beautiful daughters of the Rhine made him an easy victim, so a procession was formed, the young ladies leading and Paul and his party were marched to the hotel, where an informal reception was held. When they left Geisenheim, the press boat was literary loaded down with hampers of delicious wine.

That same evening they reached Bingen. Here the Captain was warned to beware of Bingen Loch and the Lurlei. He took but little stock in the stories about their dangers and secretly determined to dash right into the legendary whirlpool. That whirlpool which has been the theme of Heine's song, has also been the dread of Rhine boatmen from time immemorial. Legend says it is presided over by a fairy maid who lures hapless fishermen to the spot by her syren voice and rejoices in their destruction. The beauty of this part of the Rhine is indescribable. Mountains tower directly up from the water's edge, here and there dotted with historic castles. Time after time was Paul's bugle salute answered on the ramparts far above and many a fair hand waved a handkerchief. When they approached the Lurlei, the boatmen used superhuman efforts to get away from the dreaded whirlpool and hugged the opposite shore. Their cries of:

"This way Captain, the Lurlei," were unheeded by Paul who kept directly for the jutting rock which causes the eddy known as the whirlpool.

"Where are you going?" thundered out one of the members of the press, "Come to this side of the river!"

"Oh, I'm going to visit the mermaid," responded Paul and a few minutes afterward he was in her embrace; or rather in the embrace of the noted Lurlei. Instead of swallowing him up, as had been anticipated, it only whirled him around a few times; he soon succeeded in getting away with a few strokes of his paddle and rapidly overhauled the terror-stricken occupants of the press boat. He dashed alongside and with a dexterous twist of his paddle, sent a shower of water over the astounded and horror-stricken Simnick, who was sure that the voyager must be crazy to take such risks.

"Why," said Paul, "there are a thousand more dangerous eddies in the Mississippi that have never been heard of," and he laughed heartily at the danger he had passed.

At Coblentz the Strassburg boatmen refused to go any farther so they were sent home. The guiding of the press boat was now left to the tender mercies of Simnick. Some of the press men occasionally volunteered to help him. His erratic steering brought him showers of abuse, the occupants of the boat became so nervous that they earnestly desired Paul to remain as near them as possible. Paul knowing that his baggage was aboard, did not require a second invitation. Once Simnick landed the party on a bar, before they got the boat afloat again, all excepting Simnick's master, the Count, were compelled to take off their shoes and shove her off.

Shooting pontoon bridges was the greatest danger. On approaching one, all were aroused and the press men's-hearts were kept pretty close to their mouths. The Count, seated forward in his little carriage, was almost knocked over board, while the boat grazed some spar or bridge. On each of these occasions, the imprecations of the Count, both loud and deep, fell harmlessly around the stolid Simnick. The Count adopted new tactics when approaching a place where bad steering would be likely to cause serious trouble. He would, by the aid of his hands, get down from his carriage and seat himself in the bottom of the boat with the expression of his face, saying:

"Well, if I have to die, I will not have my brains knocked out."

The fifth day after leaving Strassburg, the party reached Cologne, where they were received by the booming of cannons and ringing of bells. The greatest excitement prevailed in the quiet old town and Paul was the recipient of many honors and presents. Several poems were dedicated to him, good, bad and indifferent. One very persistent poet, whose knowledge of English was rather limited, bored him considerably. He got so inflated over Paul's feigned praise, who had tried this ruse to get rid of him, that he had his poem put in a German paper and printed in English at his own expense. It was as follows:

Hall my boy! coming to us with a ton full of reason, Bringing that, what now is most of season: The best of these we did meet since years In a period of apprehensions and fears.

You are, no doubt of those good hearted fellows, Who like to lead the men through friendly meadows; God bless always your noble, humane aim, And give to it the success you do claim.

The people by his loud acclamation, May prove to you that it feels no temptation To cut the throats, to break the necks around And make a grave of all European ground.

It is a sort of cry that's rising, To prove that there are men enough despising Armstrong and Krupp etcetera With Dyrose, Snyder, Mauser, yea.

Are you returned to Uncle Sam's cottage, Then make aware your countrymen of every age: Your finding the German people sorry for human life, But not for scorn and war and strife.

And now, farewell, my boy, with your ton of reason, May God you bless at every season.

The trip on the Rhine concluded, Paul in company with Doctor Willis visited several cities in Germany, Holland and Belgium, where he gave exhibitions till the ice stopped his work. He then crossed to England and took a steamer to New York on a flying trip home, where he arrived December 28th, 1878. He had been gone about sixteen months.

CHAPTER XI.

After spending a few weeks with his family, Captain Boyton received an invitation to visit a friend in St. Louis. While there the swift current of the Mississippi, which was then flowing with ice, tempted him and he made a voyage from Alton to St. Louis, about twenty-five miles. A boat containing newspaper reporters was to accompany him down; but the weather proved too cold for them and they abandoned him after a few miles. The thermometer was below zero, and a man was frozen to death that morning in a wagon at Alton. His reception in St. Louis was something extraordinary. The deafening noise made by the steamers and tug boats as they passed the bridge was heard far beyond the city limits. Before he left St. Louis he gave a lecture for the benefit of St. Luke's Hospital, and on that occasion was presented with a massive silver service. General Sherman made the presentation speech.

From St. Louis he went to New Orleans where he decided to feel the waters in the stronger currents of the lower river. He concluded to take a run of a hundred miles and gave himself twenty-four hours in which to make the voyage. Several members of the press intended to accompany him on the trip and a row boat was procured for their accommodation. This boat was placed on board the steamer Bismarck that was bound to St. Louis. It was arranged with the Captain to drop them off at Bayou Goula exactly a hundred miles above. As the steamer, to get ahead of an opposition boat, started an hour before the advertised time, all the newspaper reporters except one, were left behind. At six o'clock the next morning, Paul and the reporter were landed on the levee at a miserable looking little Louisiana village. They breakfasted at the solitary hotel; after which they made enquiries in regard to a pilot. All agreed that a colored man named Gabriel was the best. They sauntered forth on the levee to hunt up Gabriel. They were followed by a large crowd of negroes, young and old who had heard about the wonderful man-fish. Paul was informed that Gabriel was out in the river catching driftwood, and the entire colored population appeared to join in yelling for "Gabe" to come ashore. Gabriel, who was a tall, sad looking negro, was called on one side by Paul who explained that they desired his services for twenty-four hours, he stated that there was plenty of provision aboard for him and that he would send him back from New Orleans by steamer, so that his trip would not cost him a cent. Gabriel received the communication in stolid silence. He then retired to a log where he seated himself in the centre of a number of his darkey friends. After a consultation, he returned and announced that the figure would be twenty-five dollars.

"Why, what do you mean, you black rascal!" exclaimed Paul, "it will really be only one day's work. How much do you make a day gathering driftwood?"

"Two an' foah bits a day sah."

"And you want twenty-five out of me for one day's work? I will give you three dollars."

"All right, boss, all right, sah," responded Gabriel without a moment's hesitation.

Soon after, Paul and the newspaper man were approached by a darkey, who introduced himself as Mr. Brown. He said:

"I heah dat yo' hab engage Gabe fur pilot ye' down to New Yorleans. Dat niggah don' know nofing 'bout de riber, sah, no sah, me do dough, an, me'll go down fur nothin' sah."

"Are you sure you understand the channel down the river?" asked Paul.

"Deed I do, sah, I knows mos' oh the cat-fish tween heah an' dere."

"Consider yourself engaged, providing you can get the boat away from Gabriel."

"Dats all right sah, lebe dat to me," Mr. Brown answered. A liberal supply of hay for the comfort of the reporter was placed in the row boat.

As the hour approached for them to depart, the levee was thronged with darkies of all sizes and ages, who gazed in open mouthed astonishment, when they saw the dark form in rubber appear and step into the Mississippi. By a clever ruse Mr. Brown got charge of the boat and shoved her off, much to the discomfiture of Gabriel. He returned Gabriel's maledictions with bows and smiles. They shot rapidly away on the yellow flood and were soon far below Bayou Goula. As night came on, Paul requested Brown to light his lantern and get ahead. Brown lit the lantern, but insisted on keeping behind instead of taking the lead. To all Paul's remonstrances he would reply: "Yo' doin' all right, Capen, jus' go right 'long, right 'long, sah."

Paul soon discovered that the negro knew far less about the river than he knew himself and so he threatened that if Mr. Brown did not keep up, he would be tempted to dump him overboard, where he could renew his acquaintance with his old friends the cat fish.

All night they glided between the dark forests on either side of the river. Paul frequently amused himself by startling a camp of negro fishermen.

They spear fish by the light of a fire they build close to the bank. All he had to do in order to break up a camp was to float down quietly until the glare of the fire played on him, then stand up in the water and utter a few howls to attract the darkey's attention. One sight of so hideous a figure in the rubber dress was enough. Their fishing was adjourned for that night.

About three in the morning, Paul found himself far ahead of the press boat and made the forest ring with the echo of his bugle to wake Mr. Brown up. Two or three times he had to wait for the boat. At last he decided that there was no use in dallying or he would never get to New Orleans in twenty-four hours; so he shot ahead and let the boat take care of itself. Before daylight in the morning he heard the roar of a great crevasse that had been formed near Bonnet Carre. The river bank there had been washed away for about four or five hundred yards and a great volume of water was being swept into the forests and swamps below. Without much difficulty he passed this dangerous break and at daylight his bugle called the early risers in the village to the river bank. Here without leaving the water, he got a cup of hot coffee and while he was drinking it, those on the bank informed him that there was a white boat just coming around the bend in the distance, so he concluded to wait for it. Soon after, Mr. Brown, pulling lazily along, arrived. Paul rated him soundly for his tardiness. The reporter was sound asleep, doubled up in a pile of hay at the bottom of the boat. At five o'clock that evening, exactly twenty-four hours after they started, they tied up at the levee in New Orleans where they were received by about ten thousand people, who covered the levee and crowded the deck of the steamers.

While resting in New Orleans after his run, Paul was waited on by a party of gentlemen, who announced themselves as a committee appointed to call on him and see if they could induce him to give an exhibition in……, an interesting little town up the river.

"Have you got any water that can be enclosed?" Paul inquired.

They said they had a beautiful little lake right back of the town that could be properly fenced, so that no one could look on without paying. They promised that Captain Boyton should have the entire receipts, and that they would make it a gala day providing he would come up, and assured him of the warmest kind of reception. "We'll have music too," added one of the committee men.

Being so assured, Paul promised to be on hand. The committee started for home where they commenced to rouse the country. One morning Paul, accompanied by Mr. Brown stepped off a steamboat at ………., and was received by the committee who were waiting for him and who immediately escorted him to the hotel where he was cordially invited to "limber up." After breakfast, the voyager was escorted to the lake and saw to his annoyance that there was no fence or enclosure around it. He remonstrated with the committee and said that they could never get a fence around it in time. The answer was, "Never mind, Captain, never mind. We'll guarantee that no one stands around that lake without paying."

All the morning crowds kept pouring into town. By noon, the main street was filled with wagons, ox-teams and mules with vehicles of every kind, shape and color, all carrying crowds of whites and negroes. Paul dined with the Mayor, at the hotel and after dinner commenced to dress in his suit. The Mayor informed him that there would be a parade to start from the hotel door and that he would be escorted to the lake by the guard and the band. When the hour arrived, Paul was led from the hotel by his honor and was mounted on a cart to which two white mules were hitched in tandem. The Mayor mounted with him. Behind this cart, drawn up in military array were fifty men armed with shot guns. In front of the cart rode the Grand Marshall of the occasion followed the band which consisted of a solitary hand-organ. Order for advance being given, the parade started for the lake. When they reached the water-side, Paul was requested to step into the little tent which had been erected for him and to be seated until the fence was made. The Grand Marshal then ordered all the people to fall back, while he stationed the guards with loaded shot guns at intervals around the entire lake. Then riding his horse wildly up to the crowd he informed them that "this line of guards was the fence and that any person coming within one hundred yards of the line would be shot."

"This," pointing to two of the committee men, who stood with shot guns near an old soap box in which a slit was cut to receive the money, "is the entrance gate. Niggers twenty-five cents, whites fifty cents. Now get right in or get off this prairie."

The whole exhibition was unexpectedly successful. There was not a deadhead around the lake. Paul took for his share two hundred and thirty dollars, beside spending one of the pleasantest days he remembers. This town is now a smart city and Paul withholds the name because the citizens may not relish this reminiscence.

Soon after, Paul went to Louisville, Ky., where he made a run over the Falls of the Ohio. This feat caused the most intense excitement in Louisville and vicinity. He then went to Europe and commenced his exhibition season at Amsterdam, Holland, in May, for by this time he was well launched in the show business. He exhibited with much success all through Holland and Germany. August 3d, 1876, he found himself in the town of Linz, Austria. Here he met with an accident from which he almost lost his right eye, by the premature explosion of a torpedo. He was an invalid in the hotel on the banks of the Danube for two weeks. The constant sight of the inviting water of the Danube started the desire in his heart for another voyage, and it did not take him long to make up his mind to take a run to Buda Pesth, about four hundred and fifty miles below. When he announced his intention to take this voyage, it was quickly telegraphed all over the country bordering on the river. Almost the whole city of Linz turned out to bid him goodbye as he stepped into the Danube. The current was very swift; but the river was greatly cut up by islands and bars. He could see nothing blue about the Danube. That river was almost as yellow as the Mississippi. Like all rivers it has its bug-bear. The Struden is the terror of the Upper Danube. It consists of a sharp and dangerous rapid, picturesquely surrounded by high wood covered hills. Great crowds were gathered here to see Paul make his plunge. He passed under two or three heavy waves that completely submerged him. As he was hurried away on the wild current, he held his paddle high up in acknowledgment to the cheers.

His reception in Vienna was most enthusiastic. From Presburg he was accompanied for about two miles by the swimming club and he was made an honorary member by a vote taken while he was paddling in the river surrounded by his swimming friends. He was then left alone and all that day he traveled through a barren and desolate country. He occasionally ran across parties of gold dust hunters who were at work on the sand bars. They were a wild looking lot of people and all wore white shirts and baggy trousers. His appearance as he skimmed along on the current never failed to produce the utmost consternation among the groups who had possibly never heard of him. It was a very warm day and the sun burned his face cruelly. In the evening the mosquitoes hovered around him in clouds and made his life miserable. That night he was drowsy and fatigued in consequence of his hard work all day. About eleven o'clock, in spite of himself, he went to sleep, though well aware of the danger he ran from the mills. The Danubian mill consists of two great barges fastened together by beams and decked over with a large wheel between them. They are anchored in the swiftest part of the current which drives the machinery. He was awakened from his nap by hearing a tremendous crashing noise and found himself just passing in between two barges and in a second or two would be under the rapidly revolving wheel. The current hurled him against it. Before he could recover one of the planks struck him over the eyebrows and the next struck him on the back of the head driving him completely under. His paddle was smashed in two and one half of it gone, while he could feel the warm blood running down his forehead. With the broken piece of the paddle he managed to gain the eddy back of one of the barges. The miller was awakened by his cries for assistance and the stalwart Hungarian appeared on the deck with a lantern and threw a rope to the almost fainting man. Paul grasped this firmly and was hauled up till the light of the lantern revealed his blood covered face and glinting rubber head piece. The miller uttered a cry of terror, let go the rope and ran into the mill where he securely fastened himself, thinking no doubt that some evil sprit of the Danube had appeared to him. When the terrified miller loosened his hold on the rope, Paul now almost entirely exhausted dropped back into the current and floated away in a semi-conscious condition. With his half paddle he succeeded in keeping clear of the mills and drifted till day light. His eyes were almost closed by the swelling of his forehead. Soon after he discovered a castle high up on the banks on one side of the river, the inhabitants of which he stirred up by a blast on his bugle as he was drifting helplessly. A boat shot away from shore and picked him up. The boat contained an Austrian officer and two soldiers. The officer informed him that the castle to which he was being conveyed, was the fortress Komorn. His wounds were quickly dressed by the surgeon and in two days he was sufficiently recovered to resume his trip.

From Komorn he ran all day and the following night to make up for lost time. About daylight next day great mountains towered up each side of the river that was there narrow and rapid. About eight o'clock he arrived at a little village and was informed that it was Nagy, about forty miles above Buda Pesth. Here he got some refreshments and started on his last run. A few miles below he saw a very high mountain, surmounted by a cross, up which ran a zig-zag road. At each bend of this road was erected a grotto containing some scene from the Passion of Our Lord. This Way of the Cross is a celebrated place of devotion to the pious people of Buda Pesth. As he passed the mountain he saluted a party of ladies and gentlemen standing on the shore. One of the gentlemen hailed him in German with the request to slack up a little and they would come off in a boat. Paul complied with their request and stood upright in the water and drifted quietly along. The boat was soon beside him: it contained two ladies, evidently mother and daughter, and two gentlemen. The daughter, about eighteen years of age, was, in Paul's estimation, the most lovely girl he had ever seen. He gazed with a look of admiration on her wondrous beauty and paid but little attention to the shower of questions that were put to him in Hungarian-German by the male members of the party. In his best German, he asked her what he already knew, that was, "how far it was to Buda Pesth?"

She smiled and answered in French, "about thirty-five miles. I presume you can speak French better than German?"

This was just what Paul wanted. She now acted as interpreter for the whole party and her sweet voice drove away all feeling of fatigue. As the current was driving the party rapidly down, the mother suggested that it was time that they should say good-bye. Before going, one of the gentlemen asked through the young lady, "if M. le Capitaine would take a glass of wine?"

Paul responded, "that it was pretty early in the morning for a toast, but if he was permitted to drink to the health of Hungary's fairest daughter, he would sacrifice himself."

With a musical laugh she handed him a glass filled with sparkling Tokay. A general hand shake all around followed and as Paul's rubber-covered, wet hand grasped that of the young lady, he begged her to present him with the bunch of violets she had pinned to her breast, as a memento of the pleasant moments he spent in her company. She complied with his request, he gallantly kissed them and pushed them through the rubber opening of the face piece, down into his breast.

As he resumed paddling, the thought occurred to him, that the frank cordiality of the male occupants of the boat had undergone a decided change, and their farewell was a little more formal than their introduction; but he paid little attention to that and struck away for Buda Pesth with a strong steady pull, while he hummed:

"Her bright smile haunts me still."

The news of his approach had been telegraphed to Buda Pesth. When he arrived at the Hungarian capital both banks and the bridges were black with people and the cry of, "eljen Boyton, eljen America," re- echoed on every side. The warmth of his reception in Buda Pesth was simply indescribable. In narrating the story of his voyage down the Danube, he mentioned the fair vision he had encountered at Visegrad. This was duly published with his other adventures. From Buda Pesth he returned by railroad to Vienna, where he had an engagement to give an exhibition for the Boat Club. This contract being filled and free to go anywhere he wished, he followed his fancy and took the first train for Buda Pesth again. Here he gave many successful exhibitions; one of largest was for the benefit of a girl's home at was a favorite charity in Buda Pesth. At the close of the exhibition he was bewildered by the shower of flowers and bouquets thrown on him in the water. Next day he received a letter addressed, as follows: Sir Captain Paul Boyton a Buda Pesth, Hotel Europa.

The contents of the letter were:

Sir!—Accept our hearty thanks for your generous complaisance, having succored foreign interest in a foreign land. We assure you, that your name and the remembrance of your noble action never leave the hearts of these young girls, whom we can help through your beneficence to instruct them useful professions. Let me render you our thanks, we do never forget your gentlemanlike conduct.

I remain very much obliged, your esteemer ELMA HENTALLERF, Secretary;

MRS. ANNA KUHNEL, President of the Union of Ladies. Buda Pesth, 1876,
Sept. 18.

During all this time Paul kept his eyes wide open in the hope of again meeting the beautiful young lady, who had made such an impression on his heart. One day a Hungarian officer met him on the street and said "Captain wouldn't you like to be presented to the young lady you met on the river at Visegrad?"

"Would a duck swim?"

The officer told him to be ready that evening and he would take him around to their private box in the National Theatre. Paul was ready a couple of hours before the appointed time. They entered the box and the object of Paul's dreams arose and advancing with a charming smile, said in English:

"I'm so delighted to see you, Captain."

"Not any more than I am to see you. Why didn't you speak English to me on the river?"

"Well," she exclaimed, "I was a little confused and did not remember that Americans spoke English, but let me present you to my mother and the gentlemen."

Paul was then introduced to an Austrian officer and a count who with her mother were occupants of the box. Little attention was paid to the play going on by Paul, who kept up a running conversation in English mixed with French, with the charming girl at his side, but wily diplomat that he was, he got in an occasional remark to her mother in German. At the close of the performance, Paul offered his arm to the young lady, while the Austrian officer took the mother in tow. The other gentlemen in the party took the lead at the door. They walked leisurely home through the narrow streets and the officer who was escorting the mother clinked the scabbard of his long sword in a savage manner on the cobble stones. Before they parted at the door of her home, Paul had asked for and obtained permission to call the next day. He then turned away accompanied by the officer and walked in the direction of his hotel. The officer asked him how long he intended to remain in Buda Pesth. Paul did not give him very much satisfaction as he was running free at the time and had no course mapped out. On arriving at the hotel, the Captain invited the officer to take some refreshments. While seated at the table, the latter introduced the subject of dueling and asked Paul questions in regard to the code in America. Paul easily seeing the drift of his thoughts, entertained him with accounts of hair-raising combats with bowie knives, revolvers, shot guns and cannons, assuring him they were of frequent occurrence in the part of the States where he came from. He told the officer that he did not know one of his friends who would not rather participate in a duel than be invited to a banquet. When the warrior parted from Paul he was stuffed fell of harrowing yarns, all of which he seemed to believe, at least his demeanor was much more gentle than when he had entered the hotel. Paul remained in Buda Pesth two weeks longer than he expected, during which time he was a frequent visitor at the home of the fair Irene, where he was always welcomed by herself and parents. Then followed a trip through the principal cities of Hungary.

He then went to Italy where on the 4th of November, 1876, he started on a long voyage down the Po from Turin to the Adriatic, a distance of about six hundred and seventy miles. He was determined to make this trip in one continuous run, intending it as a feat to test his endurance. Paul's knowledge of Italian was very limited and his knowledge of the river he was about to embark on, less. All the inhabitants of Turin seemed to have turned out to see him start. To carry his provisions, map, etc., he had a little tin boat made about two feet, six inches long and eight inches wide. This little craft bore the name, "Irene D'Ungeria," Irene, belle of Hungary, and was the model from which his well known "Baby Mine" was the evolution. The weather was cold and the water intensely so. Its source was the Alps, then in plain view and covered with snow.

He started on a Saturday morning at nine o'clock. The current was exceedingly strong, rushing over gravel beds on which he frequently grounded. The country in the vicinity was very beautiful with high ground on each side. At every little village and hamlet, he was received with enthusiastic "vivas" and many were the kind invitations he was tendered to stop and take refreshments. All these he declined as he had ample provisions in his little boat for a four day's run. This boat he had attached to his belt by a line about three yards long. She behaved very well; but when he reached very violent rapids he was compelled to pick her up and place her on his legs before him. About nightfall a lady and gentleman came off in a small boat and requested him to stop for the night assuring him that the danger in the river below was very great. It contained many mills under which he might be carried; but his mind was made up and he went steadily along on his perilous voyage. The night was very cold and the struggling moon occasionally lit up the valley. He struck many times heavily on the rocks and frequently entered false channels. About three o'clock Sunday morning, he heard a loud roaring noise and supposed it to be some freight train passing over the bridge at Casale, a village below, which he considered was then near. About the same time a thick, white fog peculiar to the Po, settled over the river. Through this he picked his way cautiously and as the current swept in around the bend of the river, the noise he heard before seemed to be no great distance away. The speed of the current seemed to increase and in a few minutes afterwards, he was shot over a dam and hurled in the tumbling water below. Before he could extricate himself, the little boat had been upset and was about sinking when he grabbed her. The current soon drove him far below the dam, where he landed on a bar and emptied his tender of water. He knew her contents were ruined; but it was too dark to examine, so he kept on his voyage until sunrise, when he landed and found that all his provisions were converted into a kind of pudding, dotted with cigars instead of fruit. The small flask of Cognac and a bottle of oil were the only things uninjured. A pull at the Cognac flask served him for breakfast and he paddled away on his voyage with vigorous stroke. The sun rose that morning in a deep red color and as the rays illumined the snow clad Alps, that looked so near him, the valley of the Po and the remnants of the fog were bathed in a soft red light, so that even the very water seemed turned to blood. A sight more beautiful and peculiar than this, Paul never witnessed since or before. The river now seemed to shoot from the hills into the low land. On either side was a heavy growth of willows.

He saw no one until about nine that morning, when sweeping around a bend he came on a boat containing two men with a swivel gun, after ducks. Both men were greatly excited and one of them turned the swivel in his direction. Paul shouted vigorously at him not to fire, and fortunately he did not. He ran along side and held a conversation in the best Italian he could muster. They informed him that he was nearing the village of Frassinetto and offered him provisions. He accepted a piece of bread which he ate and again started on his journey. A couple of hours afterward he came to a flying bridge, an institution peculiar to many European rivers. It consists of a long line of small boats strung together on a heavy cable, anchored in the centre of the river. The boats supported the cable. The last boat on the line is the ferry or bridge. This is much larger than any of the others and has a steering oar. When cast away from one shore, the ferry is steered diagonally against the current to the opposite side while the line of boats supporting the cable swing with it. Paul often found these bridges exceedingly dangerous, particularly at night time. Then the ferry is always tied and the line of small boats lead from the centre to the side for about a hundred yards below. The bridge men at Frassinetto were notified of Paul's approach by his bugle and never having heard of him before, rowed out in a skiff and were very indignant when they found that he would not be rescued. All day Sunday he drove ahead on the rapid current. By consulting his maps, which he fortunately saved and dried on the deck of the Irene, he found that he could not make the run in four days as he had expected when he started. Sunday evening he obtained some provisions from a miller and though feeling very sleepy and much fatigued, he kept driving along all night. The roar of the waters as they dashed against the mills, put him on the alert. Monday morning he was faint and fast becoming exhausted; but was encouraged by the hope of soon reaching Piacenza. There he expected to meet his agent, get a little rest and a full supply of much needed provisions.

The agent in question, was a Scotchman, he had met in Milan, before going to Turin. His occupation was that of a tenor singer; but he failed to make a success of it, he was open for anything that turned up. Finding that he was a good Italian scholar, Paul engaged him. He was not exactly Paul's idea of what an agent ought to be, as he showed too much fondness for the good things of this life. When seated with a dish of cutlets and truffles flanked by a generous sized bottle of wine, he was apt to make statements that were rather unreliable. Before leaving Milan for Turin, Paul told him, as the Po was to him an unknown river, he could not tell at what time he could make on it, so that he must use his judgment from the reports he would get from above, in regard to the progress he was making down the river. He then instructed him to go to Piacenza on Saturday as he expected to be able to reach that point on Sunday evening. Paul afterwards learned that instead of waiting until Saturday; his courier, full of self importance, started for that city the same day Paul left on his way to Turin. On arriving there he introduced himself to the Sindaco and newspaper men, by whom he was feted and ample opportunity was given him to indulge in his favorite dishes. On his own responsibility, he informed the journalists that Captain Boyton would be sure to arrive on Sunday evening, and at that time almost every man, woman and child in Piacenza was on the banks of the river two miles away from the town. Finding that the Captain did not appear at the time he announced and that the crowd was getting angry, the agent slipped away and got back just in time to catch a train for Ferrara much farther down the river. Most of the crowd waited on the banks until dark, then returned and commenced to hunt for the agent; not finding him, they satisfied themselves by burning his effigy in the public square.

Monday broke on Paul, chilly and uncomfortable. Once in a while a faint gleam of sunshine would light up the river and he took advantage of any long reach before him, free from mills, to take a nap. He woke from one of these naps by hearing a cry on the banks and saw a fisherman gazing intently at the floating object. He half opened his eyes, but never made a move, curious to see what effect his presence would make on the peasant. At this time the current was setting him into the shore. The fisherman ran down along the bank to a point and there stood, pole in hand, waiting to capture what he no doubt thought was a dead body. As he was thrusting the pole out, Paul quickly assumed an upright position in the water and saluted him with the words:

"Buon giorno."

The pole dropped from his hand and with one frightened shriek he rushed up the bank and disappeared. About one o'clock the bridge at Piacenza came in sight but instead of being full of people, as he expected, Paul saw only a few working men and some soldiers. No sight of the agent was visible, so he decided to run through and stop at Cremona about thirty miles below. He saluted the workmen and soldiers as he was carried under the bridge with frightful velocity. At this time his strength was almost gone and he was heart sore that he should fail in his self-imposed task; but felt that he was able to continue on as far as Cremona, about twenty-five miles below. The day grew more dreary and it seemed to him as if it would soon commence to snow. He continued working slowly and stubbornly along, when he was arrested by a cry behind him. Coming upright and wheeling around, he saw a young officer standing in a boat pulled by about twenty pontoneers. As he shot alongside, the officer stretched forth his hand to shake Paul's and said in French:

"You must come on board and go back to Piacenza. The public are greatly disappointed. Your agent said that you would be here yesterday and a great reception was prepared for you."

Paul thanked him but firmly declined to return. The officer then asked him if he desired anything and Paul informed him that he was badly in need of provisions and some oil for his lamp. He had missed the little light on the head of the Irene during the long, lonely nights on the river.

"There is a village a couple of miles below," said the officer, "and if you will slack up a little, I will run ahead and have all you need by the time you come opposite."

The pontoneer's boat shot away and Paul followed quietly after them.

When he arrived off the village, the boat again pulled out into the stream with not only the supplies desired, but a most excellent meal, consisting of boiled eggs and other nutritious edibles, along with a bottle of fine old Barolo, the sparkling red wine of that country. While eating the food, Paul, with the boat alongside, drifted slowly with the current and during that time, he ascertained that the young officer, who had manifested so much interest in him, was the son of General Pescetta, Minister of Marine. Shortly before being overtaken by the friendly Italian, Boyton was beginning to feel terribly fatigued and had serious thoughts of throwing up the trip; but under the influence of the hearty meal and the invigorating wine, his courage was renewed and he felt he could easily complete the journey. All that day he passed through lonely and miserable looking country. Swampy lands and rice fields bordered either side of the river. About five o'clock he saw two men on the bank and called out to them, asking how far it was to Cremona:

"Motto, Signor; motto," was the answer which means, "very much, very much." It is the usual reply of all Italian peasants when asked regarding distance.

Paul was so refreshed that he did not mind the discouraging answer. He was on buoyant spirits and to it seemed to him as though he could dash along forever without tiring, his strength was so great. He felt there would be no difficulty in completing his undertaking in time. This unusual animation and feeling of wondrous power, he could only attribute to the effects of the food and wine. Pulling gaily along, he suddenly felt a tremendous pressure in his head, and apparently without the slightest cause, blood spurted from his mouth and nostrils. It occurred to him that he had burst a blood vessel.

Brilliant lights seemed to be burning in front, behind and all around him, with the intensity of electric search lights. A village appeared on the bank and he concluded to stop. Pulling in shore, he was bewildered to find only the mud bank. This discovery startled him into a realization that something was wrong with his brain. The mind was wavering between the hallucinations of a fever, and lucidity. Vagaries occasioned by a high temperature, would suddenly vanish as the struggling mind briefly asserted itself. As he resumed paddling, some swaying willows became three ladies attired in the Grecian bend costume, then a fad in America, smiling and bowing to him. His mind told him they were only willows; but his eyes would not be convinced.

Darkness fell about him. He had no idea of where he was going, and the lights burst on him again with increased brilliancy. No matter where his eyes turned, the intense rays would shine into them. He thought he had arrived at Cremona, and that some men were turning the reflector to annoy him. "Keep those lights off," he shouted, "don't you see they are blinding me?"

Reason came for an instant and told him there was no town and no lights. He knew he must call for help, but several minutes elapsed before he could remember the proper Italian word. Then he cried:

"Soccorso, soccorso!"

But only the echo responded from the lonely shore.

He again reached the bank, formed by a dyke which protects the lowlands from the floods. He climbed to the top, carrying the little tender in his arms. Then he could hear the tack, tack, tack, of some one pounding, and through an open door he saw a shoemaker hammering away at the sole of a boot on his knee. Attempting to enter, he staggered against a tree. The shoemaker appeared in another direction and the sound of the hammer was continually with him. Almost overcome with fatigue he decided to sit down, and then his paddle assumed the character of a companion, remonstrating with him and advising him to move on.

"I think I'll sit down here," Boyton would say.

"Indeed you won't," answered the paddle.

"But I must."

"If you do you will die. Come on."

Endeavoring to obey the commands of the paddle he continued to stagger on, falling at every few steps; but regaining his feet and pressing forward. Intense thirst consumed him and he went often to the brink of the river and drank quantities of water, burying his face in the muddy stream; the paddle all the while urging him to move on. Along the top of the dyke he came upon three posts placed for the purpose of keeping cattle from getting off the road. These posts became sneering, laughing men, wearing cloaks flung across their breasts, Italian fashion. They were insolent, and he challenged them to fight; but they only ridiculed him.

"You are the fellows that have been bothering me all night," he shouted, and dropping on one knee, he took a sheath knife from the tender and plunged it into the breast of one of the men. In a flash of reason he saw the knife quivering in a post.

Again the fevered voyager started, the paddle all the while telling him that he would soon strike some town or village. Two or three times the overwhelming desire for water compelled him to return to the river and drink. Every time he descended or climbed the dyke he grew weaker and finally decided to lie down at all hazards and sleep. The paddle earnestly remonstrated:

"It is death. Death if you lie down. Keep on," it said.

Fatigue obtained the mastery and he sank on the ground determined to sleep. Scarcely had he stretched his limbs on the muddy dyke, than he was partially aroused by the "dong, dong, dong," of a great bell clanging on the still night air. He counted twelve strokes.

"Ah, that is another illusion," he thought; but it brought him to a sitting posture, just as a bell of different tone sounded "ding, ding, ding," and again he counted twelve strokes.

The second sound convinced him that he was near a village, and heeding the commands of the paddle, he struggled to his feet and entered a road which he followed, passing under an old arch that spanned the highway, but he was afraid to touch it, thinking that it too, would disappear. Shortly the cobble stones of a street were felt through the rubber soles of his dress. He saw houses on each side, but kept on under the impression that if he approached them they would vanish, and he also conceived the idea that he must tread lightly or he would scare them away. As he advanced through the village street, arguing with the paddle that no real village was in sight, a light shining through a transom over the door of some outbuilding, attracted his attention, and he thought he might be in the vicinity of human beings. Hearing the sound of voices he approached the door, listening. Then another mad thought came to him, that he must make a desperate rush at the door and get inside before it melted away. He did so, and the frail barrier gave way before the pressure of his shoulder and he stumbled headlong into the place. He disturbed several men who were drinking and playing at some game and as he regained his feet he observed two of the men trying to escape through a window, while the others seized chairs and benches to repel an attack of what they imagined to be the Evil one.

"Molto malado!" cried Boyton.

At hearing this, the men gained confidence and put down their weapons.

"Medico? Albergo?" inquired the voyager.

One of the most intelligent of the party, said: "Ah, he wants a doctor and a hotel. He is sick," and they went out with him into the street which was then lighted by the moon. The men advanced in a group while Paul brought up the rear and in this way they proceeded until the hotel was reached, when some of the party began to throw pebbles against the upper window to awaken the landlord. While they were doing that and shouting, Paul counted them and found they numbered twelve. He concluded they were the twelve apostles.

"Pedro, Pedro, come down," shouted one of the apostles, "a Frenchman wants to get in."

Pedro at last appeared at the door with a light in his hand; but on seeing his strange visitor in the black dress covered with mud, he exclaimed: "No room, no room."

Boyton said "vino," a touch of reason coming to his aid.

"Yes," replied the landlord, "you can have wine."

He opened the door and the entire crowd entered a large room with an earthen floor and ranged around were several common board tables polished to a snowy whiteness, while on shelves were bright colored vessels and measures. On ordering the wine, Paul noticed the landlord eyeing him suspiciously, so he took from the little boat which he still carried, a book, among the leaves of which was some Italian paper money. Throwing a ten lire note ($2.00), to the landlord, he ordered wine for the full amount, and the twelve apostles were soon enjoying it. Boyton sat down and mechanically took the measure every time it was handed to him and drank. He tried to listen to the conversation of his strange comrades, but found himself dozing. The uproar made by the twelve, who had seldom experienced such a windfall, awakened the landlord's wife who entered the room and began to question the roysterers in a very emphatic manner. Going to Boyton, she lifted the rubber from his forehead and turning angrily to men, exclaimed:

"Can't you understand? This man has febbre del fuoco."

Taking the measure of wine away from Paul, she ordered her husband to build a fire and began to take off the rubber dress, in which she was assisted by some of the men. When the tunic was off, steam arose from the voyager's body as from a boiler, and when the pantaloons were removed, the good hostess unceremoniously ordered the twelve apostles into the street. She procured a chicken which was soon broiling, and brewing some kind of tea, she compelled Paul to eat and drink, after which he was escorted to a room and snugly covered up in a big, canopied bed. He was no sooner stretched on the mattress than he was sound asleep, not waking until the sun shone through the window next day. He then heard the murmur of voices in the street. Jumping up, his feet struck a cold tiled floor which sent a chill over him. Peering through the curtain, he discovered a crowd of people looking up at his room and a buzz of voices was heard all about the house. Not remembering where he was, he pulled a bell cord and the summons was answered by the landlady, who greeted him kindly and hoped he felt better. She also informed him that two gentlemen were below who wished to see him. "Let no one up but a doctor," answered Paul; but in a few moments three men were ushered in. Boyton was unreasonably suspicious and testily told the men that he only wanted a doctor. One of the gentlemen explained in French that he was the mayor of Meletti; that one of his companions was a doctor and they had come to take care of and entertain him. Such gracious answers to rough and suspicious questions, disarmed Paul and they were soon on friendly terms. The mayor informed him that a carriage was at the door to convey him to his own house, where better care could be had. It was explained that the patient had nothing to wear except his underclothing, and the mayor immediately procured him a suit of clothes and escorted him through a gaping crowd to the carriage, nor would he permit Paul to settle the hotel bill.

After an hour's drive the voyager was comfortably installed in a mansion, under the ministrations of a distinguished physician. No one could have been better treated. He afterward learned that his host, beside his official position, was a large landed proprietor, owning most of the village, and was a member of the great family of Gattoni de Meletti.

Reports that the man in the rubber dress had been attacked by the fever, spread all over Italy, and great numbers of people came from surrounding towns to see him and inquire as to his condition. The fire fever with which Paul was attacked (febbre del fuoco), is peculiar to the districts along the lowlands of the Po, and he had been eighty-three consecutive hours in the water when it overcame him.

For more than a week the doctor was in close attendance and then Boyton was sufficiently restored to health to go about. He was treated with the utmost consideration. The mayor took pains to show him everything of interest. Among his other possessions, the hospitable Italian owned great droves of cows. The cows of that vicinity are known all over the world, the famous Parmesean cheese being made there. The mayor's herd wintered in long sheds and were so near of one size that looking along the stalls over their backs they seemed as even and as level as a floor. The stalls and everything about the sheds were as clean and as sweet smelling as could be.

The notoriety given to the town of Meletti by the presence of Boyton created much jealousy in the breasts of the people of Castlenuovo Bocco d'Adda, the town in which he first appeared. They became impressed with the idea that their village had been cheated out of considerable fame by reason of the action of the mayor of Meletti in taking him away; so in order to even things up they formed a Boyton club and promoted a big banquet in his honor. This was followed by a more stupendous entertainment given by the people of Meletti, and thus there was great rivalry between the villages to honor the distinguished guest. At the Meletti banquet people were present from Cremona, and Boyton gave an exhibition in the lake for the benefit of the poor. When thoroughly restored to health, Paul continued his voyage and was tendered an ovation all the way. On the fourth day he ended the journey at Ferrara. When he landed he found that the enterprising agent before alluded to, had pursued the same tactics there that had distinguished him at Piacenza. He had told the people that Boyton would surely be down on a certain day, while at the time he was ill at Meletti. On the day set by the agent for his arrival, great crowds gathered on the bridge and along the banks. A log floating down on the current was hailed by the agent as the voyager, much to the disgust of the people who strained their eyes until darkness sent every one home. The agent having reached the limit of his credit in Ferrara, as he had at the town up the river, secretly disappeared to the shades of Milan, where it is supposed that he resumed his operatic career.

CHAPTER XII.

After leaving Ferrara, Boyton gave many exhibitions through the interior towns of Italy; and finally made arrangements for a voyage down the Arno from Florence to Pisa, a distance of about one-hundred kilometers. All Florence was worked up to a state of great excitement when it became known that the intrepid American, as he was called, was going to start on a voyage from that city. The banks of the Arno were literally jammed with people to witness the start. The river, which is fed by mountain streams, was rising rapidly owing to recent heavy rains above and many were the exclamations of doubt regarding his ability to accomplish the undertaking. A dam, called the pescaia, spans the river diagonally in the midst of the city and it was looked upon as a dangerous obstacle by the people. The start was made shortly before two o'clock in the afternoon and the rapid current, assisted by the powerful strokes of his paddle, soon carried Paul beyond sight of the crowds and he went over the dam in safety.

At nine o'clock he arrived at San Romano where an immense crowd, including the notables of the district, together with the municipal junta of Montopoli, awaited patiently as possible his arrival. Torches blazed along the bank to show him where to land and loud huzzas rolled up from the multitude when he stood on the shore. He was escorted to a small inn where his only refreshments were two cups of tea. The crowd demanded a speech, and to quiet the yelling, Paul stepped to the porch of the inn and delivered most of the Italian words he knew:

"Signori, taute grazie di vostra accoglienza, arrivederie, ciao!"

The speech was greeted with great applause and the crowd was satisfied. He remained at San Romano but a short time and again entered the water. At some little distance below the village, there is a weir which is considered a most formidable spot by the inhabitants. They endeavored to persuade Boyton to remain until morning and not attempt its passage in the darkness, especially as the river was now much higher than when he started. Paul laughed at their fears and amidst the plaudits of the spectators, disappeared in the darkness. The weir so feared by the people, proved a mere toy for him.

A demonstration in his honor was prepared at Pontedera, where he arrived at 12 o'clock. Regardless of the late hour, the banks were crowded and torches gleamed along the entire length of the town. The whole population seemed to have turned out. As Paul came opposite, he stood up in the water, saluting the assemblage. As he resumed his recumbent position, his hand came in contact with the upturned face of a dead woman. For a moment he was horrified; but fastening the body to a line, he carried it to shore, while the band played and the people cheered, little suspecting that the voyager had such a ghastly object in tow. He called out that he had the corpse of a woman with him. Some of the authorities took charge of it; but the crowd gave it no heed as they followed up the street, cheering and tumbling over one another in their anxiety to see him. One enthusiast, who thought he was being unduly crowded, rammed his torch down another's throat. Boyton was compelled to repeat the speech he made at San Romano. The banquet was a noble success; but very trying to the landlord who appeared to be completely upset at having such unusual trade. Instead of heeding orders for edibles, he would rush into the banqueting hall every few moments and nervously count the empty wine bottles. The guests yelled at him to hurry; but those bottles were counted several times before anything was set on the table to eat. Paul remained at Pontedera until morning, simply because he did not wish to reach Pisa until the following mid-day, which was the time appointed. Consequently it was 8 o'clock in the morning when he resumed the voyage; he was escorted to the river by the same enthusiastic crowds. At noon he arrived at Pisa. A unique reception had been arranged. The mayor and all the authorities were out to meet him in those peculiar looking boats that are seen nowhere else in the world, called Lancia Pisana. Those boats are of ancient make; none of them being manufactured at the present day. They are about thirty feet long, richly carved and gaudily painted. Under the escort of these gay boats, containing the notabilities, Paul landed and again great crowds tendered him an ovation.

Under the impression that Boyton could neither speak nor understand the Italian tongue, the officials had engaged a man who was supposed to be a great English scholar, to act as interpreter for him at the feast to be given in the evening. The fellow was a burr, sticking to the outer skirts of respectable society, and when he was engaged to act as interpreter on such an occasion, he felt himself to be a great man. He was over weighted with his importance. At the banquet he sat at Boyton's right hand and at every toast proposed, he would rise and bow in the most gracious manner. This rather embarrassed Paul, who understood about all that was being said and could speak enough Italian to make himself understood. He mentioned the fact to one or two of his entertainers, at the same time expressing a desire to be rid of the interpreter. The fellow was having too much pleasure to be easily disposed of, and it was not until some very vigorous words were passed, that he concluded to abandon the scene. In the meantime he had been honoring every toast with copious draughts of wine, and was very much intoxicated when he left the hall. He wandered about the streets and the more he thought of his dismissal, the deeper became his wrath and he concluded that he had been insulted. A few more measures of wine, partaken of at the café, determined him to wipe the insult out in blood. Having made up his mind to write Boyton a challenge, he entered a hotel with an air of great importance, and called to a waiter in a voice that could be heard all over the place:

"Waiter; a pen, ink and paper. I wish to write to Captain Paul Boyton." The materials were given him and the following is a verbatim copy of the challenge sent by the accomplished English scholar to Paul:

[Image of obviously illegible gibberish]

Next morning Boyton returned to Florence and that evening while entertaining some friends in his room, one of the guests looked out at the window and remarked how much higher the river was than it had been when he started for Pisa. Some of the guests advanced the opinion that it would be impossible for him to go into the river while it was in such a flood. Paul, overhearing them, said: "Ladies and gentlemen, if you will step out on the porch and wait a few moments, I will enter the river and paddle through the city in order to show you that I am equally as safe in such water as I would be were it as smooth as glass."

While he was preparing for this short trip, the news spread over the city like wildfire and by the time he was ready, people lined either shore. When he proposed the trip, he had forgotten about the dam before alluded to, and did not know that the water was pouring over it in such torrents that it was extremely dangerous. He entered the raging current and was rapidly carried toward it. When he realized the danger he was approaching, it was too late to retreat, owing to the terrific power of the current that was bearing him to the falls. As he went over the sloping volume of water, he was met at the bottom by an immense back wave which drove him under. Where the clashing waves embraced each other, he was checked and held, being rolled like a log that is caught between a back and an undertow. Thousands of people crowded the banks in the vicinity of the pescaia and they gave Boyton up as lost. Men turned pale and women fainted. Now and again they could see an arm protruding from the dark, angry waters; then a leg and an end of his paddle which he had the presence of mind to retain. It was impossible to get a rope to him and certain death to attempt a rescue with a boat.

"Only God can save him now," yelled some excited Italian, "no man can do it."

The multitude felt there was nothing to be done but to stand helplessly by and watch him drown. And what were Boyton's thoughts? He stated afterwards: "I thought of it being Christmas eve. The news of my death would be telegraphed to New York, my mother would hear of it and it would make a sad Christmas for her." The voyager straggled with all the strength he possessed against the awful power of the contending waters and fortunately succeeded in throwing himself out on a big wave and was carried down. A great sigh of relief went up from the crowd which sounded like the rush of distant wind.

Soon after Paul was pulled from the river insensible. When he recovered from that adventure, King Victor Emanuel gave permission for him to appear in the Jardin Boboli. The excitement was so great during that appearance and the crowd so large that ticket takers were carried away from the gates, and though many thus entered free, several thousand francs were realized.

Paul was now the fashion in Italy. Songs were composed and sung in his honor at the theatres, brands of cigars and other articles were given his name; business men had their calendars for the new year printed with his adventures detailed on them, and the citizens of Meletti christened a lake after him. Managers of places of amusement advertised that he would be present at their entertainments in order to draw crowds, and everywhere could be heard the praises of the wonderful American.

From Florence Paul went to Rome, where he visited General Pescetto, Italian Minister of Marine, with whom he had a pleasant conversation, during which the meeting with his son on the Po was mentioned.

"What can I do for you?" cordially asked the General.

"Well," answered 'Paul, "my business is introducing my life-saving dress, which will be the means of preserving many lives on the coast as well as on the men-of-war you are now constructing."

"Ah, you have proved the value of your dress. I have no doubt of its efficiency; but our government has expended vast sums of money already for the benefit of shipwrecked mariners and we are not as rich as we would wish to be. The means we now have for saving life on the coast are considered sufficient, and in regard to adopting your dress on our men-of-war, I fear you do not understand the nature of the Italian sailor. If we placed a number of your dresses on the Duelio, for instance, or on any of our men-of-war, the sailors would reason that the vessels were not seaworthy and we would have much difficulty in persuading them to enlist."
"Suppose I could prove to you that it would be possible to slip under one of your men-of-war on a dark night and blow her to atoms. How would that be?"

"Ah," responded the General earnestly, "that is a different question. If you can prove that to me, I will call a commission to examine into it."

Ample proof was given as to the efficacy of the dress in the torpedo service, and to-day there are many drilled experts in the Italian navy, which serves to show how much more interest is manifested in life taking than in lifesaving. Arrangements were made for an exhibition in the bano del poplo. In preparing for this entertainment, Paul first experienced the manner most of the European artisans have of doing business and their original way of preparing bills for services rendered. It was necessary for him to engage a carpenter to build several small boats for use in the exhibition. Paul asked the landlord to assist him in making a contract with a workman. With the accommodating host's help, an agreement was made with a skilled worker in wood to build six little boats according to specifications given, for the sum of five lire each. The carpenter had the boats ready on time, and during the exhibition, constituted himself a sort of major domo, making himself very busy and very much in the way about the place, as though he had charge of the entire affair. At the close of the entertainment, he presented a bill for seventy-five lire, when according to his contract, it should have been but thirty lire. Paul refused to pay until the landlord should examine the account and pronounce it correct. When it was shown to that gentleman, he vigorously protested against its payment, pronouncing it robbery and compelling the carpenter to render an itemized account. Following is a copy of the itemized bill, which will be of interest to business men and artisans of other countries:

To six boats, per agreement................30 lire.
Wood for building.........................11
Nails......................................2
Labor and making..........................14
Pieces broken in bending...................5
Carrying boats to the bano.................2
Time lost while at exhibition.............10
Wine for poor boy who fell overboard........1

Total 75 lire

The above is a fair sample of how contracts are adhered to in many European countries. Paul paid the fellow the thirty lire that were due him, receiving the profane blessing of the irate builder. Boyton was just in time for the great Roman Carnival and had the pleasure, if such it may be called, of witnessing the spectacle of barbrie barbrie. This was cruel and dangerous sport—a horse race along the Corso, the principal thoroughfare in Rome; which is a narrow, winding street. The race was contested by five or six thoroughbred horses, nearly wild and very vicious. They were turned loose in the street without bridle or any other harness with the exception of a surcingle, from the sides of which hung like tassels, steel balls, with sharp, needle-like points projecting from their surface that served to prick and goad the animals to a frenzy of speed. The streets were lined with people and it was all the enormous force of guards could do to drive them out of danger to the sidewalks. The balconies and windows of the houses were also crowded. The start was made near the upper end of the city at the Place del Popolo, where anxious grooms held the struggling horses; until, at the firing of a cannon, the bridles were slipped and the frightened animals dashed madly down the street, with those wicked steel balls swinging in the air and cruelly beating their sides, spurring them to a terrific pace. Each horse bore a number and as immense sums of money are wagered, cannons were placed at intervals along the route which were fired a number of times to correspond with the number borne by the horse in the lead, thus indicating to the betters the number of the horse in front at the different stations. Perfect pandemonium reigned during this wild dash down the Corso. Men and women yelled as though they were mad, and the shrill voices of children were also heard above the roaring of the cannon.

At the end of the Corso a net was dropped across the street, into which the frenzied steeds plunged and were flung to the ground, a tangled and bleeding mass of noble horse-flesh. Some were killed outright and others were so maimed that they had to be dispatched to put them out of misery. More or less people were always killed at these barbarous races; but for some years the barbrie has been abolished.

While in the ancient city, Paul determined to make a voyage down the Tiber. He went up the river as far as he could get, to Orte. The distance from that town to Rome is about one hundred and ninety miles by river. News of his determination to try the Tiber having preceeded him to Orte, he was royally received by the authorities and populace. When the start was made, the mayor escorted him to the river, lustily blowing a horn all the way, like a fish peddler trying to attract attention. The Tiber is an uninteresting stream, running through the Roman Campagna, and is made up of great bends. He left Orte in the afternoon, and night came on terribly cold. Now and then he would get a cheer from people along the banks; but in a moment it was lost. He drove rapidly along all night without an adventure worth recording. About six o'clock next morning he was caught in an awkward manner in the branches of a tree that had washed into the stream and he only freed himself by cutting away the limbs with his knife, causing considerable delay. All day he drove energetically along, and the stream turned and twisted so much that he frequently passed the same village twice in swinging around great bends. At nightfall he came near frightening the life out of a shepherd. Not knowing where he was and hearing the bark of a dog he climbed up the bank to ascertain, if possible, his locality. He met the shepherd on top of the bank, who looked at him a moment and then scampered away across the plain as fast as his legs would carry him.

That night Paul was met by the Canottiere del Tevere, the leading boat club of Rome, and was accompanied by them for the rest of the journey. Next morning, when they neared Rome, they hauled up at a clubhouse for breakfast. For some miles before they reached the city, people came out on horseback and on foot, saluting them with vivas. At three o'clock they pulled into Rome and were welcomed by thousands of people, and Paul was agreeably astonished at hearing a band play Yankee Doodle in a house which was profusely decorated with American flags. In fact, the reception was something indescribable. People were crowded into every available space. A barge upset in the river, but all the occupants were saved. Boyton landed at Ripetta Grande and so great was the pressure of the throng that the iron band about the waist of his dress was crushed like an eggshell. No end of fetes followed, the citizens seeming to vie with one another as to which could give the most splendid entertainment.

Naples was next visited with the intention of crossing the famous bay. Paul arrived in that city in time for the carnival, and enjoyed seeing Victor Emanuel, that grim but good natured old king, open the festivities by driving through the streets and submitting to the bombardment of confetti. His majesty smiled and bowed as he passed along, throwing some of it back at those who were standing near. The confetti is made of plaster of Paris and easily crumbles to powder, as flour and it is thrown everywhere and at everybody by the gay, laughing people.

On the afternoon of February 16th, 1877, Boyton crossed on the steamer to Capri, having decided to start from that point. While on the island that afternoon, he visited the Blue Grotto, an opening in the island leading into a cave of rare beauty, which is daily visited by tourists. A boat passes through the entrance and directly the visitor is enshrouded in intense darkness; but the moment anything touches the water, the phosphorus causes it to light up a vivid, silver-like color. Paul put on his dress and paddled all through the wonderful grotto, the rubber appearing like a bright, silver armor as he agitated the water with his paddle.

At three o'clock next morning he started on his trip across the bay from the steamboat landing. Notwithstanding the early hour, all the inhabitants of the island were on hand to witness the start. To his surprise he found the effect of the water of the bay in the dark, the same as had been observed in the Blue Grotto. Even the fish darting about, would leave a phosphorescent trail.

When the sun rose that morning, Mt. Vesuvius loomed up before Paul in the clear atmosphere. It seemed very near and he thought he would reach

Naples before time. About nine o'clock, the bay became very rough and soon the blue waves covered him. He kept paddling on and on, yet the grim, smoke-covered mountain seemed no nearer. At three o'clock in the afternoon, he sighted a felucca bearing down on him. When near enough, he stood up in the water and hailed her. The occupants of the little vessel came to the rail, pointed at the unusual object in the water and then the great sail was veered around and they scudded swiftly away. Sailors on that bay have a superstition about picking up a dead body and they either supposed Paul was a drowned person or some mysterious denizen of the deep. At any rate they were too badly frightened to investigate. At five o'clock, the voyager was nearing Naples in a rough sea. The excursion boats went out but almost missed him. Sounding the bugle, he attracted their attention. He landed at the city at about seven o'clock before an enormous crowd, among whom were King Victor Emmanuel, the sindaco with the other authorities of Naples. The usual banquet was prepared and it was a late hour that night before the ceremonies were concluded. The fishermen of the city presented Paul with an address signed by over four thousand people connected with the water, and Marianne Aguglia, Comtesse Desmouceaux published a poem commemorating the event. Victor Emmanuel invited Paul to exhibit before him in the arsenal, or military port. The King was accompanied by his morganatic wife, the Countess of Miraflores. He was delighted with the performance, more particularly with the torpedo display. One of the pieces of timber from the explosion fell near his feet; he laughed merrily about it, while the Countess drew away in alarm. After the exhibition, Boyton divested himself of the rubber dress and stood clad in a well-worn naval uniform. He was escorted to the presence of the royal pair by Admiral del Carette. The King asked Paul many questions in his quaint, Piedmontese French, and then observing that the voyager was fatigued, he ordered two goblets of wine to be brought in, which good health and fortune were pledged. Then an officer was ordered to bring the cross, which the King himself pinned on Paul's blue shirt, knighting him with the Cross of the Order of the Crown of Italy saying:

"You are a brave man and deserve this token of our appreciation."

CHAPTER XIII.

In several engagements about Naples, enormous sums of money were taken. Then Boyton proceeded to Messina. Before leaving Naples, he had made up his mind to attempt the dreaded straits of that name, and dare the dangers of the noted whirlpools of Scylla and Charybdis. Every one cheerfully assured him that the attempt would result in death, for beside the dangers of the whirlpools, the straits were infested with sharks.

Arriving at Messina, he determined to test the report of sharks. At early morning he went to the market place and procured a large piece of meat which he took out near the fort, where the sharks were said to be numerous. He threw a piece of the meat into the water and it slowly sank. Paul, as he saw it going down, believed that the stories of the sharks were exaggerated; but suddenly it was drawn out of sight. Another piece was thrown in and had scarcely touched the surface when there was a rush and a swirl and the meat was snapped up in a twinkling. An old hat was thrown in next and it was torn to shreds in a second. This undeniable proof that sharks were plentiful in the straits, made Paul feel very blue, as he did not fancy giving up an undertaking after once setting his mind to it.

It was noised about that Boyton would attempt to swim the straits. The people of the city and surrounding country grew excited, and all manner of bets were made on the result. One night as Boyton sat gloomily at a small table in the corner of a café, he overheard a man wager his oxen that the American would not attempt the passage and that he could not cross if he did. Though much disheartened, when Paul heard this, as well as many more doubts expressed as to his ability to accomplish the feat, he determined to attempt it at all hazards. An old legend is extant among the fishermen and peasants of the locality that the only human being who ever crossed the straits without the aid of a boat, was St. Francisco, who, being pursued by his enemies, spread his cloak on the water and stepping on it was wafted across without harm and escaped. So the proposed attempt of Boyton was looked upon as certain death.

After deciding to try the passage, Paul engaged a felucca, owned by the most expert spearsman in those waters, to accompany him, and another for the invited guests and newspaper men. These boats were ready on the morning of March 16th, 1877, and sailed from Messina for the coast of Calabria, from which point the start was to be made. They arrived there at seven o'clock the same morning. The party consisted of several prominent men of Messina, among them the editor of the Gazette. Everybody was armed for sharks, the editor being especially well equipped for slaughtering these wolves of the deep and very bold in his assertions of how he would protect Boyton from their attacks.

At a small, scattered village on the Calabrian side, the felucca containing Paul and his guests landed. The dress and those on board were put ashore and preparations were at once made for the start. A sirocco was blowing at the time, setting a heavy tide in the direction of the whirlpool of Scylla, or the Faro, as they call it there. The sea grew rougher while the little party stood on the beach and as Boyton was dressing the most anxious one in the group was the enthusiastic editor. His nerve was slowly oozing out at his finger ends.

The inhabitants of the village began crowding down to the shore and when they learned what was going on, an old white-haired man approached the voyager, and in the most earnest manner, addressed him in the Calabrian dialect: "Don't go, don't go," he cried. "I had a boy such as you, who was lost out there and the devils of the straits will get you."

The appeal of the old man was interpreted to Paul and was the only occurrence of the day that had a tendency to upset his nerves.

The expert spearsman had arranged a place on his boat where he could stand and harpoon any sharks that might attack the adventurer, while the guests on the other craft thought they were pretty well fixed to keep the monsters off. Everything being ready, the felucca backed in from her cable to get the guests aboard. All were safely on except the bold editor. He was pale and his knees were knocking together. His courage was gone and he persisted in remaining on shore, until one of the sailors lifted him bodily aboard.

The sea was very rough when Boyton stepped into it. He struck away as fast as he could and both feluccas kept a sharp lookout. He reached mid-channel without encountering any danger, and stopped to look about and take his bearings. He perceived that he was nearing Charybdis. On looking around, just as the foremost boat rose on a huge wave, he saw what he thought to be a shark directly under it. He pulled his knife and prepared for an attack. He was rather nervous, and the feluccas seemed an awful distance away. He called out that a shark was in sight. Immediately, as Paul was afterward informed, the brave editor dropped on his knees and began to pray that they might not all be swallowed up. The shark was darting from side to side of the boat, but spying Boyton's black figure, it turned on its side and swam for him. Paul braced for the attack, and when the monster was close enough he ripped it under the mouth, and in going down it struck him a severe blow in the side with its tail, then disappeared, leaving a trail of blood in its wake. Boyton made away as fast as he could, glad to escape the monster so easily. He was not attacked again. The tide was carrying him right to the place where he had first discovered the presence of sharks; but a number of boats came off from Messina, their occupants yelling and splashing the water, which served to frighten the brutes away.

On the outer edge of the whirlpool of Charybdis, which is a great eddy caused by a jutting point of land on which a fort is built, and on the ebb tide strong enough to swamp a boat, Paul worked for one hour without advancing a single yard; the people all the while expecting to see him swallowed up. He held out, however, and at last landed safely at Messina. The American ships laying there dipped their flags in salute, and the entire population was filled with astonishment at the successful termination of the feat. The valiant editor of the Gazette, after feeling himself safely ashore, became quite a lion, graphically picturing the adventures of the day to admiring crowds. From the wharf to the city hall, where a reception had been arranged, the streets on both sides were lined with troops to protect Paul from the crowds. On arriving at the hall, he fainted and an examination showed that three of his ribs had been broken by the shark's tail and that the steel band of his dress was bent close to his body by the great force of the blow. He was conveyed to his hotel where he remained for two weeks until he was quite strong again. For some time after the attack by the shark, Boyton took life easy. He visited Mt. Etna, Catalana, Syracuse and other places of interest in Sicily. At Syracuse, he spent a lazy week. It is one of the dirtiest town in the world; but Paul enjoyed everything he saw. When on the street, he was generally followed by a crowd of boys who were trying to sell all sorts of little trinkets. One of them especially, was very persistent in trying to dispose of an ancient coin of the Ceasars, which he guaranteed to be very valuable and for which he would take the paltry sum of ten lire. Boyton finally told him that he knew all about the coin, and would give two lire to find the man who made it. The young villain mysteriously whispered the information, which later on was found to be correct. Some of the boys would get him ten fine oranges for one cent on being given an extra penny for going on the errand.

It was a favorite amusement for Paul and his agent to go out on the road in hope of encountering brigands, who were reported numerous and bold. They would enter some low cabriolet that was suspected of harboring these knights of the mountains. With carbines concealed under their coats, they would make an ostentatious display of rolls of Italian paper money, expecting that some of the robbers would follow them out on the road and stir up a little excitement. The brigands were either too busy at something else, or they regarded the American as rather too dangerous a customer to attack for they never materialized. Before leaving the old town, the authorities induced him to give an exhibition, which was witnessed by the entire population, brigands included. Just before the entertainment, Boyton hung his rubber-suit on a stone wall in the sun, to dry. When the crowd had gathered, he hurried on with the dress; but flung it off with much greater rapidity, when he found it was full of the little green lizards which abound on the island.

When the P. & O. steamer arrived, Paul and his agent embarked for Malta, where they had their first clash with the authorities. There is a peculiar law in that sleepy old town which prohibits the posting of any bills larger than a small sheet, about the size of note paper. The night after their arrival, they plastered the town with one sheet posters, which looked to the natives bigger than one hundred sheet stands would in this country. Next morning the inhabitants stood aghast at the audacity of the Americans in doing such an unheard of thing. They were summoned before the Governor and the enormity of their offense solemnly revealed to them; but owing to the plea of ignorance of the law, they were discharged, and ordered to take down the bills as quickly as possible. In obedience to the mandate of the Governor, they employed a sleepy-eyed native to do the work, with instructions to take his time. It required two days to undo the work of one night, but the authorities were satisfied and the exhibition was the best advertised of any that had been in Malta for years.

Paul was a great favorite with the boatmen and fishermen of Malta, and spent all of his leisure time with these acquaintances, going fishing with them almost daily. The boatmen are peculiar and their boats are queer affairs, every one having a large eye painted on each side of the bow. Paul asked a fisherman why eyes were painted on the boats, and he gravely replied:

"How could the poor things see without eyes?"

Not one of these men could be induced to go out in a boat that had no eyes painted on her.

From Malta, Paul went to Tunis, and on landing there, was genuinely surprised. The passengers and their baggage were loaded into boats for transfer to shore, nearing which, they were met by crowds of bare legged natives who waded out as far as they could and when a boat was near enough, they grabbed the baggage and trotted off with it, regardless of the remonstrances of the owners. At the custom house, the luggage was found; each native sitting stoically on whatever he had chanced to capture, with an air of absolute proprietorship. After it was passed by the custom authorities, it was carried to the hotel by the howling mob, where, with many kicks and cuffs administered by the landlord, it was reclaimed. Paul gave an exhibition at this place on which the awe stricken Moors gazed in wonder. He then returned to Italy in which country he gave exhibitions with extraordinary success. While working north, he received an invitation to visit Lake Trasmene, celebrated in Roman history. All the villages about the lake joined in a demonstration that was to take place at Pastgnano. Boyton's program was to cross from the old town of Castiglioni de Lago to the former place. The mountaineers living near the lake came out in queer boats loaded to the water's edge, in which they followed him across. He observed the wind rising and knowing that the heavily laden boats would not live in any kind of rough weather, he warned them and begged them to go ashore; but very few heeded him. Scarcely had he landed when an Italian officer rushed in to where he was undressing, excitedly shouting:

"Oh, go back. Go back. They are drowning out there."

As quickly as possible, Paul returned to the lake and saw that one of the boats had swamped. The three men who occupied it were drowned and could not be found. The accident put a damper on the festivities of the day. The bands of music were hushed and much sorrow expressed for the unfortunates. The Syndaco, however, invited Boyton to a dinner, and they were enjoying themselves very well, considering the circumstances, when a delegation of the people called and made the statement that a majority of the crowd was dissatisfied. Many were from a great distance, and demanded to see L'uomo Pesce, a name they had given to Boyton, meaning "Man Fish." Some of the leading men of the town advised Paul that it would be better for him to give some kind of an entertainment, otherwise there might be a riot. So much against his will, he went out and gave an exhibition, before the bodies of the poor fellows were recovered. The mountaineers were satisfied, however, and went to their homes with all sorts of ideas of the "Man Fish." That night after sundown, the bodies were found and the weird cries of the relatives rang dismally through the streets until morning.

Next day Paul and his agent remained over to pay their last respects and attend the funeral. They witnessed the peculiar ceremonies of the Misericordia, a society that has for its object the burial of the dead. They wear long, white robes, covering their entire person, with holes cut for the eyes, nose and mouth. They formed a grim looking procession, and as they turned those expressionless faces toward one, they sent a cold shiver down the spine. Regardless of this uncanny feeling, Boyton and his friend followed the procession into the church and by so doing, gained the good will of the villagers, who assured them that they were in no way to blame for the accident. The entire receipts of the entertainment, with a liberal addition, were presented to the families of the drowned men.

CHAPTER XIV.

Exhibitions followed in Milan, Turin, Genoa and other cities of northern Italy, then the travelers passed into France, to the headwaters of the Rhone. Paul had selected this river for his next voyage. With the intention of making the entire stream from its source to the Mediterranean, he visited Geneva, in Switzerland. Here he discovered that it would be impossible to start from the lake, as by doing so he would be carried into the great cavern known as Per du Rhone, in which the entire river disappears and makes a mysterious and unexplored passage under the mountain. He was anxious to try the underground current through the cavern and did not give up the idea until several experiments had convinced him that it would be foolhardy to make the attempt. He stationed one of his assistants at the point where the Rhone again comes to the surface and with the help of others, miles above at the mouth of the cavern, he sent in logs of wood, bladders and other buoyant objects, none of which were observed to pass through by the watcher below. The last and deciding experiment, was sending in a pair of live ducks and these, also were lost. He then concluded to start below the cavern and selected the little village of Seyssel as the best point to prepare for the voyage.

The Rhone when high is one of the most rapid rivers in the world, and Paul's trip from Seyssel to the Mediterranean was the swiftest he ever made. The entire distance is five hundred kilometers, or three hundred miles, and his actual running time was sixty hours. He was enabled to push along at this unusual rate on account of the freshets swelling the river to a flood. He passed in safety the perilous rapids of the Saute du Rhone; but near the frontier of France he had a marvelous escape from a frightful death. The authorities on the frontier are kept busy watching for smugglers who work contraband goods from Switzerland into France. A quantity of goods were smuggled through the lines by floating them down the river at night, and in order to catch such articles the officers of the Duane stretched a strong gate of chain work across the river just at the border. This gate is thickly set with sharp iron hooks which hold the packages that float against them. Paul was not informed of this dangerous bar to his progress. As he neared the frontier village he noticed the utmost excitement amongst the crowds congregated on the banks. From their wild gesticulations, he could see they were shouting; but he thought they were simply cheering him and continued his rapid approach on the swollen stream. When near enough he saw that their faces were pale and they were making motions for him to stop; but the current was so swift that such a thing was impossible. He was irresistibly carried along by the terrible force. He next noticed several guards rush out on the bridge, who, throwing off their coats, began quickly to turn heavy cranks, and then he saw the sheet of glistening hooks rising slowly from the water. Now he understood why they had tried to stop him. To be thrown with all that force against those hooks meant not only certain death, but fearful mutilation.

Swiftly he drew near the wicked looking points and slowly, oh, so slowly they rose above the water. The people watched with nervous dread. Could they be hoisted high enough before he reached them? Many a silent prayer was murmured that the guards would be successful. Bravely those men strained every muscle; but the thing was unwieldy and the work was slow—fearfully slow. The terror of the people was depicted on their faces. They now saw that the last row of hooks was nearing the surface, but Boyton was almost upon them. The panting and perspiring guards redoubled their efforts. Paul swept under and the lower line of hooks barely allowed him to pass unscathed. A great shout went up from the crowd.

The current at that point was running fully twelve miles an hour. Boyton was asked how he felt when going so rapidly: "Such lively motion," he said, "greatly excites you. Your heart beats fast; you feel as if you had enormous power, whereas you have no power at all. There is something in the danger that pleases and thrills you."

After passing under the smuggler's chain gate, his course ran between lines of hills which fringe the banks of the river. He could see here and there on the slopes, an old woman with a cow. Every cow seemed to have a woman attendant in that country. Now and again one of them would catch sight of Paul as he sped along. For a second she would gaze at the unusual object and then move off—she and her cow. One old dame happened to be nearer the water's edge than the others, the voyager saluted by standing up in the water and shouting:

"Bon jour"

She crossed herself, and fled.

Next morning he was nearing the rapids of the Saute du Rhone, and inquired of the people he saw: "How far is the Saute?"

"About two kilometers," was the answer.

"Which side shall I take for safety?"

"The left."

The next one told him to take the right, and at last he was advised to keep in the middle.

Finding he could gain no reliable information, he stood upright and looked about to see, if possible, what the danger was. Ahead of him was a rapid, running amid big, black rocks and crossed by a bridge which was crowded with people. It was too late to think of stopping himself and be swept into and through it like an arrow; but at the bottom he was carried against a wall of rock and nearly blinded. He hung there for a few moments to recover himself, and again felt the current bearing him away almost as fast as he approached. He was kindly received all along, and had he accepted one-third of the invitations to entertainments, some months would have been required to finish the voyage. On one lonely stretch, he saw a solitary countryman standing on the bank.

"Ho, ho; my good friend," he shouted.

"Who is there?" asked the startled farmer.

"The devil."

"Where are you going?"

"To Lyons."

"Well, get along, then; you are going home."

Probably the farmer had visited Lyons, and was not pleased with that city.

Paul entered Lyons at two o'clock, having been twenty-four hours under way. He was tendered a splendid reception and presented with several rich souvenirs. Resuming the journey, he traveled at the rate of fifteen miles an hour and many people accompanied him in boats for quite a distance down the stream. At places along the route, the banks were broken, the river flooded the lowlands, and he was frequently carried among groves of trees, requiring no little exertion to keep from being pounded against them by the force of the current. He paddled that night and all the next day and night without meeting unusual adventure, when he reached Pont St. Esprit, with its long stone bridge, through one arch of which, the river rushes with much force. The next day ended this rapid voyage, as he landed at Arles in safety. The entire population was out to receive him. Not thinking of his exhausted condition, a force of gendarmes who had been sent by the Mayor to escort him to the hotel de Vine, turned a deaf ear to his demands for a carriage, but insisted on his marching through the hot, dusty street, encased in the heavy rubber dress, carrying his little boat and paddle so the people would have a good chance to see him. The gendarmes meant everything in kindness; but in that case, kindness coupled with ignorance, resulted in Paul's arriving at the hotel barely able to walk; he expressed his gratitude in rather vigorous terms.

From Arles, Boyton visited Monaco on the invitation of Monsieur Blanc, who was then at the head of the great gambling institutions of that place. At the instance of this world-famous gambler, Paul gave an exhibition for which he was presented with two-thousand-five-hundred francs by his host and his agent received five-hundred francs. The evening after the exhibition, Monsieur Blanc escorted the voyager through the sumptuous gambling palace. Thinking to please Monsieur, who had been so generous with him, Paul thought he would wager a few francs at one of the numerous rouge et noir tables and was proceeding to put down a Napoleon, when he was observed by his host whose attention had been distracted for a moment.

"Don't you do it," said he quickly, grasping Paul by the arm, "there are fools enough here without your becoming one."

Monsieur drew his guest away from the table and took him into the private office where rouleaux of gold were stacked in great piles about the walls.

One of the queer superstitions of gamblers was vividly impressed on Boyton at this place. Leaving Monsieur Blanc's office he sauntered about through the rooms, deeply interested in the exciting scenes before him. It became noised around that he was in the place, and some one pointed him out. He was immediately besieged at almost every step by ladies who had been playing with ill success. They represented almost every nationality, French, American, Russian, English and Italian. Looking upon him as a lucky man, they tried to persuade him to play for them.

"Ah, Captain Boyton," one would say, "you are a man of great luck. If you put this bet down for me, I know I shall win."

That was the request made by several, when they had an opportunity to speak to him. One or two assistants would have been needed to accommodate all of them.

Leaving Monaco, Paul gave successful exhibitions in the principal cities of southern France and was honored with several decorations. At Lyons he gave an entertainment for the benefit of the poor in the Park of the Golden Head, at which fifteen thousand francs were realized. One of the handsomest ladies of the city, donned a suit and went into the water with him. As a mark of appreciation, the people presented him with a magnificent poinard, sheathed in a richly carved scabbard, ornamented with a handle of artistic design, weighing, with the exception of the blade of fine steel, ten pounds solid silver.

Exhibitions were given through Belgium until November 15th, 1877, In Brussels they took one thousand dollars a day for four days, and at a benefit for the poor given in the lake of the Bois de Cambrai, under the patronage of King Leopold, at which the Royal family was present, an enormous sum resulted. The king bestowed on Paul the medal of the First Order of Life Savers of Belgium.

November 17th, he began a voyage down the Somme, which occupied two days. He started at Amiens. On the evening of the first day, just before reaching Ponte Remy, where he intended to stop for the night, he was surprised at receiving a charge of shot. While he was drifting around a point above that place, a duck hunter who was concealed in the bushes mistook his feet for a pair of ducks and fired at them. Luckily the shot struck the heavy rubber soles of his dress and no damage was done. Boyton rose up in the water with a torrent of forcible comments in English, and the frightened sportsman rapidly disappeared in the darkness.

Starting early next morning, he arrived at Abbyville in the evening, where the customary generous reception awaited him. Next day he returned to Amiens where he gave an entertainment, and thence to Paris. He had a new tender built in the latter city, in anticipation of a voyage down the Loire. He christened the new tender the Isabel Alvarez du Toledo, in honor of a fair maid of Italy. He began the voyage of the Loire, December 8th, 1877, at Orleans, to make a run to Nantes, a distance of four hundred and nine miles. The weather was cold and miserable. The river is bad, numerous shifting sand bars making it difficult to keep the channel, and added to this are many beds of treacherous quicksands. The lowlands, through which the course of the river runs, leave a free vent for the wind to strike its surface, making it desirable for sail boats to navigate. They are mostly wood and provision boats, flat bottomed and built somewhat on the plan of canal boats. They carry an enormous square sail on a single mast, larger than any sail used on the greatest ships.

At nine o'clock in the morning the start was made from Orleans and Paul arrived at Blois in the evening, where he came very near having his arm broken by coming in contract with a pile as he was leaving, so instead of running all night as he had intended doing, he hauled up and remained at Blois, much to the satisfaction of the citizens who entertained him in the most pleasant manner.

The following afternoon he started for an all night run, in order to make up for lost time. At nightfall the weather grew intensely cold and ice soon covered all exposed parts of his dress. A small, but powerful lamp on the bow of the tender, gave him plenty of light and that evening furnished the means of some amusement. Along the frozen road which follows the river bank for quite a distance, he heard the clattering of the sabots of a belated peasant, who was singing to keep his courage up. Paul darkened the lamp by putting a piece of rubber over it, and when the profile of the peasant stood clear between him and the sky, he suddenly removed the rubber and turned, the light full on the man, at the same time sounding an unearthly blast on his bugle. The startled peasant uttered no sound; but the distant clinking of his sabots down the road, told how badly he was frightened.

About four o'clock that morning, Paul felt his dress touching bottom, the current slackened, and he knew he had wandered into a false channel. With some difficulty, he assumed an upright position and the moment he did so, found his legs grasped as in a vise.

He was caught in the quicksand.

With a feeling of horror he felt himself settling, settling in the treacherous sands, until he was slicked down nearly to the neck, his face almost even with the surface, the dark water gliding by him like some slimy serpent into the night.

The tender swung round with her bow pointing toward him, the strong light from the bull's eye glaring him in the face with its blinding rays. The little boat seemed to realize the awful situation and she tugged at the cord which fastened her to the dress, as though struggling to free him. From the moment the sands were felt, he' had worked to free himself, only to find that the effort sunk him deeper. He began to think he was not going to get out; that his time had come and not a trace on earth would be left to tell of his dreadful end. But his was not a nature to give up until the last gasp. The thought struck him that there was some chance for life by fully inflating the dress which, would have a tendency to lighten and give him more buoyancy. He seized the air tubes and in the desperation of a final hope, he blew for his life. He could feel himself lighting as the chambers filled. He had the dress inflated almost to bursting and with a powerful effort, he threw himself on his back. He was lifted clear and moved away on the gliding water, continuing the lonely journey with a prayer of thanksgiving in his heart.

At ten o'clock next morning he arrived at Tours, with nerves considerably shattered, and he accepted the invitation of that municipality to stop for refreshments. The kindness of the citizens and the officials was overwhelming, but he remained only long enough to become thoroughly rested when he again sought the river.

At every village during the entire trip, he was given a warm reception. The weather being cold, the mayors insisted on his drinking hot, highly spiced wine, and he was also invariably greeted with the question asked in all countries and all towns, American as well as European: "Are you not cold?"

The little boat was loaded down with supplies and invitations were continuous from chateau and cottage to stop and partake of refreshment.

Sometimes he would run far into the night before hauling up, but usually his rest was broken by bands of music turning out to serenade him, and at one place, where there was no band, an enthusiastic admirer blew a hunting horn most of the night under his window. It was a frightful but well intended serenade.

When he reached Ancenes he was met by a crowd, headed by the mayor with a liberal supply of hot wine. From this point a boatman who was employed in placing stakes indicating the changes of current, for the guidance of navigators, insisted on accompanying Paul. He had been on a protracted spree and proved annoying.

"I know the river well," he said, "and will pilot you down."

"I assure you there is no necessity for a pilot," Paul answered, "I have journeyed so far without one and can go the rest of the way."

He could not get rid of the fellow that easily, so he concluded to try some other plan. After they had proceeded a short distance Boyton asked the persistent boatman to have a drink, at the same time handing him a bottle of very strong wine that had been given him to use in case he needed a stimulant. The fellow, already half intoxicated, absorbed most of the contents and was soon maudlin. He ran his boat around and across Boyton to the latter's great annoyance. He became drowsy, however, and finally fell into a deep sleep. That was the opportunity Paul desired. He seized the anchor that was in the bow of the fellow's boat and dropped it in the stream. The boat swung around and hung there, and Paul paddled away. When quite a distance down he heard faint cries of "Captain, Captain, where are you?" The boatman thought he was drifting; but Boyton never saw him again.

Below Ancenes Paul was met by Jules Verne, the distinguished novelist, who came up the river on a boat rowed by some of his sailors. He accompanied the voyager all the way to Nantes, where the trip terminated. The two men became great friends, the navigator enjoying the novelist's hospitality on his yacht and also at his residence in Nantes. Monsieur Verne afterward made use of the life-saving dress to illustrate scenes in a novel entitled "The Tribulations of a Chinaman." Nantes was reached eight days from the time of starting. Excursion steamers met them and fired salutes, The Hospitaliers des Sauveteurs Bretons, the leading life-saving society of France, elected Paul an officer of the first rank and gave him diplomas and medals.

CHAPTER XV.

Until January 15th, Paul remained in Nantes, then he went to Madrid. The weather was very cold. It was his intention to make a voyage on some of the Spanish rivers. On looking over the country, he selected the Tagus as being the least known and promising more adventure than any of the others. When it was announced that he was going to attempt that river, several of the-leading residents of Madrid endeavored to dissuade him; he received letters from many prominent people telling him that the river was not navigable, running as it did, through a wild, mountainous country, and full of waterfalls. He concluded to take a look at the stream himself and so form his own opinion. For this purpose he went to Toledo and found there a narrow, turbulent river, rushing over great masses of rock. He hired a mule and rode several miles down its banks and discovered no improvement. In making inquiries of the natives about the character of the river, the invariable answer was, "Mucho malo, Senor; mucho malo." "Very bad, sir; very bad."

Boyton was far from liking the looks of the river; but made up his mind to try it anyhow, especially as everyone told him he could not do it. After deciding on a course, he returned to Madrid and witnessed the fetes attending the marriage of King Alfonso and Queen Mercedes. The young King took great interest in the proposed voyage; he sent word over the country that the American was the guest of all Spain, and requested his people to receive him hospitably. Before leaving Madrid to begin the perilous undertaking, the Minister of the Interior gave Boyton maps of the river and all the information concerning it he possessed, which was surprisingly little: The maps were glaringly incorrect, as was afterward learned. Many towns that the maps located on the river were not near it.

When all was ready Paul's agent and baggage were sent to Lisbon to await the termination of the voyage. Paul returned to Toledo to make final preparations for the trip, which was one never before attempted. In fact, as far as was known, the river had never been navigated from source to mouth. It is three thousand five hundred feet above sea level at Toledo, which accounts for its rapid descent. On his return to the famous old city, Boyton was met by an aid-de-camp of the governor, who tendered the hospitality of that official, which was gratefully accepted for one day. That day was spent in visiting interesting points. The next morning, Thursday, January 31st, 1878, Paul drove to the river through the Gate of the Sun, and found a crowd of people assembled to see him start. In a few moments he was in the water, and the people cheered lustily as he began energetically to ply his paddle. As he turned the bend at the end of the first half mile, he took his last look at the stately Alcazar, away on the Crest of the hills, and at the ruins of the Moorish mills on the riverside below. Onward, and the bright, sunlit vision faded from his view.

"Now that I was started," said Paul, detailing an account of the wondrous journey, "I felt easier and stopped at noon to partake of a light dinner. I knew I was in for a tough job and made up my mind to go through with it. The river ran all over the country and was as changeable in temper as a novelist's heroine. Sometimes it was a mile wide, running slowly, with as calm and smooth a surface as a lake. Again, at the next bend it would dart toward a range of hills, and instead of going around them as its previously erratic course led me to expect, it would plough straight through the solid rocks. Then it would become as narrow as a canal, deep and rapid as a mill race, and in some places hurried along with the speed of an express train. The country was utterly wild, and it was not an unusual thing to paddle from morning until night without seeing a human being. As I knew nothing of the river except that I was bound for Lisbon, it may be imagined that I was not perfectly easy in my mind, I did not know but that the next angle in a canyon might land me in a whirlpool or over a fall.

"A great majority of the peasants do not read and were therefore ignorant of my undertaking. They are somewhat superstitious and my first adventure was with two of them. It was some hours after I left Toledo that I spied these men. They were great, hulking fellows, engaged in rolling a large stump up the steep hill, rising from the bank of the river. Slipping quietly along the surface, I got close behind them without their seeing me. When I hailed them, they gave me one startled look, released their hold on the stump which crashed down to the river, while they ran up and disappeared in the recesses of the hill. They never stopped to look the second time.

"I thought I would reach Peubla the first night; but owing to the extraordinary bends of the river, nightfall found me in a terribly rough portion of the country. I kept dashing from waterfall to waterfall, from rapid to rapid, until two o'clock in the morning, when the barking of a dog caused me to haul in. It was intensely cold and I was very tired. I blew a blast on my bugle and some very rough looking men came down to the bank. They proved to be shepherds and very kindly took me to their hut, which was not far from the water. They had the queerest way of keeping fire I ever saw. It was made of straw, the embers banked in such a way that there appeared to be only a black mass; but when they blew on the mass, a red glow would blush from it, throwing out considerable heat. Over this fire, they cooked a little soup for me. I remained in the hut until morning, stretching out on the floor for a little rest, while they stood about, speaking their mountain patois which I could not understand. I left them early in the morning, passing through wild mountain scenery and seeing no signs of habitation. No railroad or telegraph lines cross the river until near Lisbon and there was no way for me to get word to my friends. I arrived at Peubla at twelve o'clock and owing to the fact that I ran on to an old, broken bridge which cut my dress, I was compelled to haul up. The Alcalde was out in his high, picturesque cart, drawn by a tandem team of mules. I accepted his invitation, and was driven up through the olive groves to his house, followed by crowds of people. That night there was a sort of entertainment given in my honor and having no clothing with me except the heavy suit of underwear; I had to borrow a suit from the Alcalde in order to be presentable. The women of that place were most gracious and the girls as pretty as pictures. The Alcalde's little daughter took an interest in me. She talked to me a great deal, and in fact I could understand her Spanish much better than I could the adults. What a pretty little thing she was—a perfect type of Spanish beauty. She tried her best to deter me from continuing my voyage; but next morning she went to the river to see me start. In fact the entire village was there. When I was about to step into the water and was bidding her adieu, she pressed a small religious medal into my band, saying:

"Oh, I am so afraid you will never get to Lisbon. Take this, it will help you through, The Blessed Madonna will protect you from danger."

"I kissed the little one good bye and slipped into the water amid the vivas of the crowd. I was much grieved to hear, on reaching Lisbon, that the little girl died a few days after my departure.

"Nothing of interest occurred during the day except that it was very cold and rough and a snow storm was raging. On Sunday morning I arrived at Talavera, where the kindness of the people was so great I was compelled to leave the water and rest for awhile. From there the river ran through a lower country; but wound about so that I could never see more than a quarter of a mile ahead anywhere. There was a continual change of current, now very rapid and again sluggish and smooth. Just below the town is a water fall of considerable proportions and a great crowd had gone down there to see me shoot over. In a spirit of bravado, I stood up when near the brink and was hurled over head first. Had I hit a rock, it would have killed me. The people cheered, thinking that was the way I always went over them, but I tell you I made up my mind never to try the experiment again.

"It was not long until the land began to rise higher and higher, or rather, as it appeared to me, the river seemed to sink lower and lower and settle down among the great hills. I could not tell from the maps how I was working and I was anxious to see anyone in the hope that I could get some information. During Monday I swept on a flying current around a point of rock and was glad to catch sight of two men on the bank. One stood on the ground surrounded by a group of sheep, the other was up in a tree with a knife, lopping off the young limbs, throwing them to his companion who distributed them to the sheep. I hailed them with the cry of 'Hey, brother.' The man in the tree looked around and on discovering my black figure in the water, helplessly let go all holds and fell to the ground. His companion was startled; but when, recovering from the shock, I was pointed out, he ran to the bank, yelled something that seemed to be a warning and then both disappeared. As I passed on, I saw why he had shouted. A young, gipsy-like girl stood on a shelf of rock surrounded by goats. As the current was carrying me toward her, she gave a cry of alarm and faced me, the long-bearded goats doing the same. They formed a beautiful picture. Not wishing to frighten her, I called out some reassuring word in Spanish, and to show that she was not frightened, as were her male protectors, she seized a big stone and raising it defiantly over her head, awaited my approach. As I passed, I waved her an adieu and then she dropped the stone and fled up the mountain followed by her goats.

"All day I picked my way cautiously along, using every energy to avoid the varied shaped boulders which filled the river. At one time I appeared to shoot down a very steep hill. I was hemmed in by huge rocks that rose like a high wall on either side and there was no possible way to get out. The thought struck me that I was going into some subterranean passage, the perpendicular walls seeming to close in and swallow up the entire river. I was swept down by the mighty, though narrow current, and was beginning to feel sure that I was being carried into some underground rapids, when I was suddenly dumped into a deep pool, where the course of the river was running smooth and placidly along almost at right angles with the rapids above. At this abrupt turn, evidences of former floods were plain. Immense rocks were cut and carved in spiral columns as skillfully as any sculptor could have chiseled them. Great flocks of wild black ducks peculiar to the Tagus, were continually rising at my approach.

"At ten o'clock that night, hearing the heavy roar of rapids below and the river becoming wilder, I decided to stop until daylight. I crept cautiously in shore until I found an opening and there landed. There was no wood to build a fire and I laid for several hours in my dress. At daybreak I resumed the voyage and it looked as though I was penetrating the very bowels of the mountains, whose crests loomed high in the sky. I soon discovered the cause of the roar that had arrested my progress the night before. It was an ugly rapid, madly fighting sharp, broken rocks and I was dashed in amongst them. In trying to make a passage to escape a back water, something like that I had gone through on the Arno, at Florence, I turned so quickly that the little tender was thrown into the vortex on one side, tearing loose from my belt, while I was rapidly carried down the other. I never saw her again and what was more, I was left without provisions of any kind.

"That afternoon the river increased in speed and, dashed along at a mad rate. Once in a while, as I wheeled around some sharp bend, I could hear a sullen roar that plainly indicated the presence of falls below; but it seemed so far away that I paid but little attention to it. I kept driving steadily along, enjoying the exhilaration of the rapid pace, when my attention was attracted by the report of a gun. Looking up I saw a guarda civil, the gendarme of Spain, who held his carbine aloft and vigorously waved his hat with the other hand as I shot by. The current increased and the roar below became more audible. Going around another bend I saw a number of people on the bank waving their hats with a downward motion. That is the signal used in Spain when you are desired to approach. I misunderstood it, and thought it meant for me to take the other side, which I did and found I was in a current from which I could not extricate myself. Another sharp, turn and the village of Puente del Arzobispo came into sight with the heavy spray from the falls rising high in the air. The roar was like the deep rumbling of thunder when near at hand. I paid no attention to the shouts of the people to stop, for I saw could not possibly get out of the current, so I exerted myself to pass the falls safely. I saw where the water sank on the brink and I knew that was the course of the channel, and I also knew that my only chance of safety was to reach that point. All my energies were directed to it and in an instant I was on the brink of, a series of falls, tumbling from ledge to ledge like the steps of a colossal staircase. Fortunately I struck the deep channel—my only safe course. I was covered with foam and spray and could not see. All I could do was to trust to Providence and the depth of water, and I shortly found myself twisting around in a great pool below. Half stunned and almost smothered by frequent submerging and the weight of the volume of water that had fallen on me, I drifted helplessly toward the bank. The next thing I remembered was hearing sounds above me and a hand reaching down and grasping me, while a voice in French said:

"You live!"

"It's about all I do," was my answer.

Then strong arms hauled me out on the bank. The one who had addressed me was a priest, and through the midst of a madly excited crowd he escorted me up the street to the palace of the archbishop, a quaint old building, almost in ruins. Here every possible kindness was extended from the civil, military and religious authorities. At the banquet tendered me I was dressed in a suit of clothes half clerical, half military; but I enjoyed it as well as my tired bones would permit. I excused myself as early as I could and went to bed with the intention of making a start in the morning; but when morning came I felt so broken up and sore that I concluded to remain over and rest a day.

I was taken in hand by some of the prominent people and shown the places of interest in the village. Among those visited and one that greatly interested me, was the olive mills. The town is noted for the production of a superior olive oil; but the mode of producing it is most primitive, being almost the same as that used by the Moors hundreds of years ago. They first place the round, green olives in sacks that are then set in a large stone bowl into which a flat cover lifts. An old time screw with beam attachment presses on the stone cover, and as an ass, hitched to the end of the beam, tramps wearily round and round the screw presses the stone tight on the olives, squeezing the oil into cemented grooves at the bottom of the bowl through which it flows into casks. The refuse, or pummies, as we would call them, is fed to the hogs and cattle. It struck me at the time that with our improved American machinery, we could extract about four times as much oil out of the pummies thrown away, as they got out at the first pressing.

"Another place I visited under the escort of the good padre and an officer, was the prison. This prison contained as choice a collection of murderers as ever drew a knife across a helpless traveler's throat. The news of my coming had preceded me and these free knights of the mountains stood in rows along the corridors to receive me, backed up by several well armed carbineros. The worthy padre would point out the most distinguished of these gentlemen. 'That one,' he'd say, 'is in for killing two travelers at such or such a pass. This one abducted a wealthy man and demanded ransom from his family, to whom he sent the ears of the unfortunate, and the ransom not coming, his throat was slit. The one over there, killed four men before he was caught,' and so on down the line, such cheerful histories were told. I politely saluted each artist of the knife and carbine as I passed, and on leaving, one of them stepped up and addressed me in a patois which the padre translated. The request he made, struck me as being so ridiculous, that I could scarcely refrain from laughing. It was to the effect that they all had heard of my voyage down the river and all of them were anxious to witness my departure on the morrow and knew if I would kindly intercede with the Governor, they would have that happiness.

"The request was so absurd, that I had no thought of saying anything to the Governor about it. In going out, the Governor invited us into his private apartments, and while being entertained there, I jokingly told him of the queer request the brigands had made. I was more than ever astonished at his replying:

"Como no? Senor" "Why not, sir?"

"When starting, next morning, I was frequently warned that the river was very bad; but could get no information of any consequence, except that it wound through many canyons. The whole town turned out to see me off and as I was feeling very much refreshed, I was soon ready. Going to the bank, what was my astonishment to see all those gentle murderers standing in a row with carbineros on either side, guarding them. One of the brigands, the spokesman of the day before, stepped forward and addressed me thus.

"'Illustrious Captain. We would like much to form your escort down the river as a protection against the lawless characters which we are aware infest the mountains below; but being detained here against our will, we are unable to offer you that homage. But as a mark of our pure regard, on behalf of myself and worthy companions, I present you with this purse, a specimen of our own handicraft and may you never lack means to keep it full.'

"The purse was a long, knit affair in colored yarns, looking like an old fashioned necktie. I thanked them and regretted the cruel circumstances which prevented their accompanying me, while secretly rejoicing that such a disreputable looking set of villains was closely guarded.

"I took to the stream again and the mountains once more looked as if they were closing in on the river. At times I would sink into quiet pools, requiring incessant paddling to push through and then emerge into rapids that would necessitate the utmost labor to keep from being dashed on the rocks. I ran all that day without meeting any one. About ten o'clock at night, I noticed a light down the stream and sounded my bugle. I was tired and chilly and glad to hear a hail from the direction of the light. I landed at a sort of ferry and found a man and woman awaiting me with a lantern. They escorted me to a little cabin and the woman bustled about, building a fire out of weeds and other stuff, wood being very scarce. Their patois was of the mountains and I could not understand their speech nor they mine. By signs, however, we understood each other very well and I intimated to them that I would stretch out before the fire all night. But they refused to allow me to lie on the floor. I understood them to mean for me to take the bed as the man was going away somewhere. This I did and was soon sound asleep. At one o'clock in the morning, I was awakened with an impression that some one was in the room near me. I looked up and by the dim rush light saw a tall figure standing by the bedside, upright and stiff, a three cornered hat on his head, a carbine strapped across his back and a sword by his side. In answer to my look of wonder, he simply raised his right hand and gave a military salute. I asked:

"Que esta, Senor?" "What is it, sir?"

"His reply was: 'By order of the king, I am here to offer you protection and assistance.'

"Thanking him for his courtesy, I turned over in bed and went to sleep again.

"After breakfast of wild boar bacon, which was the sweetest meat I ever tasted, the guard and my host accompanied me to the river. I carried a good supply of gold and silver with me; but all offers of money throughout the entire eight hundred miles of this voyage, were peremptorily refused. It was impossible to spend a cent. In fact, the money wore through the little bag I carried it in and I found it loose in my dress. The only place I used a cent on the trip was at Talavera. A boy who had done an errand for me, accepted a peseta. When it was found out, he was sent back with it and apologized for his conduct.

"The river now began to get very narrow and to bury itself in canyons, so that during the day the sun scarcely ever shone on the water except at noon when it was directly overhead. Since losing my little tender, I had no way to carry provisions except in a small oil cloth strapped on my breast. The host of the cabin had insisted on my taking some of the wild boar bacon with me; but seeing their stores were low, I took but very little, which I easily devoured at noon. For three days I continued the voyage through canyons and during the entire time the only signs of human life I saw was an occasional glimpse of people far up in the mountains, passing along, but too distant to attract their attention. My progress was slow owing to the long stretches of dead water I would strike, it was silent and lonely. The wild black ducks I would scare up were the only signs of life on the river. All the sleep I took was during daylight. I would haul up on some dry rock near the shore and in a moment be buried in profound slumber. At night I dare not sleep, for I could hear the howling of the wolves that are fierce and plentiful along that part of the Tagus, and their dismal yells warned me to keep to the river.

"On the morning of the third day in the canyons, I was stiff, sore and hungry, having eaten nothing but wild olives, gathered near the banks, for two days. That morning the idea struck me that I must have wandered into some false channel, or some branch from the Tagus, as I could make no headway. I came to an upright position and with every sense sharpened by hunger, listened to hear, if possible, the ringing of a bell, the barking of a dog or any sign of life; for I had about reached the conclusion that it was time for me to leave the water and climb the mountain in search of some house or village; but not a sound broke the deathlike stillness, except the distant rumbling of rapids I had passed over or those below that I must soon encounter. As I wearily sank back in the water and grasped the paddle in the hope that farther down some opening in the mountain might give me a chance to escape, something familiar struck my senses. I could not tell what it was. It was intangible, yet I felt there was something about that belonged to human beings. Again I came to an upright position, peered in every direction and listened. It was then discovered what it was that had so affected me. It was the smell of smoke which the breeze was gently carrying up the river. I pushed down on my course with all my strength in hope of finding the fire, and on rounding a sharp bend was rewarded by seeing a thin, blue streak curling up from the mountain side. I landed a little above it and commenced clambering over great, detached rocks, until I gained a terrace on a level with the line of smoke. I paused to listen and heard the muffled sound of voices near me. The voices came from the other side of a small promontory around which I crawled. My soft rubber boots made no sound, and as I rounded the rock I was surprised to find myself almost alongside of two shepherds. One of them was stooping over the fire stirring something in a stew pan, while the other was rolling cigarettes in corn husks, their backs turned toward me. Previous experiences with these simple people of the mountains had taught me how superstitious and easily frightened they are, and wishing to gain some information from them as well as something to eat, I let the point of my iron shod paddle strike a rock, at the same time saluting them with 'buonos dias mis hermanos,'— good day, my brothers. The men sprang to their feet and turned around at the unexpected salutation. Then a wild yell rang through mountain top and ravine and they dashed away like a pair of frightened deer. At every hail for them to stop they only redoubled their efforts to escape and soon disappeared up the ravine. I sat down and made a breakfast off the provender they had left behind and enjoyed it as I never enjoyed anything before. I also absorbed a pig skin flask of Spanish wine which afforded me great consolation in my exhausted condition. I then took off the dress and dried myself before the fire and rising sun, in hopes the shepherds would take courage and return; but they never came back. Before dressing I left a Spanish dollar on the upturned bottom of the stew pan, and returned to the river much refreshed and all traces of hunger gone.

"I had not proceeded more than a league when I observed a man seated on a mule, occupying a point of rock overlooking the river. The man, on seeing me, raised a bugle to his lips and sounded a merry blast, which was, answered by loud cheers further down. On arriving opposite the lookout, I was informed that the Governor of Caceres and a party of ladies and gentlemen were waiting for me at a short distance below, and in a few moments I sighted the party and landed. I was warmly received by a numerous gathering. The Governor informed me they had driven across from Caceres the day before, to intercept me; that he had had a message from King Alphonso to see that I wanted for nothing. He pleasantly remarked to me in French, that it was an old Spanish custom to say to a guest, 'my house is yours,' but he would change the saying to 'my country is yours.'

"The place at which I landed was a ford or ferry. The Governor and his party were sheltered under a large tent which had been erected for the occasion, and were attended by a troop of servants and cooks. The latter had prepared a regular banquet and oh, how I wished I was so constituted that I could take enough food aboard to last me some days. As it was, the bounteous feast deserted by the shepherds, had filled me to repletion and I could do but scant justice to the load of luxuries they spread before me. I spent the day pleasantly with them, however, and parted that evening with many kind wishes and warnings. The Governor's engineer, who was one of the party, told me all he knew about the river and said I would soon reach the terrible rapids known as the Salto del Gitano—the Gypsey's Leap.

"After leaving the delightful company, I bowled away on a flying current and ere long heard a roar below warning me that I was approaching a dangerous point. I prepared to take it, no matter what it was. The river closed in between two natural walls, as narrow as a canal, and danced away at a lively pace. The water dashed over the rocks that obstructed its passage, and was churned into foam and spray that leaped high into the air. As the roar below grew more terrible, I lost some courage and endeavored to check up, fearing to encounter backwater. In attempting to stop myself, I grasped a rock as I was being carried by; but did not have strength enough to resist the force of the current, and so was hurled along. The current ran about thirty kilometers an hour, and the rocks were so high on either side that only a small strip of sky was visible overhead. The stream took on an abrupt turn about every hundred yards and was running in the most peculiar currents. I was tossed repeatedly from one side of the river to the other by sortie unseen action and bumped against the rocks. I dashed through two or three rapids and then came to a fall that almost deafened me with its roar. I saw the water in front of me rushing together in big waves and then jumping, leaving nothing but white foam to show where it disappeared. I was drawn down and whirled and thrown about; how I came out I can't tell. I do know, however, that I was puffing and trying to breathe. It was quite a while before my head became clear after that shaking up; but I kept right along.

"All that night I ran through another series of canyons until about two o'clock in the morning, I saw in the moonlight what seemed to be a thin string across the river, but on drawing closer, it proved to be the bridge at Alcantara. It is a queer stone bridge, with two abutments and one arch stretching across from one mountain to another, high up in the air. There was no one out and I climbed up to the level of the bridge. By calling and making a lot of noise, I succeeded in rousing the bridge tender, who took me to the house of the Alcalde where all turned out and welcomed me. I stopped there over Sunday and thoroughly enjoyed myself. At night I went to a theatrical entertainment and was called on for a speech, to which I responded to the best of my ability. I was presented to many ladies and thought them the handsomest I had seen in any part of Spain.

"I started early next morning and a short distance below, came to the point where the river is bordered on one side by Portugal, and I soon noticed a Portuguese flag flying from a mast and heard loud vivas from the crew of a flat bottomed boat with a cabin, which I ran alongside of and was informed that the boat had been sent by the Portuguese government to meet me. The captain also carried a letter from the Minister of Marine stating that the boat had been placed at my disposal. At this I felt wonderfully relieved. The hard work was now all over, as I simply followed the government craft for the remainder of the journey. It was quite a novelty at first to begin taking my meals regularly again and as there was an abundance of everything, I began to thoroughly enjoy the trip. We would tie up every night and I occupied the cabin.

"At Portes de Rodas, the first town we struck in Portugal, I met with a peculiarly Portuguese reception. Every person was supplied with detonating rockets which were fired off in showers and that was the manner of showing good will at every place in the country. There were no rocks in the river now. The stream broadened majestically and the tides from the Atlantic began to be felt. At Abrantes and Santarem, the receptions accorded me took the wildest form of enthusiasm and I there heard for the first time the peculiar name given me in Portugal 'Homen das Botas',—'the man with the boots'. This name grew out of an ancient story connected with the Tagus. Many years ago the government officials wished to pass a law which was obnoxious to the people, who made a terrible clamor against it. A shrewd politician, to distract the people's attention from the proposed law, circulated the report that a man in boots was going to walk on the surface of the Tagus from Santarem to Lisbon. This was such a wonderful thing that the people lost sight of the political question, in watching the river and discussing the performance. In the meantime the law was passed. For years the people talked and at last joked about the 'man with the boots,' and so when I came down, there was some reason for their cries of 'here comes the veritable Homem das Botas.'"

As Paul approached Lisbon, he had to work tides. The river ran through a very low country and stretched into so wide an expanse, as almost to form a bay. He arrived in Lisbon just eighteen days from the time of starting, which included nine night's paddling. The welcome he received there was something tremendous. It was estimated that one hundred thousand people were out to see him land. Just before going ashore, a steam launch put out to him with dispatches of congratulations from the King of Spain and his Minister of Marine. A company of horse guards took charge of him and escorted him to a hotel. The usual banquets and entertainments followed this winding up of one of the hardest voyages he ever made.

The fact that the Tagus had been navigated, created a profound sensation throughout Spain and Portugal, and Boyton was kept busy acknowledging telegrams of congratulation. The governor of Toledo sent the Spanish consul at Lisbon a telegram which, translated, read as follows:

"I beg you to heartily congratulate Captain Boyton in my behalf for the happy termination of his difficult voyage on the river Tagus, which has once more shown his intelligence and courage."

"Before leaving Madrid to begin the journey," remarked Paul to an American friend, "the foreign colony warned me not only of the dangers of the Tagus, but also against the people along the river, who were wild and ignorant, and would kill me. On the contrary I found them kind, hospitable and generous, both in Spain and Portugal."

The Geographical Society of Lisbon requested the navigator to deliver a lecture. Though the members of the society lived right on the banks of the river, they knew comparatively little about it, and Boyton's lecture was of great scientific importance to them. Among other things, he told them of the abutments and ancient masonry he had seen while going through some of the wildest canyons, that could not be approached in any way. This masonry, he thought, must be the remains of ancient Moorish structures which stood there before the great earthquake had shaken up and changed the surface of the country through which the Tagus flows.

An expedition sent out by the Society soon afterward, verified Boyton's words and opinions.

Paul remained in Lisbon during Carnival week, and was entertained until he grew weary of so much pleasure. He gave an exhibition in the Arsenal de Marinha before the king and queen of Portugal, and received numerous presents and decorations.

CHAPTER XVI.

Paul next went to Gibraltar. On arriving there, he expressed his determination to cross the straits; but was given very little encouragement. He was repeatedly warned against sharks which were reported numerous in those waters. An English officer took him to the rear of the place where cattle are killed for the army. This building abuts on the water, and there, in the clear depth, they could see big, blue sharks laying for the offal that is thrown from the slaughter house. Even this sight did not intimidate Paul and he began preparations for the trip.

At first it was his intention, to paddle from Gibraltar to Ceuta, which is almost on a straight line across; but on account of the currents, that course was changed and Tarifa, the lowest land in Europe, was selected as the starting point, from which place he was confident he would be able to strike the African coast somewhere. Two gentlemen of Gibraltar agreed to accompany him and the Spanish felucca, San Augustine, was chartered for their accommodation, manned by a captain and crew of five sailors.

On Thursday, March 19th, they sailed from Gibraltar. As they neared the Spanish side, carrying the American flag, a Spanish gunboat put out and overhauled them, under the impression they were tobacco smugglers. It was some time before the officials could be made to understand the object of the voyage; but finally allowed them to proceed. They arrived off Tarifa at eleven o'clock at night, and lay to for a couple of hours, when, as the captain of the felucca refused to start across without clearance papers, they landed and went into the old, Moorish looking town and woke up one sleepy official after another; but it was not until seven o'clock in the morning that clearance was procured.

The danger of this undertaking was by no means confined to sharks alone; the wind and currents are usually variable. Through the middle of the strait a current may be considered to set constantly to the eastward, but on each side, both flood and ebb tides extend to a quarter of a mile or to two miles from the shore, according to the wind and weather, and are consequently very irregular.

At 7:30 o'clock Boyton had donned his dress and was ready to take the water. For the first time in the history of his voyages he took the unusual precaution against sharks, of screwing sharp steel sword blades on each end of his double bladed paddle. With these he felt confident that he could stand up in the water and rip open any shark that approached him. He also carried a large dagger fastened to his wrist. He jumped into the sea amidst the enthusiastic cheering of quite a crowd that had assembled on the beach to see him start. He paddled out to a rock close by Tarifa lighthouse, said to be the extreme southern point of Europe, which he touched, turned and waved an adieu to Spain. He was then fairly launched on his journey, steering southwest in a smooth sea and calm weather. He was in excellent spirits and fully confident of success. The southwestern course was taken as he expected to meet the current setting eastward, which would carry him toward Malabata, the point he determined to make his port of destination. His calculation, however, proved to be false, for the current turned out to be setting from the opposite direction and therefore gradually conveyed him toward the westward.

Shortly after 8 o'clock Paul was singing as he paddled along and came very near running into a school of porpoises. A couple of shots were fired into them from the felucca in order to frighten them away, as it is generally supposed that sharks are following them up. A few moments afterward another school appeared astern, when the operation was repeated with the desired effect. Paul finding that the current was setting too rapidly westward, turned his course due south and as the wind was beginning to rise, a small square sail was handed to him; but as that did not seem to increase his progress to any perceptible degree, he put it back in the boat after about ten minutes' trial. As he was passing over Cabezes Shoals the breeze freshened; but he was still being carried westward. At that stage of the journey, about 9:30, he hauled up for a moment and partook of a little bread and cheese, and before resuming work with the paddle he attached a white pocket handkerchief to a cord about eighteen feet long and fastened one end to the belt of his waist, allowing the handkerchief to drift astern. This was another precaution against sharks, as it is well known that their malevolent impulses are more likely to be excited and their attacks directed against white objects than any other. His idea was that a shark attacking the white handkerchief would jerk the cord and thus give warning of its presence in the rear, in time for him to be ready with his sword blades.

The wind increasing from the east, Paul again tried the sail, still steering south, toward Malabata Point; but again found it ineffectual. He was then about nine miles from Tarifa and though having paddled constantly, he did not show the slightest signs of fatigue. The westward current continuing, it looked for a time as though he would be carried into the Atlantic. He turned his course southeast and fought against it. At two o'clock, he was passed by the British steamer, Glenarn, eastward bound, and was loudly cheered by the people on her deck. At two-thirty o'clock, a very strong breeze with a rapid current setting eastward, caused a high sea and Boyton had great difficulty in keeping near the boat, his distance from her increasing every moment until he disappeared from view altogether. But by dint of hard pulling on the part of the sailors, for about twenty minutes, he was sighted more than half a mile to the leeward and sail was hoisted on the felucca in order to get up to him, which was done after much trouble and anxiety. The master and crew of the boat then advised him to give up the attempt to cross, as from their long experience of the straits, they believed it to be impracticable under existing circumstances; but Boyton positively refused to give up the undertaking, and forged ahead, undismayed and in the most hopeful spirits. As it was found impossible to keep up with him with the aid of the oars alone, the boat's sails were reefed and hoisted and by steering close hauled, was enabled to keep nearer him.

At three o'clock, he was about half way across, steering south south east. The wind continued to increase, and it again seemed as though he would be carried into the ocean. The sea broke over him constantly and he suffered greatly from the salt encrusting on his eyebrows and causing his face to smart. It was nearly five o'clock when he was off Boassa Point, bearing south and only distant about three and one half miles from the African coast. He made another attempt to use the sail but the wind was too strong and he was compelled to give it up. The current with heavy overfalls, caused him to be constantly taken under water, and also proved very trying to those in the boat. The overfalls are caused by two currents rushing in opposite directions, meeting with a great crash and making a tremendous wave. Paul bravely continued to paddle despite such dreadful obstacles and at five-thirty o'clock, he was bearing due south off Alcazar Point two and one half miles. One hour later, the current was setting to the west again, driving the voyager and the boat further and further away from the African coast. It began to grow dark with increasing wind and every sign of a gale coming on. The boisterous sea and wind, in conjunction with the rapid currents and heavy over-falls, again caused Boyton to drift away from the boat, so that those on board soon lost sight of him altogether. After cruising about in all directions and hailing at the top of their voices, his friends on board the St. Augustine were relieved by hearing a distant hail which proved to be a guide to his whereabouts and by proceeding in the right direction they got up to him; but not without great risk and very hard work.

On reaching him, the crew became very violent in their language and conduct and insisted on his getting aboard, as they were all drifting into the Atlantic Ocean. Boyton, however was firm in his resolve to keep on until he reached the African coast. Seeing no other way to stop him, three of the crew leaned over the boat's side and endeavored to drag him on board by main force. That movement caused Paul to become greatly excited in his turn. He stood up in the water and with the sword blade raised and pointing at the crew, he glared at them with blazing eyes and told them he would rip open the first man that dared to touch him.

The men took to their oars again. Boyton began to sing, with the intention of encouraging the men and dissipating their apprehensions.

At seven-thirty o'clock, he was again lost sight of in a heavy overfall, the current setting to the eastward at a place commonly known as La Ballesta. He was sighted after the lapse of about twenty minutes. The increasing darkness and bad state of the weather necessitated harder work on the part of those on board the boat in order to keep near him. Clouds gathered fast and a heavy mist partly obscured the moon, which wore a large circle, called by the sailors a "weather band." Directly after finding Boyton, those on board of the felucca, were startled by his cry of "Watch; oh, watch!"

In answer to excited inquiries from on board, he directed that they should stand by with arms, at the same time calling attention to the weather side of the boat, where was observed a great commotion in the water causing a bright, phosphorescent glow, which left no doubt of the unpleasant proximity of a shark, or some other huge denizen of the deep. Fears for the safety of Boyton, however, were quickly dispelled by the disappearance of the creature, whatever it may have been, and all preparations to give it a warm reception proved needless. Bonfires were at that time seen at long distances from each other on the African coast. It was subsequently ascertained that they had been built by order of Colonel Mathews, the American Consul General at Tagier, as beacons for Boyton's guidance. A current setting to the westward was encountered, which drove them in a northwesterly direction and the wind increased to a gale with a heavy sea. In answer to a hail from the boat as to whether he had been attacked or needed anything, Boyton replied: "No, thank you, all's right."

It began to rain and the boat labored, rolling heavily. At 8:30 o'clock Malabata Point was distant about four miles. The crew was again losing heart, as matters bore a very serious aspect. For the fourth time they were obliged to go about and pull in various directions in quest of Boyton, whom they missed for more than a quarter of an hour.

After nine o'clock the most exciting and anxious moments of the entire trip were experienced by all concerned. With the wind blowing violently, the current driving fast to the westward and a high sea increasing every moment, Paul was lost sight of for nearly forty minutes, in an unusually heavy overfall. It is not to be wondered at that under these most trying circumstances, the boat's crew, having nothing to eat, and exhausted by the fatigues of the day, after pulling about for a considerable time, should have dropped the oars accompanying the action with language more forcible than elegant. Happily the cessation of their labor was of short duration, for they soon yielded to the admonitions and entreaties of Boyton's friends, who sought by every possible means to buoy up their spirits, although they, as well as the crew, were of the opinion that any further attempt to find Paul would be utterly futile. The joy of all may easily be imagined when they heard the echo of a distant hail, amid the roaring of the wind and hissing of the seething water, that once more restored their hope and confidence in him and announced after all that he had not been lost beyond, recovery. A little more pulling in the right direction brought the boat alongside of him, when, despite the entreaties of the crew and the great risks he was running, he refused to get on board, but continued with undaunted courage and characteristic firmness in his endeavor to accomplish the daring task.

Boyton was missed for the last time and found again about 10:30 o'clock. At that time the severe strain he had imposed upon himself began to be felt, for when within hearing distance he stated that he had fallen asleep for a few moments and had been unceremoniously awakened by a sea breaking over him with such force on the side of the head as almost to stun him. The crew now expressed their thorough appreciation and admiration for Boyton's intrepidity and powers of endurance, and declared he had done as much as to cross the straits three times over in point of distance; but he persistently turned a deaf ear to their entreaties to get into the boat. At 11:20 o'clock the bay of Tangier opened ahead and the force of the current began to abate. They were rapidly approaching Tangier reef, which was a source of uneasiness to the boat's crew, who were afraid of being driven on it. They passed the headland between Tangier and Cape Malabata and were inside the bay before one o'clock. When within one hundred yards of the outside of a reef of rocks, forming a natural breakwater, and the landing place at Tangier, the impracticability of the boat clearing the reef (toward which the current was driving her) with the aid of the oars alone became manifest. They therefore advised Boyton to take a line as they were going to set sail and would tow him around the point, for otherwise they would inevitably be dashed against the rocks. On further representing to him that as the tide was high he ran the risk of fracturing his leg or arm in passing over the slippery obstruction, he acceded to the request, particularly as he considered that his feat was accomplished. He accordingly took the end of a line and discontinued paddling for a short while until they arrived opposite the town, within three-quarters of a mile from the landing, when he let go and shaped his course for the beach, the boat standing to the southward and anchoring.

Boyton emerged from the surf and stood on the beach at 12.55 o'clock. The moon was shining. Some of the native soldiers were aware that a man was paddling across the straits; but many were not. One of the guards on the wall surrounding the city, seeing him come out of the water, set up a terrific cry in the Arabic tongue. Soon the bells were ringing from the mosques and a great commotion was evident within the walls of the city. Paul, not knowing what the natives might do with him, walked down the beach a short distance and coming upon the upturned hull of a wrecked vessel, crawled under it. He had scarcely done so, when the gate to the city opened and a crowd of soldiers and citizens carrying torches, rushed out. They soon got on his trail and followed it to the old hulk which they surrounded with wild and discordant cries. In the midst of all the hubbub, Paul heard a voice calling in English, and he stepped out to be met by the son of the American Consul, Colonel Mathews, who explained the cause of Boyton's appearance to the natives. It was afterward learned that the peculiar cry of alarm given by the guard on the wall, was:

"Awake, awake. 'Tis better to pray than to sleep, for the devil has landed in Tangier."

All the explanation, however, did not prevent one of the natives from running back into the city with the statement that, he had actually seen a Christian walking on the sea.

When those on the boat heard all the commotion ashore, their anxiety for Paul was great. They rightly apprehended that the superstitious feeling of the Moorish guard had been excited at the apparition of so strange an object emerging from the sea at that advanced hour of the night, and might lead them to resort to violence.

In answer to Mr. Matthew's invitation to enter the city as his guest, Paul told him that he must first paddle back to the boat and Mr. Mathews agreed to meet him there. As soon as he returned to the boat, he was divested of his rubber dress, when it was found that his under clothing was completely saturated with salt water. He accounted for it by the fact that having been so frequently drawn under by the overfalls, the water had entered at the sides of the face. As soon as he had been provided with a change of clothing, he began to display evidences of the most complete prostration, coupled with acute pain in the wrists and hands which were covered with large blisters, while he was almost blinded by the action of the salt water on his eyes. A fire was lighted in the cooking stove on board, but it was long ere Paul could obtain sufficient warmth to stay the violence of his shiverings. In due time they were all gladdened by the arrival of the pratique boat alongside, with Colonel Mathew's son, who took the party to the landing stage, where Boyton was highly honored by the presence of several officials who were waiting to offer him a welcome and their congratulations, for which purpose they had exposed themselves to the discomforts of a cold and cheerless morning. The time was half past two. Accommodations were provided for the party at the house of Colonel

Mathews. In company with the Consul General next day, Paul visited the old Sheriff of Tangier, to whom he was introduced as the water god of America. The superstitious old Moor looked at Boyton with great respect and remarked, Colonel Mathews interpreting:

"I am well pleased that the water god has made his appearance on these shores as there has been a terrible drought here for sometime, and we are sadly in need of a rainfall to moisten the parched lips of our soil and I hope the great water god of your country will deign to favor us."

Boyton had been noticing the clouds since morning; his sailor training told him it would not be long before rain would fall, so he answered the Sheriff's appeal with a sly wink at the Colonel, as follows:

"The request of the Sheriff is well. I promise that rain will come before a great while."

Before they left the house, luckily for Paul, it did begin to rain and the old man was absolutely bewildered with astonishment, having not the least doubt that the rain had been called by the American. To this day, the Moors of Tangier tell the story of how the drought was ended by a wonderful American who came out of the sea one night.

On returning to the Colonel's house, Boyton was waited on by a delegation of distinguished Moors; old, white bearded fellows, in turbans and burnouse. Each of them offered a present of some kind. One of them brought a beautiful pair of Barbary pheasants, another a young wild pig in a crate; others, quaint arms, and one had a chameleon of a rare species, which he carried on the twig of a tree. An address of welcome to Morocco was read by one of their number and then they asked Paul he would not kindly walk on the water in the daylight for them as the soldiers had seen him do when he landed, so that all the people might behold him.

In response to the request, Boyton promised to favor them and on the following day, he gave a demonstration of what he could do in the water, much to their enjoyment and surprise.

After the exhibition, he was shown the pleasures of the city. One of his most interesting experiences was in encountering the great dangers afforded by a wild boar hunt. Early one morning the hunting party, headed by Colonel Mathews, mounted on wiry little Arab horses, and carrying bamboo sticks pointed with a sharp spear, rode over the hills back of the quaint old city and descended to the desert. They proceeded for a long distance and chanced on no signs of game. They were beginning to get somewhat discouraged, when they met a camel train from Fez. "I will ask some of these people if they have seen any boars on their way hither," said Colonel Mathews, "but you can place very little dependence on what they say. They are naturally inclined to exaggerate." He rode up to the leader of the train and the following conversation which the Colonel's son translated, took place:

"Mahomet protect my brothers. You came from afar; but your journey will soon be ended and you will have blissful rest," said the Colonel.

"Allah bless you, master. We are weary and glad to approach our journey's end," replied the head of the caravan.

"Have you seen the wild boar in your last day's journey?"

"We have, my master, in great numbers, not far from here."

"Good ones?"

"As large as an ass, my master."

"In which direction?"

The Moor responded by raising his hand and solemnly pointing to the south-east.

After riding in the direction given for an hour or more, the party halted on the crest of a hill, scanning the desert for game, and discovered two sickly looking little pigs running across the valley below.

"Those are not the ones the Moor saw?" said Paul.

"Oh yes, they are. It's a wonder he imagined them so small as an ass, for it is their national characteristic to exaggerate."

There was rather meager sport in running down and spearing the skinny little wild pigs, but after it was done the party returned to the city, as the experienced hunters knew there would be no use looking further that day.

One place in the queer old Moorish city which Paul never tired of visiting, was the market. There the Moorish women with covered faces, squatted on the ground displaying their little bowls of beans, peas, etc., for sale. The tired camels from the desert were laying with their noses buried in the sand, taking much needed rest, while their owners stood about and bartered the goods of which they were possessed. Once, while walking around the market place with Colonel Mathews, Paul saw a man seated cross-legged on the ground in the midst of a circle of merchants, who were deeply interested in the discourse and gestures of the central figure.

"I'll wager something that I can guess what that fellow is, though I do not understand Arabic," remarked Paul to the Colonel.

"Well, what is he?" asked the Colonel.

"An auctioneer," triumphantly asserted Boyton.

"Wrong. He is a professional story-teller. He is as imaginative as Scheherazade and the merchants here are so busy that they always have time and inclination to listen to his long fairy tales."

After each story the listeners dropped a small coin, valued at one-twentieth of a cent, into the story-teller's hat.

Another thing that amused Paul was the indiscriminate use the guides made of the stout sticks they carried, whacking the natives who got in their way in the narrow streets as mercilessly as they did the asses they drove.

The women were all heavily veiled, their faces jealously hidden from the eyes of men, except when some giddy girl with a taste for flirtation allowed her veil to slip down as if by accident, and one then, as a general thing, beheld a very pretty countenance.

Returning to Gibraltar, Boyton visited Cadiz, Seville, and the principal cities of Southern Spain, with extraordinary success, and was the recipient of continued ovations. While giving exhibitions in those cities, he concluded to take a run on the Guadalquivir, from St. Geronime to Seville. It was an uneventful though pleasant trip. His only adventure was that of being driven back into the water after going ashore to take observations, by one of the famous Andalusian fighting bulls that was feeding close by. He completed the journey in three days—March 29, 30 and 31.

Madrid was again visited on the invitation of the King, and preparations began for a grand exhibition at Casa de Campo, the royal garden, which contains a beautiful little lake. A tent was erected on its bank and every assistance rendered Boyton in preparing for the entertainment. Several small boats were built for him with which to illustrate torpedo work in naval warfare. The King took great interest in the work and in fact in everything American. He treated Paul in the most affable manner; among other attentions, showing the royal boat house and was astonished when told that boats, such as his mahogany ones, that required four men to lift out, were made in America out of paper, so light that a man could take one of them under his arm and carry it where he pleased.

On the morning of the exhibition, the finest military band in Madrid was present. The affair was private, only the notables of the city being there. When the King, Queen, and members of the royal household arrived, a signal for the exhibition to begin, was given. In one part of the entertainment, pigeons are used to illustrate the sending of dispatches. On that occasion, Paul had procured a pair of beautiful white doves. One of them when loosed flew away, while the other, bewildered, circled about and finally lit at the feet of the Queen. The Princess of Asturas, the King's sister, caught it and handed it to the Queen, who held and petted it during the rest of the time.

The exhibition was a complete success and at its termination, the King summoned Paul to land where the royal party was seated, when he congratulated the hardy navigator, as did also the Queen. As she thanked him for the pleasure he had given her, Paul said, referring to the dove that had gone to her feet:

"I hope it will prove a good omen, your Majesty." Turning her wondrously beautiful, though melancholy black eyes on him, she replied, with a sad smile:

"I hope so; I hope so."

She then conferred on Paul the order of Hospitaliers of Spain, making him for a second time a knight. He is the only foreigner ever knighted by Mercedes during her short reign. The King also presented him with the Marine Cross of Spain and photographs of himself and Queen.

Before he left Spain the beautiful young Queen was dead. Might not the erratic action of the dove have been an omen?

Leaving Madrid, Paul appeared in the principal cities of the northern division of the country and was everywhere received with the usual cordiality. At Barcelona, he gave an exhibition for the benefit of several families of fishermen who had been lost in a gale but a short time before. The fishing folk of Barcelona, as well as those of Northern France are unlike those in any other part of the world. They are peculiar in their costumes and characteristics and form a little world unto themselves. After Paul had given the benefit exhibition, he was surprised one morning to be summoned from his room. He found the courtyard of the house full of fisher folk dressed in their holiday attire, who had appeared to tender him their thanks. An address was delivered, and he was also presented with a curious, pear-shaped iron locket, inlaid with gold and silver, that had been made by one of their number who was a cripple. It was suitably inscribed and of ingenious workmanship. He values it among his most cherished possessions.

Toulouse, France, was next visited and a voyage made from that city to Bordeaux on the Garonne, which occupied six days, from May 19th to the 25th. There was nothing but pleasure on the trip down that beautiful river, which winds through the rich wine valleys of France. The greatest hospitality was shown Paul and when his little tender was not loaded down with flowers, it was filled by his admirers with provisions and rare wines.

After the Garonne he went to Paris, where his steam yacht, the Paul Boyton, which he had ordered before departing for the Tagus, was delivered to him. She was a magnificent little vessel, in which he intended to sail and steam to India, China and Japan. This was during the Paris Exposition of 1878, and he remained on board the yacht, whose dock was at the exposition grounds, most of the time. The little vessel was always full of distinguished visitors, and many pleasant excursions were taken up and down the Seine. During that time Paul became acquainted with the ex-President of Peru, Don Nicholas de Pierola, then in banishment. They became fast friends, the ex-President taking much interest in torpedo work, and they frequently made quiet experiments at isolated places down the river. Before they separated he assured Paul that if he ever regained his position in Peru, he would remember their pleasant times aboard the "Paul Boyton," and their torpedo experiments.

August 12th, Paul began a voyage down the Seine from Nogent-sur-Seine to Paris, a distance of two hundred miles, which he accomplished in four days, landing at the Exposition buildings, Champs de Mars, before an immense concourse of people. The crowds that lined the banks of the Seine were estimated at half a million by the Figaro. As he passed under Pont Neuf he stood up and dipped the stars and stripes in salute. A mighty shout went up from thousands of throats, "Vive l'Amerique, Vive Boyton."

During November of the same year, he voyaged the Orne from Lou to Caen, occupying two days. The trip was an uneventful one, and soon after he returned to America.

CHAPTER XVII.

For some weeks Paul remained in New York, much to the delight of his mother and family and he was also feted and entertained by many of the prominent citizens of the metropolis. During his stay at home, he amused himself by paddling from the Battery around to Hunter's Point and one night crossed down the bay through the Narrows, and came near losing his life in the ice off Staten Island.

On an invitation from a member of Congress, Paul visited Washington and was cordially received by President Hayes and his Cabinet, all paying him high compliments for the daring things he had performed in the interest of life saving. During the afternoon of February 1st, 1879, at the instance of the President, he gave an exhibition in the navy yard, before the members of the Senate and House of Representatives.

While in Washington, Paul received an invitation which highly pleased him. It was signed by leading citizens, asking him to revisit his former home, Pittsburgh. He was glad to have the chance of seeing the old river of his boyish gambols, and cheerfully promised to go. After a day or so in Washington he went to Pittsburgh, where met with the most cordial greeting on the part of the citizens and was also happy to see many of his playmates of former years. On the evening of his arrival, while resting in his room at a hotel, he was visited by a man wearing the uniform of the Fire Department, who grasped his hand with more warmth and enthusiasm than ordinary visitors were wont to do, at the same time remarking:

"I don't suppose you know me, Captain Boyton?"

"My memory certainly fails me in that respect," replied Boyton

"I am Thomas McCaffery, whose life you saved more than twenty years ago. Of all men in the world, I most desired to meet you," and Paul returned the warm hand pressure of the fireman.

An evening most agreeable to both was passed in recounting their adventures of other days. Before Paul left Pittsburgh, Mr. McCaffery presented him with a gold medal, commemorating the important event in his life, which, but for Boyton, would have terminated so disastrously.

Some time was spent about Pittsburgh, while preparations were made for a voyage down the Alleghany and Ohio rivers, which he had decided on making. It was the first intention to start on the Alleghany at Kittanning, but on looking over the ground, Paul selected Oil City as the starting point, distant above Pittsburgh about one hundred and forty miles.

There was great excitement at Oil City when it became known that Boyton had arrived and contemplated paddling down the river. Many people believed the attempt would not be made on account of the extremely cold weather. These were astonished when Boyton appeared on the morning of February 6th, equipped for the dreary voyage, and he was given an enthusiastic send off. His progress the greater part of the first day, was slow, owing to, the blocks of floating ice. At Black's Riffles he struck on a rock, with such force as to turn him completely over and almost knock him senseless. Fortunately his dress was not punctured by the blow and he continued the journey to Emlenton, forty three miles from Oil City, where, on account of the accident and the fact that he was almost frozen, he decided to remain over night instead of rushing on to Kittanning as had been his intention.

At all towns he passed, crowds of people lined the banks and offers of hospitality were numberless. There was great rivalry between some of the towns as to which would get the voyager to stop off, and the arguments used by the inhabitants to induce him to favor them, were very funny. A citizen of Parker come to the front with a statement which he thought would surely be a winner.

"Tell Boyton," he said to one of the newspaper men who followed by train from one station to the other along the river, "that he should stop off at Parker instead of Kittanning, because Parker is an incorporated town and Kittanning is not."

Paul was not greatly refreshed by his rest at Emlenton. He arose in the morning, stiff and swollen, his hands and face very much so, being slightly frost bitten and very painful. He was somewhat depressed in spirits and said he could not reach Pittsburgh until Sunday. He bravely entered the water, however, and that day he shot over Parker's Falls.

Before he reached Mahoning, a big crowd lined the bank awaiting his approach. In the crowd was one of those wise bodies who are never to be fooled and who knows a thing or two about the ways of the world. This individual made himself exceedingly conspicuous in the gathering and confidentially told everybody that would listen to him, that he was smart enough to size up the whole affair and that they were all fools to be taken in by the report that a man was going to swim down such an icy current.

"I'm on to the whole thing," he said, with a real knowing look, "this is gotten up by the newspaper men. They have a block of wood dressed up in a rubber suit and let it float down, while this 'ere Boyton sneaks along the river with the reporters. They can't close my eye, not much."

He was one of the front line on the bank when Paul arrived. He had made up his mind to grab the rubber covered chunk of wood and expose the whole thing to the public, and then it would be seen that he was "jest a leetle smarter than the rest of mankind." As Boyton drew in at that point and walked up on the land, the clever fellow's eyes looked as though they would burst from their sockets, and he beat a precipitate retreat, followed by the derisive shouts of the crowd.

Paul was much interested during a great part of the cold, cheerless trip, in the immense pillars of fire that belch from the natural gas wells that are numerous along the river, which runs through the famous oil country of Pennsylvania.

A reception was tendered him at Kittanning, notwithstanding that little city's misfortune in "not being incorporated," and the mayor delivered a warm address of welcome.

From the moment Paul neared Pittsburgh's suburban places there was a continued ovation until he completed the voyage at the Point, where the confluence of the Alleghany and Monongahela forms the Ohio. Thousands of people jammed the bridges and thousands lined the shores to salute the intrepid voyager. He was picked up at the Point and quickly placed in a carriage in order to avoid the crowd and hurriedly driven to a hotel. He was half frozen and his worn appearance showed how trying had been the trip, which was accomplished in a little less than four days.

After a brief rest, he made ready to resume the voyage. The start was made from the foot of Seventh Street, February 24th. The Ohio was so full of ice that it was difficult to forge ahead. The first day's run was to Rochester, where he hauled up for the night. Owing to his being behind time the band and many people who had been waiting for him, went away, while those who remained occupied their time in patronizing a convenient bar. Mr. James Creelman, of the New York Herald, who had been assigned to write up the voyage, and another newspaper man, accompanied Boyton, making their way in conveyances along the shore. When they arrived at Rochester, Paul was tired and wanted to sleep, so they repaired to a hotel as quickly as possible, and all three were put into one room. It became, noised around that the travelers had arrived and crowds gathered at the hotel. They demanded a speech and the landlord waited on Paul with the information. He was sent back to tell the people that Boyton was in bed and did not wish to be disturbed. Then they wanted him to fire off just one rocket. That was also impossible, because the "Baby Mine," the name of the little tender, had struck a piece of ice before reaching the town and sprung a leak, wetting all the fireworks. The landlord, however, thought he could touch off one of the rockets anyway, so he seized a large detonator and with a red hot poker tried to see how it would work. Finding the fuse, as he thought, too wet, he threw the rocket on the floor and left the room. Directly after, Paul heard a hissing noise and realized that the landlord had succeeded in leaving a live spark in the fuse. He simply drew the bedclothes around himself and let the rocket sizz. It went off with a terrible report, shaking the whole house and frightening his companions out of their wits. The landlord rushed into the room with a "hip, hooray," much delighted.

"That's it," he cried, "that's good," and he yelled again, regardless of the fact that his carpet was on fire and the room terribly littered up.

Between Rochester and Wellsville, Paul had an awful time in an ice gorge. He could hear it cracking and grinding below as though warning him of danger. He succeeded in climbing on a cake which saved him from being carried under, and made his way to clear water on the other side.

Below Steubenville, a native from the West Virginia side rowed frantically out to him.

"Hold on, stranger, I'll resky yo' in a minit," he yelled. When he drew nearer and Paul spoke to him, he appeared as tickled as a boy at a monkey show. "Wal, ef yo' aint jus' th' cutes' little cuss I ever seed paddlin' aroun' out here in the ice like a beaver."

However, he expressed much disgust, not to say contempt, when Boyton refused to land and take a drink of "Virginia's own Mountain Dew."

After hard work through the ice gorged river, Paul reached Wheeling and rested there until the next morning. On resuming the voyage he was frequently compelled to mount an ice cake to look for the best place to strike open water, where he could get at least enough paddling to keep up his temperature. While on one of those lookouts he heard the clear, ringing sound of an ax on the frosty morning air, wielded by the powerful arm of some hardy chopper. Looking along shore Paul discovered the wood cutter just about the same instant that worthy discovered him. The tall, lank West Virginian eyed the strange looking creature far a second, dropped the ax and started in a lope for his cabin. Suspecting that the curious landsman was going after his rifle, as it is customary for them to shoot at anything in the water they cannot understand, Boyton sounded a lusty blast on the bugle to attract the chopper's attention from the shooting iron. The man returned to the water's edge, loosened a flat bottomed boat from the ice and with an iron shod pole pushed out from shore toward Paul, who was rapidly approaching with the floe. As Boyton neared the woodcutter he thought, "Here comes another lantern-jawed individual who wants to ask me if I'm cold." To his surprise the man never opened his mouth, but ran his boat as close as he, could get it to the object of his curiosity and after a long stare turned his craft and began poling back to shore. When about twenty yards away he stopped as though he had forgotten some important matter, and seriously inquired:

"Say, mister, be yo' stuffed wuth cork or wind?"

"Wind," tersely answered the Captain.

He waited for no further reply, but poled solemnly and silently back to his cabin.

Below Pomeroy, Boyton, making his first all night run and feeling drowsy was moving along mechanically, when he was startled by hearing the paddle wheels of a steamer, which proved to be the Telegraph, bearing right on him. With all his energy he rose up and shouted: "Port, port, or I am a dead man."

Instantly the wheel was put over and the steamer glided by, barely missing him.

At six o'clock next morning, as he was nearing Gallipolis, he observed a boat putting out from one of the floating houses, or Jo-boats that are frequently met along the Ohio and Mississippi, containing two river gypsies. Boyton paid no attention to them until they were close behind. Then he stood up expecting to ask the time of day. He made that movement just in time, for one of the men, pale with excitement, was taking deliberate aim at him with a musket. Boyton yelled out a warning as the trigger was about to be pressed, and saved his life. The river pirate was profuse in his apologies.

"Great etarnal jeehosophat, straanger; I wouldn't a shot yer 'fur two dollars an' a half, I wouldn't, by golly, fur I'm loaded bang up ter th' muzzle with slugs fur geese. It were a narry escape fur me."

When nearing the mouth of the Big Sandy river, which forms the boundary between West Virginia and Kentucky, Paul was met by the steamer Fashion, loaded with ladies and gentlemen, who gave him a hearty welcome to the shores of old Kentucky. At Cattlettsburg, a banquet was spread on shore, of which he partook and slid back into the water. He arrived at Ironton at nine o'clock that night where he remained until morning.

From that point to Cincinnati, every town turned out to greet him. The banks were lined with people and bonfires were built at night. A short distance above Cincinnati he was met by an excursion steamer containing notables of that city and newspaper representatives. Madame Modjeska, who was with the party, presented him with a handsome silk flag. The river at Cincinnati was crowded with excursion boats. A large barge loaded with people, was driven against a pier and was barely saved from sinking with all on board. He made a brief stay in Cincinnati, and continued the voyage accompanied by a boat load of reporters, among whom was also Oliver Byron, the actor. The ice was then disappearing though the water was very cold. He averaged about five miles an hour on the lower river, and the rowing of the newspaper men to keep their boat up with him, was something beautifully scientific. At Delhi the two experienced oarsmen, who had been engaged to row a short distance, went ashore, leaving Creelman, Byron and two Cincinnati newspaper men to manage the lumbering boat. It was fortunate for their reputation as oarsmen, that spectators were directing most of their attention to Boyton, for such pulling was never seen before on the Ohio and will probably never be seen again. Paul felt like shedding tears every time he looked around to see how they were getting along. His own safety had something to do with his watchful care, for they came near running him down several times. The enthusiastic oarsmen first removed their overcoats; their undercoats followed and then collars were unbuttoned. One of them said it wasn't the length of the river that bothered them so much as the breadth. They worked independently of each other, and it was pretty hard to tell which was the bow and which the stern of the boat. A ragged urchin rowed out from shore to see what they were doing and sarcastically inquired if they were rowing over stumps. That was an unkind allusion to the extreme height at which they elevated their oar blades from the water between strokes. There was no revolver or shot gun in the party, or there would have been a funeral in that lad's family.

Row boats would pull out from shore all along, and the questions asked by the parties pulling them were ridiculous, and painfully monotonous. A sample of some of them: "Have you springs in your arms?" "Blow your horn. How far can it be heard?" "Are you going to travel all night?" "Are you going back to Cincinnati to-night?" "Let me sit on you." "Don't you get tired?" "Are you cold?"

When the press boat was not trying to climb the Kentucky hills, Paul would cheer himself by running alongside and converse with the boys; but as a rule he was wary of getting too close to them.

Nearing Louisville, a fleet of excursion steamers ran up to meet him. There was a heavy fog and the excursionists were so eager to see him, the boats pushing close around, that before he could bear into the city, he was carried over the falls, and was picked up five miles below. The newspaper men were also carried over and rescued by the life saving crew.

Leaving Louisville next morning, he intended to make the run to Cloverport, over one hundred miles below, without leaving the water. There was a strong head wind all day, turning the yellow waves of the Ohio over his face, and night closed in with dark, low hanging clouds. An electric storm began to rage about him. Flashing sheets of lightning ran over the surface of the water, cracking and sputtering as though angry at his presence. It was a grand, though fearful sight. Tree after tree along the shore was splintered by the sharp flashes and peals of thunder added to the terrific grandeur of nature's display. Fearing that his copper bugle would attract the lightning, he lowered it as far under the water as he could. All night he ran through that fearful storm, arriving at Cloverport very tired. He rested there several hours and ran to Owensboro. The mail boats, Idlewild and Morning Star, steamed up from Evansville to meet him, lashed together for the occasion, carrying a large crowd of people, and flying Boyton's colors, the Geneva Cross, which is the international life saving standard. Miss Maggie Morgan, one of Evansville's fair daughters, stepped off the Idlewild into the press boat and presented Paul with his colors.

An amusing incident occurred just as the flag was being presented. The commander of the steamer Hotspur, with an eye to business in running a little speculation of his own, loaded his steamer at so much per head, holding out the inducement that Boyton would give an exhibition up the river and that would be seen better from the deck of the Hotspur than from any other boat. As the young lady finished her presentation, the Hotspur steamed up, her deck black with people eager to witness the exhibition. Boyton had been told about the Hotspur by his agent who was on the other steamers and so, despite all the efforts of the captain and pilots of that boat, Paul kept the Idlewild and Mayflower between himself and her, in such a way that the people aboard of her could see nothing. For an hour or more, this amusing dance around the two steamers continued, until the Hotspur's captain, swearing and tramping his decks in a rage, ordered the boat back to Evansville, and to make matters worse with him, he could not collect a cent from the people he had inveigled aboard, having lost his sunshade during the night, his eyes were almost blinded and his face scorched by the intense heat.

He reached Cottonwood at 6 o'clock in the evening and through sheer exhaustion was compelled to leave the water for rest, after a continuous run of thirty-two hours. About 2 o'clock the next afternoon he met a heavy head wind and a high sea. He kept up a pretty good rate of speed, however, until he was struck by a storm off Hale's Point. The rain descended in torrents and darkness became so intense that he could scarcely tell whether he was going up, down or across. His matches were wet and he could not strike a light. He determined to go ashore, and if he could find no habitation, at least to remain along the bank until the storm had abated. A landing was effected in a thick woods, and there he found that he had not bettered the situation, because he was in danger of the lightning. He was debating whether to return to the water or not, when he caught the tiny glimmer of a light among the trees and he struck out for it, leaving the

"Baby Mine" under a log near the shore. The light guided him to a lone negro cabin and he unceremoniously pushed the door open and entered, frightening the inmates, a newly wedded couple, half out of their wits, until he had explained who he was. The negro took it all good humouredly, however, saying: "Yo' done scart de life mos' out o' us. I knows who yo' is now, do Boss."

"How about a little fire, my friend," asked Boyton.

"All right boss, all right, sah, yo' kin have a fiah quicker 'n yo' kin skin er cat," and the negro began tearing boards off the side of the cabin. It was too much trouble to gather fuel in the woods or cut down a tree and besides, the boards burned more easily.

They soon had a roaring fire and Paul, divested of the rubber dress, was drying and thoroughly enjoying himself. The negro was so tickled at having such a guest that he disappeared in the recesses of the forest for some time and returned with a whole delegation of his relatives, including his mother. By the time they had arrived, Paul was dry and prepared to re-enter the water. The old woman was not perfectly satisfied that he was of the earth and she looked upon him with considerable suspicion, mingled with a great deal of fear.

"Boss," she said, edging into a corner and peering over the shoulders of her stalwart son, "yo' 'suredly looks like a suah 'nough man; yo' certn'y isn't got de looks ob de debbil 'bout yo' face; but dey say de debbil's get cow hoofs an' I kaint see yo' feet."

Her son assured her that he had seen Boyton's feet and they were just like any other human beings; but the old woman kept something between herself and the Captain all the time and when he stepped out, he could hear her sigh of thankfulness as he walked off among the trees.

After leaving the cabin, another storm came up and the heavy rain turned to hail. In a short time the light on the Baby Mine was again put out by the waves which also soaked the matches procured from the Negro. In the darkness there was great danger of his being run down by the fleets of empty coal barges that were being towed up from New Orleans to Pittsburgh. Those great tows cover acres of river space and it is a hard matter to tell which way they are going to turn. Observing one of the Government lights which are now placed along the rivers as a guide to mariners, he steered for it. He landed and climbing the ladder to the lantern, was proceeding to get a light for his lamp, when a big dog rushed furiously up and held him treed on the lamp post. The light keeper hearing the victorious barking of the dog, came out with a gun and Paul could not explain his presence there any too quickly. The keeper called off the dog, gave the Captain a supply of matches, who lighted up his bull's eye and was soon forging ahead again. During the small hours of the night, he passed the steamers Osceola, James Howard and Andy Baum, all of which spoke him and inquired if he was in need of anything. At daybreak, the Osceola Belle stopped and gave him some hot coffee and the City of Helena gave him a cheer.

Around the Devil's Elbow, he encountered another furious head wind which required heavy work to go against. So vigorous were his exertions that he stopped at Bradley's, Arkansas, for the night and started next morning at 11 o'clock for Memphis which city he reached at four o'clock. Above Memphis he was met by a fleet of excursion steamers and the sight of his flashing paddle as he approached them was the signal for the firing of a salute from a ten pound parrot gun on the deck of the General Pierson. Miss Jeanette Boswell, one of the reigning belles of Memphis, handed him a banner and made a pleasant address of welcome.

Holding on to the gunwale of the gig, Paul replied in a felicitous manner as he accepted the trophy from her hands. The reception at Memphis was in accordance with the enthusiasm of the excursionists and Paul resumed the voyage Monday afternoon with the well wishes of the populace.

That night another terrific storm almost overwhelmed him. Huge trees were borne to the earth on either side of him as though they were reeds. Rain turned to hail and the river was whitened by the icy stones. So great was their forge that he was compelled to stand up in the stream to shield his head and face with the broad blade of his paddle and his knuckles were badly bruised. In a short time he experienced a sensation of leaking. He thought the hail stones had cut his dress; but next morning, landing on a sandbar, he found himself as dry as a pebble, the leaking sensation having been caused by the sudden change in the temperature of the water owing to the melting of the hail stones. In the darkness, he missed the cut off, by which he could have saved fifteen miles of paddling, and went around Walnut Bend. At daybreak, he saw a negro on the bank and inquired his whereabouts.

"Yo'se in de bend shoah 'nough Cap'en; but I'se pow'ful glad yo' missed the cut off, cause I wanted to see yo' awful bad."

Paul did not sympathize with the darkey's joy and that unnecessary fifteen miles was the hardest pull of the entire trip, to his mind.

That morning was very lonely along the river and he was still lecturing himself for missing the convenient cut off, when away around a distant bend he could hear the beating paddles of an approaching steamboat. That animated him and he pulled with renewed vigor until he met a boat which was loaded with excursionists from Helena, Arkansas. He hauled up alongside and the excursionists begged him to go ashore and visit their city. He was feeling sore and declined the kind invitation; other boats came up until he was surrounded. They insisted earnestly and so kindly that he should stop oft at Helena, that he finally consented to do so and rest a couple of hours, as his watch and lamp were smashed and that would give him an opportunity to get them fixed. He was enthusiastically welcomed to the city, and a committee of citizens was appointed to get anything he might want. The mayor and several other officials requested him to remain that night and deliver a lecture. He declined to do so, because his wardrobe had been shipped on ahead to Vicksburg, and he had nothing to wear but a suit of heavy underclothing and the rubber dress.

"That'll be all right," said the mayor, "we'll fix you up in a dress suit and attend to all the details. We'll get out bills, hire the hall, get a band and just fix you up as snug as a bug in a rug. Don't you let anything worry you; but just stay here and rest up while we make the arrangements."

The people had been so kind that Boyton could not resist their desires and consented. That evening the mayor drove up to the hotel and entered Paul's room with a swallow tail coat, white vest and tie, and a collar that was fastened around his neck without the assistance of shirt buttons. The upper half of him looked all right and quite appropriate for presentation to the public. They waited for the gentleman whose pantaloons just fitted Paul, but he did not appear.

"All right," said the mayor again, "I reckon he's gone to the hall with them and there's a dressing room there. Come on now, just hop into my carriage and we'll drive there. No one will see you."

They reached the hall and waited in the dressing room for the other gentleman to get there with the pantaloons. It was growing late and the people who crowded the hall began to get impatient.

"That's all right," once more exclaimed the ever ready mayor, "we can fix that."

He shoved a stand to the middle of the stage and taking a large table cover; arranged it so that it hung to the floor in front, thus hiding everything behind it from the eyes of the crowd. On the stand were placed the rubber dress, the Baby Mine, a pitcher of water and a glass. Then Boyton stood behind it and from the front he looked as though attired in an irreproachable dress suit. The curtain was rung up discovering him standing in the shelter of the table, the mayor on one side, ready to introduce him. In that position Paul acknowledged the introduction and proceeded to describe the rubber dress, his 'mode of navigating in it and an account of his voyages. In recounting his adventure with a shark in the straits of Messina, he became somewhat excited and without thinking, stepped from behind the protecting folds of the table cloth in all the glory of a dress coat, white vest and violently red drawers.

There was a stare of wonder, an awful silence for a moment and then a wild roar of laughter, which brought the orator to a sense of the comical figure he cut, and he fled from the stage with the unfinished shark story on his lips. The mayor after a violent effort, got the attention of the crowd and explained the situation. They took it so good humouredly that they gave three rousing cheers for Paul, and a tiger.

To make up for the time he had lost with the hospitable citizens of Helena, Boyton was compelled to make an extra long run and he paddled to Arkansas City without leaving the water, a distance of one hundred and sixty miles in thirty one hours, which was the longest continuous run he ever made up to that time. That night on the lonesome stretches of the river, he frequently started a loon from its resting place and it would fly off into the darkness with a wild, unearthly shriek, so ghostly in its echoing cadences that with a nervous start, Paul would glance around for that "dead man in a boat."

Early in the morning the voyager struck a big eddy and was twisted round and round for quite a while before he could clear himself and then found he was pretty close in shore. Through the thick growth of cottonwoods he observed a thin spiral of smoke rising, and knowing it to be from the cabin of some negro, he blew a merry blast on his bugle. Before the clear notes had faded from the morning air, a venerable darkey with whitened head and slightly bent, though walking without the assistance of a cane, appeared on the bluff overlooking the river. He raised his eyes to the eastern horizon, as though to determine the weather probabilities, and then he scanned the river up and down. He failed to see Boyton at first, and another blast was given on the bugle. Slowly, and with evidences of some fear, the old darkey bent his eyes on Paul, and then as slowly he deposited his white, broad brimmed hat on a stump by his side, reverently raising his eyes and with outstretched hands he solemnly said:

"He bloowed his trumpet on the watah. Bless God, bless God."

He remained in this attitude until Paul disappeared around the bend, no doubt expecting to be summoned any moment by the archangel Gabriel.

Directly after leaving the old negro, Boyton espied something in the river below him, which he thought was a snag or the floating branches of a tree; but as he drove swiftly along and looked more closely, he saw it was a large deer swimming across. Quickly loosening the "Baby Mine" to let her drift along with the current, he unslung the large hunting knife and started for the deer with the intention of bleeding it. He anticipated no trouble in paddling alongside while it was swimming, and putting the knife into its throat. When the buck discovered the pursuer it redoubled its efforts to reach the shore, but Paul was faster and was soon close on the antlered beauty. As he raised the knife to stab, the deer also raised and struck viciously with its front feet, and Paul barely dodged the blow which would have cut through the rubber suit like a keen edged knife. Again and again did he try to get an opening for a thrust, and as often did the deer, with eyes blazing like a panther's, beat him away with its sharp hoofs. At last Boyton concluded to follow if to the edge of the river, where he felt sure his game would sink in the mud and then become an easy victim. The animal did stick in the mud as was expected, but as Boyton was about to stab, its feet struck a bit of log so small that its four hoofs were all bunched together on it; but thus hampered, it sprang with wonderful power, landed on the bank six feet above, and galloped off into the forest, waving Paul a farewell with its white, stumpy tail.

That night he arrived at Arkansas City, very tired after his long pull. It was there he ran across a silent admirer—an extraordinary character who appointed himself Boyton's body guard. All that night he sat and watched the voyager while he slept. He put wood on when the fire burned low and whenever Paul wakened he was at his bedside with a drink of hot tea, but never uttering a word. Next morning he assisted in the dressing and when leaving, he wrung the Captain's hand as though parting with his dearest friend; yet he hadn't a word to say, nor would he accept any recompense for his services.

A short distance below Arkansas City, a blast from Paul's bugle brought a troop of negroes to the bank. As they gazed on him in open mouthed wonder, he asked them the distance to the next place; but they were so overcome either with fright or astonishment they could not answer. One old auntie, however, leaned over the bank and in a trembling voice asked:

"Chile, does yo' belong to the chu'ch?"

She drew a sigh of relief and seemed satisfied that he was a human being when he answered, "yes."

A lonely run of one hundred and forty miles brought him to Milligan's Bend where he stopped at a planter's house over night. The next day was Sunday and as he only had a twenty mile run to reach Vicksburg, he did not propose to start until rather late in the day, so that he would land at Vicksburg during the afternoon. While he was taking it easy, chatting with the planter, and enjoying a fragrant cigar, the old minister of the parish called, and was introduced to him.

"God bless you my son," said the venerable gentleman, pressing Paul's hand, "I must say I have called expressly to see you and ask you to do me a favor."

"I would be pleased to do anything in my power for you," replied Boyton.

"I knew you would, God bless you, I knew you would," fervently spoke the old minister, "my congregation is waiting along the bank of the river to see you start away and not a soul of them will enter the church until you go, if it is not until dark to-night. And I wanted to ask if you would start soon, so that I may begin services?"

The old man spoke with profound sincerity and his face brightened when Boyton told him that preparations would be made for leaving at once. He called down a benediction and joyfully departed for his little church, the weather beaten side of which could be seen in a grove not far distant. Paul immediately donned his dress and took to the water, paddling a few miles down and hauling up on a muddy bank to wait until it was time to start for Vicksburg. Though it was not so pleasant there as it was on the cool porch of the planter's, and he had suffered much from the heat, thoughts of the satisfied old minister did much to lighten the discomforts of his surroundings.

He arrived in sight of Vicksburg at four o'clock in the afternoon and was met by the steamer Silverthorn towing a big barge, loaded with excursionists. It appeared as though the entire population of the town and surrounding country had assembled on the river bank. So dense was the crowd, that it caused a philosophical negro to remark:

"Ef dose yere people keep on a crowdin' on dis en' ob town, de whole place are gwine fur to tip ober in de ribber, suah 'nough."

With the aid of the city marshal and a few policemen, Boyton got through the crowd to a carriage in which the Mayor was awaiting him. As the carriage was about to move off for the hotel, a man jumped in and seated himself between the Captain and the Mayor. Paul did not think much of the incident at the time, being under the impression, that the fellow was one of the Mayor's friends, though he noticed that official did not seem to be particularly pleased. When they reached the hotel, the man made himself obnoxiously officious, entering Boyton's room with an air of proprietorship and taking refreshments as though he was paying for them all. At last Paul made inquiries concerning him and found he was the most desperate character in all that section of country—a killer who had more than one murder to his account and who had the citizens of the town so terrorized that they were afraid to interpose any objections to his conduct. As soon as he learned that, Paul was in a rage and remarked that the citizens might submit to such intrusion, but he would not. The desperado, who had gone out of the room for a few moments, returned and was met by the angry navigator, who caught him by the neck, threw him bodily out of the room and kicked him down stairs. That cuffing did the fellow some good for it had the effect of encouraging other men to thrash him until he became mild-mannered and inoffensive.

The next run was from Vicksburg to Natchez, one hundred and nine miles. The start was made in a gale and Boyton was not much more than under way when he felt symptoms of fever. Indeed, so violent did the attack become, that he felt as though he must give up. He took an enormous dose of quinine which braced him and he kept pushing ahead until he arrived at Natchez, twenty six hours from Vicksburg. He was so ill on his arrival that he could scarcely notice the hearty reception given him; but went immediately to bed and fell into a deep sleep. A doctor called and pronounced him in danger of swamp fever, but thought it might be kept off with proper attention, and prescribed some remedy. Boyton felt considerably refreshed by the sleep, assisted, probably, by the prescription of the doctor, and one or two callers were admitted to his room. Among them was a gentleman who stated that his wife was an invalid. The windows of her room overlooked the river and as she saw Paul passing, on his way to Natchez, she had composed a little poem, which she begged the voyager to accept. The lady's name was Mrs. Francis Marschalk, and the poem follows:

Hail, King of the wat'ry world, New Neptune, grander than the old, Serene as thy great prototype, 'Mid storm and wave, mid heat and cold! Great victor! Man of nerve and will, Ingenious mind and wondrous skill, Laurels of peace are thine to wear, More blest than those of battle field; Begemmed with tears of gratitude And brighter than a Spartan shield—The world acclaims this crown to thee, And glories in thy victory.

The greatest boon of God is life, The dearest trust to mortal given And God-like 'tis to keep and save This precious heritage of heaven, This holy aim, this task divine Thy proud achievements claim as thine.

When all the waves of time are past And earth's rude storms with thee are o'er, Oh, may'st thou sweetly rest at last Upon the peaceful shining shore, And may thy spirit's pastime be Life's river and the Jasper sea.

Paul was deeply affected by so delicate a tribute from the accomplished stranger, and did all he could do under the circumstances—sent her an autograph note of grateful appreciation.

He did not stop long at Natchez, feeling anxious to finish the voyage as soon as possible. Among the crowd that followed him to the wharf when he resumed the trip next day was the doctor who had prescribed for him.

That gentleman was very earnest in advising him not to start as he was in great danger of being seized with the fever.

"You have every indication of the fever now," said the doctor, "and if it attacks you on the water you will to a certainty die. However, if you will persist in going, all I can do is to tell you that as soon as you feel the symptoms, make for the shore and get into a bed as soon as you can."

"What are the symptoms?" inquired Boyton,

"You become chilly and have a numb feeling all over."

"All right, I'll look out for them," and with that Paul waved a good bye to the multitude and struck gamely away in the teeth of the wind. As night came on he was tired and imagined he could feel the symptoms of which the doctor had warned him. He was just heading for shore when he heard a steamboat. He burned a red light for her and she slowed up. The passengers on deck cheered him and the Captain sang out:

"How do you feel, Paul?"

"All right, report me above," was the answer, and the boat headed on up the river. The diversion gave him courage to go ahead, and he struck out with renewed determination, running so well that he reached Baton Rouge at eight o'clock in the morning. From that city it was a home run of one hundred and thirty four miles to New Orleans. He started early next morning, though feeling very stiff and sore. The weather grew intensely hot, he suffered terribly and was burned almost black in the face, the skin of which peeled off. About eleven o'clock in the morning, on the glassy surface ahead, he noticed something bobbing up and down in a queer manner, and pulled away to investigate. He found it to be a dead mule swollen to gigantic size. While looking at it its tail flipped out of the water as though it were alive. It was then he became aware of the fact that a swarm of alligators were feeding on it, and he pulled away with about as much speed as he has ever been able to attain.

During the day he ran through a thickly populated country, along what is known as the lower coast of Louisiana; the river was fringed with rich sugar plantations, and a majority of the negroes who rowed out to see him, spoke the language of the French Creole. Magnolia trees were thick on either side and framed a picture of rare beauty.

While paddling for a short distance close in shore, Paul discovered a most unique and lazy style of angling. Happening to look up at the bank, he saw two pair of bare feet of heroic size, from which two fishing lines hung, the corks bobbing on the surface a few yards from the shore. The broad bottoms of their pedal extremities turned to the river, the line passing between the great and second toes to the water, and there they lay enjoying delicious sleep, waiting for a fish to swallow the bait, when the pull on the line would be felt between their toes and awaken them to attend to business. Paul took in the situation at a glance. Quietly drawing near one of the lines he gave it a vicious jerk. The negro on the other end of it flipped to a sitting posture as though he was worked on a spring like a jumping jack. When he saw the black figure as he thought, on his line, he let out a shriek that could have been heard for a mile, at the same time springing to his feet and starting on a sprinting pace for some hiding place, yelling, as he ran, to his companion:

"Hyah Bill, git away from dar; git up an' cut. I'se done cotch de debbil on my hook."

The other restful fisherman sat up stiffly as if worked on a rusty hinge, and seeing Boyton, was seized with an uncontrollable fit of laughter. He laughed as though he was never going to catch his breath, and Paul was afraid he would choke. He rolled on the ground in paroxysms of mirth, stood up and leaned against a tree shouting out such loud guffaws that it was difficult to tell whether it was through amusement or fright. Paul got out on the bank and tried to quiet him, but was unsuccessful and entered the water again and paddled away. For some distance the voice of that hilarious fisherman was borne to him on the breeze.

As evening closed in he could hear the darkies who had been paid off, it being Saturday night, singing and arguing along the shore. A dense fog soon enveloped everything, however, and he could not see which way he was going. He seized the roots of a drifting tree, knowing it would keep in the channel, mounted it and sat there for hours floating with the current. All night the mocking birds along shore serenaded him. He would have remained on the tree until morning; but he heard the whistles of steamers below. Knowing that a fleet left New Orleans every Saturday afternoon bound north, and that each would be trying to gain the lead on the other, he was afraid he would be run down, so he slid off the tree and made for shore. That course was not without its danger, also; for mingled with the beautiful songs of the mocking bird, he had heard the hoarse bark of alligators and there was no telling but that he might run right on to some of them. They are thick along shore, but rarely go out into the river, except as in the case of the dead mule, they follow their prey. Luckily he avoided those dangerous reptiles. He sounded the bugle and a Frenchman came down to the bank. Paul explained who he was and the man eagerly invited him ashore. "I am sitting up with my old master who is dead," said the Frenchman. "What was the matter with him?" inquired Boyton, somewhat alarmed.

"Oh, it wasn't the fever, you need have no fear."

Paul decided to land and wait until the fleet had passed at any rate, then he lighted his lamp and pushed off through the fog, preferring the solitude of the river to the society of the grief stricken Frenchman. The fog lifted in the morning and he found that he was on time. Ten miles above New Orleans, he was met by excursion steamers with enthusiastic crowds aboard. Captain Leathers of the famous old boat, Natchez, was determined to outdo the others in the way of welcoming the voyager, for Boyton was an old friend. He had a cannon placed on the deck of his boat, loaded to the muzzle. A crowd of negroes were jammed on a lot of cotton bales, craning their necks to catch a glimpse of Paul and Captain Leathers fired right in amongst them. The concussion was so great that at least forty of the darkies were knocked off their feet and thought they were killed by the explosion. Paul landed at New Orleans, April 27th, finishing a journey of two thousand four hundred and thirty miles. He was feted and lionized in the Crescent City until he was in danger of becoming enervated, so he boarded a train for the north, some thirty pounds less in weight than when he started at Oil City.

CHAPTER XVIII.

The summer of 1879 was idly spent. Boyton visited the most celebrated watering resorts of America and enjoyed a well earned good time. As the autumn leaves began to fall, he was seized with an irresistible desire to feel himself again afloat, so he turned his attention to the rivers of the New England States. He went to Boston, made a careful study of the maps, and concluded to take a voyage on the Merrimac; this river, with its numerous falls and rapids, he thought would furnish some excitement. The start was made from Plymouth, New Hampshire, at six o'clock in the morning of October seventh. The river was too rough for him to tow the Baby Mine along, a fact which he very much deplored. Boyton had not paddled many yards from the shore ere he found the water so shallow that he was compelled to wade quite a distance before getting fairly under way, then he soon left the cheering crowd in the distance. About nine o'clock, approaching a bridge, he heard a rumbling sound. Looking up he beheld the figure of a man and horse outlined against the sky like a shadow picture. The countryman also discovered the queer looking figure in the water. He craned his neck, jerked his arms up and with mouth and eyes wide open slapped the reins on the horse's back and galloped off at a faster pace than the good agriculturalists in that locality are wont to ride. He had not read the newspapers.

An hour later, Paul blew his bugle in front of a farm house that stood near the river. The people ran to the water's edge and began firing a broadside of down east interrogatives with such rapidity as to nearly swamp him.

"Ain't yeou nearly drowned?" "Ain't yeou afeard yeou will be?" "Ain't yeou hungry?" "Ain't yeou cold?" "Ain't yeou hot?" "Kin yeou keep awake?" "Ef yeou cain't, would yeou sink?" "Air yeou a orphing?", "Dew yeou like the water?" "What circuse dew yeou belong tew?" "Who hired yeou tew dew this?" "Why on airth dew yeou travel this way fur instead of in a boat?"

Paul could not stand the rapid fire system of the New Hampshire rustics, and with a pained expression on his face he, pulled silently out of hearing. The narrowing river brought him closer to the banks, and as he was forging ahead an old gentleman hailed him. Paul stopped for a moment and was sorry for it, as the man tried to chill his blood with doleful stories of the dangers in the river below. "Yeou air goin' straight ahead tew destruction," he bellowed, "thar's a whirlpool jist ahead, where six lumbermen was drowned one time."

Boyton had no fear of sharing the fate of the lumbermen, so he pushed ahead, leaving the old man standing on the bank with clasped hands and pained expression.

The voyager shortly reached the junction of Squam river, and there encountered the first waterfall. A crowd of men and boys had assembled on the bridge and anxiously watched him dash down on the rushing waters, in which he was for the moment lost. Emerging from the boiling foam at the foot of the fall, he scrambled on a rock and stood up to look for the channel. From that point he had a wearisome pull in dead, choppy water, until he reached New Hampton. At many places along the route, well disposed persons were liberal with their advice to give up such an "outlandish" mode of traveling and to "git on land like a human critter." Though the advice sounded well, Paul noticed on one occasion at least, that their methods of travel were not devoid of the danger ascribed to his. Above him, on the grim rocks of a bluff, he saw the wreck of a light wagon, and floating along with the current, were the seat and one wheel.

"Where is the driver of that wagon?" inquired Paul. No one knew and he plied his paddle vigorously in the hope of overtaking the unfortunate man who had evidently been hurled from the bluff into the stream; but no trace could be found. Below the sound of rapids was borne to his ear. The smooth water began to break and start as if suddenly impelled forward by some subtle influence that meant to tear the rocks from the bed and crush every obstacle in its course. With all his care in steering through that rapid, he was thrown against a rock with considerable force, but caught hold of it and stood up to determine the course of the channel. Seeing an old lady standing before the door of a farm house, he rang out a cavalry charge on his bugle. She threw up her hands as though she had heard the last trumpet of the Day of Judgment, and rushing into the house she alarmed all the occupants. The look of horror they gave the Captain as he stood on that rock in the midst of the rapids, beckoning to them with his paddle, was evidence that they took him for his Satanic majesty or one of his courtiers.

"Lan' sakes, 'Zekiel!" exclaimed the boldest one or the party, who chanced to be a tall, raw-boned female, "go git gran'pap's old blunderbuss, an' shoot it."

Zekiel was rooted to the spot with fear and heeded not the exhortation of his strong-minded relative. Boyton, who feared the people who did not keep posted by reading the papers, more than he did the rapids, relieved them by taking to the water, and was flashed from their sight as he was drawn into another and larger rapid. He was whirled into a place where he had a hard struggle over a bed of round, slippery rocks in shallow water. He could not find the channel, and if he stood up to take an observation, his feet would be swept from under him. He was fully an hour getting over the rocks, walking, crawling or paddling as best he could. At five o'clock he reached Bristol. There he was advised to go no further and a telegram from his agent below, told him the river was too dangerous to travel at night. The next morning the landlord's daughter drove him to the bank and a large crowd watched as he paddled away toward the whirlpool, against which he had been warned. It was a rough passage, but he reached Franklin in safety at one o'clock. All the way he had kept a sharp lookout for the driver of the wrecked wagon, but could discover no trace of him. Before reaching Franklin a fleet of boats rowed up to the falls to meet him, and bonfires were built along the shore in his honor.

The voyage was resumed at eight o'clock next morning, and at ten o'clock he shot Sewell's Falls, a rather rough place, and from there the river was lonely until West Concord was reached. Here the booming of cannon announced his safe arrival to the people. He was met by a fleet of boats and informed that they had been looking for him two days. He was warned to look out for Turkey Falls, and before proceeding he asked a countryman which side of the falls he should take, and received the cheering answer that, "whichever side he took he would wish he had taken the other." Both banks of the falls were lined with people, Paul always noticed a larger crowd at every point where he was likely to be killed. He went over Turkey Falls, and for a few seconds was lost to sight. The spectators waited in breathless silence to see his lifeless form rise from the foam, but beheld only the flashing paddle moving gaily along in smoother water, and so a hero was not lost at that uneventful spot, and there would be no legend of the place to hand down to posterity.

One mile from the falls, the Captain encountered the first dam, below which there was a stretch of dead water for seven miles. It was there he met the first steam craft—a small launch that had sailed up from Suncook. It was a long, tiresome pull through the dead stretch, and he arrived at Suncook at dark pretty well fagged out. Invitations to remain were plentiful; but he continued two miles further to Hookset where dry clothing awaited him. Next morning an early start was made and he was able to have the Baby Mine with him for the rest of the journey. The water from Hookset to Manchester is heavy; but by constant paddling he reached the latter place at noon. There were more signs of life as he progressed. Children ran along the banks calling to him, and one little girl cried: "Paul, come in here I want see you," as though she had known him for years. He passed two of the five falls that barred the progress to Nashua, when darkness fell with such intensity that he was compelled to depend on shore sounds to determine in which direction he was going. At eight o'clock, seeing lights on shore, he summoned some people with a blast on the bugle and inquired the distance to the next falls. As was the case above, he had to listen to diverse and widely different opinions, with the usual result, that he took his own course, and succeeded in reaching Nashua in safety at ten o'clock. The next day dawned dull and rainy and he had a tiresome pull on a sluggish stream until he reached Tyngsborough. Nearing a crowded bridge at that place, volleys of questions were fired at him. He was choking with thirst and without looking up, asked: "Is there a hotel here?"

"Naw," shouted a gruff voice, "ner yeou kaint git naw liker hure nowhere neether."

"I'll take an oath that you never colored that nose of yours with river water," quickly replied Boyton.

The retort happily hit the mark, for the fellow was the possessor of a richly tinted proboscis of carmine hue, that was somewhat of a landmark in the village. The crowd roared in approbation of the home thrust and the man, hastily elbowed his way through the crowd until he was beyond hearing.

A number of small boats ascended the river from Lowell to meet Paul, and he accepted an invitation from the Vesper Boat Club, of that city, to land at their club house, which he did at five o'clock. He remained over Sunday in Lowell and resumed the journey Monday morning. He shot Hunt's falls in safety and there met a steam launch with newspaper men from Lawrence, aboard. At Lawrence the river begins to be affected by the tide, on account of which he was compelled to wait until four o'clock next morning before continuing the trip. He made a landing at daylight at a frame house over the door of which was painted the word "confectionery" and he thought he could get some breakfast. He was given a room, but it was soon filled with obtrusive questioners. A farmer, seeing the look of hunger in his eyes, volunteered to procure some breakfast. The Captain was prepared to do justice to the kind of a meal he had been wishing for, when the farmer returned with a genuine country breakfast consisting of several pieces of apple and mince pie and a liberal supply of assorted pickles. It was fortunate for Boyton's digestion that he was obliged to stay at that place for five hours, owing to the flood tide.

Directly after resuming the voyage, he was met by a fleet of boats, one of them being occupied by Sir Edward Thornton, the British Minister at Washington, and his beautiful daughter. Being old acquaintances, Paul enjoyed a pleasant chat with them, and a few moments later, he landed at Newburyport. The voyage was ended. He had made two hundred miles of very rough going, in seven days.

Boyton rested but a short time ere he was ready to begin a run down the Connecticut, the largest and most beautiful river in New England, from as near the headwaters as he could get, to Long Island Sound. His arrival at Stratford, New Hampshire, from which place he had decided to start, occasioned a great deal of comment in that and neighboring villages. The inhabitants concluded he should have more than ordinary recognition, and in lieu of a cannon they put a pair of anvils together and succeeded in making quite a respectable noise. At night a deputation of citizens called on him with a request that he would not start until daylight next morning, so they would have an opportunity to see him off. At six forty-five o'clock the following morning, a goodly sized company was present to witness the start. After passing the railroad bridge at Coos, he had about six miles of rapids, the river being only about forty yards wide and rather speedy, the voyager averaging about five miles an hour. At eleven o'clock he passed Stratford Hollow and inquired of a countryman there how far it was to Northumberland:

"Seven mile b' road an' twenty-b' river, b' gosh," was the native's reply.

Though laconic, the answer was correct, for the stream bowed and bended frequently, and at one time he passed the same farm house twice in an interval of two hours and a half, giving him an opportunity to observe both sides of it. About two o'clock in the afternoon a heavy rainstorm blew up, while the booms and logs in the river also caused a great deal of trouble. Whenever a person on the bank could speak to him he was invariably warned of the Fifteen Mile Falls.

"Look Bout, straanger, fur them 'ere Fifteen Mile Falls. They'll jus' squeeze yeou sure'n daylight," was almost always the style of warning.

Paul hauled up to question one man who looked like a waterman, concerning the falls. The fellow said he had gone over once on a raft, when the water was much higher. "An' would yeou b'lieve it," he added, "one o' them 'ere wimmen were boun' an' determined tew come wuth us."

"Did she go?" asked Paul.

"Neow yeou jus' bet she did."

"Well, how did she act?"

"I'll tell yeou straanger. I tol' her tew go astern an' hol' on hard tew th' stake. She went aft ju' afore we got tew Holbrook's Bar, an' then we jus' tuk it. Slap, bang we went, jus' run pitch right under thet 'ere rushin' water'n come up b'low all right."

"What did the woman do? How did she act?"

"Wall, sir, yeou wuden't b'lieve it. She jus' guv one loud snort, shuk herself out'n went right erlong."

The loss of his paddle caused Paul to remain at Northumberland all night, and fortunately it was found among a lot of driftwood next morning, enabling him to drive ahead again.

One of the drawbacks of the voyage was the difficulty experienced in getting proper provisions at many places. Numbers of people were either thoughtless, or they looked on Boyton as an uncanny sort of creature, whom they did not care to have about. When he did get food, it consisted of pie, which seemed to be the staff of life with most of the country people. He inquired of a voluble fellow where he could be best accommodated at Northumberland.

"Oh, stop at th' hotel, b' all means. They feed yeou tip top; high up," said he, "I've been ter dinner there w'en they've hed all o' seven kinds er pie on ther table t'onct."

"Have they got apples and squash?" jokingly asked the Captain.

"Yeou kin jus' bet on thet," was the enthusiastic answer.

Just below Northumberland, which place he left at nine o'clock, he encountered a dam and very rough water. The weather became squally, with a cold and cutting snow beating into his face; but he plied the paddle vigorously and made remarkable progress, reaching Lancaster at one thirty o'clock. Countrymen whom he passed would stare at him and then burst out into loud guffaws of laughter as though immensely tickled at the idea of a man paddling down the river in a driving snow storm.

At length Paul began to feel the livelier motion of the water as he was nearing Lunenburg, where the Fifteen Mile Falls begin. Wishing to enter that dangerous stretch a fresh man, he pulled up for the night and luckily found a hospitable farmer in the person of Mr. Frank Bell, who entertained him handsomely until morning.

He was prepared for heavy work when he started early next day, and well it was that he was fortified for the occasion, as the Fifteen Mile Falls proved about as rough an experience as he had ever gone through. At Holbrook's Bar, the last pitch of the falls, M'Indoe's Dam, Barnet Pitch and other place, he encountered many dangers in the way of whirling currents and jagged rocks. He suffered but a slight bruise in the descent though his dress was cut and he was obliged to stop and repair it at Lower Waterford where he remained over night. At a little settlement above that village, someone in a small gathering on the bank said:

"Hure comes that pesky swimmer aroun' th' bow, an' he's a cumin' like forty."

"Who's a-comin'?" asked a broad shouldered Green Mountaineer. The very thought of a man paddling down the river seemed to suggest some scheme of the fakir or dodge of the showman to separate him from the coins that jingled in his pocket. The old Vermonter, turning a quid of sassafras from one corner of his mouth to the other, drawled, with all impressiveness of a judge to whom some knotty law point had been presented: "Wall, I wunder what he gits out'n this? He mus' be a darned critter tew resk himself in thet ere fashion; an' I swan whar th' profit comes in is agin me tew tell."

The Vermonter's inability to understand what Boyton was going to get out of such a trip, appeared to be the subject about which most of the people along the Connecticut were puzzling their brains. They would invariably ask: "How dew yeou make it pay?" "Ain't yeou cold?" Many of them would not respond when asked for information regarding the currents and rough passages; but would permit him to paddle along uninstructed in order that they "might have the full benefit of the show."

After cutting his dress he became chilled by the inflow of cold water and was helplessly numb. A little stimulant would have done him a world of good; but he could neither beg, buy nor borrow anything from the spectators. When he reached Lower Waterford Bridge, his agent met him with supplies, and there he stopped to repair his dress. He was only about midway of the Fifteen Mile Falls. The suit was injured in the first pitch and the accident might have been averted had any one in the large crowd that watched him start in, given him information. As he approached, he asked the onlookers where the channel of the river was. They stared at him and on the question being repeated, looked at one another and put their eyes on the river again. Almost immediately the current swept Boyton toward the rocks.

Off Morris' place, Paul hailed a fellow in a turnip patch and as he cautiously approached the river, the Captain removed the cover from an air-tight jar suspended from his neck, took out a cigar and holding a match in the rubber tube of his dress, lit the weed. The rustic removed his hat, closed an eye and scratched his head in great perplexity.

"Wall, I swaw," he ejaculated, "ef yeou hadn't spoke er I'd er taken yeou fur th' devil an' swore yeou that ere durned cigar Wuth th' end o' yer tail, I wud, b'gosh. But ain't yer cold?"

Valley Hotel was the name of the tavern at which Paul and his party put up for the night at Lower Waterford. How long before Boyton's visit the last guest had registered there is problematical, but the landlady proved hospitable. During the evening, her sitting room, which Boyton and his party occupied, reviewing the incidents of the voyage, was overrun with fellows who stalked in and looked at "the show" just as if it was a menagerie of wild beasts into which they had free admission. They gathered at the country store opposite and poured across the street, in sixes and sevens, like so many reliefs on army duty. A gang would enter the sitting room occupying the chairs and sofa, look on with open mouths for ten or fifteen minutes and listen to what must have been enigmatical to them; then looking one at the other, the entire party would rise together, stalk back to the store, where they would relate their experience to others, who in turn would brace up and make a descent on the lion of the hour. They did not rap for admittance, did not remove their hats on entering, did not wait to be asked to take a seat, did not say a word to anybody while present, did not say "good evening" when they went out—in fact did nothing but stare in the most ignorant and saucy manner. An excuse may be made for there in the fact that Waterford is isolated from civilization, there being neither railroad nor telegraph communication with the outside world and few newspapers are ever seen to say nothing of being read. Paul bore the inspection good naturedly and joked pleasantly as each "relief" went out.

Just before starting in the morning, an old gentleman met Boyton on the porch in front of the hotel and expressed real pleasure at meeting him—in fact, claimed close acquaintanceship. The Captain was glad to meet an old friend and was inquisitive enough to ask where they had seen each other before.

"Wall," the old fellow answered, "yeou remember w'en yeou crossed th' English channel?"

"Yes," Boyton remembered it.

"An' that ere rubber suit you wore?"

"Certainly."

"Wall," continued the old man, apparently tickled to the end of his toes because Paul had not forgotten. "Wall, I saw thet ere suit at the centennial in Philadelphia in '76; I was thar." He looked triumphantly around to catch the admiring gaze of his townsmen.

The above are only a few samples of many similar incidents and episodes which occured during the voyage. In shooting Dodge's Falls, a lumberman called out to Paul to hug the New Hampshire shore and he would get over safely. That was the only sensible word of warning or information he received through the entire Fifteen Mile Falls.

He reached Woodville Monday evening after escaping many dangers, pretty well used up. The worst of the run had been accomplished, though there were still several falls and dams to be shot and long stetches of dead water to be paddled. Nearing Bellow's Falls, the people were more enlightened and many offers of hospitality were sung out to him from shore. The citizens of that place displayed a deep interest in his attempt to shoot the falls and rendered all the assistance in their power. He shot them in safety, though narrowly escaping a big log that was dashed over directly behind him. From that point to the completion of the voyage, he everywhere met with kind words and encoragement.

On the evening of November seventh, he landed at Saybrook light, sixteen days from Stratford Hollow.

The winter of 1879 and 1880 was spent in Florida, hunting, fishing, alligator shooting and canoeing. He and a party of friends made a canoe voyage far up on the St. John's river and through the Kissimmee to Lake Okeechobee, where they had a great deal of sport shooting deer, bears and alligators; but at the same time the numerous moccasins and rattlesnakes afforded more amusement than was relished by several of the party. Returning north to Jacksonville, Paul made a run down the St. John's river to the sea, crossing the shark infested bar at the mouth of the river.

On his way north during the spring, he made short trips on the Savannah, Cooper and Potomac rivers and the Chesapeake Bay. In June he paddled down the Delaware from Philadelphia to Ship John's light. That trip was a very laborious one on account of the sluggish tide. The moment the tide would turn against him, he would have to strike for the flat Jersey shore, where in the long grass the myriads of energetic mosquitoes almost set him frantic with their attention. Later he paddled the entire length of Lake Quinsigamond, and in September he ran the Narragansett from Rocky Point to Providence.

CHAPTER XIX.

One day in October, while Paul was walking down Broadway, New York, a gentleman tapped him on the shoulder, saying: "This is Captain Boyton, I believe?" On being answered in the affirmative, he continued:

"I have just returned from Europe, where I was looking for you. I have a message for you from Don Nicholas de Pierola, but as I am known as an agent of the Peruvian government, it is hardly safe to talk to you here, as there are Chilean spies in New York as well as Lima. Meet me to-night at this address." He slipped a card into Boyton's hand and stepped quickly away.

That night Paul entered a house in Thirty-fourth street where he met the stranger, who immediately proceeded to business by stating that Don Nicholas de Pierola wanted Boyton to start for Peru at once, with a full equipment of dresses, torpedo cases, electrical appliances, and everything necessary for the destruction of Chilean vessels. It did not take Paul long to arrange the preliminaries and before he left, a contract was made by which he was to enter the Peruvian torpedo service, with a commision of Captain. He was to receive one-hundred-thousand dollars for the first Chilean vessel destroyed; one-hundred-and-twenty-five thousand dollars for the second and one-hundred-and-fifty thousand dollars for the third. Three Chilean vessels that were desired most to be destroyed were named. They were the Huascar, Blanco Encalado, and Almirante Corcoran.

Next day Boyton was busy getting the necessary equipment together, happy in the thought of more adventure and chances of big prize money. He also received credentials as a newspaper correspondent under the name of Pablo Delaport. He told his family he was going to take a little run to Panama, but said nothing about Peru. On October 10th, 1880, accompanied by his assistant, George Kiefer, he embarked on the steamer Crescent City for Aspinwall, arriving at that port on the 19th, whence they crossed to Panama and were compelled to wait there two days for the Columbia to bear them south, to Peru. One of the passengers from New York, was a curious and erratic character, who was the possessor of a weighty secret. After much mystery, he decided to make Boyton his confidant, and he solemnly revealed to him the matter that was bearing on his brain. It was to the effect that a great treasure was buried on a distant island and he was about fitting out an expedition to go in search of it. A female relative, who was a clairvoyant, had located the treasure and he was sure of finding it. He was anxious for Paul to join him in the search, and displayed almost insane disappointment at receiving a refusal. At Panama, the fortune hunter purchased an outfit of arms, including a commander's sword which he strapped on and strutted about with the air of a bold buccaneer. He chartered a vessel in which he sailed for the treasure island; but, as Paul afterward learned, returned after great suffering and loss, minus the treasure.

A Chilean man-of-war, the Amazonas, was anchored at Panama on the lookout for a torpedo launch that was expected to arrive for the Peruvian government from New York. In his capacity of a newspaper correspondent, Boyton went on board the man-of-war to inspect her, with an idea that he might have an opportunity sometime to feel her bottom with a one-hundred-and-fifty pound torpedo. He was escorted through the vessel by her Captain and took copious notes of her construction and armament. As he was over-going the side into the boat to return to shore, an English engineer spanned him carefully and remarked: "Your face seems familiar to me. Where have I seen you before?"

Paul replied that he could not possibly tell as his duties led him to all parts of the world, and he hurriedly entered the boat.

The next day they set sail and on the 24th, sighted Dead Man's Island at the mouth of the Guayquil river. From a certain point the island bears a startling resemblance to a gigantic man afloat on his back. Hence its name. They steamed up the river about sixty miles to Guayquil. The chattering of parrots and paroquettes along the shore was almost deafening. Flocks of them would hover over the vessel for several minutes at a time and fly back to the forest.

Guayquil is one of the hottest towns on earth, though not one of the cleanest. The stenches arising from the filthy streets and byways are overpowering, and fever flags fly from nearly every third or fourth house. The steamer lay in the middle of the river while discharging her cargo into lighters and the passengers took advantage of the wait for a trip across into the city. From the landing place crowds of boys followed them, offering monkeys and alligators for sale. The latter were from six inches to three feet long, strapped on boards to keep them from biting. They are much quicker and more savage than the North American alligator.

After the cargo was discharged, the vessel was again put under way and on the 26th they anchored off Paita, the first Peruvian port. Paul took a long walk on the beach at that place, and for the first time saw the curious, blood red crabs that dwell in myriads along the shore. At a distance they look like a big red wave; but as they are approached, quickly disappear into holes in the sand, and on looking back, they are seen in countless thousands in the rear. Their habits are similar to the hermit crab. They are small and not edible, quick as rats and difficult to catch.

Chimbote was the next place in Peru at which the steamer anchored. That port was then in the hands of the Chileans and the stop was only long enough to take on the mail, when they headed for Callao, the principal port of Peru. As the Chilean fleet then blockaded the port no steamers were permitted to land there, but when off the city, the Columbia steamed through the blockaders, much to Paul's anxiety, because of a man on board who had been questioning him rather closely regarding his intentions in visiting Peru and Boyton had every reason to believe him a spy, and looked every moment for him to signal one of the blockading vessels; but fortunately the Columbia was allowed to proceed on her way unmolested to the port of Chilca where there are only a few miserable houses. The steamer landed there at night and Paul with his companion and five other passengers were put ashore in a small boat. Accommodations for the entertainment of travelers were very poor, but they made the best of it for the night, though they were nearly devoured by fleas, which, combined with the fact that it was necessary to guard closely their baggage, prevented the enjoyment of any repose. A train of mules was chartered next morning to bear them across the pampas to Lima. All day long they bestrode those razor backed mules, riding through wild country, now over bleak and desolate hills, then across barren plains. The absence of even a spear of grass bespoke the unfruitfulness of the soil, while large condors and galanasas hovered overhead, waiting for man or mule to fall, overcome by the heat; then they would alight with exultant cries to a horrible feast. The water of the caravan was rapidly exhausted and they suffered the pangs of thirst. Toward evening, with parched throats and weary bodies they reached an oasis in the shape of a poor village. There was water in abundance however, and that was more precious to the wayfarers than the sight of great palaces. Being refreshed, they proceeded to the town of Lurin, where they arrived late at night and found the place occupied by Peruvian troops. An ambitious officer of the company, selected Paul for a victim and placed him under arrest as a Chilean spy. The officer would listen to no explanations, but compelled his prisoner to travel on that night, though he was so fatigued by the day's journey that he could scarcely sit on his mule. There was no help for it, so Kiefer was left with the baggage and Paul, closely guarded, rode off into the sultry night During the small hours of the morning, the troop arrived at Chorrillos, at which place, Boyton positively refused to go further, being too nearly exhausted to proceed. The officer decided to remain until daylight and go on to Lima by rail. As tired as the prisoner was, he could not sleep on account of the ravenous attacks of fleas which drove him almost mad. At daylight he was taken by railway train to Lima and on arrival there was immediately marched to the palace, where he was to be presented as a spy to his friend, Don Nicholas de Pierola, the Dictator.

The impertinent officer arrived at the palace with his prisoner, under the impression that he would receive a handsome reward for making such a notable arrest. When Paul pulled out a packet, addressed to Don Nicholas, the fellow was rather surprised; but continued to treat the supposed spy with overbearing harshness, until Boyton was released from his presence and taken before the Dictator, where he was cordially received and many references made to their former pleasant meeting in Paris.

"But how did you get here so soon?" inquired Don Nicholas, "other passengers who were on board the Columbia have not yet arrived."

Paul related the story of his capture at Lurin and of his all night ride on mule back. The Dictator sent for the officer, who, thinking he was going to be rewarded for his cleverness, entered the reception room with a peacock strut that was admirable. By the time Don Nicholas finished a reprimand, he slunk away like a whipped cur and it is likely he was more careful to investigate thereafter when making arrests.

The Dictator sent Paul to the Hotel Americano, where fine quarters were prepared for him and he took a much needed rest, not waking until the next day when a message was conveyed to him from Don Nicholas to the effect that they were going to Ancon that day to try some torpedo experiments. Much refreshed, he was quickly ready to accompany them.

Ancon is a small seaside resort about fifteen miles from Lima. At that time it was almost entirely deserted on account of the frequent bombarding by the Chilean cruisers as they passed up and down the coast. Whenever those aboard the cruisers wished amusement, they turned their guns on Ancon and knocked over a few houses.

The party consisting of the Dictator, several high government officials, Boyton and Major Rabauld, who had been transferred to him as an aid, went down on a special car drawn by a little engine named the Favorita, furnished by the railroad company, which was largely owned by Americans.

The experiments took place between several rocky islands, that have probably been detached from the mainland by volcanic action, and the shore. The torpedoes were tried on dummy vessels, while a troop of soldiers stood guard at all the approaches to the place in order to prevent inquisitive individuals as well as Chilean spies, from learning the nature of the work going on. Don Nicholas was highly pleased and was in fine spirits at the thought of getting rid of some of the powerful vessels that darkened his harbor with their frowning ports. On their return trip, the Favorita had proceeded less than one mile, when the little engine ran plump into a sand pile that had been carried up by the wind, and was thrown from the track on to a plain that had once been a burial place of the ancient Incas. All efforts to put the engine and car back on the track were fruitless, and a messenger was sent back to Ancon to telegraph to Lima for an extra engine to assist in righting the little train. As the telegraph service was extremely slow, the party was compelled to wait all day for the relief engine. In the meantime, Don Nicholas and his staff, went out on the pampas and stood about the sand hills talking over the struggle they were having with their neighbors. During that time, a Chilean cruiser passed about one mile off shore, and had the importance of the little group been known to those on board, they could have captured the Dictator without a great deal of trouble.

The soldiers gathered up the skulls and bones of Incas that were strewn about and amused themselves by playing ten pins on the hard sand, sticking the bones up and rolling the skulls at them. Don Nicholas paid no attention to the gruesome sport; but stood calmly conversing with the officers who surrounded him.

It was almost dark when the relief engine came puffing into sight; but a short time sufficed to place the car on the track and the party arrived safely at Lima.

On the following day, Paul went down to Callao, bearing a letter from the Dictator to General Astate, commander of the fort, requesting him to furnish Boyton with the best small vessel obtainable for torpedo work. The General received Paul in the kindest possible manner, and took him out to the Punta del Mar Bravo, where fortifications were located, and calling his attention to some American parrot guns, patted one of them and smilingly remarked:

"These are some compatriots of yours."

With that, the General gave orders to fire at the Chilean fleet which was then laying near San Lorenzo, an island several miles out from Callao and so high are its cliffs that they penetrate the clouds. Four or five shots were fired at the blockading vessels; but they were too far off, as the iron balls could be seen throwing spray in the air at some distance to the landward of them. "That is a salute in your honor," remarked the General.

That evening, after having overhauled every available craft in the harbor, General Astate gave Paul a little sloop, the only thing that could possibly be used in torpedo attacks; but far from being the powerful little steam launch that had been promised. The Peruvian steamers at that time were all corralled in the harbor at Callao. They were not strong enough to grapple with the powerful men-of-war of the Chileans that so saucily watched the port, hence they remained inside under the protection of the guns at the fort and at the point, while great piles of sand bags were erected to the seaward of the docks as a shield against Chilean cannon balls.

Paul was therefore compelled to enter upon his torpedo work, terribly handicapped by the poor equipment of the Peruvians; but determined to make the best use of the means at hand. The little sloop was called the Alicran. She was quickly provisioned and a crew shipped. Before embarking on her, Don Nicholas sent for Boyton and commissioned him as Captain in the Peruvian Navy. She was then sailed around to Chorrilos, as Paul considered that the best point from which to begin operations on the Chilean fleet. There he made his headquarters at a hacienda which a wealthy Peruvian turned over to him and anchored the sloop close in shore under the shelter of the cliffs, and began the manufacture of torpedoes. One thousand pounds of dynamite had been sent down to him in wagons from Lima, and under his directions, the crew was soon engaged in stowing it away in the rubber cases.

When the torpedoes were ready, he began cruising to the seaward in order to reconnoiter the movements of the blockading squadron, which every night would trip anchor and stand off to sea. The Chilean's fear of torpedoes deterred them from laying in to shore at night. Paul drilled the officers that were placed under him in the use of the rubber dress and in handling torpedoes; but he did not find them overly energetic in their work. They spent most of their time among the islands, that were formed by great rocks which had been cast from the mainland by earthquake or volcanic action, watching the movements of the Chileans. All day long the blockading vessels would lay in sight; but at night they would steam further out to sea and stand slowly up and down the coast. Night after night Paul and his crew watched for an opportunity to place one of their torpedoes under the dark hull of a Chilano; but the latter were on the alert for them, having been informed that Boyton had been engaged by Peru. The phosphorescence of the water at night was also against them. The least disturbance on its surface would cause a glow of silver to flash in the darkness that could be seen for quite a distance.

One night as they were watching from Chorrillos, a cruiser was sighted steaming slowly up the coast and Paul determined to test her alertness at all hazards. He put on his dress and taking a one hundred pound torpedo in tow, paddled out as carefully as possible until he saw her head toward him. Then he set the fly torpedo across what he thought would be her track and pulled in shore. Had the cruiser picked the line up with her bow, it would have thrown the torpedo along her side, setting an automatic wheel in motion that would explode it. When he had reached a safe distance, he turned to see the vessel blown up and to his intense disappointment, the cruiser turned a gatling gun on the torpedo. The Chileans were more watchful than he had given them credit for.

After the Chilean had discovered the torpedo, the little sloop barely escaped by putting out her sweeps and drawing close up under the land, by that means reaching Chorrillos next morning in safety. A party of marines from the cruiser were landed on an island near where they had discovered the torpedo, next day, to hunt out those who had placed it. Fortunately for Paul and his crew they had eluded the cruiser under cover of the night. For some two months after the above adventure, the torpedo men laid under the shelter of the batteries on the top of Moro, a high bluff. They made sorties every night; but the Chileans were on the watch for them, besides the sloop was so slow as to be almost useless, and Paul's Peruvians had a wholesome dread of the enemies' guns which could be turned with great rapidity in any direction. Daily they sailed to some barren, desolate island, hoping for a chance to blow one of the Chilean's vessels out of the water. The Huascar stood up and down the coast at times, almost within range of the Peruvian guns. As she was one of the vessels Paul wanted to get, he determined to lay in her track and risk an attempt to destroy her. With such intention, he ran the sloop out as far as he could, one night, and went overboard in his dress, with a screw torpedo, that would have blown the Huascar as high as the topmost peaks of San Lorenzo. It was a favorable night—dark, with a choppy sea that turned the phosphorescent lights up, all over the surface, so that no single object could be distinguished in it. He sighted the Huascar crawling slowly along the coast, with not a light to be seen aboard of her. Being short of coal, her fires were banked and she was carried forward by her own momentum. When there was danger of her losing steerage way, her engines would be started again and then shut down as before. Thus she was slowly creeping along the coast line.

Her bow glided by Paul not more than twenty feet away. He moved cautiously to her side expecting to catch hold of her rudder chain. He saw one-hundred-thousand dollars in his grasp. Now, he thought, "one of the most powerful enemies of Peru will be put beyond doing damage." When he was about midship and was preparing to reach for her chain, the steersman's bell rang a signal to the engineer, her wheel began to revolve and she slipped by him out of danger, of which those on board were unconscious. Paul was terribly discomfited at the result of that attempt which was so near being successful. He left the torpedo floating on the sea and struck out to reach shore before daylight discovered him, knowing that it would be impossible to gain the sloop.

The next move of the torpedo men was to sail to all the outside islands, which are literally alive with seals and sea lions. So thick were those mammals, that the guns were frequently turned on them. Their numbers so emboldened them that unless frightened away, they would attack the intruders on their territory. From those islands Paul took observations of the movements of the Chileans and came to the conclusion that they were running so short of coal that all of their vessels did not steam out to sea at night; but some of them anchored back of San Lorenzo. He made up his mind to visit that island some night to assure himself that his idea was correct. One end of it is detached from the main body as though split off by an earthquake, and is called Fronton. Both Fronton and San Lorenzo are honeycombed by numberless caves, cut out by the continual beating of the sea forced by the two trade winds against the rocks; so too, is the entire coast of Peru sieved by caves whose length or depth have never been explored.

Paul decided to make the reconnoiter of San Lorenzo by running the sloop to Frouton, then paddle himself across to the main island and make his way over it as far as he could until he discovered whether or not the Chilean soldiers guarded the approaches to the night anchorage of their vessels. He waited for a dark night and then put his scheme into operation. He placed two one hundred pound torpedoes aboard the sloop and stood away for Pronto. The crew displayed signs of nervousness at running so close to the dreaded torpedo boats of the enemy, and it was with some difficulty he kept them close at work. They glided along in a heavy fog; but having dead bearing for compass and allowance for currents all made, the fog did not bother the Captain in the least. The crew was armed with carbines and ordered to make no noise as the sloop, with a light wind, nosed in through the fog. Suddenly, as if coming from the thick mist high above them, the sound of approaching oars was heard. The men were ordered to get ready and hold their carbines at ease; but to Paul's consternation, he observed they were ready to give up even before they saw an enemy. They said the Chileans were sure to hang them for being in the torpedo service even if they were not shot down in fight and it mattered little which way they went so long as there was no chance for escape.

Knowing that prompt and harsh measures would be the only means of handling the quaking cowards, Boyton seized a carbine and in a determined manner told them that the first man who refused to fire when the order was given, would receive a bullet through his head.

"Now stand by and await orders, no matter who or what is coming," he thundered.

A moment later, the strokes of the sweeps were almost under them.

"Que venga," hailed the Captain.

The oars were immediately stopped and a trembling voice answered in Spanish:

"Fishermen, fishermen; don't shoot."

Seeing nothing more formidable than a couple of poor fishermen who were willing to brave the vigilance of the Chileans for the sake of a catch, the crew at once became very brave and bustled about as though they were willing to sail right into the entire fleet of the enemy.

In a short time the breakers were heard booming in on the rocks of Frouton and the sloop was run to a safe anchorage under the cliffs, in smooth water. Paul prepared for the trip to San Lorenzo and ordered the crew to remain by the sloop until three o'clock in the morning as that would give them ample time to reach the mainland before the Chileans could sight them. Launching the two torpedoes, he paddled across the narrow but rough channel, intending to plant the torpedoes for future use. He struck under the towering cliffs of the island and pursued his way along them looking for a safe landing place. At times he passed great openings in the cliffs, into which huge waves rolled and sounded back as though dashing against some obstruction far away in the bowels of the island, and the heavy, saline smell of seals and sea lions escaped through the openings. At length he came to a place where he could land without being flung against the rocks. He hauled the torpedoes up on a smooth beach, placed them carefully under a shelf of rock, removed the rubber dress and in his stocking feet began to climb the steep side of the island with the intention of discovering how far the Chilean outposts extended in his direction. It was a tiresome climb. Up over guano beds and broken rock, and as the wind was off shore, scarcely a breath of air came to cool the heated atmosphere and as he toiled on, the perspiration fairly streamed from his pores. When he reached the top, a cool land breeze fanned his perspiring face and with an exclamation of pleasure, he seated himself on a rock to rest and cool off. At the same moment, a dark figure started up, not thirty yards away. There was a flash of fire, a report and a bullet passed close to Paul's head. He drew his revolver with the intention of shooting at the figure which was retreating; but not knowing how many soldiers there might be around, he refrained. There was a lapse of but a few seconds, when gun after gun was heard cracking in nearly every quarter and that was proof to him that sentries were stationed all over the island. Knowing that a general alarm had been given, he began a rapid descent of the cliffs, well aware of the fatal consequences if the Chileans captured him. Every moment he expected a company of soldiers to pounce upon him, or that their torpedo boats would capture him at the foot of the cliff. Shot after shot followed him as he made for the place at which he had concealed his dress, with all the speed with which he was possessed. Being less cautious in the descent than he had been in going up, he loosened great masses of guano and rock that rolled down ahead of him. When he reached the breakers again, an avalanche of guano had covered his dress. He hurriedly searched up and down the beach until he discovered one foot of the rubber pantaloons sticking out from under the guano. He pulled it out and was soon paddling across the gut again. As he ran under the cliff where the sloop had been anchored, he could not see her; but as he rose on the waves he discovered her nearly out of sight, standing away for the mainland, with all canvas spread. The crew had heard the firing, had weighed anchor and sailed for the protection of their own guns, under the impression that their Captain had been killed; in fact, such was the report they made on their arrival at Lima.

Appreciating the fact that he would surely be discovered by the enemy if he attempted to paddle to the mainland in the dress; if not during the night, certainly in the morning, for he could not hope to reach safely before daylight revealed him. What should he do? He now knew that San Lorenzo was heavily guarded and there was no hope of shelter on Frouton. It were better to challenge the mercy of the monsters of the deep than that of his human foes, so he quickly made up his mind to return and conceal himself under the crags of San Lorenzo in one of the caverns which he had passed. He paddled back through the heavily rolling waves and got under the cliffs of the island, looking every moment to be run down by a torpedo boat; but fortunately his pursuers missed him and he felt a wave of hot air, impregnated with that saline smell which betokened the entrance to a cave. Then he could see a blacker spot than the darkness that surrounded him, which he knew was the entrance. He unhesitatingly struck for it, the mountain seeming to close over and swallow him as he entered the mysterious chamber of the sea. Cautiously he made his way back, not knowing what creatures he might encounter. Slowly and with straining eyes he advanced through the thick blackness, until he could hear the breathing and stirring of what he rightly conjectured to be seals. He sounded with his paddle and found it to be of insufficient length to show him the depth of water. Reaching a ledge of rock which had been rendered slippery by the constant sliding of slimy seals over it, he drew himself up, having to use great care not to cut the dress on the sharp edges of numberless shells which he found everywhere wedged in the interstices of the rock. When he reached a place against the back wall where he thought he could keep himself from sliding into the water, there was an ominous growl, one or two splashes below, then for a moment all was quiet again except the mournful washing of the waves far back in the mysterious depths and the heavy breathing of the sea animals about him; but what they were he was not sure, whether they would attack him or not, he could not tell, and could only trust in Providence to keep him safe. The noise of snapping, snarling and growling was kept up and through the watches of that dreadful night, he never closed an eye.

As the rays of the tropical morning sun began to penetrate the gloom, Paul looked around him. Everywhere along the sides of the cavern were ledges and shelves of rock; covering these was an army of seals and sea lions waking from their night's rest. They would raise their bodies half upright from their stony beds, stretch their flippers and yawn, much after the manner of a human being, then drop into the water and make off toward the open sea in search of their breakfast. Stretched on his ledge, in the black rubber dress, Paul was probably taken for one of their own species, for hundreds of them passed without noticing him. Some of them, however, did discover him to be a strange intruder in their lodging house. These would turn their great, round eyes on him, circle off from the ledge, then with a quick flip of their flukes dart toward the opening, gracefully cutting the water as they steered for their fishing grounds. Some returned with a fish in their mouths, shining like silver, and all day he had a chance to watch their movements.

He was greatly interested in the peculiar manner in which they climbed upon the ledges. They would raise their bodies almost out of the water, place their flippers on the edge of the rock and with a quick flirt of their flukes, project themselves to the shelf in the most graceful manner. Later in the morning, Paul noticed one enormous brute on a ledge opposite him and about fifty feet below. It appeared to be heavy and sleepy. Around it were clustered several smaller ones, seeming to be its immediate retainers or most intimate friends. The big fellow was uneasy. Several times he lifted his head, looked about with his blood shot eyes and then dropped back again as though to finish a nap. Paul expected an attack and braced himself for it. The monster finally edged slowly over and plunged into the water. He did not appear again until he had passed Boyton's ledge, then he came to the surface, gave a loud snort, either of defiance, fear or astonishment, sank again and went out to join his comrades.

Paul dare not venture out of the cave in the daylight. He sat there in his dress and dozens of baby seals crawled up on the ledge beside him, playing all over and around him, some of them sucking the fingers of his gloves with mouths like red coral. Sometimes the anxious mothers swam in and bellowed at their young; but as they grew accustomed to the stranger and saw no injury came to the little fellows, they became quiet.

At sundown, the seals began pouring in again and climbed to their respective couches, uttering the most weird cries, snarling and bellowing as though quarreling about their beds. Paul had had nothing to eat or drink all day; but owing to the dampness of the cavern, he felt no thirst. Twilights are short in that latitude and nightfall followed fast in the wake of sundown; so he quietly unlimbered himself, slipped off the rock so as not to disturb the seals and dipping his paddle gently in the phosphorescent water, slid out of the gloomy jaws of the cave into the starlit night. He made a wide sweep against the tide around Frouton and by steady, cautious pulling all night, was close under the fortifications of Callao by morning.

Not wishing to land until daylight for fear of being shot by some of the sentinels, he laid off and then came very near getting what he had waited to escape, for in the grey light of the morning, he discovered a sentinel with a gun aimed at him. He shouted "Peru, Peru," several times before the guard would understand and lower the rifle.

Landing safely at last, he immediately proceeded to Lima to report to the Dictator, and hurried back to take command of the sloop again.

The reconnoiter of San Lorenzo had convinced Paul that the island was watched from end to end in the closest manner and it was useless to attempt to work from there with the means at hand. He determined to lead out in a different direction to accomplish his designs, and his next move was a cruise due southward to the island off Pachacamac and generally called by that name. The little sloop wound her way in and out among the numerous rocky islets off the coast. Under their close shelter she picked her way hidden from the Chilean cruisers that turned their guns on everything not of their own kind, on the sea. The coast is extremely wild and utterly deserted, formed of lofty ledges of rock, hollowed into caverns underneath, by the insidious beating of the trade wind waves. The chiseled doorways to those caves are rare specimens of Nature's mysterious work; some large, some small and of queer, fantastic shapes; that black-mouthed gape at chance passers, while towering high above, a roof of table land—arid, scorching pampas, is just as uninviting as the water way below. So desolate is that part of the coast that it is but little known. Don Nicholas and a group of Peruvian officers to whom Paul described the caves, expressed the utmost astonishment, though born and bred within twenty five miles of their mysterious recesses. The desert above is traversed only by a narrow trail and is seldom used, while even the fishermen give the caverns below a wide berth, being superstitious and fearful of the strange cries that are heard echoing from their depths. That is why they are so little known and never explored.

During the day, when a Chilean cruiser nosed around uncomfortably close, the little sloop would be hugged under the lee of one of the islands, sail lowered and anchor dropped. Paul was thus given an opportunity of exploring the caves. Sometimes he paddled into them encased in his rubber dress; but generally he used a little gig, carrying an ax, knife, carbine and a few biscuits, spending whole days in those lonely places whenever the sea permitted. Once while exploring along the coast, he observed a great table rock that had been washed down until it rested upon two natural pillars, forming the capstone of the entrance to a great cave. The sea was rolling heavily at the time, but by cautiously backing the gig, he succeeded in entering. A scene of marvelous beauty met his wondering eyes. High above, the rays of the tropical sun pierced the numerous cracks and crevices in the arched roof of the cavern, illuminating with gorgeous coloring the submarine vegetation which hung like long snakes from roof and walls. Here the curling vines and tendrils glowed a deep purple; there, owing to changing light, a dark green; everywhere, light greens, dark reds, pinks, crimsons, yellows, greys, bright reds and every conceivable color. Sea fans and, sea plumes there were in endless variety, while outside, in the scorching heat, no sign of vegetation relieved the eye, inside was cool and beautiful with the luxuriance of the flora of the sea. The sides of the cavern were filled with molusca—radiantly colored shells, sea urchins and innumerable specimens of marine life. Along the pale green surfaces of shelving rocks, sea foxes, a fur bearing animal on that coast; bright, wicked little fellows, darted about, uttering shrill cries at the intrusion of the stranger as he drifted slowly back into their fairylike abode. Paul felt as though he would like to have one of the little fellows and raised his carbine to shoot; but it seemed profanation to disturb the grand serenity and beauty of the scene. The weapon was lowered and the animals allowed to play undisturbed.

The gig was backed slowly through the brilliant arches until the light became dim and the darkening recesses wore a gruesome look. Thinking it unsafe to penetrate further the vast, unknown aisles, Paul rowed out of the yawning mouth after picking up many shells of every hue.

Next evening anchor was weighed and the sloop headed for Pachacamac. It was beautiful moonlight. About midnight, sailing close in shore, they were passing a white, sandy beach when one of the crew asked Boyton if he would like some turtles, as the place they were then passing, swarmed with them. An affirmative answer being given, the sloop was hove to, while Paul and the sailor entered the gig and pulled ashore. Under the strong rays of the moon, the turtles on the white sand appeared to be as thick as ants. Selecting two or three of the smaller size for their game, hundreds of them being too large to be turned over by their united efforts, they quickly threw them on their backs while the others ran into the sea with astonishing celerity considering their very poor reputation for speed. Paul and the sailor transferred their capture to the boat and in a short time the ugly animals were turned over to the scientific ministrations of the cook. About ten o'clock next morning they put into a little bay, bound in by rocks and well hidden, on the shore side of the island of Pachacamac. There they passed several days, and many fruitless attempts were made with floating torpedoes to destroy the steamer Pilcamo. They worked only at night time and laid under the friendly shelter of the rocks during the day.

It was their custom during the daytime to explore the ruins of the ancient Inca buildings, the island having been the site of their temple and used also as a place of burial; for their strange tombs are numerous there. One of the crew was an expert in locating those Inca tombs. By sinking a pointed rod in the sand he could easily tell when a grave was below and after some laborious digging, the oven shaped top of the tomb was exposed. With a heavy pick an opening would be made through the sun burnt brick, and instantly a rush of foul air assailed the nostrils, though the bodies had been buried there for perhaps thousands of years.

When a hole large enough was made, Paul and the expert sailor would drop through it into the oval space below. There they invariably found several mummies seated in a circle, with their heads on the knees around which their arms were clasped. Some of them were encased in wicker work, others in cloth made of alpaca wool in brilliant colors and gorgeous with curious designs. The bodies were wonderfully preserved. In the center of these weird circles were found earthenware vessels containing petrified corn. As the sun streamed in lighting up the awe inspiring groups, whose history runs beyond all knowledge of the present day, one could but think of the deep and wonderful secrets which the grave conceals.

Paul gathered many curious things of prehistoric workmanship and only regretted that the limited quarters of the sloop prevented his taking all he desired. He was so deeply interested in excavating the tombs, however, that regardless of his inability to carry more relics, he prosecuted the search in the hope that he might discover something that would throw mote light on the habits, customs and peculiarities of the strange race. It struck him, however, that laborious digging through the hot sand was not the best method of reaching the mummies, and he overcame the difficulty by dropping a charge of dynamite which blew an opening with sufficient force to have given the dried up Incas a headache had they been sensible of feeling. He found many stone idols, specimens of pottery, bracelets, anklets, chains and other ornaments fashioned out of gold and silver and of strange designs.

Several days passed while exploring the mysterious tombs in the daylight and watching for a chance to place a torpedo at night, when it was discovered that the cruiser they were after had hauled off; so the necessity of their staying there being removed, the sloop was headed for Chorrilos. From the latter city they made short runs among the islands in that neighborhood While on those trips, they frequently passed an island on one of the ledges of which, they often saw a monster sea lion—the largest among the thousands in that locality. One of his crew assured Paul that that lion was known to all the fisherman and was remarkably cunning. Boyton at once made up his mind to capture the brute. With that purpose in view, he ran the sloop for several days to a point behind the island near the big lion's resting place, in order to get him accustomed to their presence. He was always found occupying the same ledge of rock, surrounded by smaller lions. For the first two or three days, when the sloop approached, the monster would rise on his flippers, bellow and dive off into the sea. Following his plans, Boyton made no attempt to molest him; but brought the sloop close under the island where the men would either sleep or spend their time at fishing. In a few days the lion became so accustomed to the sloop, that instead of diving he would lay on the rock and watch curiously. If he did go off, he returned again after satisfying his hunger. When it was thought he had lost all fear of them, Paul gave orders to the men one morning to stand by with carbines ready to fire as soon as the word was given. Sail was lowered and the sloop allowed to drift in as close as the monster would permit. As soon as he raised his great head and showed signs of uneasiness, the man forward let go the anchor and the crew pretended to busy themselves about the deck without regarding his presence. For a few moments he hung his ponderous body from side to side and settled down to sleep again. He was not disturbed for an hour or more and then Paul ordered his men to get ready. Raising his carbine, he fired over the head of the lion. The shot had the desired effect, for the brute sprang, to his flippers, presenting his broad breast to the crew and at that moment the order was given to fire. The beast staggered and attempted to reach the sea; but fell over, while the smaller ones dropped off the rock in fright. Convinced that the monster was dead, Boyton ordered the boat lowered; but strange to say not one of the crew would get into it with him, they were so terrified. Taking a knife, ax and revolver, he persuaded one of the men to back him to the rock along which the sea surged heavily and when near enough, made a spring for it. He managed to draw himself upon the ledge where the monster laid, though the sea caught him to the arm pits before he could do it, and found his prize to be fully fourteen feet long from snout to flukes. He plunged the knife into its throat to make sure of the work. Then he called to the crew to get ashore as there was no danger; but the men were afraid to risk it, the other sea lions being greatly excited, and Boyton began to remove the skin as best he could without assistance. The only way to do it was to run the knife along the stomach and cut away the blubber, rolling the skin back as he did so. He took out the entrails and flesh, so that instead of removing the skin, he really hewed the body out of it, throwing the offal into the sea. While the cutting was going on all appeared to go well with the other sea lions that were swarming about in a great state of excitement; but when he chopped at the flippers or any bony obstruction with the hatchet, they leaped on to the rock in such numbers that he had to shoot into them to frighten them away. After two hours or so of hard work lie had the body with the exception of the head and flippers out of the skin. He ordered the crew to haul in close and throw him a line which he made fast to the skin and it was pulled aboard, while the small boat backed in and took the Captain off. They sailed back to Chorrilos where some fishermen were engaged to trim the pelt and spread it on a roof in the sun to cure. It was the finest skin Paul had ever seen and he was very proud of it.

The next morning he was ordered to appear at the palace in Lima and was detained there for three days on business connected with a new submarine boat. When he returned to the sloop, he was surprised to see great flocks of galanasas (a species of buzzard) and condors hovering over the beach; but at the moment paid no attention to them any more than to think some dead body had been washed ashore on which the scavengers were feeding. Hastily ascertaining that everything was in order on board the sloop, he went to the roof to see how the sea lion's skin was curing. To his intense disgust, he found nothing left but the polished skull of the monster. The birds had torn it to fragments and eaten it. The artistic expression of his overpowered feelings at the discovery, would have frightened every galanasa and condor from the coast had they been familiar with the English, French or Spanish languages.

Orders were received from Lima to sink torpedoes as far out in Chorrilos Bay as they could reach without being shot by the Chileans. As there was only a lot of old Russian torpedoes on hand and no dynamite to spare, Paul decided to set dummies, knowing they would have the same effect on the Chileans, who would watch the work through their powerful glasses, from San Lorenzo. He procured a lot of empty kegs and had them painted a bright red. With these aboard, he pushed out as far as safety permitted, and in an ostentatious manner placed them across the entrance to the bay, so they would float within three feet of the surface and were plainly visible through the transparent water. The approach of a steamer from the seaward when the work was about finished, caused them to hoist sail and stand in. The steamer opened fire on the retreating sloop, but the shots fell short and her guns were answered by those on El Punte. A few days after, they had the satisfaction of seeing two Chilean men-of-war expending thousands of dollars worth of ammunition at one of the empty kegs that had loosened from its anchorage and showed on the surface. From that time, the little sloop was frequently made a target by the enemy's long range guns. One day while Boyton was lying under the awning of the sloop, he heard a whizzing cannon ball strike the rocks above where they were anchored. He leaped to his feet and scanned the sea in every direction; but as the atmosphere was a little hazy, he could discover no vessel from which the missile could have been thrown. Thinking that it was possibly a chance shot from the fort, he paid no more attention to it, until he was aroused by another one shrieking overhead and striking the cliffs a few hundred yards below. Then by closer observation, he could see the dim outlines of a Chilean ship fully twelve miles away. It proved to be the Huascar, that had received some new and powerful guns, practicing. The sloop was anchored in a less exposed place in a very few moments.

The next morning Boyton engaged in quite a lively adventure. He was about to dive over from the side of the sloop into the cool water for a bath, when he saw some dark object moving on the bottom and checked himself. It was well that he did so for the object proved to be an octopus, or devil fish, edging its way nearly under the sloop toward the shore. Its great tentacles stretched out nine or ten feet from its round body and a more repulsive or dangerous looking creature is hard to be imagined. One of the crew, who was an experienced fisherman, told them all to keep perfectly still as the fellow was going ashore among the rocks, which those creatures sometimes do; but for what purpose is not known.

The fisherman was correct, for in a few moments they saw one of the powerful tentacles reach up and grasp a rock which was just bare at low water. A party of fishermen near by, were called to assist in the capture. They were armed with oars, spears, guns and boat hooks and formed in a circle outside the dangerous brute, where they began yelling and splashing the water with their weapons in order to prevent its returning to the sea and to drive it upon the shore. It moved toward the beach, only a few yards distant, and whenever it was submerged discolored the water almost to inky blackness. At last, harrassed on all sides, it put its slimy tentacles on the gravelly beach. Its round, pudgy body was no sooner out of the water, than an expert, in the person of a half naked fisherman, rushed in and struck it a blow on the head with a heavy club dexterously leaping away in time to avoid the waving tentacles. At every blow, all the colors of the rainbow could be seen glowing through the body of the octopus. Once it lifted its powerful tentacles, clinging to the suckers of which were stones and gravel and either in pain or anger, hurled them in all directions. Nearly every one in the party was hit. At last, after an exciting battle, it was dispatched and cut up for division. According to the unwritten laws among those fishermen, one half of it belonged to the sloop, and Paul was just telling them he did not want it, when the landlord of a little hotel in town, who happened to be on the beach, made a proposition to give a supper that night if he was given Boyton's share. The unexpected offer was quickly accepted and sure enough, that night a magnificent spread was laid with the octopus served as the principal dish. It was sometime before Paul could be persuaded to taste it, and then he found it to be the most delightful fish he had ever eaten—delicate of flavor and flesh of a slightly viscous nature. The native fishermen look upon them as a rare luxury and always have a feast when one is caught.

Notwithstanding the very poor appliances possessed by Peru, two Chilean men-of-war were blown up during the struggle, by very clever tricks. They were the Loa and the Covodonga. As has been previously stated, it was the custom of the Chilean blockaders to pick up anchor and cruise slowly up and down the coast during the night, to keep out of the way of torpedoes. One foggy morning as the Loa was crawling back to her moorings after her customary night's cruise, her lookout discovered a small sloop containing a crew of four men, who appeared to be in a great state of alarm. One was up on the mast endeavoring to repair the peak halyards that were hanging down as though having been disabled. A gun was immediately turned on the boat by the Chilean and a shot fired over it. At that the sailor hastily descended from the mast and the four men hurriedly jumped into a light gig and began pulling with powerful strokes for the mainland. A boat was also lowered from the man-of-war and chase given, while shot after shot was sent after the fugitives. The man-of-war's boat had no chance of overhauling the quicker and lighter Peruvian gig and when the Chileans reached the sloop, they abandoned the chase. On discovering the prize they had taken, cheer after cheer rang over the sea. The sloop was loaded down with baskets of fruit, crates of chickens, vegetables, in fact the very things the Chileans mostly needed. A line was quickly fastened to the prize and she was towed alongside the Loa, and the entire crew joined the captors in cheering when they saw the good things. All hands went to the side of the vessel to look at the lucky find. It was short work to begin sending the cargo up. Almost everything had been passed aboard when the sailors took up what seemed to be a heavy crate of vegetables. The moment it was lifted clear of the deck, there was a terrific explosion— a mighty upheaval of the sea. A mountain of water shooting skyward, mingled with fragments of the steamer and bodies of men. As the spars and timbers dropped back into the sea, there floated on the surface but splinters where a few seconds before the proud steamer had stood. The Loa and her crew had been swept into eternity. It was then a cheer rang out from the little gig far in under the shore. A bold, dangerous game had been played and won.

The most emphatic orders were issued after the destruction of the Loa, by the Chilean officers to their crews, to pick up nothing without the utmost care and the most rigid examination. On an afternoon several days after the above order had been issued, the Covodonga steamed slowly along in bright, calm weather, on a cruise to the southward of Callao. One of the crew sighted a pleasure row boat. The man reported it and the Captain was about ordering the guns turned on it, when an officer approached him and said:

"Let us examine it. We may learn something."

The Captain consented to the officer going off to the little boat; but with repeated instructions to examine carefully before touching it. It proved to be a beautifully built lady's pleasure boat that had broken from its moorings and drifted seaward, a piece of frayed line still hanging from her bow. She was painted white and gilded, elegantly furnished with cushioned seats and handsomely ornamented. An open book was found on one seat and a single oar rested on the bottom. The officer carefully examined her, passed a boat hook underneath her and concluded she was harmless. She was towed to the steamer and the Captain assured that there was nothing suspicious about her.

"She will make a beautiful present for your wife," said the officer. The Captain responded:

"If you are certain, send her aboard."

Lines were lowered and hooks fastened to the fairy craft. As they tightened on the polished brass rings in her bow and stern, a deafening roar told the fate of the Covodonga. She was cut completely in two and only sixty of her crew were picked up and saved.

The little boat had been made with a thin false bottom in which was placed a quantity of nitro-glycerine. The friction pins were connected with the brass rings and the moment her weight was on them the pins were pulled out and the explosive discharged.

It may be imagined that after such costly experiences, the Chileans redoubled their watchfulness. They would not approach anything seen floating on the water; but turned their guns on whatever they saw at long range. They were known to fire at a seal that had wandered away from its usual haunts. Paul and his crew were compelled to keep close under cover. The Chileans were daily drawing their lines closer to the doomed city of Lima. Boyton dispatched an officer to Don Nicholas with a request to be sent with his torpedo crew down to Pisco where he expected the Chileans would attempt to laud troops. The answer he received was "Impatience is a bad counselor. Wait for orders."

If Paul had followed his own instincts, he could have knocked two or three Chilean vessels out of the water, for they landed at Pisco a few days later and no very sharp lookout being kept, he might have put torpedoes under them at night.

As the enemy was gradually closing in by land and sea, Paul was ordered to Callao to take charge of a submarine boat that had been built by a Swiss engineer. The boat was to be run by compressed air under water and by steam on the surface. It was a complicated affair and Boyton had but little confidence in it and that confidence was considerably lessened when the inventor himself refused to go down in her. However, it was decided to try her. Having managed all the details of her construction, Boyton ordered her swung under a big pair of shears and from their support hung the boat on chains, so that in case she would not run to the surface by her own power, she could be hoisted by the machinery above. She was then lowered to the water. Paul and two of his crew entered, but before descending to the bottom, gave orders to those manning the shears, to hoist at the expiration of twenty minutes. After fastening the man-hole, the valves were closed. There was an ominous hissing of air that sounded peculiar; but when she got her weight of water, she slowly settled on the mud bottom in twenty-three feet of water.

"Now get at your compressed air and see how she will go on the bottom," said Paul to the engineer as soon as they felt they were down.

She wheezed and groaned and moved slightly on the mud; but she refused to rise. Groping about with his lantern, the engineer found something was the matter with the valves as lie could not get one of them to work and he grew excited. He was advised to keep cool as there was no danger but they would get out all right. For five or six minutes, which seemed an hour to the men thus caught in a trap, they tried every possible way to get the machinery to work; but it was useless. The boat refused to rise. The oxygen became rapidly exhausted and the lights grew dim. Even the valve supplying fresh air for the nostrils of the occupants of the boat would not work and the situation grew more desperate with the flight of every second. As the atmosphere became oppressively heavy, Boyton wanted to knock the valve off with a hammer; but the engineer showed him if that were done, they would be drowned.

It began to dawn on the minds of the three men that they were doomed. They sat and looked into one another's pale faces. Paul consulted his watch and estimated that twelve more minutes must elapse before those above would haul up. He felt that it would be impossible for them to last so long for already they were beginning to gasp for lack of air. They became weak; but again tried the valves to no purpose. The least exertion exhausted them. One of the lanterns flickered out and the other was very dim.

At last Paul seized a hammer and going up the little iron ladder, struck three or four blows on the cover of the man-hole, under the impression that those above might hear. The effort was too much for him and he fell to the floor where he laid in an almost unconscious condition. He dimly remembered hearing the straining of chains, then the man-hole was opened and a voice inquired: "How is it?"

There was no answer to the inquiry and the rescuers only found out how it was when they entered the boat and dragged the three unconscious men out to light and air where they quickly recovered. The inventor of the boat made an examination of her machinery and found that the valves had been tampered with and rendered useless. It was fortunate that Boyton had taken the precaution of swinging the boat to chains, for otherwise they would have died like rats in a trap and remained in their iron coffin at the bottom of the bay.

The inventor went to Lima to report the occurrence and that night Boyton received a message warning him to keep a sharp look out as there was a Chilean spy among the crew and it was he who had tampered with the valves. At midnight two officers arrived from the capitol and the crew was summoned before them. They had an accurate description of the spy and after close scrutiny, an officer placed his hand on the shoulder of one of the crew, saying: "This is the man." Then followed one of the quickest court martials on record. A small group of men walked a short distance out on the dock in the darkness. There was a click of a revolver and a dead Chilean.

The Peruvian troops were now marshaled at Chorrillos to repel the further advance of the Chilean army that had landed at Pisco. The flower of the Peruvian forces marched out of Lima in happy anticipation of battle. The brilliant ranks were composed of young men in gorgeous uniforms, who sang gaily as they marched on to Chorrillos. The native troops were the Cholo Indians that who had been driven in from their homes back of the Cordilleras and almost forced to fight. They marched stolidly through the streets, turning their eyes neither to the right nor to the left, though hundreds of them had never seen a town before. They were followed by a wild though picturesque rabble of rabona women, carrying great bundles tied on their heads or backs, shrieking and chattering in their native tongue like gariho monkeys. These women formed the commissary department of the native troops. Whenever there was a halt, the rabonas would quickly unlimber their bundles and in an incredibly short time be engaged in the preparation of some sort of soup which they sold to the Indians for one cent per bowl.

The Chileans had advanced beyond Pisco and the first battle near Lima, on the plains outside of Chorrillos, was imminent. Paul and his crew with several torpedoes, went down the coast in a boat in the hope of being able to get under a Chilean vessel; but those vessels fired on the boat and sunk her, while the Captain and his men hastily gained the shore and joined the army on the heights. On January fourteenth, 1881, the Chileans began the attack on Chorrillos, the fashionable watering place about three leagues from Lima. Colonel Yglesi with but a handful of troops made a brave defense and had reinforcements been sent him from Miraflores, where the main body of the Peruvian army was stationed, the tide of battle would have been turned. As it was, he held out as long as he could and then retreated to the main body, after killing three- thousand of the enemy, just double the number of his original command. On his retreat, the Chileans swarmed into Chorrillos, more intent on plunder and wanton murder than honorable warfare, while the Chilean fleet continued to pour a storm of shot and shell after the retreating fragments of the little command. That night the Chileans broke into the liquor store-houses and soon drunkenness increased their natural blood thirstiness. Prisoners were murdered in cold blood and women were wantonly shot down. They even fought among themselves, many being killed in that way. Next morning the streets of Chorrillos presented a sad and bloody spectacle. Dead and dying were everywhere. Even the poor rabona women had not been spared. Their bodies could be seen all over the place. Many dead were seen on the beach where they had fallen when cruelly bayoneted off the cliffs.

While Boyton and a brave Peruvian officer, Colonel Timoteo Smith, were hastily crossing a meadow, they saw a young Chilean officer fall from his horse, wounded. They noticed that he wore the iron cross of Germany on his breast and ran forward to save him. Before they could reach him, a Peruvian Indian, knife in hand, bounded to the spot, cut the young man's throat from ear to ear and tearing the decoration from his breast, quickly disappeared. On examining the body it proved to be that of a young captain or lieutenant. It was learned afterward that he was the nephew of the celebrated General Von Moltke, the German soldier and strategist. His death was outright murder.

After the retreat to Miraflores, a truce was declared and an effort made to arrange terms of peace. The foreign diplomats, among whom was United States Minister Christiancy, and high military officers were holding a conference, while the two armies faced each other. During the peace conference, a gun was fired. It was said at the time that a Peruvian soldier fired at a cow. At any rate, the Chileans began the attack at once. The crack of their guns along the line sounded like the running of a finger over the key board of a piano. The bullets began to shatter the house in which the diplomats were conferring. They suddenly became aware of their danger and fled in all directions. Minister Christiancy was seen in his shirt sleeves valiantly running across the fields towards Lima along with many others. Not to speak flippantly, it was a genuine go-as-you-please hurdle race, for they had to jump the low, mud walls forming the fences. The Peruvians were utterly routed. When Don Nicholas saw the battle going against him, he gallantly mounted his charger and rode to the front; but it was too late. He turned in despair and fled to the mountains followed by a few of his immediate troops.

One of the leading causes of Peru's defeat, was the fact that her soldiers were armed with two makes of rifles of different caliber. The cartridges became mixed and hundreds of soldiers were seen to throw down their guns and flee because their shells would not fit. The ammunition, too, was strapped on mules that scampered away out of reach after the first fire.

Paul with hundreds of others, fled to Lima. The city had been taken possession of by a mob of drunken sailors and soldiers, who went about in large bodies, robbing and killing indiscriminately. The streets were strewn with the dead. Next day the foreign residents banded themselves together to put down the mob. Boyton took command of a company of Americans and went through the streets shooting down the rioters wherever found. On a street at one side of the palace a row of little houses was occupied by Jewish money changers. This was an especial point of attack by the rioters on the first night. They were under the impression that loads of money would be found there. Next morning the narrow street was full of dead rioters, showing the desperate and successful defense made by the Jews, who shot the robbers through holes made in their doors and walls.

Hundreds of Chinamen were shot and their valuables taken. The foreign patrols soon beat the mob into submission, and then collecting silks and other goods that had been taken from the people, they placed them in a general repository where they could be claimed by the owners, if alive. While the rioting was going on in Lima, the Peruvians set fire to all the shipping in the harbor at Callao, to keep it from falling into the hands of the conquerors. The patrols were kept busy until the twentieth of January, when the Chileans marched triumphantly into Lima. The city presented a queer sight. From almost every house the flag of some foreign nation was flying, to save it from pillage and destruction; but scowling faces appeared at the windows. The first act of the Chilean army was to break in and rob the custom house. An attempt was made to restrain the men, but some awful scenes were enacted before it was done.

During this time, Paul and some friends had a chance to visit the battle-fields of Miraflores and Chorrillos. And the sights they witnessed! The gallant, young soldiers who had left Lima in brilliant uniforms, with high hopes of success, and gay songs on their lips, lay a confused mass of bloated corpses. Four days of tropical sun had made them burst, and the stench was horrible. Dreading contagion, for the field of death lay near to Lima, the Chileans had forced the Chinamen of that city to gather the dead, cover them with kerosene and fire.

After nightfall, the blue glow rising from these awful funeral pyres, lit up the whole field. Bands of Chinamen leading mules who carried panniers containing vessels of kerosene, passed around, and whenever they saw a corpse not burning, they struck a hole in it with a spade, poured in the oil and fired. At other points on the road, lay heaps of mangled dead, while the earth around was torn up in most unaccountable manner. This was caused by ground torpedoes placed in the road by some fertile genius, who thought that he could thus destroy the advancing Chileans.

After two or three of those hidden mines had exploded with dreadful effect on the Chilean soldiers, they compelled the Peruvian prisoners to march ahead, and when these were destroyed they set a drove or cattle ahead in self-defense. Chorrilos, where Paul's headquarters had been so long, lay a mass of ruins. Bodies in every fallen house gave forth the awful stench of human decay.

Paul stood on the cliffs overlooking the pleasant bay, in whose waters his little sloop had been anchored so many times, and beheld the result of a charge of the Chilean army. Bodies of the dead soldiers lay thick under the foot of the cliff, Chilean and Peruvian grasped in each other's arms as they had been hurled in the fury of battle to death below.

Along the beach from the cliffs to the ocean, lay numbers of the soldiers who had been wounded, and while endeavoring to reach the tempting waters and quench their thirst, had perished. Others, who in their delirium had drank its brine, died in more agony, and lay in strings along the side washed by the waves.

At the approach of a human being, flocks of hideous galanasas and great droves of condors would rise lazily, too heavy from their ghastly feast, to flap their monstrous wings.

It was a sight to sicken one forever of the vaunted glories of the battlefield.

Soon after the occupation, General Backadana issued a proclamation requiring all Peruvian officers to surrender. The Chileans knew that Boyton was in the country, and for what purpose, but he surrendered under his assumed name "Delaport," an engineer.

He was paroled, and went to Ancon, a village on the coast that had been deserted, and no Chilean guards had been placed there.

Plans were laid for his escape; but he found it impossible to get off to a steamer.

He procured a little boat and spent most of the time on the islands off the coast and among the caves, his American friends in Lima sending him provisions. For a companion he had a young Peruvian officer who also thought it well to keep under cover. For three weeks they amused themselves fishing, hunting, exploring, and several times they rowed far out to sea, in the hope of being picked up by some passing steamer and taken north, but the hope was not realized.

From almost any other country in the world escape would be easy. But north and south of Peru lay thousands of miles of sun-parched pampa, on the west lay the rolling Pacific patrolled by the enemy's ships, eastward lay the Cordilleras soaring into the clouds—the only passage through them held by Chilean soldiers.

One morning while they were cruising among the outer group of islands, Paul noticed a cave opening into one of them, the entrance to which was far above the water and so peculiar in its appearance that he determined to explore it. Backing the boat in and taking a shot gun, he jumped ashore, while his companion pulled quickly away to keep the boat from being dashed against the island which was formed of an almost perpendicular rock. Boyton climbed to the entrance of the cave and found it ran like a slanting shaft through the island. Far below he could see the green, surging water lashing the adamantine walls. Picking his way down over the slippery rocks which almost choked up the passage, he had proceeded about half way down the incline, when his attention was attracted by a strange cry. Turning, he saw something that appeared to be neither bird, animal nor fish; but partaking something of the character of all three. He had often heard of the existence of such creatures in the remote caverns, but had scarcely credited it. Fishermen had spoken of them though few claimed to have ever seen one. They are called ninas del maris-children of the sea. He had heard they were gentle and affectionate in captivity but savage in their wild state.

He raised his gun to shoot; but on second thought concluded to try and capture it alive. He made his way down the incline as rapidly as possible in order to cut the nina off from the water, knowing that it would not make its exit from the cave by the upper opening. When he reached the bottom, a wonderful scene unfolded. He could easily imagine that he had unconsciously stumbled into the playhouse of Neptune's rollicking subjects. The water formed a great pool surrounded by an amphitheatre of towering crags of most fantastic shapes, which reached far up toward the sky, there being no roof to its vast extent. The waves beat in from the sea; but as no opening was visible, a subterranean passage surely formed the entrance. Hundreds of grey ducks were startled and circled around him or flew back and forth to their nests as if fearful the intruder intended to do them damage. These nests were built unlike those of any other duck he had ever seen, or in fact, those of any aquatic fowl, being hung in the cracks and crevices of the rocks precisely like the nests of the common barn swallow. The sight was so strange and unexpected, that for a time he forgot all about the nina; but recovering himself, he started back, watching closely to prevent the queer creature from slipping past-him. With all his care he could discover no trace of it and had made up his mind it had escaped through some hidden passage, when he heard the cry again. By close examination in the direction of the sound he found a little pocket in the rocks and instead of one, two children of the sea were hiding in it. He was so anxious to capture them, that without thinking of the consequences, he ran his hand into the pocket and caught one by the neck. After a struggle he got it out and threw his arms around it, holding it to his breast. With one vicious kick of its claws and flippers, it stripped his clothes off almost from chin to waist and scratched his body considerably. He soon learned that though small, it was very powerful. Having secured it, however, he left his gun and carried it to the mouth of the cavern and called for the Peruvian to throw him a line. With the line he tied the nina's mouth, lashed its legs securely and as the boat was backed under, dropped it in the stern. He returned for his gun and was surprised to see the other nina sitting stupidly where he had left it, having made no attempt to escape. He captured it easily, but took the precaution to put his soft felt hat over his hand before seizing it. The second prize was landed safely in the boat and the two explorers pulled back to Ancon. As there were only two or three fishermen in the entire village beside themselves, there were plenty of vacant houses in which to put the new pets, but Paul put them into a room in which he had previously placed a young condor. When the lashings where taken off the ninas, they waddled to a corner and sat there.

The children of the sea are a species of penguin. Their bodies are furnished with a downy covering which is neither hair nor feather. They stand about two feet eight inches high and have very short, but very strong legs terminating in web feet. They are of a grey color with white breast. Their necks are short surmounted by a bird shaped head with a powerful but stumpy bill, the lower part is V shaped into which the upper snugly fits. They are also armed with a pair of minute flippers much of the same conformation as those of a seal and their eyes are large, round and soft, surrounded by a black circle. They walk, or rather waddle much after the manner of an over fat man. When resting, their bodies never touch the ground; but bend over to within an inch of it, giving them the appearance of doing a very difficult balancing act, though as a general thing they sit upright.

Paul's prizes were very sullen and refused to take the fish offered them, so the door was shut and they were left alone with the condor. That night the Captain and the Peruvian, who slept next door, were awakened by an awful uproar in the room where the pets were confined.

"Ah," exclaimed Paul, "do you hear that? The condor is killing the children of the sea."

They were too tired and sleepy to investigate, however, and in a little while the noises ceased. At daybreak, after their usual plunge in the surf, they went to ascertain the condition of their pets. To their amazement they found the condor gasping its last breath, while the ninas were comfortably pluming themselves in their corner. Two or three days passed before the ninas could be induced to take food; but they would snap viciously when approached. At last the male took a small fish from Paul's hand, and then he knew they were conquered. Both began to feed and in a few days became the most affectionate pets, following him around like dogs. They would swim into the breakers with him without showing the least inclination to escape to their former haunts.

Paul seeing no hope of escape from Ancon, returned to Lima to consult with some American friends. These informed him that there was little chance of escape from there.

Paul then formed a resolution to wait on General Patricio Lynch, who was in charge of Callao, six miles away.

From his name, Boyton judged he was some good natured soldier of fortune who would be only too happy to aid a brother in distress.

With this intention he called at the headquarters at Callao, and informed the aid-de-camp that he desired an interview with the General.

That officer told him to wait a few hours, which he did. Waiting there, Paul planned the interview to suit himself. He intended to say: "General, my name is Boyton; down here just like yourself, from the States, etc." He pictured to himself how cordially the General would receive him, give him his passport, perhaps, invite him to dine. Paul regretted that his clothes were dusty and torn.

Eventually the aid-de-camp approached and said: "You may now see the General."

Paul was ushered into a large room and the officer retired. Paul looked around, and saw no one but a white-haired, mahogany-faced old man who sat writing at a table. Advancing, Paul stood silently waiting to be noticed. At last a pair of cold steel gray eyes were turned up to him which confused him so that he stammered in English:

"Is this General Lynch?"

"Si," was the sharp reply.

In English, Paul continued: "General, I am a patrolled prisoner who came down to see if—"

At this moment he was shocked by a heavy hand crashing on the table and a stentorian voice rang out in Spanish:

"Speak you Spanish, speak you Spanish. Muerte Dios, I understand not much English."

Paul mumbled a request in Spanish to have his parole transferred to Callao. "No, No, Anda!" pointing to the door, Paul retired and soon after rejoined his companion at Ancon.

Three days after this he received a message from his friends at Lima which caused him considerable alarm. It was to the effect that the Chileans were making a diligent search for him and to be very careful as there was yet no chance to get on a north bound vessel, every passenger being closely scrutinized and it would be impossible to cross the mountains.

Late one night, shortly after receiving the above message, he was awakened by a hammering at the door, he leaped out of bed to find the house surrounded by a squad of Chilean cavalry. The officer in command told him he was wanted at Lima and to prepare to accompany the squad at once. He was taken to the capitol and ushered into the presence of General Backadona.

"What is your name?" thundered the General, striking the table with his fist.

"I surrendered to you General," replied Boyton, "my name is Delaport."

"You were in the torpedo service?"

"Possibly; I held a commission from Don Nicholas de Pierola."

"But your name is Boyton and no one by that name held a commission."

Boyton neither affirmed or denied the charge, and the General ordered him to be confined in the quartelle with the other prisoners, where he was kept for some weeks while the victors were awaiting dispatches from Chile that would decide his fate and he could readily surmise what that would be.

Almost daily during his imprisonment he could hear the barbaric blare of the Chilean bugles outside the quartelle, the gates swing open and a party of Chilean soldiers enter. An officer would call the names of the prisoners wanted and surrounded by a firing party, the unfortunate wretches were marched out, followed by white robed priests who walked by their side administering words of consolation. With gay music, the prisoners were escorted to a convenient place for the execution, which was usually the back of some store or the front of a public building. The condemned were strapped on a plank, their feet resting on a step two feet from the ground. This was placed against a wall. Then followed a sharp order, a bright flash, the crack of rifles and the poor fellows were sent to their long home. After the execution the planks with the bodies on were placed on the death wagon to be unstrapped at the grave.

Paul expected every morning to hear his name called. Every time that fatal gate opened he thought it meant his farewell to earth, but strange to say, he became hardened and did not dread the summons. His friends on the outside worked like beavers for his release or escape. His belongings had been placed in the care of the railroad company and were safe; even the "children of the sea" having been brought up from Ancon.

For several days he noticed a Chilean who seemed to be some sort of an official within the prison, watching him. One day this officer carelessly passed near him and in a low voice asked if his name was Delaport. Paul said "yes" and the official walked away.

Next day four officers who looked like the bearers of dispatches rode in at the gate. The prisoners looked significantly at one another, remarking:

"There's news from Chile."

"Yes," replied Boyton to one of them, "I guess my death warrant is there."

The officers leaped from their horses, allowing them to stand unhitched in the quartelle and entered the palace through a side door. As Paul was patting and caressing one of the foam flecked steeds, the officer who had before noticed him, touched him on the shoulder and whispered the one word:

"Venga," —come.

Without hesitation, he followed the Chilean, who opened the same door into which the dispatch bearers had disappeared. Once inside, his conductor turned with a finger to his lip and silently passed on. They descended several steps into what appeared to be a basement, where they groped among pillars and underground apartments until they came to a heavy door, through the chinks of which a little sunshine was streaming.

Boyton's conductor drew the bait and with a gentle push shoved him out, whispering:

"Anda,"—go.

The Captain found himself in a street as the door softly closed, and at that moment a party of Chilean soldiers rode by. He dropped his hat and stooped to pick it up, keeping his face toward the ground until they had passed. He then started in the direction of the railroad, in the neighborhood of which he expected to find some friends. When he reached a bridge over the track, he saw a train dispatcher of the road, whose name was Campbell, of Alleghany City, Pennsylvania, standing below. He made a sign to Paul, who quickly descended and entered an old warehouse. He was followed by Campbell who handed him a paper, saying:

"Here is safe conduct through the lines. You are a submarine telegraph man going down to the coast to repair the cable. Outside is a mule equipped and ready for you. In one side of its saddle bags is one of your rubber suits and a jointed paddle, covered with coils of wire. In the other side are coils of wire, telegraph instruments and some provisions. To all inquiries, you must answer: 'Comision especial telegrafos del sue marina.' There's an English steamer going north to-morrow, the Captain of which is fixed all right. Your baggage and all your traps will be aboard of her. Go to Ancon and get to the furthest island out and stand boldly off; the Captain of the steamer will pick you up. Your greatest danger will be in leaving the city and passing the lines. You must depend on your own resources to get through them."

Campbell then placed a purse of money in Boyton's hand bade him God speed and disappeared. The Captain unhitched the mule, mounted, and started across the Pizzaro bridge over the Rimac. At the other end of the bridge, he noticed a Chilean soldier eyeing him intently. He thought the fellow was one of the guard who might recognize him; but knowing that any quick or startled movement would instantly excite suspicion, he leisurely rode the mule up to a cigar stand, dismounted and purchased some cigars. This move seemed to allay the suspicions of the guard and he walked away. Lighting a cigar, Paul remounted and kept on to the outskirts of the city. Night was falling when he reached the first line of sentinels and he heard that sound which made his blood surge:

"Halta, cavagna," shouted by the sentry.

"Comision especial telegrafos del sue marina," he answered, displaying his forged pass. The officer scanned the paper and gave him permission to pass on. At the second outpost, which was quite a distance from the city, the same program was enacted; but at the third or outer line of sentries, that occurred which caused cold beads of perspiration to start on Boyton's forehead. A young officer was in command who posed as a strict disciplinarian and acted up to his idea that there was very little else in the world for him to learn. He critically examined the paper and then looked into the saddle bags that were swung over the mule's back. Then strutting haughtily about, said:

"The pass is not correct, you will have to go back to Lima."

It was a terrible blow to Paul's chances for escape and though his heart was in his mouth, he kept as cool as possible and assumed a careless air. He presented the officer with a cigar, talked about the weather and other interesting subjects, while a guard was being formed to escort him back to the city.

"I hope," said he, "that you will be pleased to command the guard that escorts me back. I assure you that the society of the beautiful senoritas at the capital is far preferable to me than to proceed with the wet, cold work I have been sent to do."

The officer was polite enough to regret that he could not accompany the guard.

"I would be sorry to see a brave officer like yourself get into any trouble over this," continued Paul. "You know how anxious your superiors are to have the wires repaired in order to re-establish communication with Chile, though I am sure I do not fancy the work and am well satisfied to have my journey interrupted."

The officer took the pass again and carefully ran his eyes over it, as Boyton, apparently in the most happy humor, puffed away at his cigar.

"I think you are all right," said the officer at last, returning the paper, "you can go on."

Paul's heart gave such a thump of joy that he was afraid the Chilean would hear or see it; but the latter observed nothing. With assumed reluctance, he bade the officer good night, mounted his mule and rode slowly away. As soon as he was out of sight and hearing, he dug his heels into the mule's sides and was galloping swiftly across the pampas toward the coast. He could detect no signs of pursuit and in about an hour he heard the sweetest music that had ever soothed his ears.

It was the booming of the breakers near Ancon.

Riding close to the edge of the cliff, he stripped everything off of the mules and with a "good bye, old fellow, you have served me well," and a gentle pat on the neck, he turned its head toward the pampas and it scampered away. The next work was to fling all the wire and telegraph instruments into the sea. He then donned the dress, and with his paddle firmly jointed, began descending the cliff. Reaching the water in safety, he plunged right into the breakers and paddled with all his strength from the shore. Island after island was left behind and at daybreak he was to the seaward of most of them. He selected the one that stood furthest out and steered for it. It appeared like a huge rock standing straight up out of the water; but he found a narrow strip of sandy beach on which to land, being escorted by a whole troop of seals which offered him no harm, however. Climbing to a high ledge, he removed his suit and found that from his perch he commanded a good view and could see the smoke of the steamer as soon as it left the harbor of Callao.

The sun came up with a dull, red color promising a hot day. By nine o'clock, the heat was so intense that he began to suffer from thirst and then discovered that he had made one grievous mistake. He had neglected to supply himself with fresh water. After partaking of a little breakfast, he began a tour of exploration in the hope of finding some cave in which he would be sheltered from the rays of the sun; but none was to be found and he only kept cool by wading into the sea at intervals, yet such immersions increased his thirst. All day long he scanned the horizon in the direction of Callao, looking in vain for the black smoke of the steamer; but hour after hour passed and there was no sign of it.

During the afternoon he found a shelf of rock under which there was some shelter from the heat. He sat under its shade suffering terribly from the intensity of thirst. Then his mind was somewhat disturbed by seeing a tremendous cloud of pelicans headed for the island. They circled round arid round and lit in a confused mass on the narrow beach. There were several thousand of them and he gazed at them with interest. They went through a regular drill, in squads, which is the habit of those queer but unclean birds. The smell from them was almost overpowering. They would stand straight up in long rows, looking wise and solemn, while two very dignified birds marched up and down in front of the lines for all the world like military grandees reviewing a dress parade. Their drill must have occupied at least two hours, then the ranks were broken and they went into the sea in search of fish.

Paul's suffering from thirst became almost intolerable, his tongue was swollen and his mind was being affected. At last he saw the smoke of the steamer as the sun was going down. He was seized with an idea that she would miss him in the darkness and he decided to return and give himself up if she did, preferring to be shot rather than to die of thirst on that desolate island. He put on his dress and paddled out until he could see by the steamer's mast that she was head on, then he laid still and awaited her coming. Close and closer she approached until he could see the lookout. He waved his paddle vigorously and they saw him. To his intense joy, she slowed down, a boat dropped from her side and he was soon on board and hurried below much to the amazement of the passengers. He was received kindly by the Captain and made comfortable. Everything had been attended to by his friends, all his luggage, even to the pets were aboard.

The steamer only touched at one more Peruvian port, Paita, and while they stopped there, Paul went below and turned coal heaver; but on account of the wires being destroyed no news of his escape had reached that port and no search was made. Next morning they steamed up the river to Guayquil and he felt himself free.

To Panama was but a short run and the twenty-five dollars in gold that he had to pay for his trip across the isthmus from there to Aspinwall, left him almost penniless. At Aspinwall he found the same steamer on which he had sailed from New York, the Crescent City, and he put up his baggage for a passage home on her. No trouble was experienced in making such an arrangement for the trip north, for as soon as the Captain learned who he was and the straits he was in, he was received with open arms and every attention paid him.

Eight days after, Paul stood in Broadway, New York, without a cent in his pocket, instead of the hundreds of thousands he had anticipated earning when he cast his fortunes with Peru. But he felt rich in the joy of his mother and family, who welcomed him as it were from the grave.

Kiefer, who had gone south with him, succeeded in making his escape for the mountains where he remained several years, collecting antiquities and shipping them north. He died of consumption soon after his return to the United States in 1889.

CHAPTER XX.

In less than a month after his return from South America, Boyton was in St. Paul, Minnesota, ready to start on a voyage of one thousand and eight miles down the Mississippi river to Cairo, this trip being undertaken in order to complete the length of that river from source to mouth. Though there were no adventures of extraordinary interest in this voyage, it was the stormiest one he ever encountered; and he was diverted on the way by two peculiar characters that accompanied him, being almost continually provoked to mirth by the humorous incidents which befell them. His companion was a celebrated German artist, Dr. C., who was on his first visit to America, as a representative of that famous publication, the Gartenlaube. The Doctor was a scholarly gentleman, but being unacquainted with American characteristics, which had been sadly misrepresented to him by some of his countrymen who were inclined to joke, he had an exaggerated notion as to how he must dress and act for such a trip as he was going to take. When he was at St. Paul, he thought he was on the skirts of civilization and it behooved him to appear in such a manner as not to be imposed on as a novice. So when he was presented to Boyton, he was gaily attired in a buckskin suit, with revolver and bowie knife trimmings, looking rather out of place with the scholarly spectacles that bridged his nose. He really outdid the most fanciful cowboy of the far western ranches. Such an outfit he imagined just the thing for a trip among the wild characters on the Upper Mississippi. The other member of the party was a broad nosed, Herculean negro whom Paul hired to pull the row boat he had purchased for the Doctor's accommodation.

Boyton found that the scenery on the Upper Mississippi was more beautiful than on any river he had yet traversed. There was not that startling grandeur which characterized the shores of some of the rivers; but it was beautiful—with high buttes and pleasant shores, while the people throughout its entire length are exceedingly hospitable. If the loveliness of this river were better known, it would be more generally visited by tourists in search of rest or recreation. On the morning of May nineteenth, 1881, the start was made, the usual crowd of people lining the banks to see them off.

Several of the Doctor's enthusiastic friends presented him with a keg of beer. It was placed in his skiff. Unfortunately, they forgot to give him a faucet. All that day was very hot, and the entire party longed for a drink from its cooling depths. Late that evening a steamer, towing a raft, came slowly down the river. Paul told the negro to pull alongside and have the raftsman open the keg. They had no faucet but they had an auger, with which they willingly started to bore into its head. A moment afterward a white fountain shot to the sky and all hands held their hats to catch the descending shower.

They ran along without other adventure, until the second day out, when Lake Pipin was reached, where they were met by a heavy head wind and an enormous sea, that almost swamped the Doctor's boat; but they hauled up at Lake City in safety, where they passed the night.

The first reception accorded the voyagers was at La Crosse, where they were greeted with a blaze of fireworks and the roaring of cannon.

Below La Crosse as they were swinging along between the willow-laden banks of the beautiful river, whose waters, unlike the thick yellow of its lower half, where it partakes of the character of the Missouri, are clear and pure, the Doctor developed a taste for hunting and asked permission to use the shotgun that had been stowed away in the boat. Boyton readily consented; but seeing that the Doctor knew nothing about handling the weapon, which was an improved breech loader, some pains were taken to instruct him in the use of it. It looked so simple that the Doctor thought he had mastered it without any trouble at all. The negro, however, was not so confident and eyed the gun in the Doctor's hands with great suspicion.

"Ise not sayin' nun' Cap'en" he remarked to Paul, "but that man aint been rised aroun' whar da do much shootin', suah's yo' libe. Dar aint no tellin' whar he gwine fur to pint that weepin' an Ise running chances in hyah wid him. Dat's right, Cap'en."

He was assured that there would be no danger; but he was far from being satisfied and kept an anxious eye on the Doctor's movements.

After further instructions and admonishing the Doctor to be very careful, Boyton resumed his paddle and was soon ploughing ahead of the boat. He had not proceeded a mile when he heard a report of the gun and turning, saw both the Doctor and the darkey gazing intently into the sky at a gull that was sailing leisurely around a half mile or so above them. The Doctor nervously rubbed his glasses and looked again, at a loss to determine why the bird did not fall. When the boat dropped alongside, Paul explained to the astonished Doctor that a shotgun only carried a short distance and he could not expect to hit anything so far away.

As the sun was sinking that evening, Boyton heard the negro yelling:

"Great Lawd, come hyah Cap'en! Oh, my soul, come quick! quick! Dis hyah Dutchman gwine t' kill me suah!"

Wheeling around, Paul witnessed the most ludicrous spectacle. The Doctor, with the muzzle of the gun turned on the negro, was excitedly hammering a cartridge into the breech, while the negro was stretched on his back nearly over the gunwale of the boat, with the broad sole of his foot held as a shield toward the muzzle, yelling at the top of his voice. The doctor saw some blackbirds in the bushes and not remembering how to put a cartridge in the gun, was pounding it in with the handle of his bowie knife. Of course it was liable to explode at every stroke, and the poor negro knew the danger.

After some expostulation, the Doctor was persuaded to put the gun away.

Below Dubuque, the weather grew stormy and so continued for the rest of the voyage. They were treated to some marvelous lightning effects. Its forked tongues lapped the water in the most eccentric manner—fearful, though intensely beautiful. The poor darkey cowered in fright on the bottom of the boat with covered eyes, while Paul and the Doctor were so impressed with the grandeur of the manifestation, as to be unmindful of the danger. After that, whenever dark masses of clouds began to roll up in the sky and the wind commenced to sough mournfully through the willows, no power on earth could prevent the darkey from pulling in shore and staying there until the storm had passed.

"Ole Mastah above kin hit me evah w'en he wants to; I knows dat; but den Ise gwine to climb fur the shoah foah dat lightnin' play tag aroun' dis niggah's head agin, dat's shoah as yo' libe," he explained to Paul after one of his hurried retreats into the bushes.

Twelve days after the start the party arrived at Davenport. Paul had been greatly retarded in his progress on account of false channels and sloughs into which he wandered and through which he paddled many weary miles. Early one morning, emerging from one or these sloughs just as the sun was rising, he was treated to a concert such as he had never heard. The music seemed to him almost heavenly—so exceedingly beautiful that he remained motionless on the water, charmed by the entrancing melody. It burst from the throats of thousands of birds on one side of the river, and the refrain was taken up by a swelling chorus of feathered warblers on the other shore. It was a concert that paid him for the labor of a thousand miles of paddling.

At Davenport, and in fact at all the river towns, the party was tendered enthusiastic receptions. All the members of the boat clubs at Burlington rowed up to meet them and formed an interesting flotilla into the city. They frequently encountered rafts of logs, containing millions of feet of lumber. The raftsmen were always glad to meet Paul and converse with him as long as he would paddle alongside.

Below Davenport, the Doctor's passion for hunting was again displayed, much to the disgust of his dusky boatman. He insisted on firing at some blackbirds and the promise of a quarter to the negro, persuaded that worthy to row him close in shore. He took deliberate aim and fired into a tree that was covered with birds. Not one of them fell; but a cow that had been drinking among the willows, ran wildly up the bank with her tail in the air, bellowing mournfully. The darkey received the promise of another twenty-five cents for pulling away from the scene as fast as he could. It had usually been Paul's complaint that the boat was too far behind; but after the cow incident, it was just the other way. They were always so far ahead that it was hard to keep them in sight. The darkey was bribed to this unwonted exertion by presents of neckties and other fancy articles which the Doctor sacrificed from his wardrobe. The latter had visions of that cow's owner in vengeful pursuit.

While paddling along one morning, the boat being quite a distance below him, Boyton heard a terrific fusillade from the gun. He thought the Doctor was shooting away all the cartridges. The boat was surrounded by smoke and Paul drove ahead to see what was going on. As he drew near, he saw the doctor holding a small object in his hand while a look of pride glowed on his countenance. It was a little squirrel.

"See what I have killed," enthusiastically cried the Doctor in German.

"Yaas," chimed in the darkey, "dat squi'l him swimmin' de ribber an' de Doc, he shot an' shot an' den I kill um wid de oah."

After leaving Quincy, the Doctor again distinguished himself, by firing into some ducks that he saw in a slough on the Missouri side. The negro had encouraged him to shoot and to his intense satisfaction, he accidentally killed one. He made the darkey row in and pick it up, and a few moments later, a gruff voice was heard on the bank:

"Pull ashore; nigger."

Looking up they saw a gigantic Missourian with his rifle pointed at them and the negro pulled in as though he was trying to escape another lightning storm.

"Mister; I want six bits fur that er pet duck of mine," the man remarked to the Doctor.

The price demanded was promptly paid and the Doctor was glad to get away from that wicked looking weapon which the Missourian handled as though familiar with its use. After that adventure, he lost all interest in hunting.

On June nineteenth, the party pulled into St. Louis, where they were welcomed by a crowd of about thirty-thousand people, and the screaming of whistles was something deafening. The Mayor was on one of the steamboats and extended Paul the freedom of the city. He was hospitably entertained, and after a short visit, began the last stretch of his journey, two-hundred miles to Cairo, which he intended to finish without a stop; the longest continuous run he ever made. On this trip he had a great deal of trouble with the boat as both the Doctor and the darkey would persist in sleeping, after they had been on the route a short time. On one occasion, after the boat had been lost from him for a couple of hours, Boyton saw something limping down the river in a lopsided manner, which he could not believe was the boat; but on its nearing him, he saw it was the Doctor pulling away as though his life depended on it, with one oar and a little staff to one end of which was fastened a small German flag. Both occupants had gone to sleep and lost an oar, and the Doctor had utilized the flag staff that had been proudly placed at the boat's stern. They arrived safely at Cairo, forty-one hours from St. Louis. The Doctor poorer in clothes and the darkey much richer in wardrobe, parted with each other and Paul at this point.

At Cairo, Boyton met a friend who was going up the Mississippi to St. Paul on his own private steamer, a handsome little boat fitted up with every luxury. He invited Paul to accompany him and knowing no more congenial way to rest, he consented. They made the trip by easy stages stopping at places where good hunting promised and thoroughly enjoyed themselves. The little steamer was full of pets they picked up at various points; coons, foxes, opossum, crows and squirrels.

Above Burlington they ran across somewhat of a snag in the shape of a pilot's union. They were compelled to hire a pilot to see them up the river, (though they were perfectly able to handle the boat themselves), or be compelled to pay a fine of fifty dollars. They were hauled up at the wharf of an Iowa village when they heard this, and rather than have any trouble, they concluded to hire a pilot. On inquiry, they learned that there was no pilot in the village except the editor of the weekly paper. He had a license and could do the work if he was so inclined. This placed them in a rather awkward position. They did not feel like asking so distinguished a gentleman as the editor of the paper to pilot them. Several conferences were held on the subject; but the stubborn fact still stared them in the face, that the editor was the only man in the village who could do the work and if they proceeded to the next town without a licensed pilot they would have to pay a fifty dollar fine. At last in a fit of desperation, Paul said he would call on the editor and see what kind of a man he was, anyway, and if he proved to be all right, he might be induced to join them as a guest, which would be a more polite way to put it. They were willing to give twenty-five or thirty dollars; but they felt a delicacy in making such a proposition to an editor.

At any rate, Paul called at the office. After climbing a crazy flight of stairs on the outside of a little rheumatic looking frame building, he found the editor seated on a stool at a case of type, setting up some matter for his next week's issue. Boyton introduced himself.

"Well, I'll be doggoned, Paul," exclaimed the editor, jumping from the stool, "I'm almighty glad to see you," enthusiastically shaking his hand, "where in thunder are you swimming to now?"

"Oh, I'm just going up the river on a pleasure trip, with a friend of mine, on a little steamer."

"Is that so. Well, I'm glad to meet you any way. I'll make a note about it next week."

"Yes, we are having a little pleasure excursion; hunting, fishing, and all that sort of thing and we thought you might enjoy a trip with us a little way."

A cunning gleam shot through the editor's eagle eye, as he replied:

"Um, I guess you want me to pilot you up, don't you?"

"Well, yes. If you want to put it that way. You might assist our regular pilot if you felt so disposed. I can assure you a good time. Plenty of everything on board."

"I'll be doggoned if I wouldn't like to go up, Paul; but don't see how I can do it. In fact it's impossible. You see I couldn't get out my paper next week. Have to disappoint all my subscribers and you know that would hardly be right." "We would have a good time," persisted Boyton, "you could take a little vacation, you know, and you might get some one to put out the paper for you." "Couldn't do it. There aint a man between here and Chicago that could get out this paper. No sir. If I went, I'd have to disappoint all my subscrib—"

"Well, what will you take to pilot us up?" interrupted Paul in desperation, willing to offer fifty dollars if there was a chance. "You see I would have to disappoint all my subscribers and then the advertisers would kick and want to knock off on their bills. Taking all those things into consideration, I don't see how I could go up for less than three dollars." Of course he was taken along and luxuriously entertained as well as paid the three dollars. The week following the editor's return, his paper contained an item to the effect that "owing to illness in his family, the editor was compelled to disappoint his subscribers last week."

At St. Paul, Boyton began preparations for the longest voyage he had yet undertaken—down the Yellowstone and Missouri.

CHAPTER XXI.

There being many dangers to encounter on his contemplated voyage down the Yellowstone and Missouri, every precaution was taken that might possibly lessen them. General Terry kindly sent information to all the military posts and Indian agents along the rivers of Boyton's voyage and requested them to tell the Indians so that they would not shoot him in mistake for some strange water animal.

On the 15th of September, 1881, Boyton arrived at the terminus of the railroad at Glendive, Montana, then a little town made up of rough board houses and tents, which was the highest point on the Yellowstone he could reach. He went to a hotel and asked if he could be accommodated with a room. "I reckon you can," said the landlord, "there's only sixty in there now."

He was not compelled to occupy that general sleeping room, however, as the superintendent of a construction train provided a place for him in one of the cars. He remained two days in Glendive, completing preparations for his journey. Besides his usual equipments in the Baby Mine, he added an ax, a double barreled gun which could be taken apart and made to occupy a very small space. This was a necessary weapon, as he knew he would have to depend largely on his own exertions for provisions through a greater part of the country he was to traverse. These with signal lights, rockets, compass, maps, etc., completed the Baby's cargo. As he knew he had three-thousand five-hundred and eighty miles of river to haul under him, he determined to put into practice a theory he had long maintained, that hardship can better be endured without the use of alcoholic liquors. As a substitute, he reduced two pounds of strong black tea to liquid form, to be used as a stimulant when one was necessary, and his subsequent experience proved that his theory was correct.

General Merritt was in command of the post at Glendive and did everything in his power to assist Paul in his preparations. During the last evening spent at the post, the General asked him what time he would start in the morning.

"At five o'clock," was the answer.

"For goodness sake," facetiously replied the General, "don't start so early. At that time our sentries sleep the soundest."

The river at Glendive is narrow and quite shoal, the channel not being more than eighteen inches deep. The bottom is composed of gravel, but having been solidified by the alkali, is like a solid rock. The channel runs in every direction and is at times diverted by great sandbars strewn with the most beautiful agates, on which no human foot had ever trod before Paul touched them.

In deference to General Merritt's wishes and a fellow feeling for the sleepy sentinels, Paul did not start until seven o'clock on the morning of the 17th. All the inhabitants of the town went to the river bank, among them, the General's handsome daughter, who presented Paul with a set of colors, which he flew on the Baby throughout the trip. A cannon salute was fired and he began his lonely and dangerous journey.

In an incredibly short space of time he was away from all signs of civilization and running very fast on the lonely river. He had been warned at the start to look out for hostile bands of Crow Indians who were hunting in that vicinity, so he made fast time all day. Now and again he struck rapids and had to exercise the utmost care to keep his suit from being cut on the rocks. He saw any quantity of game along the route, particularly black tailed deer that frequently came to the water's edge. He amused himself by blowing blasts on the bugle and watch them dash up the banks and disappear in the timber. That evening he decided to camp on a bar across which a cottonwood tree was lying, that promised an excellent back log for a fire. Either shore was heavily wooded. Taking off his suit, he gathered a quantity of brush; but was careful not to create too much smoke for fear of guiding Indians to his resting place. He cooked supper and leaving a little fire smoldering, put on the rubber pantaloons, using the tunic as a pillow and laid down, the hooting of owls furnishing music to soothe his slumbers. Being somewhat anxious about Indians, he slept lightly and about two o'clock, he was startled by what seemed to be a canoe landing on the bank near by. He rose cautiously from behind the cottonwood log. Instead of a canoe full of hostile Indians, he saw a magnificent elk sharply defined against the dark background of the shore, his sides glistening like silver, being wet from his swim across the river. The huge animal was uneasy, throwing his splendidly antlered head back, sniffing the air and pawing the ground. Boyton raised his revolver and fired. The great head swayed from side to side and the noble animal dropped to his knees. Thinking the shot was fatal, Paul seized the hunting knife and sprang forward to slit its throat, having first flung a lot of brush on the smoldering fire. As the flames shot up, the elk rose to his feet and commenced to retreat slowly across the bar. Fully expecting to see him fall at every step, Paul followed as fast as the cumbersome rubber pants would permit. Instead of weakening, as Boyton thought he would, the elk gained strength and speed and went crashing through the timber out of all possibility of pursuit. Boyton returned disappointedly to the camp, where the blaze of the fire was casting a reflection almost across the river. Excited and blown after his chase, he sat down to rest, when to his surprise he saw the paddle in the fire, nearly burned in two. Hastily snatching it out, he found one blade utterly ruined and it was anything but cheerful to contemplate his helplessness in those wilds without the means of propelling himself; like a steamer without her wheel. He was not a man to be easily overcome by trifles, however, and he did not helplessly contemplate the situation for long; but seizing a hatchet, he chopped down a small sapling and with his knife, began whittling out another. He worked steadily until ten o'clock next morning before it was completed and then pulled away to make up for lost time. If anything, the river was rougher and wilder than it had been the day before; running between high buttes which formed the upper edge of the Bad Lands. Late that afternoon, just as he had noticed a break in the hills, a tremendous roaring sound struck his ear. The river seemed to quiver and dance. He thought there was an earthquake; but he soon discovered the cause of the unusual commotion. A herd of buffalo was approaching the river. They came down the slope as thick as ants, waded out as far as they could and swam across. The river was perfectly brown with them and they were fully three-quarters of an hour in passing. The last to cross were the calves and a few stragglers. They paid no attention whatever to Paul, who was hanging to the root of a tree for safety; he pushed ahead as soon as he could get by. The river for miles was churned to foam by their passage. It was the last great drove of buffalo to cross the river, as they were nearly all killed off in a very short time after.

About sundown he decided to camp under some high buttes. He built a fire, removed his dress and then, in his stocking feet, climbed to the heights in the hope of seeing some habitation; but as far as the eye could reach, there was no sign of anything human. The only living thing in sight was a herd of antelope, crossing an opposite hill, and far to the southward he could see the mysterious buttes of the Bad Lands. Returning to camp, he partook of supper and slept soundly all night, pulling away before daylight next morning. For two days he was utterly lonely. Not a thing in sight except wild game; but nearing the Missouri river, he was suddenly informed that there was something else around. A bullet struck the water just below him. He stood upright, placing the Baby between himself and the near 'shore and blew a blast on the bugle, discovering the Indian who had fired the shot as he did so, with the smoking gun still in his hand. Paul yelled lustily at him but he did not stop to investigate; he sprang away through the woods.

Late that afternoon, Paul saw a number of buildings ahead, with a pole on which a flag hung at half mast. He had reached Fort Buford. He sent a rocket whizzing in the direction of the fort and in a moment the bank was lined with soldiers who received him hospitably. On inquiring the cause of the flag being at half mast, he was informed that they had just received the news of President Garfield's death.

He remained at Buford two days, a soldier making him a splendid paddle during that time. He also visited the settlement of Ree and Mandan Indians near by, and it was by them he was given the name of Minnewachatcha, meaning spirit of the water. The Indians exhibited great curiosity and asked all manner of questions. When he started again, the entire garrison as well as the Indians assembled on the bank of the Big Muddy, shouting a good bye as he was borne away. The officers of the fort had warned him about a party of Indians that had gone out hunting before they had received word from General Terry, and Paul did not fail to keep a careful eye on the banks until he reached Fort Stevenson.

The currents and whirls on the Missouri were more savage than on the Yellowstone and the bends were something indescribable, as he took every point of the compass within the space of a couple of hours. If the Yellowstone was lonesome, the Missouri, after leaving Buford, was doubly so. The scenery was wild beyond expression. Great buttes towered darkly on either shore and they were being continually undermined by the swift and erratic current, causing avalanches of yellow soil to slide into the water, so that it was necessary to keep well out in the stream in order to avoid the dangerous banks. There was not a sight nor a sound of human presence in all the vast territory through which the river wound. To see a pile of wood or a stump which the crew of some boat that had wandered up that far when the river was higher, had cut, was cheering amid that awful loneliness. A blast from the bugle was echoed from butte to butte, caught in the recesses of one hill to be thrown back with double force into the solitude of another; until, from far below, the blast was returned with such distinctness, that Paul would strain his ears to catch the sound again, sure that his call had been answered by some being down the stream.

He began to make thirty-six hour runs, camping every second night. His program was to make an early start, run all that day and night until sundown next day, when he would land. His manner of camping and except on a few occasions, always the same, was to pick out the lee of a bank where there was plenty of driftwood, Just before leaving the water, the gun would be put together and one or two ducks knocked over without difficulty as they were so thick everywhere that it required no hunting to get them. These were put on the Baby and hauled ashore at the place selected for camp. Landing, the suit was removed and a fire built. Two stakes across which a stout pole was laid, were driven in the ground and the suit hung up to dry. He then skinned the ducks, drew some thin strips of bacon from the stores of the Baby with which he fried the most tender parts of the fowls, cooking enough for breakfast so there would be no necessity of delaying the start next morning. Supper was usually eaten with a little hot beef tea. After the evening meal, as soon as the dress was thoroughly dry, it was reversed and a pile of wood gathered for the purpose of replenishing the fire during the night. The softest place to the windward of the fire was selected for a bed, the suit donned, his alarm clock wound, hatchet and arms placed on the deck of the Baby near at hand in case of danger. Then as night closed in on the lonely buttes, the pipe was filled and he would lie down to the full enjoyment of a most delicious smoke, soon to be lulled into sound sleep by the melodious gurgle of the swift flowing river. Often during the night he was awakened by the "honk," "honk" of immense flocks of wild geese on their way to the southward, or by the whistling of wild ducks that flew closer to the water. Whenever awakened, he replenished the fire and consulted the clock. He became possessed with an unaccountable desire to push ahead and was jealous of every moment that detained him. This was a feeling he had never before experienced. He knew that winter was following him closely and the river would soon be freezing behind him; yet that could scarcely account for the unusual desire for haste. The moment he heard the whirr of the little alarm clock, he was up. Hurriedly swallowing breakfast, he slipped into the river for another thirty-six hours run.

Driving along one afternoon, he thought he saw a man in a tree and spurted ahead in the hope of obtaining some information as to his location, to say nothing of the pleasure of hearing A human voice. The man proved to be a cinnamon bear standing with its face toward the trunk of the tree, reaching for some kind of nuts or berries. The bear looked gravely at Paul as he passed; but paid no more attention to him, though he yelled, blew the bugle and splashed the water. A shot from the revolver, however, caused the big fellow to skin down the tree in a hurry.

Whenever the wind blew up stream, which in the northern part of Dakota was very often, the current turned to a choppy, yellow sea that was trying. While beating against a head wind of that kind one morning, half blinded, he saw a covered boat fastened to the shore, from which a man was emerging, gun in hand. Looking up the river he discovered Paul and raised the gun to his shoulder. The voyager blew his bugle in a hurry and waved his hand in sign of amity.

"Wall, stranger," said the man as Paul drew up to the boat, "thet er's a lucky horn for you. I took yer fur a bar on er log."

Paul was invited in and learned that the man was a hunter and trapper. He was exceedingly hospitable and insisted on his guest partaking of a breakfast of beaver tail which is considered a great delicacy, but which the voyager found rather too fat to agree with his palate. Noticing that his guest was not particularly fond of the beaver tail, the trapper wanted to go out and get a deer. He said he could get one in an hour without the least trouble, as he would only have to go over the hill and shoot one. The huntsman was as highly pleased to have some one to talk to as Paul was and wanted him to remain on the boat for a few days; but the necessity for haste was too pressing, and Paul could spare but an hour.

According to program, that was the regular camping night. Heavy clouds began rolling up before sundown. The high, caving banks on either side were dangerous to approach, as the least touch of the treacherous soil might loosen an avalanche that would bury him. Seeing no suitable place to land, he pulled ahead extemporizing songs to cheer himself into the belief that he was not tired. His idea was to run until nearly morning when the chances of finding a suitable place to rest would be more favorable. After nightfall as he was moving rapidly along, singing at the top of his voice, the glow of a fire ahead claimed his attention and stilled his vocal efforts. He was debating whether friend or foe was nears when a gruff voice called from the bank:

"Hello, there. Who are you?"

"Hello; I'm Paul Boyton. Who are you?"

"Pull in, pull in."

"Can't see where you are."

"Come just around this point, you can get in all right."

Paul pulled around as directed and saw the fire plainly. Three or four men approached the bank, heavily armed and carrying torches made of knots. He heard a whispered conversation, betraying astonishment at his appearance; but he was greeted kindly and invited to the camp. Nearing the fire through the woods, his nostrils were assailed by a horrible smell which one of the men explained by saying he had just shot a skunk. There were eighteen in the party, comfortably fixed with two good sized tents and an abundance of buffalo robes. After he had removed his suit the cook prepared an excellent meal and urged him to eat heartily which he was not loth to do. They also had a large supply of liquor, but he refused to touch it and they did not insist. Refreshed by the warm meal, he lit his pipe and began to talk. He told the men his object in making voyages and described some of the rivers he had navigated. When he told about crossing the English Channel, one of them jumped up, exclaiming:

"Great snakes! I know you now. I've just been tryin' to place you. Why, I read all about you in an almanac."

"Well," said another, "when I first heard you out there, I thought you was a deserter from the fort. The're about the only people we see comin' down the river this time of the year."

The same man also volunteered the information that they were traders, and Paul afterward saw that the woods were full of cattle. Seeing he was growing weary, the men insisted that he should turn in under the buffalo robes and take a good sleep, though he told them he could stretch out anywhere by the fire and not deprive them of their robes. He did as they desired and the moment he was snugged under the warm covering, the men showed their thoughtfulness by lowering their conversation to whispers so as not to disturb him.

At daylight they called him up as he had requested, and after a splendid breakfast he started, with the Baby loaded almost to the water's edge with provisions. All the cattle dealers accompanied him to the bank, cordially shook his hand and wished him God speed.

About ten days after the above adventure, Paul learned that his hospitable friends were notorious "rustlers" the western name for cattle thieves, and that on the very day he left their camp, they had been rounded up by a party of ranchers and every one of them shot to death.

During the forenoon after leaving the camp of the rustlers, Paul was hurled violently against a snag and his dress began leaking. Though not more than twenty yards from the shore, he was filled to the neck with the icy water before he could land. Fortunately there was plenty of driftwood near and he soon had a roaring fire. He dried and warmed himself while repairing the damaged suit, which he completed just in time to escape a violent rain storm that followed him all day. Toward evening, as he was entering a narrow passage between the buttes, he felt as though he was leaking again and landed on a bar to investigate. He found that though slightly wet, the leak was not occasioned by another rent; but owing to the improper adjustment of the belt. As his matches were too damp to light a fire, he gathered a pile of driftwood and placed one of his signal lights in the barrel of a twelve caliber pistol, made for the purpose; the signal light fitted the barrel like a cartridge and threw out a strong, steady blaze when exploded. He shoved the pistol into the center of the pile of wood and pulled the trigger. Instead of lighting the fire he was hurled several feet away, and righted himself with a numb feeling in his arm and only the pistol stock in his hand. It was several minutes before he recovered sufficiently from the shock to discover that he had received no serious injury. He found the pistol barrel had exploded into countless fragments and the wonder was that he had not been wounded by some of the flying pieces. The thought of the horrible predicament he would have been in had some of those fragments struck his eyes and left him blinded in those lonely wilds, almost sickened him. It was a providential escape and he kneeled on the bar and earnestly thanked the Almighty.

The incident so weighed on his mind, that he concluded not to build a fire, but to push right along. Seeing that the belt was properly fastened, he resumed the journey. That seemed to be his unlucky day, however. As night was coming on he was driving along at double speed trying to get up temperature enough to dry his underclothing. Between eleven and twelve o'clock, he found himself in a place where there was no current and realized that he had lost the channel. He tried to stand upright to see where he was; but his feet struck the slimy, working mud at the bottom. It appeared to grasp his legs and he immediately threw himself on his back again, putting forth extra exertions to extricate himself. He could make no headway and the mud seemed to get thicker all around and he could feel it touching the under side of the band of his dress. He then realized that he was in one of the dreaded mud sucks that are numerous on the Missouri. They are something in the nature of quicksand or quagmire and it is seldom anything escapes from their slimy embrace. Seeing no way out, he grew exceedingly nervous. He beat around in every direction without success. Now and then he put his hand down and could feel the deadly suction right under him. He had turned and twisted so much that he had no idea where the channel was. The shore seemed near at hand but impossible to reach. A cold perspiration started from every pore as he began to realize the frightful situation. Then he thought of the tactics he had employed in the quicksands of the Loire and he inflated every chamber of his dress to its utmost capacity. That raised him higher, but he could not get out. Then he thought he would remain perfectly still until daylight, when he might see his way clear and get the direction of the channel. And in his helplessness he begged for aid from Heaven. While lying there half exhausted, he was startled by a brilliant light. It looked like the blaze of an enormous lamp. He could see it rise as if from the ground below him, and sail silently and solemnly over to the side of a butte where it lodged. The thought occurred to him that perhaps God had sent the light to guide him to the channel, and pointing his feet toward the spot where it was shining with great brilliancy, he made an almost superhuman effort to break through the suction in that direction. To his intense joy, he found that after a little while, he was slipping off the slime and getting into deeper water. When he felt the current under him and knew he had struck the channel, he stood up and gazed in awe at the light which was still glowing against the butte, and he uttered a heartfelt prayer of thanks.

Boyton is in no way superstitious; but that incident is so strongly impressed on his mind that he often speaks of it. He understands that he saw only an ignis fatuus, a phenomenon easily explained; but he believes that it was sent that night by the great Pilot to guide a helpless human being out of danger.

Two days later he saw the Indian agency of Fort Berthold on a bluff overlooking the river. He sounded the bugle and soldiers and Indians swarmed to the water's edge. The latter covered the sloping bank, standing like statues, watching for the water spirit whom they had been told was coming down the river. Each one wore a blanket of bright red or blue and they formed a picturesque foreground to the high bluff and sullen fort. As Boyton came opposite, he stood up in the water and lighted a detonating rocket. Not a breath of air was stirring and the thick white smoke from the rocket hung on the surface of the water, hiding him from sight. Indeed, it looked to the Indians as though he had disappeared entirely, and when the rocket exploded over their heads with the roar of a cannon, their superstitious hearts could stand it no longer and they rushed up the slope like a flock of frightened sheep, tumbling over one another in their anxiety to get out of the way.

That night he stopped with the Agent who informed him that the tribe had pronounced him good medicine, (lucky) at one of their pow wows. This opinion of the red men was a source of much annoyance to Paul, for they stole every little thing belonging to him they could put their hands on for their medicine bags. The Indians belonged to the Ree and Mandan tribes and have been peaceful for many years. They have one stubborn custom which all the talk of the agents and assurances of the military officials, will not remove. In the early days the Sioux were their deadly enemies and made frequent disastrous raids on their villages. Though years have passed since they have been disturbed, a lookout is constantly kept. Every warrior in the village takes his turn at stated times, to mount an elevation where he stands, like a statue, watching the distant hills for their ancient foes.

Next day, prior to Paul's departure, all the chiefs shook hands with him exclaiming, "how;" which, by the way is a most elastic word. It means goodbye, how-do-you-do, expresses anger, friendship, pleasure, sorrow, hate, insult, and in fact, almost every feeling of the human heart, all depending on the intonation given the voice and the manner of uttering it.

About twenty miles below the fort, Paul was again shot at, this time by an Indian boy whose aim, luckily, was bad. He scampered away when the voyager stood up and shouted: "How, how, cola."

That night Boyton ran into Fort Stevenson, where he was kindly entertained, and next morning started on another thirty-six hours' run, beating against head winds and heavy weather through another wild stretch of country. The next camping place was in a sort of circular basin that had been cut out of the prairie by the floods, and was surrounded by high mud banks. He found plenty of drift in the eddy and picked out the driest; but experienced great difficulty in starting a fire with it. He only succeeded in getting sufficient heat to cook his supper; he was not able to coax enough blaze to warm himself. Night came down black as ink and he heard the distant yell of a coyote which was answered from all directions by others. In less than half an hour the top of the bank was covered with a horde of the dirty little beasts, snapping and snarling at one another, their eyes shining like balls of fire through the black night. They were frightened away by a shot or two from the revolver; but soon returned, to set up such howls as would freeze one's blood, though they are arrant cowards. Paul concluded that the river was more pleasant than their company and he started away, making a two days and two nights' run. He had hard work to keep his eyes open during the night and possibly would have dropped off to sleep but he heard the water swashing against an occasional snag of which he had a wholesome dread.

Day broke cold and chilly with the same threatening sky as had darkened the heavens the night before. Head winds fretted him and he felt cold and miserable. Toward evening, utterly tired out, he began looking for a camping place. There was no sound of life. Below he saw a belt of timber which looked promising and just as he struck out for it, he was surprised to discover on his right, at the edge of a small bit of prairie, a log cabin. He immediately sounded the bugle, but there was no response. Note after note failed to stir up any signs of life, so he headed for the place pulling vigorously to clear the swift current which he was compelled to cross. He reached a muddy shore scantily mixed with sand, which extended a considerable distance from the bank. He landed and on testing the soil with his foot found it unstable. Fearing another mud suck, he put the Baby down and made his way with quick steps to the cabin, the soil bending under him like rotten ice. He then saw that the hut had long been deserted. Grass grew high and rank all around it, while elk and deer antlers, bleached white by the sun, were strewn everywhere and strips of blackened deer skin were nailed over the chinks in the door. Pushing his way in he stood in a single room with a big fire place at one side and two rude bunks covered with old hay.

Paul was delighted with his find. Here was a royal shelter from the threatening storm and a famous place to take much needed rest. He felt himself a king in his palace. Going outside, he gathered several pieces of wood which he placed one after another on the treacherous soil making a series of steps to the water's edge, on which he could walk without so much danger of sinking. Shouldering the Baby, he soon had her safely deposited in the cabin and then removing his suit, gathered a big supply of wood which he stowed on one side of the fire place, closed and fastened the door securely, just as the storm broke with considerable fury. Over a blazing fire he cooked an excellent supper, which was eaten with a keen appetite, filled his pipe and threw himself on a pile of hay which covered a portion of the floor between the fireplace and bunks, that was boarded. There he reposed, toasting his feet, watching the fragrant smoke from his pipe curling to the browned rafters, smiling at the battling elements outside and congratulating himself on the good fortune that had directed his eyes toward such a castle. He was dozing off into a comfortable sleep, when he felt a movement in the hay under his back. Thinking it was a field mouse or a mole, he paid no attention to it; but when the pressure against his back became stronger, he leaped to his feet and was horrified to see the shining, hissing head of a snake rise out of the hay. The reptile elevated its head two feet or more from the floor, swaying from side to side in an angry fashion as though indignant at the unusual intrusion. As it continued to uncoil its hideous length, Paul seized a piece of wood and aimed a blow at its head. It quickly disappeared and he could hear it drop somewhere underneath, hissing as it went. Removing a portion of the litter, Paul found a kind of pit covered with boards, apparently six feet deep, made, no doubt, for storing provisions during the winter. Not caring to investigate further, he dropped the board in its place and covered it again. He determined not to be driven from his rest by the snakes, as he had been by the coyotes, so he put on the dress and laid on the floor away from the pit, covering his face as that was the only part of his body exposed, and was soon sound asleep.

It was almost sunrise when he awoke. He replenished the fire and cooked breakfast. The storm had passed and the sun was rising in a cloudless sky, promising a fine day. After breakfast, when everything was prepared for a hasty departure, he concluded to find out what had become of his friend, the snake. Removing a few boards from the mouth of the pit, he took up a burning brand from the fire and thrust it into the dark hole. The sight sent a chill through every vein. Had he looked upon it the night before, he would have trusted himself to the mercy of the storm rather than sleep where he did. The place was alive with a squirming mass of hideous reptiles, hissing and gliding about at being disturbed. They were probably in their winter quarters and the fire had roused them from their torpor. Quickly throwing the burning wood amongst them, he dropped the planks and seizing the Baby, quitted the den and was in the water like a flash. Many miles below, in a sharp bend that headed him toward the northwest again, he saw a column of smoke standing straight up in the sky and knew it was the burning Cabin of the Snakes. He had not intended to fire the house, but on the whole, was not sorry.

During the afternoon of the following day, a lazily moving flat boat attracted Paul's attention as it drifted with the current at some distance ahead. It was desirable to see and talk to any human being and he increased his speed. As the flat boat with its unwieldy load was in no particular hurry, he soon overhauled it and a blast from the bugle caused the navigator of the craft to cast his eyes up stream. He gazed curiously at Paul for a moment and exclaimed:

"Wall, drat my buttons, I never thought I would see a human critter goin' down the Missouri in sich a rig as thet."

He leaned back and awaited the "critter's" approach. He was a tall, raw boned man with a shock of reddish grey hair and tangled beard; a pair of keen grey eyes shown from behind deep, overhanging brows. Though he had the appearance of a farmer, he might have been anything from a deacon to a rustler, so far as could be judged by his appearance. The craft he was piloting down was loaded with a miscellaneous collection of household effects and a couple of sad eyed hounds were the man's only companions.

Paul quickly observed all this as he pulled up and heard the boatman's remark. Reaching the side of the boat, he asked:

"How far are you going down, stranger?"

"Ain't pertic'lar how fur so as I git outen this country. I had a farm on this river once; but she's gone now, stranger, gone slick an' clean. River cut under and rounded me out an' I reckon the feller on the other side owns my land now."

It is a fact that the constantly changing currents of the Missouri, frequently cut into and swallow up acres upon acres on one side only to leave exposed as much land on the other and the owner of the land next to that left exposed, becomes richer by so many acres, while the man on the other side becomes impoverished to that extent. Thus the expression is common in the Upper Missouri country that "a man may go to bed owning a fine farm on one bank and wake up in the morning to find it owned by the fellow on the opposite side."

"Well, where do you propose going to now?" inquired Boyton.

"I don't propose goin' anywhere. I only want to git outen this country. She's a holy terror an' I stood it jest as long as I could. All thets left of my farm is on this ere boat an' I don't reckon its goin' to cost me much trouble to take care of it an' locate anywhare outside of this country. This ere cantankerous river has done me up, done me up brown, straanger."

"It is a curious sort of river."

"Cur'ous! Wall, I should snicker, Cur'ous ain't no name for it. I think God Almighty built her all right enough, but I don't think He's made up His mind whar to locate her yit. She's running wild, straanger; she's runnin' wild."

He leaned back against a worn mattress with a melancholy sigh and his boat dropped astern.

The next day was dark and gloomy and Paul felt an unaccountable falling of spirits. The atmosphere was oppressive and he could not overcome a premonition of evil that effected him all day. About the middle of the afternoon, he was startled by a peculiar noise above him. Black, heavy clouds hung low on the prairie lands. An ominous roar caused him to look up stream and he beheld a funnel shaped cloud driving to the eastward across the river. In less than half an hour, another one bore down from the buttes and swept across with a terrible roar, about one mile below. While congratulating himself on having been sandwiched between these fearful whirlwinds and thus escaping them, he was horrified to see another bearing directly on him from the west. He made all possible speed to reach the willows on the windward shore; but before he could grasp them, the outer circle of the cyclone struck him and he was enveloped in a whirling mass of buffalo grass, twigs and dust. He grasped the Baby close to his sides fearing to be separated and the next moment felt himself lifted with a great volume of water and borne away as if he was of no more weight than a feather. When he recovered from the shock, he found himself stuck in the mud on the opposite shore. It was some minutes before he recovered sufficiently to proceed on the journey, fortunately uninjured.

Paul was favored with fairly good weather after the cyclone and in a few days ran into Bismarck, where he was welcomed and entertained on board the Northern Pacific transfer boat, by Captain Wolfolk. He was joined there by the correspondent of the New York Herald, Mr. James Creelman, who was sent out by that paper to accompany him the rest of the way and write up the Indian country.

After a brief rest at Bismarck, Boyton continued his course down the muddy river followed by Mr. Creelman in a canvas canoe. Contrary to his usual custom, he did not start until afternoon, in deference to friends in the town, and they had not proceeded many miles until night came on and camp was struck on a muddy bar. They were under way at sunrise next morning, and all day the river ran through a lonely country. Ranges of buttes stretched away from the banks until they were lost in the distance and from every gully, purling streams flashed their clear waters into the yellow of the river. The banks were blushing with the glory of autumn and vines hung among the trees like curtains of the richest pattern. Game was utterly fearless until frightened away from the water's edge by a blast from the bugle or a shot. A bar was utilized for a camp that night and at ten o'clock next morning, the white tepees of an Indian village were seen, and piles of wood along the river indicated the approach to some settlement. On rounding a great bend, Fort Yates and the Standing Rock Agency were sighted. Paul was warmly received by the officers of the Fort and entertained in the most hospitable manner. Among the notorious Indian chiefs whom Boyton met at Standing Rock, were Rain-in-the-Face, Gaul, Low Dog, Long Soldier, the young chief Flying-By and others.

On the morning of October 5th, they resumed the journey, the banks being crowded with soldiers and Indians to see them start. After passing an Indian village a few miles below Fort Yates, the country through which the river twisted and turned, again assumed a lonely aspect. Mile after mile was passed without the faintest sign of civilization. Sand bars divided the river into five or six different channels and it required careful paddling to avoid the countless snags which stuck out of the water, sullen and threatening. The shores were strewn with driftwood,—logs that had floated from far up the river; red willow and cottonwood trees that had been gnawed from their roots by beavers; horns and bones of wild animals and the countless ingredients of drift piles were heaped on all sides. Amid all this desolation the Big Muddy flowed, making fresh ruins at every turn. That night camp was pitched on the bank and a wild goose was the leading feature on the supper bill of fare. The next day proved another lonesome one. Not a single habitation on the rusty hills that rose on either side and hid the fertile country beyond. Toward evening a ranch was sighted and they landed to test the hospitality of its proprietor, who proved to be a squaw man, the name applied to white men who marry Indian women. The travelers were cautiously received and finally invited to remain over night, on condition that they furnished their own provisions. Several comely half breed children sat around the room while supper was being prepared by a good-looking Indian squaw. Noting the inquiring looks of Boyton and his companion, the rancher said:

"Yes, them's my children and that's my wife. She cost me a tidy bit, too. I gave up a durned good horse fur that squaw."

"How long have you been married to her?" inquired Paul.

"Wall, I ain't been married very long to this 'un. I had another almighty good lookin' one, that I lived with some years; but she got tired workin' an' run away to the tribe. This un's a good cook an a hard worker."

Supper was announced by the woman, who spoke to her husband in the Indian tongue, as she had not acquired English. The travelers and the master of the ranch sat at a small table, while the woman and the children retreated to a dark corner near the fire, where they ate.

"Will not your wife eat with us?" politely inquired Boyton.

"Eat with us!" exclaimed the rancher in breathless astonishment, "I shud say not. Do you think I'd eat with a durned Indian?"

After breakfast next morning, the travelers again took to the river, the squaw man extending an invitation to drop in on him again if they ever chanced up that way. As they passed below the mouth of Grand river, the scenery began to change. Instead of grassy buttes, the prairies were crowned with clay hills, riven as though by volcanic action and the river flowed under huge cliffs of a peculiar slate color. Wild vines twined their tendrils over shores ancient and fossilized, that were trod by tribes whose camp fires had burned out before Columbus ever dreamed of the new world. About four miles below Grand river, on a bluish cliff that shot out in the water almost at right angles, they landed and found many beautiful specimens of petrifaction—fish retaining their prismatic beauty of exterior. The mother of pear-like shells of the extinct anomite lay about as though the place had once been the bed of a mighty ocean. The shore was covered with agates and looked gray and instead of mud sucks, there were pebbly beaches for some distance. Sometimes a bank that had been eaten away by the water, would exhibit strata of clay and soil so variegated in color that they resembled vast cameos. At many places the soil was rich and black for six or seven feet deep, showing its wonderful agricultural properties, while here and there the alkali deposits seemed like frost work. The storms had eaten some of the massive cliffs into forms of castles and there were galleries of arches and columns sculptured by the rain, stretching for miles on either side. At nightfall the scene was ghostly and imagination easily peopled the dark galleries with strange images.

At midnight the sky began to threaten rain. Paul sounded the bugle again and again in hope of reaching the ears of some hospitable rancher; but only the musical echoes were returned, until he was about to land and camp on the shore when he was hailed by a voice which proved to belong to another squaw man and the weary travelers slept on the floor of his house until morning. The ranchman had several grown up half breed sons who could not speak a word of English. One of them had just returned from a hunt on which he had slaughtered two-hundred buffalos, taking their hides and leaving their carcasses to fester on the plains.

The start next day was the beginning of a long and tiresome run to Fort Bennett. During the afternoon, several geese and ducks were shot and a number of deer were seen in the timber points. When the sun went down, the country was lit up by remarkably beautiful hues, which died away as the moon rose clear and bright, and when it shone high above, the spectacle was magnificent. In some bends of the river the voyagers seemed completely landlocked and allowed the current to carry them safely through the quagmires and sand bars. They floated among a number of white swans and the whole flock flew upward with shrill cries, startling the cranes that stalked in the shadows and sending clouds of cackling geese and ducks whirling up from every gloomy nook and ravine.

Toward morning a heavy head wind sprang up that was very trying and just as dawn was approaching they entered a bend which was twenty-five miles in length, while the distance across by land, was but four miles. By hard pulling Fort Bennett was reached at four o'clock in the afternoon and Paul and Creelman were conveyed to the house of Major Love, the Indian agent, in an army ambulance after twenty-eight hours of incessant pulling. They determined to rest next day and were shown everything of interest at the Cheyenne Agency, where there were over two-thousand Indians. The principle chief was Little-no-Heart and among the others were Rattling Rib, White Swan, The Charger and Four Bears. These men were all peaceably disposed and belonged to the tribes that farm and raise stock on the reservation. They were driven about two miles from the fort to a tree in which a number of Indians, according to the custom of their tribe, had been buried. It was a goodly sized elm that had grown straight out of the ground to a height of twenty five feet, at which point the trunk forked into a dozen gnarled and twisted limbs, the peculiar black bark of which, gave them an unnatural appearance. Everywhere among the yellow leaves were perched heaps of decaying garments and bones. In some places, storms had torn away the gaudy funeral paraphernalia and whole skeletons were exposed. All the implements which the dead are supposed to need in the Happy Hunting Grounds, were placed at the side of the corpse and in one branch there was a trunk belonging to the skeleton just underneath it. So many Indians had been placed in the branches of this ancient elm, that it was said to have had a more vigorous growth than any other tree in its neighborhood in consequence of the fertilization afforded by the bodies. Since the establishment of the agency, however, the Indians have not been permitted to keep up this disgusting practice.

There was an Indian school on the reservation, which was also visited. The officials have a hard time of it to get the children to attend the school. The older ones are opposed to educating the youngsters and do not want them to learn to speak English. Some of the boys who were able to speak it fluently were ashamed to do so. They are apt pupils and can comprehend ideas with wonderful accuracy; the Government hopes that time will remove their prejudices and so they will become more civilized.

The journey was resumed next day at noon, pulling against a head wind; but their long rest gave them strength to contend with it, and the storm died out with the setting sun. Some of the buttes below Fort Sully are shaped wonderfully like pyramids; walls and cones loomed up against the sky and one could easily imagine himself on the Nile floating past the sphinxes and temples of Egypt. Occasionally the voyagers would be startled by the splash of a gigantic catfish as it leaped out of the water, and the loons driven southward by the approaching winter, filled the air with their melancholy cries. Shortly after midnight a gale sprang up which quickly churned the water into heavy waves and before daylight a regular hurricane was blowing. Acres of fine sand eddied and swirled about in the air, making it impossible to see more than a yard or two ahead and almost suffocating them. By daylight the fury of the storm was so great that the voyagers laid down on the bank to take a much needed rest. When they started again, they found the town of Pierre only one mile below where they had camped.

A halt was made at Pierre for a brief rest, the travelers stopping at a comfortable little hotel. Paul had no more than arranged himself to enjoy his pipe before sleeping, than he was called on by the editor, a bustling, little man who was warmly enthusiastic on the resources of the country about Pierre. He flitted into the room, introducing himself in a breezy manner, and immediately produced a bottle from his hip pocket and two glasses from the recesses of his coat tails; they were a recent purchase for the straw had not yet been removed from them. His astonishment at Paul's refusal to drink was so great that it quieted him for a moment; but he soon broke forth again on the resources of the country, depositing divers samples of what appeared to be black mud on the table, which he called gumbo.

After a restful sleep, Paul and Creelman visited some of the sights of the town, among which was the grave of "Arkansaw." He was a desperado whose crimes were said to throw the exploits of Rocky Mountain ruffians into the shade. Something over one year before, "Arkansaw," who was then living at Fort Pierre, expressed a determination to visit Pierre, on the other side of the river and "clean out the town." With this philanthropic purpose in view, he crossed the river one bitter cold night on the ice; but found a party of gentlemen, called vigilantes, awaiting him and while he was loading in some liquid courage at the principal bar of the place, some one called him to the door and he was shot full of holes. They buried him next day and the funeral was a very enthusiastic affair. One of the chief executioners, who was also principal mourner at the burial, made the following characteristic speech which was heartily endorsed by the citizens present:

"Arkansaw was a good feller, boys, and no mistake. He on'y got off his bearin's w'en ther idee struck him thet he cud clean out this ere town. But he were clear game. Three cheers fur the corpse."

The cheers were given with a will and another vigilante cried:

"A tiger fur Arkansaw."

With that the hero was lowered into the grave which is one of the sights of the town.

It was freezing cold the following day when Boyton and Creelman resumed the voyage, and Paul knew the rest of the journey would be a race against the winter which was now following close. He paddled between gumbo hills all afternoon. These black masses are composed of a sticky substance which becomes quite slippery in wet weather. Not a blade of grass will grow upon them except here and there where the natural soil rises to the surface. Ducks and other wild fowl cowered in the niches or wherever they could gain a foot hold under the banks, to escape the keen wind. The sky was overcast and not a ray of sunshine appeared except a momentary gleam during a slight rain storm which occurred late in the day. Shortly afterward, the river narrowed considerably and they were forced to paddle through a field of snags close to the west shore. The presence of the snags was explained by the hundreds of beaver slides which were worn in the muddy slopes, showing that that industrious little animal was far from extinct as commonly reported. The banks were hived with beaver holes and several trappers were encountered who made a business of catching them.

Night came on cold and cheerless and at midnight they entered the greatest bend of the Missouri. Two steamboats were sighted aground on a sand bar. Paul sounded a salute on the bugle, but received no answer. Later on the eastern sky was lighted up with a dull glare which soon brightened into a blaze and they could see a long line of flame and smoke racing across the prairie before a stiff breeze. At the mouth of Medicine river, the air was literally clouded with feathered game, hurrying into warmer latitudes from the frosty air of Montana and Dakota. At nine o'clock in the morning a landing was effected at the elbow of the great bend and breakfast made from choice bits of two ducks, shot just before. About noon they entered a great curving stretch of river, completely walled in on one side with hills, which resembled a vast causeway or an arched cathedral. The rain had worn a wondrous fretwork upon their sides and ribs of blue clay lent this effect to the whole.

As Paul and Creelman had paddled all night without stopping, the approach of the second night found them weary and numb with cold. There were no signs of the Crow Creek Agency and they began to fear that the settlement had been passed in the darkness. At midnight such a gale sprang up that they were compelled to land on the east shore under the shelter of a high cliff. A fire of driftwood was built and supper cooked. Next morning the sun was melting the ice on the hillsides and the frost had converted the wild grapes that hung above them into clusters of pearls. But the beauty of the scene faded into nothingness when they found they had withstood the cold of the night, while the Crow Creek Agency was just on the other side of the river. The journey was resumed in silence and a few miles below, a glimpse of the Stars and Stripes was caught through an opening between two hills as they neared Fort Hale, where they were heartily welcomed by the officers and were soon resting in snug quarters. They remained at Fort Hale over Sunday.

Monday broke clear and there was not a ripple on the surface of the Big Muddy. By this time, Mr. Creelman had returned to his appetite. At the start he could not think of drinking coffee made from the dirty river water and his stomach turned at the thought of eating blue bacon fried in a pan that was open to receive any little thing that might chance to drop in. He was now so hardened that he could eat a piece of duck washed in the thick water, or would snatch a piece of bacon off of the mud and swallow it with considerable relish.

Early in the afternoon they reached the little town of Chamberlain and the entire population was out on the bank to see the voyagers pass. An hour later, the Lower Brule Agency came in sight. Doctor Bergen, of Fort Hale, and one of the agency officials accompanied them for a few miles in a canoe, relieving the weary monotony by their pleasant conversation, while they also gave valuable information regarding several dangerous points below. Before reaching White river, Boyton frightened an Indian who was fishing from a bar out of his wits. He darted away leaving his catch and tackle and they had fresh fish for supper that night. While eating, a skiff containing two Indians approached and when within a few feet of the bank, asked Paul in good English, if he had any whisky to sell. He drove them away by threatening to sink their boat with a hatchet which he picked up from the deck of the Baby. This incident showed that there were still whisky smugglers plying their trade among the Indians. A short distance below they heard wild lamentations issuing from a clump of trees near the bank and saw the Indians were waking the corpse of a deceased friend. The mourner was attempting to sing; but the rhythm was so rude and incongruous, that it was really a series of howls. At the end of each stanza, the air was rent by a burst of war whoops that were calculated to make one's blood run cold. The weird chanting could be heard on the still night air miles below and the voyagers were convinced that there are many things more cheerful than an Indian wake. The night passed without incident and after breakfast next morning, Paul had to spend some time in fixing one or two weakening places in his dress.

Large flocks of gulls were now seen, which was looked upon as a good sign—that they had traveled south faster than the cold weather and would reach St. Louis before winter commenced in earnest. Strange as it may seem, these birds are found near the head of the Missouri river. They start from the sea coast in the spring and follow up the streams for over five thousand miles, retracing their course as winter approaches without ever going astray. That evening Paul and Creelman were greatly puzzled by the remarkable spectacle of what seemed to be a sunset in the east and west at the same time. At last they discovered that a number of large prairie fires were raging to the eastward and the reflection of the flames on the sky, caused the apparent dual sunset.

After midnight it was found that mud sucks and snags were so thick as to render further progress in the dark extremely hazardous, so the voyagers landed under a mud cliff and built a camp fire. They slept soundly until sunrise when they were astonished to see a number of Indian women performing their morning toilet at the water's edge. One of them was examining the Baby Mine in bewilderment and when Paul approached them they ran up a path in the side of the bluff and disappeared. He determined to ascertain where they were going and hastening after them, heard a stern "halt." Just ahead of him in the path stood a colored army sentinel. The soldier said they were near Fort Randall, and he was one of the guards over the Camp of Sitting Bull and other Indian prisoners of war, who had surrendered themselves to the United States authorities after the disastrous outbreak that drove them over the border into the British Possessions. Word was sent to the fort of Paul's arrival and a conveyance was dispatched to carry him and his companion to the garrison, where they were warmly received. A steaming breakfast was prepared to which full justice was done, after which, under the guidance of an officer, they visited the hostile camp, situated on a level stretch of ground about one mile distant from the garrison. There were thirty-two tepees, accommodating one hundred and sixty-eight people, forty of whom were males over sixteen years of age and the rest women and children. The tepees were arranged in a circle with a large space in the center, around which braves, squaws and almost nude children squatted or lay in the sunshine. One solitary white man was seen standing in front of a tepee. He was dressed in a dark pair of pantaloons, brown duck overcoat and his head was surmounted by a large, broad brimmed, drab felt hat, with a big dinge in each side of it. The white man proved to be Allison, the government scout and interpreter. It was he who entered the hostile camp the previous year and brought in the main body of the Sioux warriors, led by Crow King. The scout was a medium sized man, compactly and strongly built; a peculiar expression of shrewdness distinguished his face, and his eyes were keen and searching.

It was Allison's special care to look out for Sitting Bull, the famous Uncapapa chief, and after greeting the visitors, he led them into the presence of the dreaded Sioux leader. Whatever may be said of Sitting Bull, he certainly had the appearance of a man born to lead men. He was five feet ten inches tall and weighed probably one hundred and eighty pounds. His face was an unusually intelligent one and his forehead large. He was dignified, though modest, as he invited the travelers into his tepee and seemed to feel keenly his condition as a prisoner. A number of Indians also entered at the request of Sitting Bull, among them his young fighting nephew, Kill-While-Standing, who wore eyeglasses which gave him a student-like appearance. The two wives of the chief shook hands with every one present and exhibited several half naked and very dirty children, heirs of the Bull family. Among them were twins whom the ladies of the garrison had named Kate and Duplicate.

An instance of the wonderful power of Sitting Bull over his people and his remarkable shrewdness in retaining that power, the following scene enacted that evening, will illustrate: Paul and some of the army officers, with the interpreter were seated in the tepee conversing with Sitting Bull, when a deputation of Indians requested an audience with their chief. It appears they had been arguing among themselves about the mysterious manner in which Minnewachatcha floated upon the water without effort, although he appeared to be constituted the same as other men. Not being able to reach a conclusion, they referred the matter to Sitting Bull. The great chief had no doubt been ruminating considerably on the same subject without being able to settle it to his own satisfaction; but he was too shrewd a politician to display the least ignorance of the question. In fact, Bull considered no matter too trivial to use as a means of displaying to his people his own great store of knowledge and he would feign to know all about things of which he was ignorant, frequently claiming to have received his information from the Great Spirit above. So when the question regarding Minnewachatcha, was propounded, he took it as a matter of course that when a thing of importance presented itself, his people must come to him for information. His dignified manner would have done credit to a great statesman. Facing the deputation, with Paul standing at his right, he began a harangue in the Sioux tongue, using gestures that were at once impressive and graceful.

Briefly, his speech as interpreted by Allison, was to the effect that he was a great chief, that the Great Spirit made known to him all things. He knew all about Minnewachatcha, who was good medicine. (Then he would lightly tap Boyton on the shoulder and step back impressively.) In his examination, he had found that Minnewachatcha, though he appeared like other men, was not, because he was possessed of no internal arrangements as other men, hence he could float on the water like an empty can.

The government sometimes issues canned provisions to the Indians. When they extract the contents and throw the can in the water, it floats away, and Bull used that as a simile, knowing they would all understand. The deputation appeared perfectly satisfied with the explanation and went away thoroughly convinced that Boyton was supplied with no interior mechanism in the way of lungs, stomach, etc.

Sitting Bull conceived a strong friendship for Paul and they exchanged gifts, and Minnestema, Bull's daughter, who was really handsome for an Indian girl, looked upon him as second only to her distinguished father in greatness. Paul thought to flatter Minnestema, and through the interpreter, told her that he had heard her praises sung far up the river, that she was the toast at every fort and that the fame of her beauty had even spread to the great cities of the whites. Her copper countenance expressed much pleasure at this; but she dispelled the romance by immediately asking Paul in broken English, if he had any plug chewing tobacco.

The friendship between Paul and Sitting Bull lasted until the latter was killed in the ghost dance excitement during the winter of 1891. When the old chief was on a tour of the east in 1885, his face lighted up with joy when he met Boyton and gave him a cordial welcome.

Paul left Fort Randall, October 20th. After he had encased himself in his rubber dress, the Indians could not be induced to shake hands with him. A little girl put her hand into his and all the chiefs, in admiration of her bravery, exclaimed, "how".

White Dog, Scarlet Thunder, Kill-While-Standing and One Bull were anxious to see the "Water Spirit" float away, but they kept at a respectful distance from Paul as he stood on the slope before slipping into the water.

The afternoon was pleasant and as they glided down on the current followed by the wondering eyes of the soldiers as well as the Indians, Paul and Creelman felt refreshed and vigorous and made good time. Just after dark, they passed the Yankton Indian Agency and were cheered.

That night was dark, even the stars being obscured by the clouds. A number of prairie fires threw some light on the water, but barely enough to make the passage among snags and sand bars feasible. At daybreak the villages of Niobrara and Running Water were passed. A couple of hours later the weary voyagers hauled up on the bank and cooked breakfast. When barely under way again, a boat containing a rough looking stranger approached. He carried a shot gun and rowed along sometime without uttering a word. Though silent, he appeared to extract a great deal of satisfaction from his contemplation of Boyton.

"What are you going to do with that gun?" questioned Paul at last.

"Kill a goose," was the laconic reply.

"Oh, I see. You intend to commit suicide," said Creelman.

Not a muscle of the stranger's solemn countenance moved; but he rowed away suddenly and disappeared among the sand bars, followed by a peal of laughter.

Springfield was passed at noon and the citizens rushed to the bank at the first sound of the bugle.

From Springfield to Bonhomie, the river was smooth and straight. At the latter place it narrowed until the current ran at the rate of six miles an hour and the travelers were swept under the high cliffs on which the town stands in a roaring sea of whirlpools and riffles. Cheer after cheer was sent up by the people as they shot past; but the voyagers had no leisure to examine the banks, as they had all they could do to avoid the snags which stuck up everywhere and made navigation exceedingly difficult. Eight miles below, a landing was effected on a pile of driftwood; a fire built and supper cooked. It began to rain and they huddled over the fire to keep warm. At three o'clock the fire was out and a heavy fog hung on the Missouri. Paul thought it was better to keep up the temperature of the body by paddling than to sit in the mud shivering, so they resumed their voyage. The cold rain dashed into their faces in such torrents that it was more a matter of chance than skill that they progressed, as they could not see ten feet ahead. In the midst of the storm, they ran against a snag, but fortunately, no damage was done. At daybreak another halt was made and breakfast eaten. When the mists cleared, they found themselves within sight of Yankton, where they were received an hour later by the citizens.

Leaving Yankton, they arrived at Sioux City without incident and began to think they were once more within the limits of civilization. They were greeted by shouting multitudes that followed them to a hotel and would scarcely permit them to rest. Next morning the same enthusiasm was manifested when they departed. But there were yet two-hundred good miles of snaggy river to paddle before they could enjoy the luxury of a bed at every stage. Less than a dozen miles below Sioux City the weather grew threatening again and Boyton decided not to rest that night, but to push on steadily toward Omaha. During the afternoon the wind blew from every point of the compass. He hoped it would go down with the sun, but as night approached, the storm continued to develop. The increase in the speed of the current had the effect of cutting away high banks of timber and as they dashed along, they ran by immense trees sticking out of the water with the leaves yet upon their branches, showing that the channel was shifting. At midnight it began to rain and they tried to land, but failed to find a safe place as the banks on either side were undermined and caving constantly. An hour later they entered "Hell's Bend" and, the roaring of the water as it tore among the snags was almost deafening. The river was full of obstructions and suddenly Boyton and Creelman in his canvas canoe, were flung on a snag, the latter losing an oar. Regardless of his own danger, Paul struggled to release the canoe, when a large wave lifted them both clear. They were unable to continue their way in the darkness and managed to get ashore, where they built a fire and waited until daylight. The little village of Tieville was just below and when the villagers heard that Boyton was in the river, they flocked to the camp where the weary paddler lay stretched out in the mud asleep, looking more like an alligator than a man. Several experienced boatmen remarked that there were only two steamboats on the Missouri that could navigate the bend at the point where the voyagers had spent a portion of the night.

The journey was resumed at eight o'clock and not long afterward a new oar was procured for the canoe, at Decatur. A disheartening struggle against adverse wind followed until noon, when it abated. They passed the reservation of the Omaha and Winnebago Indians during the night. As the voyagers were watching for the lights of Blair early that night, a smoky smell directed their attention to a camp fire built at the water's edge. Two men were seen about it, one of whom was maudlin drunk and trying to sing. Boyton hailed them and was invited to land and get some roast goose. As the night was favorable for paddling, the invitation was declined, when the drunken one raising his gun, yelled: "You wont come in, wont you?" and fired, the shot striking the water within a few feet of Paul's head. He had a strong desire to return and punish the fellow, but concluded that to continue down the river was of more importance, besides, he could hear that the men were fighting between themselves and thought they would administer their own punishment.

At daybreak the travelers sighted Florence and discovered that they were only sixteen miles from Omaha and at the next bend they landed to cook breakfast and rest. One of the bores encountered all the way down after striking the towns, was the man who persisted in telling them all about the great flood of "last spring." He was found at every town and village and the voyagers were given all the various details of that flood until it became nauseating, so much so, that it made Boyton irritable whenever mentioned. As he lighted a cigar and stretched his limbs on the sand bar to enjoy a rest before proceeding to Omaha, he remarked to his companion that they would not be annoyed by flood fiends there; but his confidence was without foundation. In less than ten minutes after he made the remark, a man landed from a little skiff and seating himself on a log, while a gleam of satisfaction shot from his eyes, said: "Strangers, you couldn't a laid down on that bar so comfortable and easy last spring. The big flood—"

"Hop into that boat and get away from here," fairly yelled Paul, springing to his feet, "or I'll pitch you into the river, where you can tell your miserable flood stories to the fishes."

The man looked at the threatening navigator a moment, boarded his boat and with disappointment lining every feature, pulled a short distance away, then resting on his oars, triumphantly shouted: "It was high enough over thet ere bank." A club was flung at him as he drifted out of sight around the bar.

Resuming the voyage, Omaha came in sight as they rounded the next bend and beheld the Union Pacific bridge that spans the river.

"Ah," joyously exclaimed Creelman, "We're out of the wilderness. There's the first bridge."

At that point a party of friends and representatives of the press, met the travelers and escorted them to the city, where thousands of people lined the bank to extend a welcome. One man, who probably intended to commit suicide, threw off his coat and shouting that he could swim as well as that fellow, jumped in and was drowned. Boyton had great difficulty in getting through the crowd to a carriage which conveyed him to a hotel.

That evening, after a wash and getting into suits of clothes which they had shipped ahead, Paul and Creelman met a party of friends and newspaper men in their room and entertained them with an account of some of the adventures of the trip.

On leaving Omaha after a pleasant rest of a day, the voyagers realized that winter was sweeping down from the northwest with such rapidity that it was necessary for them to exert their best efforts if they would reach St. Louis before ice enclosed them. The character of the country through which they now passed was entirely different from that above. While there were still many wild stretches, instead of bare buttes covered with buffalo grass, the hills were loaded with timber, and well kept fences told that instead of a strictly cattle grazing country, immense farms stretched from either shore. At places, corn stalks rustled for miles along the bank and fat swine came to the shore to wallow in the mud.

The first night out from Omaha, they passed the mouth of the Platte river and next morning reached Nebraska City. Many towns and villages were passed and at every place large crowds were looking for the voyagers and expressed much disappointment when they refused to halt even for a few moments. As they were enjoying their pipes over a splendid camp fire one night some miles above St. Joseph, they were somewhat startled at hearing a gruff voice call out, "Hello, there." And immediately two men heavily armed, stood by the fire. One was a tall, muscular fellow and the other shorter and slighter built, both having the appearance of men that were not to be trifled with. They were very friendly, however, and chatted pleasantly for some time; inquiring all about the trip down the river and displaying a keen interest in everything concerning it. They were intelligent conversationalists and the two hours they remained in camp passed quickly. On going away they shook hands and wished the travelers good luck. Later, Paul found out that the midnight visitors were no other than the notorious Jesse James and his pal Bob Ford who afterward assassinated him.

The voyagers sighted St. Joseph at sunset next evening but having grounded in the mud they did not reach the city until after dark and found the bank jammed with people. They had been watching for them at St. Joseph all day. During their stay they were honored by a continual round of receptions, serenades and other entertainments and on leaving, the crowd was just as enthusiastic as on their arrival. They were joined there by Mr. Baker, a correspondent of a Kansas City paper, who had been assigned to accompany them as far as that city. He bad purchased a rather unwieldy skiff in which to accomplish the trip, and started along with them pulling a vigorous stroke. Toward night the weather grew very cold.

Every drop of water that splashed into the boats was quickly frozen. Paul's head covering was iced. About eleven o'clock he pulled alongside the boats.

"Boys," he said, "this is going to be a rough night on you and the best way for you to get along is to pull one hour, turn about and sleep one hour. I will keep time and call you up."

The plan met with favor and was immediately put into execution. Creelman was to pull the first hour and Baker rolled himself in the buffalo robes and laid on the bottom of his boat. He was fast asleep in a moment. At the expiration of fifteen minutes, Creelman softly called Boyton alongside.

"Say, Captain, Baker hasn't pulled all the way do n from Bismarck. He's fresh. Suppose we wake him up and you tell him it's twelve o'clock," he suggested.

Paul fell in with the spirit of the joke and after pulling away from the boat, he blew the bugle and aroused Baker with the information that it was twelve o'clock. The Kansas City man took the oars and Creelman rolled up for a good nap. After fifteen or twenty minutes, Baker hailed Paul, who hauled up.

"Say, Captain, Creelman has pulled all the way down the river and is innured to this sort of thing. I'm not. It's just about knocking me out. Suppose you call him and tell him his hour is up."

"All right," said the Captain, and in a moment Creelman was rubbing his eyes.

"Confound it, Captain. It seems to me that was an almighty short hour," he said.

"It's one o'clock," sung the Captain, "time's up. Creelman took the oars without the least suspicion that Boyton would play a joke on him.

"Call Baker up again," he said to Paul after pulling several minutes, and Baker was called up accordingly.

"By George," exclaimed Baker, rubbing his eyes, "I must have slept awfully sound. It doesn't seem to me as though I have been down ten minutes."

He went to work, however, and Paul enjoyed himself calling them up, each thinking he had the best of the other. At three o'clock, they began to scan the horizon for daybreak. According to the hours they had pulled, it should have been five o'clock. As daylight did not appear, Creelman began to grow suspicious and as Baker was called up again he saw Creelman with a lighted match consulting his watch.

"What time is it?" inquired Baker.

"Three o'clock," replied Creelman in a mournful voice.

"What?" almost screamed Baker, "only three o'clock?"

They favored each other with a cold, hard look and each seized his own oars again. So they rowed through the bitter morning hours.

Leavenworth and other towns were saluted, crowds always cheering on the banks, and the following afternoon, almost frozen, they landed at Kansas City, where for two miles the bank was a solid mass of humanity. Among those who greeted them was an uncle whom Paul had never seen, Mr. Peter Behan, a famous guide and one of the first who ever piloted a wagon train across the plains to California. The voyagers were tendered the freedom of the city and were hospitably entertained. Next morning the journey was resumed amid deafening plaudits.

Speed was now the one thing necessary and Boyton knew there would be some chance of finishing their trip on skates if they did not reach St. Louis ahead of the cold wave that was setting down the river. They passed the United States snag boat, Wright, directly after leaving Kansas City and in the evening paddled by Berlin. Wild geese and ducks were still seen in great numbers at places and several mud hens were run down and killed. At Camden and many other towns, bonfires were built by the enthusiastic citizens who were determined to catch sight of the hardy navigator, whether he passed by in the night or day.

They had now four hundred miles ahead of them. The winter had closed in with great severity. The ice formed rapidly in the river and they met daily snow storms. At the same time the river raised and increased their speed so that they easily made ten or twelve miles an hour.

Below Wellington, at two o'clock one morning, the voyagers mounted a pile of driftwood to rest. Building a fire they went to sleep, but toward daylight they were startled to find their camp was afloat, which caused them to resume the journey rather earlier than they had intended.

Below Lexington, Paul shot a beautiful pair of white heron measuring seven feet from tip to tip. After passing Booneville, the banks of the river became more permanent and they passed through a rich grape growing country, populated mainly by Germans, who have established large wine vaults and make much wine. At Jefferson City, they were met by the Mayor and tendered the freedom of the city. That night they were shown through a wine vault and learned that the soil in that country was as rich and identical with that of the best wine growing districts of the Rhine.

Wagon teams were crossing on the ice along the upper river. Paul was much reduced in flesh, and his face bronzed like an Indian's.

At last, one Sunday morning, sixty-four days after the trip was begun, they camped for the last time at the mouth of the Missouri where it empties into the Mississippi. St. Louis was twenty miles away. They entered that city during the afternoon and were given a tremendous reception. This voyage of 3,580 miles was the longest and roughest journey Boyton ever made.

CHAPTER XXII.

The long, trying voyage of the Yellowstone and Missouri gave Paul a keen relish for a few week's rest at home. He recuperated so rapidly, however, that when he received an invitation from a friend to go on a hunting expedition aboard a private steamboat, he was ripe to accept it. The steamer was then on the Mississippi and Paul joining her at Memphis, her nose was turned for southwestern waters. They steamed up the Arkansas to Bayou Meta, and were soon far in the depths of the woods. Though the water of the bayou was very deep, it was so narrow at places that trees and vines had to be cut away so the boat could push her way through. Several weeks were spent in shooting deer and bear, catching coon, opossum and other game. At their manufactured salt licks, they succeeded in taking all the deer they wanted. Boyton's love for pets quickly manifested itself and every odd corner of the little steamer had an occupant. Among these was a cub bear, captured after killing the old one, by throwing a coat over it. It was a vicious little brute at first, spitting and clawing at everything that went near it, and it seemed impossible to train. After many things had been tried without avail, a stick with some honey on its end was thrust between the bars of the cage. The little fellow struck at it wickedly at first, but noticing the honey on its paws, began to smell, then to taste it. The honey was so much to its liking that it was soon eating out of Boyton's hand and in a short time it was as tame and playful as a kitten.

Tiring of hunting, Paul was taken with a desire to feel the current of the Arkansas, to which river they returned and with such intention, he packed his dress and tender and proceeded to Ft. Smith, starting above that city at the mouth of the Poteau river, Choctaw Nation, Indian Territory, January 12th, 1882, for a four hundred mile run to Pine Bluff. The weather was cold and the chill of Rocky Mountain snow was in the river. The course was rather lonely, winding amid bleak hills and for long stretches there would be small signs of life. At the end of the first day's paddling, he hauled up at a farm house to request shelter for the night. A woman told him that the men were not in yet, but she "reckoned he could stay, though there was no bed." Paul told her he did not require a bed and when the men came in they tendered him the comforts of the cabin. After supper the time was passed in chatting over their pipes around a spacious fireplace, in front of which, Paul was to sleep. During the evening he admired a beautiful little girl four years of age. She was as shy at first as she was pretty; but finally mustered sufficient courage to edge timidly up to his side and ask:

"Please sah, gimme a chaw tobacca?"

"Why, my dear little girl you do not chew tobacco at your age, do you?" exclaimed Paul.

"Yo' bet she do, stranger," answered the father, "she's jus' a chawer from away back," at the same time giving her a goodly sized piece of the weed.

The mother, who was attending to score domestic affairs, overheard the conversation and turning to Paul, remarked:

"Now, stranger, do yo' raily think uts right t' give a chile like thet tobacca?"

"Decidedly I do not," said Paul.

"Look ut thet; look ut thet, Dan," she exclaimed triumphantly, addressing her husband, "even a stranger don't think uts right. What hev I allus been a tellin' yo'?"

The farmer laughed as he replied: "Oh, she'll git over thet w'en she gits sixteen an' goes sparkin' an' wants t' whiten her teeth."

Leaving the hospitable farm house with the tobacco question still unsettled, an early start was made for a run to Ozark. Before reaching, that place, he was driven past a high wood-covered butte when he heard the rhythmic melody of a plantation song and observed an old negro pulling across the stream below. For the purpose of a little amusement, Paul stood up and shouted:

"Aha, I've got you now."

The darkey facing around, caught sight of the curious figure. The look of fright which shone on his black features, was woeful as he struck for the shore, yelling:

"'Taint mine; 'taint mine, sah; it's de kunnel's, 'taint mine."

When within four feet of the shore, he sprang out, leaving the dugout to drift. Not wishing to frighten the darkey into the loss of his boat, Paul pulled in and ran it up on the bank. He then noticed that she had a cargo of stone jugs filled with "Arkansaw lightning," held in with corn cob stoppers. The negro was engaged in the missionary work of smuggling the liquor to Indians on the reservation. As Paul swung off into mid stream, he saw a pair of frightened eyes shining at him from among the bushes.

That night he rested at Ozark. For two days following, the weather was very bad. The first night he was compelled to camp on a sand bar for a few hours and build a fire to thaw himself. The rest so invigorated him that he paddled into the night of the second day. Sleet coated his dress until he resembled a cake of ice and his paddle became so thick that he could scarcely handle it. About nine o'clock he went ashore and found a cabin, the light from a blazing fire within shining through the chinks between the logs. He hammered on the door and was invited to enter. As he pushed in, a line, of black, kinky heads raised from beds on the floor, and several pairs of eyes gazed inquiringly in the direction of the door. When the glistening black figure was discovered, some shrieked and covered their heads. A powerful negro jumped up and seized an ax, moving rapidly toward Boyton with it uplifted.

"What's the matter with you?" said Paul, stepping back a few paces toward the door, "put down that ax. I am on a trip down the river and seeking shelter."

After some persuasion, the negro put the ax down in a handy corner and gave his queer guest permission to sleep in front of the fireplace, while the family peered at him curiously from under their bed clothes. At daylight they all crawled out to see him start and they formed quite a large gathering. It was the sight of a lifetime with them and their yells of delight were unrestrained as he pulled away towing the Baby, which was covered with ice.

As Boyton approached Dardenelle, a party of reporters met him in skiffs. He was informed that a steaming hot breakfast was prepared for him at a hotel and invited to stop; but feeling in good shape, he thought he would go ahead. Mr. James K. Perry, a merchant of Dardenelle, whom Paul had met in New Orleans, rowed up and was so pressing in his offers of hospitality, that the voyager could not refuse. A perfect mass of humanity had gathered at the wharf and a carriage was there to convey him to the hotel. He was soon divested of his rubber dress and made quite comfortable. An invitation from Mr. Perry to dine at his house was refused because of lack of clothing; but the hospitable citizens would not allow a little thing like that to stand in the way of his pleasure, and they attired him in a brand new suit from head to foot. The pantaloons had to be held up as he walked along the streets and were the source of much amusement. There were numerous other guests at the dinner and he spent a most pleasant day and evening.

Next morning was dark and threatening when he resumed the voyage. He hoped to make Lewisburg that night. Toward evening he again ran into rain and sleet which almost blinded him and the numerous islands made it difficult for him to keep the channel. Seeing smoke pouring from a cabin that stood dangerously near the brink, he sounded the bugle in hope of stirring up some one from whom he could glean a little information. A frowsy individual sauntered out, glanced over the river and without displaying the least interest, was proceeding to arrange some crocks and pans about the cabin door.

"Hello, my friend," shouted Paul.

The man slowly turned and ramming both hands into his breeches' pockets, calmly eyed the figure in the water. As he was turning toward the cabin again, without a word, Boyton asked:

"How far is it to Lewisburg?"

"Its a putty good distance," slowly answered the man. "How far do you call that?" "I don't never call ut as I knows on."

"Look here, my good-"

"Ain't I a lukin?"

"Well, is Lewisburg one mile, five miles or a thousand miles from here?"

"I reckon its one o' them numbers."

Paul was beginning to feel out of humor, but realized that he was conversing with a lineal descendant of the "Arkansaw Traveler;" he determined to get some information. Pointing to an island just below, he again put a question:

"Which side of that island shall I take?"

"Any side thet you're a mind to."

"On which side is the channel?"

"Sometimes on one side, sometimes t' other."

"Which side do you consider best?"

"I aint 'tendin' t' other people's business."

"Which side do the steamboats take?"

"Its owin' to what captain's on."

"Wouldn't you kindly advise me which side to take?"

"Reckon I bes' not."

"Why?"

"Frien's o' mine on both sides wants to see you."

"Plague take your incivility; how long will it take me to reach Lewisburg?"

"'Ts owin' ter how fas' yo' travel."

"How long does it take you to go?"

"I don't never go."

"How long did it take you to come from there?"

"Tuk me right smart while; but the team broke down."

"Confound it. Do you know what I think of you?"

"Nothin' thet ud spite my appytite."

"I think you are the blamdest fool in Arkansaw."

"Know what I think o' yo'?"

"What?"

"Thet yo're the devil come up ter cool himself off."

The fellow deliberately entered the cabin and closed the door, and Paul luckily struck the channel around the island.

The Arkansas river cuts under its banks much after the manner of the Missouri. Several places were seen where they had been undermined and sunk carrying sheep down that had been grazing near the edge, leaving the poor things hemmed in on one side by high banks and on the other by water. There they would starve rather than take to the river to get out. Whenever Boyton ran across such places, he would either drive the sheep off or tell some one below to go up and get them.

Four days from the time of starting, he ran into Little Rock, the State capital, where he was pleasantly entertained. When the voyage was resumed, he was accompanied by Opie Read, the famous humorist, who enjoyed the river experience. They amused themselves during the day with the negroes, many of whom thought Boyton was a drowning man floating along. They would run close to the water's edge and yell at Read, who was pulling leisurely behind in a row boat.

"Hyah, man. Doan yo' see dat ar man drownen? G'on an pick him up."

"Not much, I wont pick him up." Opie shouted, "I'm going to let him drown."

"Hi, Eph; git yo' boat. Drownen man in de ribber. Spec he done drownded now," excitedly yelled one old auntie to a broad shouldered darkey who was running to the bank. Then as both boat and Boyton swept by, they could hear her say: "Dere's de onliest man ebber I see dat'll let a fellah human drownd afore his eyes. Him de wickedest man in de worl'."

One old negro with an armful of ear corn, dropped it with a look of horror and stood as if petrified, as far as the voyagers could see him.

Below Little Rock as night came on, a small steamer was encountered tied up to the bank and Paul and his companion spent the night aboard of her.

It was that night that Boyton succumbed to something worse than rapids, quicksand or waterfalls. They had lighted their pipes after supper and were lounging about the cabin talking of their adventures, when Paul asked Read what kind of smoking tobacco he used.

"Old natural leaf," said Opie, "have some?"

"Don't care if I do."

The pipe was refilled and puffing away, Paul continued relating some adventure.

It was an interesting experiment to his listeners and they watched anxiously. They knew that that kind of tobacco must form a man's acquaintance gradually. It will brook no sudden familiarity. The smoke curled in fantastic wreathes about Boyton's head and the stories became less thrilling. His eyes gradually became yellow and his swarthy countenance turned a pale green. The words tumbled over one another and, got mixed up woefully.

"Look here," he said, struggling to keep his eyes open, "where did you get that tobacco?"

"In Little Rock."

"Whew! its stronger than the falls of the Arno," and turning over, he slept, perhaps to dream of red oak tobacco sticks, and bare legged boys with green hands, killing worms. He succumbed to "Arkansaw natural leaf."

Next morning they pulled out for Pine Bluff, the last run of the voyage. Above the city, the steamer Woodson met them with a party of excursionists on board. Capt. F. G. Smart, of Jefferson, was detailed to deliver an address of welcome to Boyton as soon as they met him. The Captain was an enthusiastic admirer of the voyager and had taken numerous doses of "Arkansaw lightning" for the purpose of inspiring his oratorical powers. As Boyton swung into sight, the Captain sprang upon something laying near the rail and throwing both hands up as though a highwayman had him covered with a Winchester, he began his speech.

"Standing here on this sack of salt," he roared, "I say standing here on—"

"Git offen me," yelled a colored roustabout who had laid down and upon whom the Captain had planted himself.

"Get out of my way then," shouted the orator, "don't throw yourself in the attitude of a rostrum unless you have credentials. I say, ladies and gentlemen, we have assembled on this boat, to come up to meet a man coming down. It is my principle never to shove a man down; but on this occasion, I stand merely as a spectator. As a rule, a man goes down on whisky, but this man goes down on water. May we all meet on that beautiful shore, where every man can show a life saving suit of clothes."

The Captain's voice was drowned in a round of cheers and the sound of the steamboat's whistle, as she was headed down stream to escort Boyton to Pine Bluff, where he was warmly received, completing his voyage of four-hundred miles in six days.

Again embarking on his friend's little steamboat, a cruise down the Mississippi to the mouth of Red river followed, where some time was spent in hunting and then the boat was headed for New Orleans.

For two years following, with the exception of a run down the rapids of the James river at Richmond, Boyton was engaged in business. During that time he became an agent of the Haytien insurgents, as a purchaser of supplies and he barely escaped going out on the ship Lapatrie, which was captured and all on board executed by order of Hippolyte.

In 1884, Paul decided to give up his adventurous life, and settle down. He continued in business on shore until 1886, when his health became so affected by confinement that he was advised to resume his old outdoor life for a time, to recuperate. So he concluded to limber his joints with another voyage. On looking about for a course, he found he had made all the rivers in America that promised adventure, except those of the far west. He went to San Francisco and prepared for a run down the Sacramento from Red Bluff, four-hundred and fifty miles.

He entered the water, March 26th. It was a beautiful morning and the people from the town and surrounding country gathered to see him start. A boat load of reporters accompanied him, intending to go as far as Tehama. As Paul felt his well beloved element under him again, he answered the characteristic California salute of the good people of Red Bluff, with rockets and bugle and was soon carried out of sight. When the noise of the town was left behind, the newspaper men were surprised to see him throw his paddle in the air, and catch it with a whoop of almost boyish pleasure. He answered their inquiries by saying that he could not restrain his joy at feeling himself at home once more.

Directly after the start, the Baby was discovered to be leaking. Her long sojourn ashore had subjected her to the malevolent attacks of rust, which had eaten a small hole in her bottom that had been overlooked. How to stop the leak was a serious problem. No solder was obtainable. They used some of the tar off the bottom of the reportorial boat; but it would not stick. The dilemma was overcome by a young gentleman in the boat who had been suspected of a tendency to ape the fashions of the effete east. When he blushingly produced a slug of chewing gum, they were satisfied that their suspicions were well founded. The gum proved efficacious, however, and the leak was plugged up.

Tehama was reached about noon, where they were saluted by volleys fired from shot guns, rifles and revolvers. Paul hauled up and sent a messenger for glycerin and oil to use on his face which began to feel the effects of the burning sun. As he lay in the dock answering a shower of questions, about his name, age, fighting weight etc., an old gentleman stepped to the front and said:

"Captain, why don't you come out? Tehama is famous for its widows. They are handsomer and more of them than will be found in any other town of her size in the world, and if you ain't married, I guarantee you will be in an hour after you're ashore."

The widows present shyly smiled.

After being supplied with the glycerin, he left the newspaper men and struck away alone. He kept on all night and passed Chico bridge early next morning. Before sun-rise he noticed a tree that was strange and wonderful. It was full of what appeared to be large white clusters of feathery-like blossoms, which swayed to and fro as though alive, yet not a breath of air was stirring. His wonder at the beautiful spectacle was so great, that he ceased moving the paddle and drifted with the current toward the snowy looking tree. When opposite, he saw it was a roost for some sort of water fowl. He shouted and a cloud of white heron rose in the air and soared away.

He now entered a stretch of river that was very lonely. The ranches were far away from the banks. The sand bars were full of geese, ducks and heron, while many buzzards sailed gracefully above. He noticed one large flock of these scavengers, that hung over him and which gained in numbers as they moved along, no doubt mistaking him for a dead body, floating. He had commenced the voyage on Friday and the old sailor superstition affected him. He did not like the persistence with which the ill-omened birds kept him company; but they were far out of range of pistol shot. He grew so nervous looking at the buzzards that he could see nothing else along the river. Then he thought of a plan to get rid of them, which he immediately put into execution. Taking a powerful detonating rocket from the Baby, he fired it into their midst and it bursted above. They darted away toward the Sierras and he was annoyed by them no more.

There was one companion he could not get rid of, however, that was the snow clad peak of Mt. Shasta. It appeared ever present and always at the same distance. He would think he had left it in the rear, when at the next bend of the river, it again loomed up in front of him. He saw it at sunrise and at sunset for days, gloriously colored as the variations of light bathed its towering sides.

At Grimes' Landing, a Sunday school picnic was encountered. Arches and banks of flowers, made bright a beautiful grove. On one arch were the words, "Baby Mine," spelled out in roses. Boyton had not intended to stop, but could not resist getting out and shaking hands with the little ones. That night he stopped at a wood cutter's camp.

Next evening he was met by a gentleman in a boat with a servant, who extended a most cordial invitation to spend the night. They repaired to an elegant residence on the river bank and the gentleman proved to be the Hon. John Boggs, proprietor of one of the great ranches which make California famous. He was profuse in his hospitality, sending messages by his private wire to Sacramento and San Francisco. His ranch consists of eleven thousand acres, requiring hundreds of men to work it; herds of cattle and droves of sheep, numbering into the tens of thousands, graze on the ranges. Ocean vessels are docked at his warehouses and loaded for foreign ports. Boyton always remembers the night spent at that California ranch as one of the most pleasant of his life.

Next day Colusa was reached and for some distance below, people were numerous on the banks, school children sometimes running along a mile or more. At one place a tall, raw boned woman, who looked as though she possessed a mind of her own, gathered up her skirts and trotted along the bank for same time, talking to Boyton. She wanted to know if he lectured.

"No; I am taking notes so as to write a book," replied Paul.

"Well, you're just the fellow I'm looking for. I want you to take notes about the slickens that are filling up this river and go for the miners, good and strong, who make them." With that she dropped her skirts and pointing her index finger impressively at Paul, concluded: "Now don't forget that, young fellow," and turned to retrace her steps.

The slickens spoken of by the strong minded female, is refuse from the mines filling the channel of the river and ruining navigation. It is produced by hydraulic mining, powerful streams of water washing the dirt down from the hills into the river. Boyton found the slickens very trying to the eyes.

At the mouth of Feather river he met a boat load of Sandwich Islanders, who were up that far fishing, they kept along with him for several miles and he found them to be very intelligent companions. That night he landed at a ranch and sounded his bugle. No one answering, he climbed to the top of a high hank and discovered a number of Chinamen coming toward him. At sight of him they all returned to the house in a hurry and Paul knew it was useless to apply for accommodation there. He entered the river again and paddled on until he reached another ranch. At the call of the bugle, a man came out and in answer to Boyton's request for lodging, said.

"Why, certainly Captain, glad to have you come in. I've heard all about you."

On entering the house, the host explained that he was a bachelor and all alone, at the same time bustling about, baking biscuits and boiling eggs. Next morning there was the same liberal supply of eggs and as Paul was devouring a goodly share of them, the bachelor remarked:

"You needn't think, Captain, that because we had eggs last night and this mornin' too, they're cheap. No, sir. Why, 'pon honor, Cap, them eggs is worth fifteen cents a dozen in Sacramento."

The Captain assured him that they were most nutritious food and that he heartily enjoyed them. Before resuming the voyage that morning, Paul discovered, that back of the ranch, thousands of acres of splendid land was overflowed and rendered useless by the slickens falling into the Sacramento.

From the egg producing ranch, the river took on the appearance of a southern bayou. Trees and festoons of vines hung in the water, which was clear and beautiful and numbers of water snakes were continually crossing and recrossing. Seeing one handsome yellow fellow, Paul paddled after and captured it. It made no attempt to bite; but coiled tightly around his wrist and hand. It was three feet long and beautifully marked. He stowed it in the Baby and it remained his companion for the rest of the journey.

Groups of Chinamen were occasionally seen, fishing from the banks or the branches of overhanging trees. Some of these stared at him while others ran away. During the afternoon, he saw two celestials in a tree. He silently ran under them and uttered a terrific yell. One of the Chinamen was so frightened that he let go all holds and dropped into the water, while his companion remained in the tree, his teeth chattering like castanets.

Further down Paul encountered beating head winds and suffered from the slickens. His face was badly burned and the skin peeled off in flakes. On April 1st, he reached Sacramento and the usual hearty California reception was tendered him. For five days after leaving that city, the going was heavy and tiresome, having struck tide water directly below. The runs through Suesun and San Pablo bays were very trying. Saturday, April 6th, he made John's Lighthouse at the head of San Francisco bay, and remained there until four o'clock in the morning, intending to start on the last run to San Francisco on the ebb tide. He made Angel Island at seven o'clock, where he was compelled to stop because the tide as it then was, would have carried him through the Golden Gate to the Pacific. When the tide turned, he again struck across the bay and was met by a fleet of boats to escort him in.

Foremost among these was the yacht of Mr. Matt. O'Donnell. Calling to him, Boyton said: "Halloa Matt, I have a present for you." The boat was pulled alongside and Paul took the yellow snake out of the Baby, putting it into his friend's hand so quickly, that the latter did not have a chance to see what it was. The reptile coiled about his wrist and with an exclamation of fright, he shook it off on the deck much to the consternation of those aboard. As Boyton sheered off, O'Donnell, assuming an oratorical attitude, called out:

"Thanks for the snake."

Before Paul could reach his destination, the wind and tide suddenly changed and he was swept in the direction of the ocean, so he hauled around and headed for Sauscilito where he became the guest of the yacht club for the night. Next morning he made his way across and landed safely at San Francisco, after a laborious journey of twelve days.

He will long keep green in his memory the royal hospitality he received from the Californians.

Paul next decided to go to Salt Lake City and try the waters of its wonderful inland sea. After a few day's rest in San Francisco, he found himself on the shore of the Great Salt Lake. He had been told that the water was so dense that he would be able to walk on it in his rubber dress; but actual experience did not verify the assertion. In fact, he could discover but little difference between the water of the lake and that of the ocean. He might, possibly, float higher on the surface of the former, but very little. He found the water as clear as a crystal; but a veritable dead sea so far as animal life was concerned. There is no life in its depths except little worms that are found around the bottom of piles or on pieces of submerged wood, and these turn to flies. Wishing to prove to his own satisfaction that fish would not live in the lake, Paul procured some trout and turned them in. The moment they touched the briny water, they died as though shot by an electric current.

On the second evening after his arrival, Paul entered the water to paddle out to Antelope Island, about fifteen miles from shore. He was warned of danger in case of a wind; but thought nothing of it at the time. After slipping over the glassy surface of the lake for about ten miles, he noticed a heavy cloud coming down from the surrounding mountains and in a short time it was churned into a short, choppy sea by a squall blowing thirty or forty miles an hour. The waves were not very high, but slashed about him in such a manner that his eyes, nose and mouth were filled with the salty foam which caused intense agony. He still struggled for the island, hoping to reach it before he would die of suffocation. He steered by the sound of the waves washing against the shore. At last he heard the flap, flap, of the breakers and he was swung against the rocky coast of Antelope Island. He knew that no human being lived there; only a flock of sheep that had been taken thither in flat boats to graze. He also knew there was something else on the island for which he longed—fresh water. He groped about for a time until he could open his eyes to see a little and fortunately discovered a spring not far from where he landed.

The gale continued all night and he dare not enter the water while it prevailed. Next morning a little steamer that was sent out to hunt him, found him on the island and conveyed him back to shore, pretty badly used up. He remained at the lake some time after, but did not make any more excursions.

During the month of March, 1887, Paul, who had returned from a short visit south, was feeling a trifle malarious. Regardless of the time honored and tested remedies for this complaint which were prescribed freely by his friends, he believed that the only thing for relief was a run in the ocean in the rubber dress, with the Baby as his sole companion. He also felt the necessity for a practice voyage before going down the Hudson, a trip which he then had in view. Getting his paraphernalia together, he boarded the pilot boat, Fannie, on a Wednesday, and on Saturday, attired in his dress, he slipped over her side with the intention of paddling to the Jersey coast, which he hoped to strike in the vicinity of Cape May.

The weather was not very cold when he went overboard and the sea was fine and smooth. Bye and bye the wind commenced to blow off shore and as he wanted to go to the westward, he had a hard fight against it all day and night. He sighted a great many vessels and signaled them to pick him up; but they did not see him for they all continued on their way. The constant battle against the stiff land breeze began to tell on him toward morning. The compass would not work and he was compelled to determine his course by the stars. The morning sun showed him that he was out of sight of land. During the forenoon, the wind shifted to the east which was more favorable, though he could take but little advantage of it on account of being stiff and sore from the severe buffeting to which he had been subjected during the night. All day Sunday, he continued working to the westward. About four o'clock he sighted the smoke of a steamer to the south and pulled across her course. He fired three rockets to attract her attention and waved his flag, the "union down" fastened to the paddle. His heart sank when she glided by apparently without seeing him; but to his joy, after passing a short distance she stopped and he saw a boat lowered. He was taken aboard and learned that she was the William Lawrence of the Norfolk and Baltimore line, Captain M. W. Snow. When picked up, he was sixty miles off Sandy Hook. Captain Snow and everyone on board treated him with the utmost kindness. Directly after getting on board he turned in and slept for twelve hours. He landed at Providence on Monday, and he immediately wired his friends in New York that he was all right.

The contemplated voyage down the Hudson river, was delayed on account of ice; but on the fifth of April, a freshet broke it up and the voyager started from Hudson, accompanied by several representatives of the New York papers, who occupied a boat which was in charge of the famous oarsman, Wallace Ross assisted by George Whistler. The voyage was not of unusual interest, outside of the difficulty of forging ahead through the ice floes and considerable suffering from the cold. On that account and from the fact that the party were compelled to watch for favorable tides, progress was somewhat slow. They were enthusiastically received at every town and village and at several places, physicians advised Boyton to abandon the trip, fearing that the exposure would prove fatal but he made light of their fears.

One of the most interesting sights was encountered in the middle of the Tappan Zee. An enormous tow of one hundred canal boats and five schooners was passed, drawn by four powerful tugs. Six hundred people inhabited this floating village and they stood on the decks of their migratory houses, going north with the spring, like the ducks, and hurrahed, and each tug screamed a salute. The oyster dredgers cheered and schooners changed their course to hail Boyton.

Less than seven days from the time of starting, Paul landed in New York, having been escorted down the North river by a large party of friends aboard a gaily decorated tug. Fully 20,000 people saw the finish. To Wallace Ross, who rowed the reporters' boat, much of the success of the trip was due. He watched Boyton with the anxious care of a trained nurse. He stood by regardless of his own fatigue, keeping a careful eye on the tides and was ready at all times to exert his skill and muscle for the success of the undertaking. George Whistler, too, who has been Boyton's attendant for years, withstood the fatigues of the journey and attended manfully to his duties.

In March, 1888, the Captain had a thrilling experience in Lake Michigan. For the purpose of reducing his weight, he began to take short runs through the icy water. On the 27th he left shore, intending to paddle a few miles out in the lake. A fresh west wind was blowing. He pushed through the ice for some time and then encountered great floes onto which he climbed. Heavy clouds obscured the sun and the wind had gathered the ice together. He struggled for a time with what he judged to be the western border of the field and then ran into a sort of pocket. Through this he pulled until he again encountered floes. A heavy fog now shut down on the lake and all trace of land had vanished, and on stopping to take his bearings, he was horrified to find that his compass was lost. There was nothing by which he could determine his position or the direction of the city. He began to get drowsy from the cold and knew he would perish if he did not labor incessantly to keep up his temperature. He concluded that he only had to pull away from the ice to reach Chicago, and for at least five hours he worked in what he considered to be the right direction. Still there was no sign of the city. Then he changed his course and pulled with all the energy of desperation. The ice gathered about him again and when night came, he was fighting it for his life. Sometimes he would dodge the drifts, at others he climbed upon the cakes and crossed them. He got a flash view of the moon when it rose and then saw that he had been working wrong. He had crossed the field in the morning when he got into what he thought was an opening and all the long day he had been driven toward Michigan. The turn he had taken sent him south. Observing the moon he changed his course, and in a couple of hours saw the glare from the furnaces of South Chicago. Taking his bearings from them, he sighted the lights at the water work's crib, where he arrived at midnight and aroused Captain McKay by a blast of the bugle and was hauled up. He was given refreshments and retired. He had been seventeen hours in the water.

During the spring, Paul made a run of eight hundred miles down the Ohio from Wheeling to Evansville for amusement, and another of two-hundred miles down the Missouri from St. Joseph to Kansas City.

Late in the winter of 1889, he again visited the Pacific coast. His object was the capture of sea lions which he knew to be plentiful on the shores of Oregon and Washington. He went to Astoria and located a large rookery below Tillamook Head; but found it could be reached only by a most difficult trail. He made up his mind to take chances although it was not according to his idea the best mode of traveling. It was not until the 12th of March that everything was in readiness and on that day he left Astoria accompanied by his assistant, fully supplied with nets and everything necessary to effect the capture of the lions in the easiest way. They went to Seaside where they secured pack horses and launched boldly into the trail for Tillamook. This route proved to be all that had been described and a great deal more that had not been mentioned in the way of roughness and almost insurmountable difficulties. They occupied eight long and weary hours in traversing seven miles to a ranch on the coast which they proposed to make their headquarters.

To add to the unpleasant features of the trip, they were tartly received by the owner of the ranch when they arrived there at night worn out and hungry. The proprietor was very ill natured and did not conceal his aversion to entertaining them. Boyton made several polite attempts to engage him in conversation; but was answered with frowns and monosyllables. There was no other place where food and shelter could be procured and they were obliged to put up with it.

At supper some very fine meat graced the table and was more than relished by the hungry sea lion hunters. Paul thought he could reach the rancher's heart through praising the excellence of his viands, and innocently asked:

"Is that elk meat, sir?"

The man became very much excited at the question and angrily answered:

"No, sir. Do you suppose I would kill elk out of season, and a law against it at this time of year?"

Paul apologized for having unconsciously insinuated such a thing and remarked that if he was in the woods with a gun and saw an elk, he would be likely to shoot it.

"It would be wrong to violate the law in that way, young man," replied the host, "and I would be the first one to inform on you if I caught you at it."

Next morning while Boyton was out looking over the position of the seal rocks, his assistant informed the rancher who he was. A change took place at once in the man's demeanor. He proved a most generous and entertaining host. "Why, Captain," said he, "I thought I knew you. I helped you take off your suit once at Hock Ferry, Liverpool."

The sullen host became bright and cheerful and wanted Paul to go out elk hunting with him every day. His strange conduct at first was explained; he had been under the impression that his visitors were spies in search of violators of the game laws.

The nets were finally unpacked and Boyton with his assistant and three men from the ranch, started for the rocks. As they proceeded through the forest, they could hear the lions' bellowing above the noise of the breakers.

They reached the cliff which towers several hundred feet above the beach, and from which they had a glorious view of the rocks and rookeries below that were literally alive with sea lions. Finding a break in the cliff, they made an easy descent. Paul then donned the rubber dress and taking one of the nets, succeeded in passing the first line of breakers without much trouble; but he reached the island with considerable difficulty. His appearance did not seem to create any alarm among the horde of mammals on the rock, even when he approached near them. He went around the island to see where he could make the safest landing. Having gained the shore he cast loose the net and then worked cautiously toward a promising young lion, about a yearling, that was sleeping, and had no difficulty in throwing the snare over it. It beat around for a time, but quieted down as the running line was pulled that tightened the meshes. Making fast, Paul returned to the mainland where he joined a rope to the line of the snare and gave the signal for his assistants on shore to pull away, at the same time pushing the captured lion off the rocks. It snapped viciously at him but did not bellow or make a noise, and was landed without disturbing the others.

In half an hour another was captured and landed by the same process and two others quickly followed. Just before capturing the last one, Paul crawled into a large ravine where there were a number of lions. There was a magnificent one, about five or six years old and fully developed; but however much Boyton would have liked to capture it, he did not have confidence in the strength of the net or his own ability to hold it. He was going to make the attempt, nevertheless, when in his excitement, he arose from a recumbent position and frightened the prize away. He says he can never forget the malevolent look of those green eyes as the lion rolled off the rock and snapped at him.

The fourth net was followed ashore and they began to devise means to get their catch up the face of the cliff. They first tried to pack them up; but the effort was futile as the earth gave way under their feet. Finally three men went to the top of the cliff and let down a half inch cotton rope which was attached to the leading string of one of the nets. The men pulled and succeeded in lifting it half way up, when it caught on a stunted bush that grew out from the rocks. They tried hard to free it, when the rope which had been worn weak in places, from contact with sharp rocks, parted and the sea lion dropped like a shot and was smashed into a jelly on the boulders one hundred feet below. As darkness was coming on, with a storm brewing, they decided to leave the other lions in the nets where they were until morning, when they could get the horses to the edge of the cliff to draw them up.

That night, a terrible gale, which left many wrecks on the coast, sprang up and next day the trail was impassible by reason of fallen timber. Late in the afternoon, they reached the beach again and finding it impossible to pull the three lions up, or to get them to civilization if they did, Paul took off the traps and liberated them.

At daylight next morning, they started back across the trail to Seaside. It was in a much worse condition than when they went in, and they were until dark traversing the seven miles. Every time they missed stepping on a root or stone, they sank in the mud to their knees, until they became so tired that they thought seriously of abandoning their apparatus.

Fishermen at the mouth of the Columbia river consider the sea lion to be more dangerous and cruel than a shark. They accuse it of mutilating in the most horrible manner, bodies that have been drowned off the bar. An incident of its vicious nature came under Boyton's notice during his stay in that vicinity. An old Indian who wished to secure the skin of a lion, went out to the rocks at low tide. He was barefooted and walked noiselessly to where a lion lay asleep. He had just raised his ax to strike it over the head when his foot slipped and he fell. In an instant the animal was awake and upon him and fastening its teeth in his shoulder, stripped his arm bare to the bone down to the finger nails. The lion then jumped off into the sea and the Indian was rescued and carried ashore where he died soon after.

On Paul's return to Astoria, he determined to visit the North Beach. He and his companion missed the regular steamer and as they were impatient, they decided to risk the trip across the bar and along the coast in a small boat. The trip to Ilwaco was made without any startling adventure and the next day they visited Sand Island and captured several seals. On Sunday they were storm bound; but Monday they proceeded on their voyage up the coast in the small boat. They started against the advice of the fishermen, the men at the life saving station and everybody else.

They made it all right through the heavy sea until they passed Sand Island, when the waves struck them. To save the boat from being swamped, they had to throw her bow up and drift "nose on." They were tossed about on the turbulent water, and to add to their discomforts, they had neither food nor drink and were drenched to the skin. That night they got under Scarborough Head where they had smoother water and succeeded in making a landing. A blazing fire and a square meal put them in excellent spirits and the following day they returned to Astoria, to disprove in person a story that had been published along the coast to the effect that they were gone to "Davy Jones' Locker."

CHAPTER XXIII.

"Well, thank goodness, we are through, and I can get out for a little air once more."

Such was the remark made by Boyton when the preceding chapter, which completed the history of his adventures, was finished.

He little relished the confinement to which he had been subjected, while getting into shape such a mass of notes and memoranda. Several times he was on the point of abandoning the work altogether.

"One thing that gratifies me," he added: "I'll never have to talk about myself or my voyages again. The book tells the story."

Though before the public so many years, Paul Boyton is still in the prime of life. It is possible that he will not attempt any dangerous voyages again; still the ruling passion is strong. He may frequently be seen poring over maps and charts of distant rivers and often discusses the probability of adventure on them.

During the summer he is almost daily in the water with his company of aquatic experts.

In the winter season, he devotes the greater part of his time to inventing and perfecting new devices in the way of water amusements.

In the large basement of his home he has fitted up one of the most curious work-shops in the world. Water-shoes, sails, marine bicycles, torpedo and submarine boats, paddles, etc., lie around in bewildering confusion to a person unaccustomed to aquatic traps. But Boyton knows where each belongs, and insists on its being kept there, his early sailor training making him a martinet of order.

He has never lost his old love of animals. Adjoining the work-shop, is a large tank for the accommodation of his water pets. This is also a favorite spot for his three little boys who often take a plunge. Sometimes the first mate of the home is compelled to make a clearance, when the pets become numerous and the youngsters bathe too frequent.

It may be well to state in these closing remarks that a cause of considerable business annoyance is the persistence with which many people spell his name, Boy-n-ton instead of Boyton. This mistake happens only in America.

One thing Boyton seriously regrets, is his inability to remember names and faces. Consequently he is spoken to every day by those who have met him in various parts of the world, and it is a source of much embarrassment that he cannot always call their names as readily as they remember him, for being of a social disposition he is always glad to meet his acquaintances.

While keeping himself pretty busy in his shop over his charts during the winter he still finds time to make runs in his rubber dress on Lake Michigan, near his home, "Just to keep his hand in," he says.

He also goes on frequent hunting excursions.

Like most men who have led a roving life, he is fond of his home and a pleasant smile always lights his face when his little children are climbing over him asking for a story.